Teaching Children's Literature

Teaching Children's Literature

A Resource Guide, with a Directory of Courses

by ANNE H. LUNDIN
and CAROL W. CUBBERLEY

with a foreword by
JILL P. MAY

McFarland & Company, Inc., Publishers
Jefferson, North Carolina, and London

Frontispiece: "All in Their Gay Vacation Time" from *Wide Awake*, volume 15, number 3, September 1889 (courtesy of the de Grummond Children's Literature Collection at the University of Southern Mississippi)

British Library Cataloguing-in-Publication data are available

Library of Congress Cataloguing-in-Publication Data

Lundin, Anne H., 1944–
    Teaching children's literature : a resource guide, with a directory
of courses / by Anne H. Lundin and Carol W. Cubberley ; with a
foreword by Jill P. May.
      p. cm.
    Includes bibliographical references (p.) and index.
    ISBN 0-89950-990-8 (lib. bdg. : #50 alk. paper)
    1. Children's literature—History and teaching. I. Cubberley,
Carol W. II. Title.
PN1008.8.L86 1995
809'.89282'07—dc20   94-32679
                                                        CIP

Manufactured in the United States of America

McFarland & Company, Inc., Publishers
  Box 611, Jefferson, North Carolina 28640

Contents

Acknowledgments   *vii*

Foreword (by Jill P. May)   *1*

Introduction   *5*

PART I

1   Reference Works for Teaching Children's
Literature   *15*

2   Journals for Teaching Children's Literature   *31*

3   Textbooks for Teaching Children's Literature   *37*

4   Teaching Children's Literature to Adults   *61*

5   Teaching Children's Literature to Children and
Young People   *109*

PART II

Eight Representative Syllabi   *155*

PART III

Directory of Courses   *229*

Author/Title Index to Part I   *343*

Subject Index to Part I   *353*

v

Acknowledgments

The authors wish to express their appreciation to publishers who contributed examination copies for this book. We wish to offer special thanks to the librarians at the University of Southern Mississippi who assisted with our research: Dee Jones, curator of the de Grummond Collection; Karolyn Thompson, interlibrary loan librarian; and Eleanor Robin, microfilms librarian. The University of Southern Mississippi was also generous in granting us financial support, and for this we would like to thank Karen Yarbrough, vice president for research and planning, and James R. Martin, university librarian.

We also wish to note the kindness of the professors of children's literature who allowed their syllabi to be published as sample course descriptions. These distinguished faculty members are Joan Atkinson, School of Library and Information Studies, University of Alabama; Jill May and Darwin Henderson, School of Education, Purdue University; and Jan Susina, Department of English, Illinois State University. These individuals not only allowed their creative coursework to be displayed, but also their names and institutions to be included. Knowing a few good people is often the best resource in any field.

The purpose of this book is to document the interdisciplinary nature of children's literature. We want to demonstrate the richness of the field and the diversity of approach to the literature on this subject, and are grateful to the people named above, and to others, for aiding us in that goal.

Foreword

It is fitting that the two authors of this book worked together while they were librarians in the Cook and the McCain Libraries at the University of Southern Mississippi. Located in Hattiesburg, Mississippi, a quiet little town that is both genteel and progressive, the Cook and McCain Libraries hold rich collections that encompass both traditional resources for literature studies and unique materials that cannot be found at many larger, more affluent universities. As faculty librarians at the University of Southern Mississippi, Anne Lundin and Carol Cubberley have perused a variety of materials that fit within today's studies of children's literature.

Cook Library's extensive microfilm collection includes the Confederate Imprints, a vast collection of music, children's school books, political publications of the Confederate States, and popular literature found in the Old South during the Civil War. Cook Library also houses current reference guides to literature, education, and library science.

The McCain Library houses Cleanth Brooks's personal library. Brooks was an important champion of New Criticism who advocated close readings of literature in order to place the reader's attention on the literary aspects of the text rather than the author's intent or the reader's immediate reactions to the religious or moral implications found in the text. Anyone who is interested in literary studies in the United States and its future in American public schools would find this collection invaluable.

Even more important to those of us who study children's literature is the de Grummond Collection, also housed in McCain Library. Researchers will find this collection a jewel for their work. Rare children's books, reference materials that explicate the collection's

1

holdings, and a rich assortment of primary source materials, including the Ezra Jack Keats papers and correspondence of several award-winning children's authors and illustrators, are carefully catalogued and maintained at the de Grummond.

Anne Lundin worked as a librarian in the de Grummond Collection, after teaching English for many years at various levels. Her diversity of talents and interests aided children's literature researchers in their scholarly pursuits. She also taught children's literature at the University of Southern Mississippi and the University of Alabama. As a researcher whose Ph.D. dissertation centered on historical children's literature, Anne's knowledge of the academic needs for scholars in children's literature is vast. As a researcher who is interested in reader-response theory and its values for the serious study of children's literature, her understanding of the field's varied audiences is unique. She is now on the faculty of the School of Library Studies at the University of Wisconsin–Madison, where she enjoys the proximity to the Cooperative Children's Book Center (CCBC).

Carol Cubberley brings a different set of skills to this project, to complement Anne Lundin's expertise in the field of children's literature. An amateur, in the best sense of the word, in the field — a reader, a writer, and lover of children's books — Carol Cubberley's contribution is in organization, research, and the editing skills she developed as editor of *Mississippi Libraries*. With a background in teaching English, Carol serves as director of technical services at University Libraries, the University of Southern Mississippi.

There are many things to recommend about this title, but I am most impressed with the fact that *Teaching Children's Literature* has been completed by two academic librarians and faculty members who have chosen to be inclusive rather than exclusive in their listings, who consciously created a nonrestrictive, annotated listing of reference materials, journals, books, and articles which discuss children's literature as literature, and who included a sampling of syllabi from undergraduate courses in order to bridge the interconnections of all studies in children's literature.

This book holds the most extensive directory of undergraduate children's literature courses in the United States. In an effort to identify all avenues of scholarship in the field, the authors have listed every course that could be identified on U.S. college and university microfilm listings. Those of us who teach children's literature will find this directory most reassuring. Children's literature is flourishing, and in a variety of ways. All of us who argue that children's literature is serious stuff and that it deserves to be a significant part of the academic milieu will find this directory impressive proof that children's literature is a viable part of twentieth-century Americana.

Jill P. May
Professor of Curriculum and Instruction
School of Education
Purdue University

Introduction

Children's literature is the Cinderella of academia. Iona and Peter Opie remind us that Cinderella was never a rags-to-riches story, but one that celebrates the recognition of true identity and worth. They point out that fairy tales, unlike popular romances, are not stories of wish-fulfillment, but of testing. The magic is made by people being shown to be what they really are, "of reality made evident."[1] Alison Lurie makes a similar comparison in her Pulitzer Prize–winning novel *Foreign Affairs*. The narrator, a children's literature professor in an English department, observes how isolated she is from her colleagues, who snub her research into childhood folklore. She writes:

> For the truth is that children's literature is a poor relation in her department — indeed, in most English departments: a stepdaughter grudgingly tolerated because, as in the old tales, her words are glittering jewels of a sort that attract large if not equally brilliant masses of undergraduates. Within the departmental family she sits in the chimney-corner, while her idle, ugly siblings dine at the chairman's table — though to judge by enrollment figures, many of them would spout toads and lizards.[2]

Now, a decade later, the status of children's literature has improved. At the very least, Cinderella is at the ball, where she is dancing with many partners. She is coming of age. Her worth is finally recognized or noticed anew by academia. In truth, more than a century of criticism in the field exists, with extensive reviewing from the mid-nineteenth century on. Children's literature was much more in the literary mainstream of the past century than in the present one, but things are changing.

A marked increase in the amount and variety of scholarly work on children's books is influenced by new trends in higher education: a blurring of genres, an emphasis on the humanities, a greater respect for popular culture, interest in the history of childhood, debate on cultural literacy, and heightened attention to women and minorities. As disciplines open up, new opportunities exist to include the study of children's books. Children's literature is being investigated in diverse fields. Betsy Hearne, in her study of contemporary children's book research, notes its interdisciplinary connections to literature, librarianship, education, psychology, sociology, anthropology, history, and art. Each discipline brings its own goals and methods of study. Library science and education are more thematically and practically oriented; literature is textually based; history looks to context; psychology and sociology are concerned with therapeutic values; anthropology examines childhood folklore; and art is graphically analytical.[3] The heightened interest in whole language approaches to teaching young children has stimulated the market for trade books instead of basal readers: books of multiple meanings and uses.

The definitions of what constitutes "children's literature" remain puzzling. To the influential historian Harvey Darton, a child's book was one that sought to provide pleasure, however defined by the age. John Townsend has described it pragmatically as any book that a publisher promotes for children. Brian Alderson sees the genre as comprised of a semi-didactic and semi-recreational character. Peter Hunt defines the book in terms of the reader rather than the intentions of the author or the text itself. Much of the criticism of the field struggles with the notion of what constitutes children's literature. Children's literature, for the purposes of this book, is defined as books written or read by children from infancy through mid-adolescence—not just books written for the audience, but all books that children are capable of reading. Young adult literature is included, although the emphasis is on a broader definition of children's literature that includes some of the books written for older readers. An inclusive definition extends the boundaries of "literature" to whatever children are reading in order to gain information and entertainment. Children's literature exists in the context of childhood and of literary experience.

Children's literature may still be a stepchild, slighted by the divisions created across disciplines—the lack of communication between one department and another. Betsy Hearne notes this bifurcation as detrimental to communication. Jill May attributes the reluctance to take children's literature seriously as part of the body of literature to current philosophies of undergraduate education. Emphasis is placed on childhood as a distinct phenomenon, without the necessary interconnections to lifelong developmental education. Children's literature fits in a niche as a teaching tool, a means to teach other concepts, rather than an effective experience in itself.[4]

Children's literature is young, and consequently still developing its place in academia. The study of children's books presupposes a literature of childhood. The publishing of children's books goes back only a little more than two centuries, to the pioneer works by Thomas Boreman, Mary Cooper, and John Newbery, who each contributed to the establishment of children's books as a separate publishing venture. Children learned to read by hornbooks, which were single sheets of paper containing the alphabet and a prayer mounted on a board and protected by a slim sheet of horn. Children heard nursery rhymes and fairy tales, which were considered more as folklore, as they were not written expressly for children. John Newbery's efforts, which Harvey Darton calls a "commercial volcano," stimulated the growth of publishing for children into diverse genres and formats: nursery rhymes, informational books, illustrated books, magazines, and the novella.[5] Newbery's emphasis on amusement as well as information indicated a new shift in the priorities for children's education. The extent of his publishing was prodigious: between 1742 and 1802 he and his family members published over 400 books for children. His innovations are honored by the Newbery Medal, given annually by the American Library Association to the author of a distinguished book for children.

The nineteenth century witnessed an enormous expansion of children's literature as an important branch of the book trade. Romanticism, in its emphasis on innate imaginative powers, inspired the publishing of fairy tales, folk myths, ballads, and romances; and new research by feminist scholars now encompasses domestic tales of nurturance and community.[6] A number of scholars have established a link between the Romantic concept of childhood and the content and narrative structure of children's literature. The idealization of the child with cult status brought child-study to the forefront of scholarly and popular interests. Victorian children's books addressed a dual audience: the innocent, receptive child and the regressive, nostalgic adult, anxious to experience a second childhood in the children about whom and to whom they were reading. Romanticism became increasingly secularized by the end of the century. A new vision of the child emerged at the turn of the century with the creation of fantasies featuring the child as storyteller, as in the works of E. Nesbit.

Children's literature enjoyed a prominence in the mainstream of literary and intellectual life from the mid-nineteenth century to the close of the century. The elevation of children's books as works of art indicated a dual audience for picture books, an aesthetic autonomy, and a perceived status as the apotheosis of art culture. The popularity of books by Walter Crane, Randolph Caldecott, and Kate Greenaway demonstrates the importance of children's books as a commodity. The lack of rigid demarcation between adult and children's literature created broad appeal for picture books and adventure fiction and encouraged the participation of the literati. Children's books were regularly reviewed in the leading literary journals of the day. Noted authors like Robert Louis Stevenson and Rudyard Kipling followed Lewis Carroll's lead in writing books especially for children. Successive editors of the *Atlantic Monthly* — Thomas Bailey Aldrich, Horace Scudder, and William Dean Howells — all wrote works for a young audience. Publishers created a niche for children's books which became ever larger through expanding literacy as well as periodical coverage in reviews, commentary, and advertisements. The result was a context of rich cultural discourse between adult and child, which could only have existed within a notion of childhood that encouraged the production of books.

The twentieth century reveals far less crossover between children's literature and the literary mainstream. While there is a cultural obsession over the inherent problems of childhood, few major twentieth-century authors have written for children. As higher education developed over the past century, the study of children's books has been relegated to schools of education and library science. Criticism of children's books has largely been the province of a small enclave of writers and critics whose background is more in practice than in theory. Much of the writing about children's books has focused on classic works within a particular elite tradition of fantasy and has slighted the phenomenally popular fiction of Horatio Alger in the nineteenth century, to the adventures of Nancy Drew and the Hardy boys in the twentieth.

Modern children's book research demonstrates a contextual approach. Children's books offer an innocent mirror to what a culture decides is important to pass on to the next generation. R. Gordon Kelly, who has written extensively on American popular literature for children, describes this formation as "cultural definitions of what *is*, what is good, true, and beautiful; what things go together."[7] Children's books are not solely viewed as reflection but as construction. Scholars now look for the ways that children's literature shaped writers' sensibilities and influenced the culture. Research in developmental and cognitive psychology has changed the conception of a child's potential. Children's books are now more aware of different delineations of social reality appropriate to children's needs and interests. Books for children have always been constructed from an adult world and its assumptions of children as resources to be molded by a particular social standard. As Mary Jackson writes in her revisionist history of early children's literature, "Children's literature was rooted in the conditions and imperatives of the adult world and was regarded first and foremost as a tool to shape the young to the needs of that world."[8] While Jackson applies that judgment to early children's literature, its truth is still operative to some extent today. Betsy Hearne notes the traces of didacticism in children's book dialogue — the necessity for justifications not being needed in consideration of adult literature. The notion of text as tool, of literature as a function, is still very much alive in contemporary research and studies in the field.

While social values are commonly explored in studies of children's literature, recent developments in literary criticism have placed new value on the reader. In short, critics of language and literature have moved from a locus of study on the text to the reader's response. Critics like Louise Rosenblatt have argued that we should begin with real readers. Scholars have broadened the notion of what constitutes a "text" and have come to consider any text in relation to its readers. Since many of the "texts" that exist in the world bear some relationship to children's books, the genre — as well as its readers — is studied. Controversy over the canon — the officially sanctioned works of literature — has subverted traditional notions of classic works. Instead of viewing literature as possessing intrinsic values that speak from one generation to the next, critics approach literature as a dynamic within a cultural environment. The question is not whether a book is "good" or "bad," but rather, how subtle or persuasive is its message or meaning for the reader. Children's literature is unique among branches in its definition in terms of the reader; the demonstration of the intimacy of the text and the reader. As its audience determines its identity as a piece of writing, a work of children's literature ceases to exist as such when it is no longer read by its audience. Historical children's books can cease to be "alive," a determination which is hard to apply to adult literature. What exists as "children's literature" today will be markedly different from what was considered appropriate in another age for children to read. Thus, as Peter Hunt observes, a fracture exists between contemporary and historical literature through shifts in the concepts of childhood.[9] The variable in definition makes the study of children's literature particularly problematic.

Traditionally, children's literature was rooted in schools of library science and education. Occasionally, some courses were offered in English programs. In the 1950s Frances Clarke Sayer taught children's literature as literature in the English department of UCLA. She had been employed previously as superintendent of work with children in the New York Public Library, where she worked along with Anne Carroll Moore, the legendary giant in the field of library service and reviewing. Librarians have always played a key role in the development of the genre. Betsy Hearne notes the prominence of library science in first recognizing and fostering children's literature.[10] The first library schools introduced the program at the turn of the century, and librarians worked closely with publishing firms, who often expanded into separate children's book divisions, with librarians as their editors. Librarians have been the chief consumers, reviewers, and promoters of children's books throughout the century, although bookstores are beginning to usurp some of the prerogatives of the children's librarian. As public and school library budgets shrink, parents look more to bookstores to provide their children's reading. Bookstores do not necessarily depend on the professional counsel of librarians, or the reviewing networks that have functioned over the years in heralding certain children's books. The commercialization of children's books, which seems to be bypassing the librarian as mediator, creates troublesome concerns for all those who question what literature does *for* or *to* children.

This book seeks to introduce faculty members in diverse disciplines to the rich potential of children's literature as an academic study. Its teaching concentrates on concept, method, and content.

As part of the larger literary whole, children's literature has discovered a unique voice that offers a plurality of meaning and response. Children's literature inspires a literature of and about childhood as well as a framework of courses that reflect and shape this interest.

The annotated entries contain books and journal articles on the teaching of children's literature and the use of children's books in schools and libraries. These sources provide a point of reference, a sense of direction as to where the literature has been and where it is going. Progress is not always implicit; historical studies offer a sense of continuity of concerns. The angle of approaches is wide, while the reality of a child audience necessitates a practical end. Pragmatic concerns are increasingly shaped by theoretical perspectives. Developmental psychology informs the suitability of books as bibliotherapy. The historical-bibliographical approach provides a context within which books fit with other books. Social and cultural issues are woven into texts for children in a way difficult to find in any other literary genre. The problems of a multidisciplinary field are inherent in the selections. The list of secondary sources is a sampling, without the attempt to be comprehensive for the whole subject of children's literature, which ranges from reading textbooks to artistic analysis. The resources provide a wealth of information on what to teach and how to teach it.

While all method in scholarship grows through practice, this field, perhaps more than any other, is intricately involved with support and input from practitioners. A syllabus reveals the critical priorities and power structures of higher education. Eight sample syllabi from courses offered in education, English, and library science programs are also presented.

This book provides a directory of courses offered in children's literature at four-year colleges across the country. The existence of a body of criticism and a curriculum in higher education is interrelated. The goals for these courses are often twofold: introducing students to books and helping students find affective pleasure in the arts. Students must be able to view children's books as adult readers before they can introduce them to children. Some of the questions implicit in course descriptions include audience, purpose, literary merit, and social and educational value. The diversity of course offerings across departments indicates the breadth of the field, which consists of pragmatic purposes and a humanistic appeal. A blend of literary study and practical school-based approaches is familiar. Most courses include a literary approach with the practical application of children's literature to children.

The resources and curriculum delineated in this book survey the serious interest in academia in what children read. Some common concerns emerge and call for relationships between disciplines. The institutionalization of children's literature, as Aidan Chambers noted in 1979, needs to encompass the study of literature, the study of the act of reading, and the study of children's literature.[11] An uneasy peace exists as to the function of literature for the young. While the uses of books are well established, the issue that books are *for* children is still unresolved. As Samuel Pickering points out, children's literature reflects society's concerns more rapidly than other literary studies. Children's literature research, criticism, and teaching can become the model for other interdisciplinary studies.[12] A growing confidence characterizes the literature of children's literature. There is no doubt that children's books are culturally formative and that children's literature is an enormous field, a scholar's paradise, in all of its unfinished business. Scholars and educators recognize the imperative of early reading as a precursor to literacy. Divisions still exist as to the uses of literature. Are books designed only to teach reading, or to produce an emotional response from the audience? To what extent is reading more than a means of instruction — moral improvement or spiritual regeneration — but also the core of the intellectual words and imaginative experience of childhood? How can teachers and librarians promote the love of literature, in and for itself?

Children's literature exists within the delicate balance of child reader and adult creator. Adults may intend for books to carry certain messages, but the truth lies in the individuality of books and of readers. A dialectical relationship between author and audience, between text and culture, is present. Complex questions remain regarding the literary and social interrelations that shape the history, inventory, and structure of children's books. These questions define what the *literature* of children's literature is all about.

Notes

1. Iona and Peter Opie, *The Classic Fairy Tales* (London: Oxford University Press, 1974), 11-13.

2. Alison Lurie, *Foreign Affairs* (New York: Random House, 1984), 6.

3. Betsy Hearne, "Problems and Possibilities: U.S. Research in Children's Literature," *School Library Journal* (August 1988), 27–31.

4. Jill May, "What Content Should Be Taught in Children's Literature?" *Children's Literature Association Quarterly* (Winter 1991-92), 275–77.

5. F. J. Harvey Darton, *Children's Books in England: Five Centuries of Social Life*, 3d ed., Bryan Alderson, ed. (Cambridge: Cambridge University Press, 1982), 260.

6. James Holt McGavran, Jr., ed., *Romanticism and Children's Literature in Nineteenth-Century England* (Athens: University of Georgia Press, 1991).

7. R. Gordon Kelly, "Children's Literature," *Handbook of American Popular Literature*, vol. 1, ed. M. Thomas Inge (Westport, CT: Greenwood, 1978).

8. Mary V. Jackson, *Engines of Instruction, Mischief, and Magic: Children's Literature in England from Its Beginnings to 1839* (Lincoln: University of Nebraska Press, 1989).

9. Peter Hunt, *Children's Literature: The Development of Criticism* (London: Routledge, 1990).

10. Hearne, "Problems and Possibilities," 28.

11. Aidan Chambers, "Letter from England: Teaching Children's Literature," *The Horn Book*, vol. 60, no. 6 (December 1979): 710.

12. Samuel Pickering, Jr., "The Function of Criticism in Children's Literature," *Children's Literature in Education,* vol. 13, no. 1 (1974): 16.

PART I

Chapter 1

Reference Works
for Teaching
Children's Literature

Courses in children's literature depend on a strong collection of reference works. Many of these books are written by practicing teachers and librarians with a great deal of experience in the literature. These titles represent works that are frequently included in reference collections of academic libraries and in specialized research collections of children's literature. While there are a prodigious number of professional books in the field, the selections in this chapter are resources most applicable to the teaching of children's literature at the college and university level.

A more comprehensive listing, although not current, is Harriet Quimby and Margaret Kimmell's *Building a Children's Literature Collection* (1983), which suggests a basic reference and children's book collection for academic libraries. Glenn Edward Sadler's *Teaching Children's Literature* (1992) includes a section titled "Readings and Resources." Kay Vandergrift's *Children's Literature* (1990) lists many recommended readings. The *Subject Guide to Books in Print* lists a large number of available books under the headings "Children's Literature — Bibliography" and "Children's Literature — Bio-Bibliography." Most textbooks include a bibliography of reference materials for further study.

1. Bingham, Jane, and Grayce Scholt. *Fifteen Centuries of Children's Literature: An Annotated Chronology of British and American Works in Historical Context*. Westport, CT: Greenwood, 1980.

This book surveys representative periods and landmark American and British children's books from the sixth century to 1945. Each time period is introduced by an historical background for both Great Britain and the United States that presents the social, economic, and political climate of the age as a context for the development of a literature for children. Each period is examined for three concepts: historical background; development of books; and attitudes toward and treatment of children.

The periods include: Anglo-Saxon (ca. 523–1099); Middle Ages (1100–1499); Renaissance to the Restoration (1500–1659); Restoration to American independence (1600–1799); nineteenth century (1800–1899); and the first half of the twentieth century.

After each period introduction, a chronology highlights the works published in specific years. This is valuable in determining works appearing simultaneously and of possible literary influence.

Additional features include chronological checklists of American and British periodicals for children; a listing of facsimile editions with a key to the publishers; a key to book collections in Great Britain, Canada, and the United States; a bibliography of secondary sources; a name index to authors, illustrators, and publishers; and a title index to approximately 9,700 books.

2. Carpenter, Humphrey, and Mari Prichard. *Oxford Companion to Children's Literature.* London: Oxford University Press, 1984.

This ready-reference encyclopedic guide contains more than 2,000 entries, covering a wide range of historical and contemporary authors, titles, subjects, and characters from children's literature. Numerous cross-references build on related topics. Traditional and popular genres are covered, including popular culture formats like films, television, radio, comics, and dime novels. While the range is international, the emphasis is on British children's literature.

The book was first proposed by Iona and Peter Opie in 1958 as a work to be similar to the *Oxford Companion to Literature.* In their words, it was designed to be "a true companion to children's literature," with a scope wide enough to contain "much out-of-the-way information on juvenile pursuits and the lore of childhood." When Oxford University Press finally became interested in the project, the Opies were committed to other projects. Humphrey Carpenter and his wife, Mari Prichard, became the compilers, and the work is entirely their own.

The approach is descriptive, including background and summary information, as well as some evaluative judgments of authors and works. No formal bibliography is included, but some important sources are listed within the course of individual articles. The authors acknowledge the following books to be leading sources in their own research: Harvey Darton's *Children's Books in England*; Mary Thwaite's *From Primer to Pleasure in Reading*; John Rowe Townsend's *Written for Children*; Gillian Avery's *Childhood's Pattern*; the *Osborne Collection of Early Children's Books*, a catalog edited by Judith St. John; and *Twentieth-Century Children's Writers*, edited by D. L. Kirkpatrick.

3. Carroll, Frances Laverne, and Mary Meacham. *More Exciting, Funny, Scary, Short, Different, and Sad Books Kids Like About Animals, Science, Sports, Families, Songs and Other Things.* Chicago: ALA, 1992.

This annotated bibliography is a personal reading guide for child readers. The books selected include those titles that librarians most often recommend in answering children's requests for books. The title indicates the various divisions, which focus on books with strong developmental interests to children. Originally published in 1983, this second edition serves as a companion to the previous edition, with very little duplication of titles. The book covers 75 subject areas that are relevant to children's reading interests. Practicing librarians compiled the lists of books currently recommended to children. Fiction and nonfiction are covered. The annotations are designed to provide a brief description of the book and appeal to children with a suggestion of suspense or mystery. The emphasis is on elementary-level books, from second to fifth grades; the maximum upper range is the eighth grade. The book is valuable as a readers' advisory for librarians, teachers, and parents, as well as for children themselves. Index.

4. *Children's Literature Review.* Detroit: Gale, 1976-.

Launched in 1976 to provide a permanent, accessible record of criticism of juvenile literature, and to provide an opportunity for selectors to make informed choices, CLR provides a wealth of information on individual authors, illustrators, and storytellers. Each volume features approximately 15 international biographees of all eras and a variety of genres: picture books, fiction, nonfiction, poetry, folklore, and drama. Each author section includes a portrait, biographical information, a general presentation of the oeuvre, excerpts of criticism of the oeuvre and of individual works, and illustrations. Indexes include a cumulative index to authors, a cumulative nationality index, and a cumulative title index.

5. Commire, Anne. *Yesterday's Authors of Books for Children: Facts and Pictures About Authors and Illustrators of Books for Young People, from Early Times to 1960.* Detroit: Gale, 1977–.

This series, which numbered just two volumes by 1992, follows the same general format as *Something About the Author,* but covers authors who died before 1961. Although emphasis is given to authors still read by children, some attention is given to earlier writers who are of interest to researchers. Although new volumes are slow to appear, each entry represents a major research effort, and some are quite lengthy and comprehensive.

6. *Dictionary of Literary Biography.* Detroit: Gale.

This series presents career biographies of authors by topics, period, or genre. At present, four of these volumes deal with children's literature: *American Writers for Children Before 1900,* volume 42, edited by Glenn E. Estes; *American Writers for Children, 1900–1960,* volume 22, edited by John Cech; *American Writers for Children Since 1960: Fiction,* volume 52; and *American Writers for Children Since 1960: Poets, Illustrators, and Nonfiction Authors,* volume 61, both edited by Estes. These volumes stand alone and can be purchased apart from the full series, although the entire series will be found in most college and university libraries. Each entry includes not only biographical information but also drawings, paintings, and photographs of authors at various stages of their careers, and illustrations of their families and homes. Facsimile reproductions are provided of title pages, dust jackets, and manuscripts. Each volume editor is responsible for preparing appendices surveying the major periodicals and literary and intellectual movements associated with their volumes, and a list of further readings. In preparation are the first two volumes to deal with British authors and illustrators of children's literature.

7. Freeman, Judy. *Books Kids Will Sit Still For: The Complete Read-Aloud Guide.* Second edition. New York: Bowker, 1990.

This book guides teachers and librarians toward good read-aloud books and literature-based activities. Explanatory chapters discuss read-aloud techniques, booktalking, creative dramatics, storytelling, poetry, and nonfiction. The chapter "101 Ways to Celebrate Books" lists additional creative activities centered on literature. Over 2,000 books are annotated, all of which have been tested with groups. Each entry includes full bibliographic citation, plus additional information as to subject headings and the number of chapters, pages, stories, and/or number of sittings required to complete the reading. Each annotation includes a simple plot statement and practical ideas for curriculum connections, activities, and related readings. The titles are organized into separate chapters covering fiction for preschool and kindergarten through grades 1-2, 2-4, 5-6. Folktales and fairy tales, myths, and legends are divided into chapters on single stories and collections. Poetry, nonsense, and language-oriented nonfiction are examined apart from nonfiction and biography. An extensive professional bibliography lists textbooks; reading, writing, and booktalking resources; and books on storytelling and creative dramatics. There are author, title, illustrator, and subject indexes. The subject index indicates recommended reading levels for titles.

8. Gillespie, John T., and Corinne J. Naden. *Best Books for Children: Preschool Through Grade 6*. Fourth edition. New York: Bowker, 1990.

The primary aim of this reference book is to provide a list of books that satisfy recreational needs of children as well as curricular needs of schools. The age range is preschool through elementary school level. The over 12,000 titles were determined by recommendations from two review sources plus additional criteria of availability, currency, accuracy, usefulness, and relevance. The book is designed to be used as a tool to evaluate collections, as a selection guide, as an aid-in-reading advisory, and as a base for preparing bibliographies and reading lists.

Book entries are organized under large divisions of literature, biography, the arts and language, history and geography, social institutions and issues, personal development, physical and applied sciences, and recreation. Each of these categories is divided into smaller subject areas. Full bibliographic information is provided, plus a brief annotation and review citations. Indexes access author, illustrator, book title, and subject/grade level.

9. Haviland, Virginia. *Children's Literature: A Guide to Reference Sources*. Washington, DC: Library of Congress, 1966.

This annotated bibliography, compiled by the head of the children's literature center at the Library of Congress, is an important research tool. The work contains extensive references to books, dissertations, articles, pamphlets, newspapers, recordings, and catalogs. Excluded are works that examine children's literature as literature; this excludes a number of major classic authors and their works.

The work is organized into eight divisions: history and criticism; authorship; illustration; bibliography; books and children; the library and children's books; international studies; and national studies. The

1,073 entries contain descriptive as well as evaluative annotation, commenting on a work's reputation, usefulness, and interest.

Three supplements (1972, 1977, and 1982) add new entries and subsections. The first supplement adds a section on the publishing and promotion of children's books under history and criticism and another on teaching children's literature after the teaching section. The second supplement adds a discussion of research in children's literature after the teaching section. French Canadian books are added to national studies. The third supplement is extensively updated.

An appendix lists professional associations and agencies that publish titles cited, and the index covers authors, titles, and subjects.

10. Hendrickson, Linnea. *Children's Literature: A Guide to the Criticism.* Boston: G. K. Hall, 1987.

This reference tool is a source for criticism: journal articles, chapters from books, reviews, and dissertations. The purpose of the annotated bibliography is to draw together significant criticial analyses from diverse disciplines published in scholarly as well as popular publications. The breadth of disciplines is particularly valuable, covering professional periodicals from English, education, library science, social sciences, and general publications. The sources are selected for particular relevance and do not represent a comprehensive listing of what is available in the literature. A source may be listed even if it just includes several pages, rather than an entire chapter, on a particular subject. Reviews are highly selective, emphasizing literary reception or scholarly analysis.

Children's literature is defined as imaginative writing for children between the ages of one and 16. The genres covered include picture books, wordless books, comics, periodicals, fairy tales, folklore, series books and popular fiction, young adult fiction, drama, poetry, and nonfiction. No criticism is included of film, television, or textbooks. Criticism of the authors of classic children's books is restricted to recent sources.

The arrangement is by authors, illustrators, titles, subjects, themes, and genres. Annotations are descriptive rather than evaluative, with a brief indication as to scope and contents. The emphasis is on contemporary books and issues, although classics and traditional genres are included.

The appendix lists reference works and journals in the field. The index includes critics, authors, titles, and subjects.

11. Katz, Bill, and Linda Sternberg Katz. *Magazines for Young People.* Second edition. New Providence, NJ: Bowker, 1991.

This is a revised edition of *Magazines for School Libraries* and a companion volume to *A Children's Magazine Guide*. Approximately 1,000 titles are selected and evaluated, the majority of which are appropriate for young adults. Titles are organized into three large sections: children's magazines, for children ages 4–14; young adult, for ages 14–18 (and older); and professional education and library journals. The section on professional journals is useful as a guide to the literature in the field and for publishing sources. Within these categories are subject divisions, selected to fit the needs of a young audience. Evaluative criteria determine certain titles as "First Choices" for selection or reference use.

The introduction presents the problematic considerations in selection policy: what is indexed, what is found acceptable by experts, what is purchased by school libraries of various sizes, price, intrinsic quality, relation to subject covered, point of view, format, advertising, curriculum, and use. The entries provide a full bibliographic citation and an extensive annotation, which places the source within the subject area and delineates its contents and utility. There are indexes of titles and major subjects.

12. Kohn, Rita. *Once Upon . . . a Time for Young People and Their Books: An Annotated Resource Guide*. Metuchen, NJ: Scarecrow, 1986.

This resource guide lists materials on printed and nonprinted children's literature. Materials are English-language trade books or booklets designed for infants to young adults, or professional materials for teachers and librarians. While the emphasis is neither critical nor comprehensive, the book serves as a guide to available resources for particular subject areas. Some 829 titles are listed with full bibliographic citation, and most include a brief annotation as to contents. Subject headings are listed under each item and indexed in the back. The appendix includes resource locations for recommended reading lists and other publications for young people; review sources; and addresses of publishers. There are title and subject indexes as well.

13. Lima, Carolyn W., and John A. Lima. *A to Zoo: Subject Access to Children's Picture Books*. Third edition. New York: Bowker, 1989.

This is the most comprehensive subject guide to children's picture books. Picture books are defined as a fictional or nonfictional book whose illustrations are as important as text and whose concepts or text is suitable for preschool to grade two. The first edition was based on the

San Diego Public Library's collection of picture books for children; subsequent editions have expanded the information base. The book contains nearly 12,000 titles organized under 700 subjects. The introduction examines the historical development of picture books, from their roots in the oral tradition and manuscript illustration, through landmark books and illustrators, to twentieth-century technology and current trends. A bibliography lists pertinent sources on the picture-book genre.

The book can be used to discover related titles under particular subjects and to ascertain bibliographic information on authors and illustrators. Subject headings are cross-referenced under bibliographic entries. Indexes list authors, titles, and illustrators.

14. McElmeel, Sharron L. *Bookpeople: A First Album*; *Bookpeople: A Second Album*. Englewood, CO: Libraries Unlimited, 1990.

The two volumes present profiles on leading authors and illustrators in the children's book field. The goals are to make connections with literature and to encourage reading. The books are one of a series on programming, which also includes *An Author a Month (for Pennies)* (1988), which features nine authors/ illustrators and includes capsule units for three other authors/illustrators. The two volumes of *Bookpeople* introduce over 80 authors and illustrators of books for elementary and middle school readers. Each of the three books contains a similar format: a biographical introduction, a picture, selected titles, and response/activity ideas. *Bookpeople: A First Album* concentrates on authors and illustrators of picture books; *Bookpeople: A Second Album* highlights those who create books for intermediate grades and middle school readers. The appendices contain addresses of authors and selected publishers and other sources. Index.

15. Meigs, Cornelia L., et al. *Critical History of Children's Literature: A Survey of Children's Books in English from the Earliest Times to the Present*. New York: Macmillan, 1969.

Originally published in 1953, this is one of the earliest studies of American children's literature. The focus is on American books for children with their English and European literary antecedents. The authors — Cornelia Meigs, Elizabeth Nesbitt, Anne Thaxter Eaton, and Ruth Hill Viguers — speak with authority from the perspectives of writer, critic, teacher, and librarian. Meigs writes the initial section, "The Roots of the Past." In "Widening Horizons," Anne Thaxter Eaton surveys the Victorian age in both England and America. Elizabeth

Nesbitt examines "A Rightful Heritage," the works of Rudyard Kipling, Howard Pyle, Walter de la Mare, and Beatrix Potter in the period of 1890 through 1920. Ruth Hill Viguers explores the modern period of 1920 through the mid-1960s in "Golden Years and Time of Tumult." The introduction is written by Henry Steel Commanger. Bibliographies are included in each chapter. Authors and titles indexes are included.

16. Moir, Hughes, Melissa Cain, and Leslie Prosak-Beres. *Collected Perspectives: Choosing and Using Books for the Classroom.* Boston: Christopher-Gordon, 1990.

This annotated bibliography includes 500 recommended titles for use with K-12 students. These contemporary books were reviewed between 1984 and 1988 by the staff from the Cooperative Services for Children's Literature at the University of Toledo, where they publish a review journal, *Perspectives*, promoting literature-based reading programs. The reviews are written by practicing teachers, librarians, and education professors engaged in programming and curriculum for children and young adults.

The reviews are organized by genre: picture story books; fiction for younger readers; fiction for older readers; poetry; and nonfiction. The editors seek a broad audience for each book, recognizing that some picture books are appropriate for all ages.

Each review examines a book from various points of view: the child or young adult reader's response as well as that of the teacher or librarian. The annotation includes summary, evaluation, awards, curriculum topics, and suggestions for follow-up activities. The reviews suggest companion books and related sources of information. Many multicultural books are included.

A title-author index, a subject index, and a listing of publishers are included as well.

17. Moynihan, William T., and Mary E. Shaner, editors. *Masterworks of Children's Literature.* New York: Stonehill, 1983–86.

This eight-volume set takes two approaches. The first seven volumes comprise an anthology of children's literature by period. Volume 1, *The Early Years (1550–1739)* presents ballads, poetry, fables, fiction, and religious verse. Representative authors are John Bunyan, Edmund Spenser, and Andrew Marvell. Many of the entries are, of course, anonymous. Volume 2 continues this period with religious prose, illustrated textbook, drama, science, and two bibliographies. In the science section selections are printed from such books as Thomas Cogan's *The*

Haven of Health. Volumes 3 and 4, *The Middle Period (1740-1836)*, begin with an essay on children's literature in England by Robert Baton, continue with representative selections, and conclude with a bibliography. Volumes 5 and 6, *The Victorian Age (1837-1900)*, begin with an essay by Robert Lee Wolff, offer selections by Thomas Hughes, Charlotte M. Yonge, John Ruskin, Charles Dickens, Frances Browne, and others, and conclude with a bibliography. Volume 7, *Victorian Color Picture Books*, reprints illustrations by Randolph Caldecott, Walter Crane, Kate Greenaway, Eleanor Vere Boyle, Richard Doyle, Andrew Lang, and R. M. Ballantyne. Volume 8, *The Twentieth Century*, has a different format. As Moynihan points out in the introduction, there is no need for an anthology of works published in this century, as they are readily available. Instead, the volume offers a series of essays "surveying the major developments in twentieth-century English and American children's literature." The introductory essay "places children's books within a critical and historical context and surveys the gradual shift from the middle-class subject matter of nursery and nanny to stories about broken homes, hostile adults, and a mass-media society in crisis." Following this are "Realism in Twentieth-Century Children's Literature" by Mary E. Shaner; "New Realism in Children's Fiction" by Rosanne Donahue; "Black Images in American Children's Literature" by James A. Miller; "Twentieth-Century Children's Fantasy" by Shaner; "Children's Science Fiction" by Thomas J. Weber; and "Small Wonders: Baby Books and Picture-books" by Ann Devereaux Jordan. An appendix describes 17 book awards and lists winners up to the year of publication.

18. Nilsen, Alleen Pace, ed. *Your Reading: A Booklist for Junior High and Middle School Students*. Eighth edition. Urbana, IL: National Council of Teachers of English, 1991.

This annotated bibliography is directed toward junior high and middle school students. The book is primarily designed as a readers' advisory for older children and young adults; it is also useful for teachers and librarians in selecting titles and planning units. The more than 1,000 books are arranged by subject so that students can find books in the following categories: connections; understandings; imaginings; contemporary poetry and short stories; books to help with schoolwork; and books just for you (self-help, how-to, hobbies, and careers). Within these larger categories are smaller divisions. Each chapter is prefaced with a short description that relates that subject to the interest level of junior high youth. The books are chosen from those published between 1988 and 1990; a list at the end of each chapter recommends books published before 1988. A rating system of stars at the end of the annotations indicates inclusion on a "best book list." A cumulative listing of books that appear on two or more "best books of the year" lists for 1988–90 is included in the appendix. Students are encouraged in the introduction to write to authors in care of their publishers, whose addresses are given at the back. An appendix for teachers and librarians indicates some of the criteria and considerations in compiling such a list of recommended books. Part of the NCTE Bibliography Series, which is frequently revised. Author, title, and subject index.

19. Olendorf, Donna, editor. *Something About the Author: Facts and Pictures About Authors and Illustrators of Books for Young People.* Detroit: Gale, 1971–.

As stated in the introduction to volume 68, "*Something About the Author* is an ongoing reference series that deals with the lives and works of authors and illustrators of children's books." Included are both well-known and lesser-known authors and illustrators. The scope of the series includes the complete time range and all genres of children's literature, primarily authors from English-speaking countries and international authors available in English translation. There are two indexes that cumulate in alternate volumes: an illustrations index and an authors index. The following sections appear under each entry: personal; addresses; career; memberships; awards and honors; writings; works in progress; sidelights; references; and illustrations (both author portraits and illustrations from publications). This work is essential to any collection supporting studies at any level in children's literature. It should be found in both elementary school and high school libraries.

20. Pellowski, Anne. *The World of Children's Literature.* New York: Bowker, 1968.

This is a valuable guide to international children's literature. The book grew out of a joint project of the International Board of Books on Young People (IBBY) and the International Youth Library (IYL), which surveyed 30 countries in 1955 and published their findings in a booklet.

The purpose of the book is to present a picture of the development of children's literature in every country where it exists. The author presents an overview of the history and contemporary (as of 1968) publishing of children's books and library services.

Following this introductory commentary, the author then presents an annotated bibliography of articles, books, and dissertations related to children's literature for that country. Historical as well as contemporary sources are listed for a broad range of topics related to children's reading, special exhibitions, and reference sources. Books are the main emphasis, with some periodical coverage of significant articles. Periodicals devoted to children's literature are listed, without annotations for particular articles. The annotations vary in length and include a summary of contents and occasionally an evaluation of the source.

The countries are listed under geographical regions: Latin America; Western Europe; Scandinavia and Finland; Eastern Europe, Turkey, and Greece; Arabic-speaking North Africa, the Arab States, and Israel; English-speaking Africa; French-speaking Africa; Asia and the Pacific; and a large section composed of Australia, New Zealand, Great Britain, Ireland, the West Indies, Canada, and the United States.

Although the book is dated, much of the information is still relevant and would be useful as historical background or in locating reference sources on a particular country's literature for children.

21. Pellowski, Anne. *The World of Storytelling.* Bronx, NY: H. W. Wilson, 1990.

Here is a comprehensive treatise on storytelling, beginning with a description that is both historical and multicultural. The various uses of oral storytelling are reviewed, as well as the different settings, such as camps and libraries, where storytelling may take place. Training for storytelling, props used, and storytelling festivals round out the topics covered.

In chapter 14, "A Brief History and Survey of Training Methods," Anne Pellowski discusses traditional methods of apprenticeship, library school courses, in-service training, and training manuals. A lengthy bibliography is provided and the book is well indexed.

22. Pilla, Marianne Laino. *Resources for Middle-Grade Reluctant Readers: A Guide for Librarians.* Littleton, CO: Libraries Unlimited, 1987.

This book is intended as a selection and resource guide for librarians working with reluctant readers in the middle grades. The book can also be useful for teachers in knowing what literature, media, and software exist in the field. The book presents an overview and identification process of the characteristics of the "reluctant reader," the importance of recreational reading, reading preference, and the role and services of the library in meeting these needs. Guidelines for selecting and processing materials include readability formulas by Dale-Chall, Fry, and software programs and high interest/low vocabulary books.

Library programs, teaching suggestions, and software programs that can motivate reading are described.

A selected annotated bibliography groups books by categories of adventure, animals, biography, family and friends, fantasy and supernatural, folktales and legends, history and historical fiction, humor, modern fiction, movies, mystery, science and science fiction, sports and recreation, and trivia. Magazines, series books, and software oriented to this age group and reading level are listed. A general bibliography includes much research in education and library science. Subject index.

23. Rahn, Suzanne. *Children's Literature: An Annotated Bibliography of the History and Criticism.* New York: Garland, 1981.

This annotated bibliography selects and evaluates secondary sources in the history and criticism of children's literature as literature. Children's literature is defined by its primary audience being children. The genres covered include fiction, entertaining nonfiction, drama, and poetry. Adult fiction adopted by children, traditional folktales, and educational, religious, and didactic works are excluded. Studies of illustration and its history are excluded, and only limited illustrators whose work is known for text as well as art are included. Also excluded are works on child development, librarianship, or education. Selection is based on a work's historical perspective and criticial approach.

The book is organized into studies of aims and definitions of children's literature, the history, genres, and authors. The introduction surveys the development of critical interest in the field, beginning with Mrs. Trimmer's reviewing in the late eighteenth century up through the 1970s. The author concludes that much of the recent scholarship in the field is mediocre and she calls for higher standards for historical or critical work.

The annotations briefly summarize the contents with some evaluation of usefulness, impact, or literary quality. The section on authors includes a selected listing of major works. The appendix describes specialized periodicals which regularly publish articles on the history and criticism of children's literature. The index includes names only.

24. Reed, Arthea J. S. *Comics to Classics: A Parent's Guide to Books for Teens and Preteens.* Newark, DE: International Reading Association, 1988.

Even though this book is directed toward parents, it is a valuable resource on young adult literature for teachers and librarians. Few books exist in the field that approach this age group and recommend readings. The first three chapters discuss the stages of adolescent development as related to reading interests and practices. The author focuses on strategies for encouraging reluctant readers. The next section explores the nature of adolescent literature, the adolescent as reader, and a recommended reading list of fiction and nonfiction appropriate for the age. Titles are organized by subject and annotated with general age ranges indicated: preadolescent (ages 10–12), early adolescent (ages 13–15), and late adolescent (ages 15–18). Other symbols indicate gender interest and reading-aloud favorites. The third section examines reading aloud, book discussions, and television, video, and computer as literary aids. The final section covers selection principles, library services, reference books for personal use, and resources about adolescents, including popular books and professional literature. The appendix includes a list of book publishers.

25. Rollock, Barbara. *Black Authors and Illustrators of Children's Books: A Biographical Dictionary.* Second edition. New York: Garland, 1992.

This book offers biographical sketches of leading black authors and illustrators of children's books. The first edition, which appeared in 1987, contained 115 sketches; the second edition includes over 150. The author's intention is to expand knowledge of contemporary black authors and artists beyond the narrow scope of a few well-known names. The coverage is international. The only authors excluded are those who are primarily adult authors with only one book for children. The emphasis is on works with original subject matter and literary quality that have been issued by trade publishers.

Biographical material is supplied for each entry. Bibliographies of books by that individual or reference sources for further information are included. The appendix to the second edition adds publishers' information and awards. An index lists 500 titles. A list of references used in compiling this book makes a good bibliography of biographical sources on black creative artists.

The author's experience as coordinator of children's services for the New York Public Library makes her particularly knowledgeable in the field.

26. Simpson, Mary Jett, editor. *Adventuring with Books: A Booklist for Pre-K–Grade 6.* Ninth edition. Urbana, IL: National Council of Teachers of English, 1989.

This volume recommends over 1,800 children's books published between 1985 and 1988. The intended audience is composed of teachers and librarians interested in selecting titles and planning instruction from a list prepared by the Committee on the Elementary School Booklist of the National Council of Teachers of English. The titles are selected for their literary and artistic quality from over 8,000 titles considered.

The books are organized by genre and special interest categories that highlight particular instructional needs. The chapters consist of the following: books for babies and toddlers; concept books; wordless books; language and reading; poetry; classics; traditional literature; fantasy; science fiction; realistic fiction; historical fiction; biography; social studies; science and mathematics; fine arts; crafts and hobbies; sports and games; holidays; professional books; teaching literature; and book awards and booklists. Books are listed with some indication as to age range and format. The annotations describe the contents and evaluate the usefulness of the book for the classroom and curriculum connections. The book is useful in finding current books on specific subject areas, professional readings, and for information on awards and booklists. Its limitations are the publishing dates of entries, which are exclusive to a three-year time span.

It is part of the NCTE Bibliography Series, which is frequently revised. The appendix consists of a directory of publishers. An author, illustrator, subject, and title index follows.

27. Smith, Laura. *Children's Book Awards International: A Directory of Awards and Winners, from Inception through 1990.* Jefferson, NC: McFarland, 1992.

The purpose of this directory is to record awards given for writing and illustrating children's books from around the world. Books from 47 countries are cited. The directory is organized alphabetically, first by country and then by award name. Each award listing gives the formal name of the award, the sponsoring organization, the address and telephone number, a contact person (when available), and the origins and nature of the award. Four indexes list awards and sponsors, authors, illustrators and titles. Information on international award books is hard to secure, which makes this book a valuable reference tool for multicultural literature.

28. *Something About the Author. Autobiography Series.* Detroit: Gale, 1986–.

In this series, authors of books for upper elementary through high school are invited to write an essay of approximately 10,000 words addressed to their readers. The writers also are requested to supply a selection of personal photographs to include with the essay. Included at the end of each essay is a bibliography listing publication information for each book's first printing in the United States and Great Britain. A cumulative index lists all essayists in the series as well as subjects mentioned: for instance, personal names, titles of works, and geographical names.

29. Williams, Helen E. *Books by African-American Authors and Illustrators for Children and Young Adults.* Chicago: American Library Association, 1991.

This bibliography identifies children's and young adult books written and illustrated by black writers and artists. Other sources list books about black children and culture without designation of the racial background of the authors or illustrators. This book assists in the identification of multicultural materials, particularly those by black artists.

While not comprehensive, the listing includes a representative collection of 1,213 works published during the twentieth century up to 1990. The books are grouped around three academic levels: preschool and primary grades; middle and junior high school level; and young adult and senior high level.

One chapter focuses on 52 black illustrators and their works, and describes their styles, media, color languages, and compositions. The terminology is explained in a glossary in the appendix. A bibliography of their works is also included, with cross-referencing to works by black authors listed in the bibliography section.

The book includes a listing of awards and prizes, the glossary of art terms, a short bibliography, and an index.

Chapter 2

Journals for Teaching Children's Literature

This section lists the wide range of periodical material on children's books. Most of the sources are applicable to the teaching of children's literature to adults and or to children, while some titles appear on the list to demonstrate the extensiveness of media interest in children's books. Instructors of children's literature should be aware of the rich periodical literature which exists — and has for well over a century — on reviewing and literary criticism of children's books.

The publications are briefly described as to scope or contents related to children's literature. Further information about these titles can be found in two standard reference tools: Ulrich's *International Periodicals Directory* and Katz's *Magazines for Libraries*.

30. *The ALAN Review.* Assembly on Literature for Adolescents, National Council of Teachers of English.

Reviews, news, and articles on young adult literature. 3/yr.

31. *Appraisal: Science Books for Children.* Children's Science Book Review Committee.

Reviews of juvenile science books by librarians and science specialists. Introductory essay. 4/yr.

32. *The Book Report.* Linworth Publishing.

Articles for junior and senior high school librarians. Author profiles, articles, book reviews, and booktalks. 5/yr.

Articles and reports on literature for children and young adults; international news; and professional reading. 4/yr.

33. *Bookbird.* The International Board of Books for Young People and the International Institute for Children's Literature and Reading Research.

34. *Booklist.* American Library Association.
Book lists for youth, middle readers, older readers, and the young; bibliographies on special subjects; translated books and international titles; and reviews. 23/yr.

35. *Bulletin of the Center for Children's Books.* University of Illinois Graduate School of Library and Information Science, University of Illinois Press.
Editorial essays, reviews, and professional sources. 11/yr.

36. *CBC Features.* Children's Book Council.
Information about publishing, booklists, interviews, and materials. 2/yr.

37. *CCL (Canadian Children's Literature).* University of Guelph, Ontario, Department of English.
Journal of criticism and reviews of Canadian books for children and young adults and on general subjects of interest; bibliographies; and interviews. 4/yr.

38. *Childhood Education.* Association for Childhood Education International.
Columns on "Books for Children," "Professional Books"; and special articles. 5/yr.

39. *Children's Literature.* Modern Language Association division on Children's Literature and the Children's Literature Association.
Literary criticism of children's literature; reviews; and notes on dissertations. 1/yr.

40. *Children's Literature Abstracts.* International Federation of Library Associations.

Comprehensive bibliography on international authors and their works, historical and contemporary. 4/yr.

41. *Children's Literature Association Quarterly (ChLA).* Children's Literature Association.
Critical essays; theme issues; reviews; professional news; and annual bibliography. 4/yr.

42. *Children's Literature in Education.* Human Sciences Press.
Critical essays on modern authors or single works, analysis or commentary on social issues reflected in books, interviews, accounts of classroom practice and theory. 4/yr.

43. *Emergency Librarian.* Rockland Press (Canada).
Articles and booklists for children's and young adult librarians; professional readings; and curriculum and programming emphasis. 5/yr.

44. *English Journal.* National Council of Teachers of English.
Columns on "Resources and Reviews" and "Books for the Teenage Reader"; essays on response-theory criticism and young adult literature; and professional news. 8/yr.

45. *The Five Owls.* The Five Owls.
Feature articles and bibliographies; profiles of authors and illustrators; and reviews. 5/yr.

46. *The Horn Book.* 6/yr.

47. *The Horn Book Guide to Children and Young Adult Books.* The Horn Book.
Oldest journal in the field includes reviews of recommended books; articles about children's literature; and professional news. Guide evaluates books of the year. 2/yr.

48. *Instructor.* Scholastic.
Columns on "Poetry Pages" and "Author Study Teacher Guide"; essays on language arts; and children's fiction book reviews. 9/yr.

49. *International Review of Children's Literature and Librarianship.* Taylor Graham publishers.
Feature articles, research reports, and literary criticism. 3/yr.

50. *Journal of Reading*: *A Journal of Adolescent and Adult Literacy*. The International Reading Association.

Columns on "Books for Adolescents," "Classroom Materials," and "Professional Materials." 8/yr.

51. *Journal of Youth Services in Libraries* (*JOYS*). American Library Association, Association of Library Service for Children.

Formerly (until 1987) called *Top of the News*. News and articles of interest to children and young adult librarians. 4/yr.

52. *The Junior Bookshelf*. Woodfield and Stanley.

Introductory articles, awards, and new books. 6/yr.

53. *Language Arts*. National Council of Teachers of English.

Essays on all facets of language arts learning and teaching; theme issues; and column, "Bookalogues: Talking About Children's Literature." 8/yr.

54. *The Lion and the Unicorn*. Johns Hopkins University Press.

A critical journal that focuses on themes in children's and young adult literature; with essays and book reviews of professional reading. 2/yr.

55. *Multicultural Review*. Greenwood.

Feature articles, bibliographies, and reviews on ethnic, racial, and religious diversity; and column, "Chalkboard," that focuses on materials for teachers. 4/yr.

56. *The New Advocate*. University of Georgia, College of Education, Christopher-Gordon.

Articles on the use of children's literature across the curriculum; interviews; literary criticism; and reviews of multicultural books. 4/yr.

57. *The New York Times Book Review*. The New York Times.

A page of reviews of children's books appears nearly every week. 52/yr.

58. *The New Yorker*. The New Yorker Magazine.

Lengthy feature articles on children's books in a November issue each year; with cartoons often featuring folktale characters. 50/yr.

59. *Nineteenth-Century Literature.* University of California Press (Berkeley).

Literary criticism, new research, comparative studies, bibliographies, and reviews. 4/yr.

60. *Phaedrus.* 1973–88, published irregularly, Columbia University, School of Library Service.

Although no longer published, this is one of the best sources for information on international research in children's literature; articles; bibliographies; and reviews.

61. *Publications of the Modern Language Association* (*PMLA*). Modern Language Association.

Articles on literary criticism that include studies of children's books. 6/yr.

62. *Publishers Weekly.* Reed Properties.

Regular column on children's book publishing; interviews with authors and illustrators; and reviews. 52/yr.

63. *The Reading Teacher.* International Reading Association.

Articles, reviews, and a column on "Children's Books." 8/yr.

64. *The School Librarian.* School Library Association (U.K.).

Articles, news, and reviews for school librarians. 4/yr.

65. *School Library Journal.* Cahners/Bowker.

Articles and reviews for children's and youth librarians, and school and public libraries. 12/yr.

66. *School Library Media Quarterly.* American Association of School Librarians.

News and reviews for school library media specialists. 4/yr.

67. *Signal: Approaches to Children's Books.* Thimble Press (U.K.).

Critical essays on literature and pedagogy. 4/yr.

68. *Storytelling Magazine.* National Association for the Preservation and Perpetuation of Storytelling.

Articles on storytelling; stories; profiles; and resources. 4/yr.

69. *Teaching K-8.* Early Years/Highlights for Children.

Articles and reviews for teachers and librarians; interviews with authors and illustrators; and professional readings. 8/yr.

70. *Times Literary Supplement.* Times Supplements (U.K.).

Book reviews that include attention to new works of literary criticism or art history related to children's literature. 52/yr.

71. *Voice of Youth Advocates* (*VOYA*). Scarecrow.

Reviews and articles for professionals who work with young adults. 6/yr.

72. *Wilson Library Bulletin.* H. W. Wilson.

Columns on "Picture Books for Children," "Middle Books," and "The Young Adult Perplex." 10/yr.

73. *Yellow Brick Road.* Viceroy.

Profiles of children's book authors and illustrators; and activities and books on related themes. 6/yr.

Chapter 3

Textbooks for Teaching Children's Literature

The use of textbooks in the teaching of children's literature has a long tradition. Many older texts in the field exist, although most are out of print. Harvey Darton's *Children's Books in England* (1932, revised by Brian Alderson in 1982) is a notable exception. Courses in education and library science departments generally use single-volume textbooks, often supplemented by another paperbound book, such as Jim Trelease's *Read-Aloud Handbook*. English courses tend to use anthologies or paperbound copies of children's books, occasionally supplemented by a book of critical readings, such as Sheila Egoff's *Only Connect*.

The titles listed are designed for general survey courses in children's literature. Some texts may not be represented here if their publishers did not send a copy when requested.

The curricular offerings cited in the directory (chapter 8) mention a wide range of related courses, such as storytelling, illustration, or fairy tales. Texts for these courses are not specifically listed here, as they would require more specialized texts. For example, a course in storytelling might want to draw on Anne Pellowski's *The World of Storytelling* or Augusta Baker and Ellin Greene's *Storytelling: Art and Technique*. A course in illustration might use Uri Shulevitz's *Writing with Pictures*, Nancy Hands's *Illustrating Children's Books*, or Perry Nodelman's *Words About Pictures*. A course in fairy tales could draw on diverse collections by Iona and Peter Opie, Jack Zipes, or U. C. Knoepflmacher, among many others.

The *Subject Guide to Books in Print* lists a large number of available books under the heading "Children's Literature — Study and Teaching."

74. Burke, Eileen M. *Early Childhood Literature: For Love of Child and Book*. Boston: Allyn and Bacon, 1986.

This beautifully designed and made book contains a wealth of information and ideas. It would be a good textbook for a children's literature course taught in a College of Education, and possibly for future librarians as well. But even if it is not used by students, it is a valuable resource for instructors.

In the first few chapters Eileen Burke discusses literature for children in general terms, indicating its value and describing the qualities of good books. In later chapters various genres and levels are developed. These include picture books, song and activity books, mysteries, fact books, books dealing with violence and problems, humor in literature, and so on. A chapter on storytelling is included. Each chapter includes activities for the student and extensive bibliographies of professional reading and relevant children's books. Many of the suggested activities involve interaction with and observation of children and their reactions to literature. These activities are of interest to practicing teachers and librarians as well as students.

75. Burke, Eileen M. *Literature for the Young Child*. Second edition. Boston: Allyn and Bacon, 1990.

Children ages three to eight are the focus of this introductory text to children's literature. The author first examines distinctive behaviors of this age group and links genres and specific titles to these characteristics. Basic critical needs of young children are related to literature. Literary elements are explored in terms of the particular readership. In addition to the standard components of characterization, plot, setting, style, and theme, the author adds the consideration of format. Story preferences of young children are discussed, with recommended titles for books illustrating these qualities. Storytelling, story reading, and story living are distinguished from each other, with specific techniques and recommended titles. Variations in book design include toy-like features in many books.

Poetry, music, nursery rhymes, and alphabet books are examined together for their rhythmic quality. Comic elements are traced through poetry, picture books, series books, and puzzle, riddle, and joke books. Picture books are explored for their value to young children, with specific criteria for evaluation and examples. Folktales are distinguished by oral or written versions and types of folktales.

Ethnic collections and related folktales are cited along with other extension activities. Realistic fiction and fantasy are related to meeting the emotional or social needs of young children. Information books, divided into concept books and counting books, are analyzed and evaluated.

The final chapter examines response to literature and proposes "a story-rich curriculum, with selected sources cited for planning." The appendix includes strategies for selecting, adapting, and preparing stories for telling; a list of Caldecott Medal books; and sources for teacher-parent communications. Each chapter includes quotations from noted authors, artists, educators, and critics along with discussion topics and recommended children's book titles and secondary sources.

76. Butler, Francelia. *Sharing Literature with Children: A Thematic Anthology.* Prospect Heights, IL: Waveland Press, 1989.

First published in 1977, this was one of the first anthologies to appear in the field. It has recently been republished in paperback format. The author is one of the first in the field of English to advocate the inclusion of children's literature as a serious study. Her efforts led to the founding of the Children's Literature Association. She continues to edit the Children's Literature annual.

This anthology is organized thematically rather than generically, which is often the most common form of presentation in textbooks. The themes are chosen to be the ones most deeply felt by all human beings: toys and games, fools, masks and shadows, sex roles, and circles.

Four criteria for selection of material include feeling, values, quality, and balance. Genre distinctions, appearing as subcategories under each theme, include myth, biblical writing, fable, folk rhymes, folk plays, folktales, fiction, fantasy, biography, poetry, and critical essays.

Suggested activities for active participation, suggested readings, and critical essays accompany each thematic section. There is an index.

77. Corcoran, Bill, and Emrys Evans. *Readers, Texts, Teachers.* Upper Montclair, NJ: Boynton/Cook, 1987.

This anthology is a theoretical and practical guide to reader-response theory in the classroom. The book contains a collection of essays on reader-oriented approaches, emphasizing the transactive criticism of Louise Rosenblatt and Wolfgang Iser, with some attention to other approaches, including deconstruction.

After a background discussion of the historical placement of reader-response theory, the text focuses on the culture of the classroom: creation of readers, the accessibility of literature, connections to the writing process, and poetry and drama. Children and young adult novels are used as examples throughout the text. The authors and other contributors are British, and most of the examples are British contemporary classics, with a few Australian and American selections. An extensive bibliography contains a crossover of disciplines: reader-response theories, research studies in language and literature development, literary texts, and children's books.

78. Cullinan, Bernice E. *Literature and the Child*. Second edition. San Diego: Harcourt Brace Jovanovich, 1989.

Bernice Cullinan is a New York University professor of education who is well known in the field. She presents a comprehensive, activity-based literature program for children at the nursery, elementary, and junior high levels.

The text is divided into three parts. Part 1, "The Child," explores developmental childhood education, including children's social, emotional, and cognitive growth. Drawing upon Piagetian theory, the author argues for selecting books appropriate to developmental needs.

Part 2, "The Books," focuses on genres and themes that coordinate with the school curriculum: picture books, folklore, fantasy and science fiction, realistic fiction, historical fiction, biography, and nonfiction.

Part 3, "The World of Books," examines multicultural and historical children's literature. Five racial and ethnic groups are discussed in terms of their contributions to children's literature. In addition to a survey of the history, a time line of major authors, illustrators, and books appears in the endpapers.

The author emphasizes the importance of critical analysis throughout the book. Teaching ideas, activity projects, landmark books, and bibliographies are regular features in every chapter. The appendix cites children's book awards, book selection aids, other professional books and periodicals, children's magazines and publishers, and birthdays of selected authors and illustrators. Indexes are included.

79. Darton, F. J. Harvey. *Children's Books in England: Five Centuries of Social Life*. Third edition. Cambridge: Cambridge University Press, 1982.

First published in 1932, this book is still considered the definitive history of children's literature. The second edition was revised in 1958 by Kathleen Lines, and the third and most recent edition was revised in 1982 by Brian Alderson.

The history is chronologically explored from Caxton's *Aesop's Fables* to the work of Stevenson and Kipling. The emphasis is on British children's literature, with some attention to American adaptations and classic works. The subtitle reflects the author's prevailing interest in the social context of children's reading. Darton comes from a family long involved in children's book publishing, a special knowledge which makes this book unique.

Brian Alderson's revision expands the text with new research. Checking on all of Darton's sources, Alderson makes some amendments in the notes section. The booklist is expanded and organized into categories of primary and secondary sources; these are subdivided into specific areas of interest.

The appendix includes information on Victorian and Edwardian titles unknown to Darton; an outline of the history of the publishing houses of Newbery and Darton; a listing of books written by Darton; and an essay, "The Youth of a Children's Magazine," Darton's own recollections of his editorship of *Chatterbox*. The third edition is well illustrated.

80. Demers, Patricia, editor. *A Garland from the Golden Age: An Anthology of Children's Literature from 1850 to 1900.* Toronto: Oxford University Press, 1988.

This anthology contains selections from the Golden Age of children's literature, considered to be its richest period for literary quality. The selections include John Ruskin's *The King of the Golden River*, Thomas Hughes's *Tom Brown's Schooldays*, Charles Dickens's *The Magic Fishbone*, Oscar Wilde's *The Happy Prince*, Kenneth Grahame's *The Golden Age*, Christina Rossetti's *Sing-Song*, and Robert Louis Stevenson's *A Child's Garden of Verses*. More obscure works are also represented, once popular books by authors such as Frances Browne, Jean Ingelow, Flora Shaw, Hesba Stretton, Lucy Clifford, and Annie Keary.

To offset the widely held belief that the Golden Age was a British phenomenon, the editor intentionally includes works that show the importance of North American writers. Excerpts from the stories and poems of American writers Helen Hunt Jackson, Thomas Bailey Aldrich, Joel Chandler Harris, Howard Pyle, and James Whitcomb Riley are included, as well as writings from several Canadian authors: James De Mille, Margaret Murray Robertson, Norman Duncan, W. A. Fraser, and Catherine Parr Traill.

The selections are organized into genre chapters that move from the fairy tale to the allegorical narrative, evangelical writing, children's novel, nursery fiction, school stories, stories of adventure, penny dreadfuls and dime novels, animal stories, children's periodicals, and children's poetry. Each chapter is introduced with commentary and historical background. Each selection is briefly prefaced. The bibliography includes references and readings for each chapter. Index.

81. Demers, Patricia, and Gordon Moyles, editors. *From Instruction to Delight: An Anthology of Children's Literature to 1850.* Toronto: Oxford University Press, 1982.

This anthology of early children's literature is organized around the development of the literature "from instruction to delight." This book is one of the few sources for selections from landmark works that are normally just mentioned in historical textbooks. The book chronicles the rise of a more playful and pleasurable spirit in children's books from its more austere beginnings.

The book is divided into eight sections: books of courtesy and early lessons, the "hell-fire" tales of the Puritans, the lyrical instruction of Isaac Watts, chapbooks and penny histories, John Newbery, rational moralists, Sunday school moralists, and harbingers of the Golden Age. Each section is introduced by critical commentary and historical background, and each selection is briefly introduced. The bibliography lists books for each chapter. Well illustrated. Index.

82. Donelson, Kenneth L., and Alleen Pace Nilsen. *Literature for Today's Young Adults.* Third edition. Glenview, IL: Scott, Foresman, 1989.

This textbook is designed for courses in young adult literature in English, education, and library science departments, as well as for professionals who work with youths between the ages of 12 and 20. "Young adult literature" is defined loosely as "any book freely chosen for reading by someone in this age group."

The authors begin with an introduction to young adults, their psychology and literature, and follow with a look at contemporary books and readers together. Censorship is covered in a separate chapter that examines its history, the state of censorship today, assumptions about censorship and censors, attacks on materials, important court decisions, strategies, and a bibliography. The history of the field is included in two chapters which explore its origins and connections to popular culture.

Criteria are cited throughout the text for evaluating various kinds of books. Each chapter includes profiles of contemporary authors and recommended readings, which cite the hardbound publisher.

The appendix cites books of distinction, book selection guides, and professional readings. Indexes.

83. Egoff, Sheila, G. T. Stubbs, and L. F. Ashley. *Only Connect: Readings on Children's Literature.* Oxford: Oxford University Press, 1980.

This collection of essays is a landmark as one of the earliest anthologies of criticism on children's literature. Most of these essays were inaccessible at the time, although many have been reprinted since this publication. Originally published in 1969, the collection focused on children's literature as part of all literature, to be studied and judged like any branch of writing. While the emphasis was on writing contemporary to the 1960s, the editors also included landmark essays such as those by T. S. Eliot and C. S. Lewis.

The second edition updates some of the historical coverage and includes writing on the problem novel, science fiction, racism and sexism, and the book trade itself.

The book is divided into five major areas: books and children; fairy tales, fantasy, and animals; some writers and their books; illustration; and the modern scene. Of particular interest is Sheila Egoff's historical survey, "Precepts, Pleasures, and Portents: Changing Emphases in Children's Literature."

The contributors are noted figures in the field. Many speak from a creative perspective as authors or illustrators. Their biographies are included at the end of the book. A selective annotated bibliography describes and evaluates important resources in the field.

Sheila Egoff is a distinguished Canadian critic whose other works include *Thursday's Child: Trends and Patterns in Contemporary Children's Literature,* and *The Republic of Childhood: A Critical Guide to Canadian Children's Literature in English.*

84. Farrell, Edmund J., and James Squire. *Transactions with Literature: A Fifty-Year Perspective.* Urbana, IL: National Council of Teachers of English, 1990.

This collection of 12 essays honors the fiftieth anniversary of the publication of Louise Rosenblatt's *Literature as Exploration.* The book contains the following essays: "Fifty Years of Exploring Children's Books" by Rudine Sims Bishop; "Fifty Years of Literature for Young Adults" by Kenneth Donelson; "Students Exploring Literature Across the World" by John Dixon; "Literature as Exploration and the Classroom" by Robert Probst; "The California Literature Project" by Mary A. Barr; "Exploring a Poem" by Stephen Dunning; "Fostering Literary

Understanding: The State of the Schools" by Arthur Applebee; "New Directions in Research on Response to Literature" by Richard Beach; "Can Literature Be Rescued from Reading?" by Alan Purves; "Retrospect" by Louise Rosenblatt; and two annotated bibliographies: "Materials and Approaches to Literature Instruction" by James Bradley, and "Research on Response to Literature" by Richard Beach and Susan Hynds.

These articles show the extensive influence of Rosenblatt's work in the field of children's and young adult literature. Attention to the responses of readers stimulated new interest in the literature itself, to critical standards by which it could be judged, and its enhanced use in the classroom. The perspective of literature as a transaction between book and reader encouraged the development of strategies to enhance the transaction. Emphasis on reader response broadened research to include the literary transaction as literary experience.

85. Gallagher, Mary Elizabeth. *Young Adult Literature: Issues and Perspectives*. Haverford, PA: Catholic Library Association, 1988.

This textbook is designed for a wide audience of teachers, librarians, and parents. The book seems most appropriate for librarians and other professionals who want to learn more about the wealth of authors who write for young adults.

The book is organized around three critical components of the adolescent literary transaction: the psychology and developmental needs of young adults, the producers and promoters of literature, and the literature itself. Two areas are intentionally omitted: the history of the field and methodology for teaching. Historical perspectives on library services to youth and on major authors from the 1930s through the 1980s are presented. The emphasis is on the promotion of leisure and recreational reading. Bibliographies of suggested readings and related media are offered for each chapter. Most book titles are annotated. A list of material selection resources, glossary, and index are included.

86. Glazer, Joan I. *Literature for Young Children*. Third edition. New York: Merrill, 1990.

This book focuses on young children's developmental growth, literature as an art form, and the ways that literature enhances children's development. The intended audience is preschool and in-service teachers, day care professionals, and all who work with preschool and primary age children.

The first three chapters explore the range of literature for children, demonstrate standards of literary excellence, and suggest methods of book selection. Chapter 4 presents the idea of grouping books for class presentation, so that children can discover the interrelatedness of literature. Chapters 5 through 9 examine the ways children's books support child development in language, intellectual, personality, social, moral, aesthetic, and creative areas. The final chapter gives various ways of presenting a book, using one book as appropriate for preschoolers and another for primary grade children, and offers evaluative material for literature programs. Each chapter includes research findings and recommended references, as well as recommended children's books.

The appendix cites Caldecott Medal awards. Charts and illustrations and indexes are included.

87. Hickman, Janet, and Bernice Cullinan. *Children's Literature in the Classroom: Weaving Charlotte's Web.* Norwood, MA: Christopher-Gordon, 1989.

This collection of essays is a festschrift for Charlotte Huck, noted author of the text *Children's Literature in the Elementary School.* The authors are former students and friends of Huck at Ohio State University. They reflect on her influence on their work and their own continued use of literature in schools.

The book is organized around Huck's favorite genres, her research and writing interests, and her convictions about children and books. The prologue presents a biographical sketch of Charlotte Huck through a vignette of her personal and professional life. Part 1, "Beginnings: Understanding the Uses of Literature in the Classroom," contains essays about Huck's philosophy on literary quality, early literacy, reading aloud, writing from literature, and literature across the curriculum. Part 2, "Strands: Celebrating Books and Authors in Four Genres," deals with the genres of picture books, fantasy, historical fiction, and poetry, with selected essays written by noted authors and illustrators. Part 3, "Patterns: Developing Literature-Based Programs," includes discussions of literature within the school curriculum and a survey of professional literature in the field.

The epilogue, "No Wider Than the Heart Is Wide," is a landmark address given by Charlotte Huck in 1976 to the International Reading Association. The address was instrumental in promoting more attention within the organization to the place of children's literature in the reading program.

Each chapter includes discussions of recommended books for children. Professional references are listed at the end of each chapter.

A comprehensive listing of all children's books cited appears at the end. This book is particularly geared toward teachers, librarians, and administrators.

88. Huck, Charlotte S., Susan Hepler, and Janet Hickman. *Children's Literature in the Elementary School*. Fifth edition. Fort Worth: Harcourt Brace Jovanovich, 1989.

First published in 1961, this standard textbook is used for children's literature courses in library science, education, and English. The book is organized with a triple focus on the reader, the book, and teaching. The emphasis is on research and practice. Part 1 examines the values and criteria for choosing and using literature with children at various developmental stages. An historical survey of children's literature is included, which explores the ways the literature has evolved. Part 2 explores children's book genres and establishes evaluative criteria for each one. Part 3 focuses on teaching methodology, curricular use, and literature-based reading programs.

The new edition contains samples from children's work, taken from real literature-based classrooms. Multiculturalism is emphasized as part of each genre or subject area. Special sections on resources for teaching include charts, models, activities, and bibliographies.

Appendices address children's book awards, book selection aids, and publishers' and book club addresses. A list of 110 recommended books for reading aloud is contained in the endpapers. The instructor's manual is written by Mary Lou White. Index.

89. Hunt, Peter. *Criticism, Theory, and Children's Literature*. Cambridge, MA: Basil Blackwell, 1991.

Peter Hunt, a British critic and children's book author, examines the relationship between literary criticism and children's literature, the present state of children's literature, and definitions of children's literature. The book uses criticial theory to help readers understand children's literature, and children's literature to help readers understand critical theory. The result is a critical approach that emphasizes the child as reader, or what Hunt calls a "childist" criticism.

Hunt defines criticism in terms of reader response: "what happens when we read, and how we can perceive and talk about a book or make a reasoned selective judgment." Hunt prefers not to analyze literature in terms of the literary elements of plot, setting, or character, but instead to begin with the reader and the book, examining each for appearance or effect, background, skills required, the circumstance of reading. The relationship of the child to the book also depends on the book as a material object, what Hunt calls "the peritext," its textual and graphic layout, as well as text, its style, and structure. The emphasis is on how the reader relates to these elements, how the conventions of genre affect the text, and how the conventions of text affect the meaning. The exploration then moves outside the text, to the ideological implications and cultural production of children's books. His approach is toward understanding ways of reading texts rather than on biographical, educational, or practical applications. Subjects covered include reader response, stylistics, narrative theory, illustration, and criticism and children's literature.

Extensive notes and a selective bibliography are included.

90. Jackson, Mary V. *Engines of Instruction, Mischief, and Magic: Children's Literature in England from Its Beginnings to 1839.* Lincoln: University of Nebraska Press, 1990.

Mary Jackson's book is the most current source on the history of children's literature. The focus is on British children's literature in its early history up to 1839, the beginning of the Victorian period and a new respectability for children's books. Her emphasis is on children's books as social artifacts, related to the marketplace of ideas and commerce of any given time. Conflicting ideologies created what Jackson calls "the continued tussle between piety and fantasy." The focus on children's literature as reflecting diverse social influences from the adult world gives a modern slant to this interpretive history. Jackson's premise can be applied to contemporary literature of childhood.

The study begins in the mid–eighteenth century with John Newbery's pioneer enterprise in the children's book trade and then traces its origins. Children's literature emerged from earlier prototypes of adult literature: alphabets, romances and fairy tales, ballads, fables, chapbooks, and religious works. The Puritans are credited as the first creators of books for children's leisure reading.

The innovations of Thomas Boreman, Mary Cooper, and John Newbery mark a new era in book publishing: the establishment of children's books as a distinct branch of the trade. Reformists used children's books as the vehicle for educational change, literacy, and moral improvement. The French Revolution produced a conservative reaction toward earlier ideas of class mobility and romanticism, creating a more utilitarian approach to books for children. The apostles of fancy countered with the publishing of poetry, nursery songs, nonsense verse, and fairy tales. Ahead were the technical innovations to come in illustration and the great classics of the Victorian and Edwardian eras.

The bibliography includes selected primary and secondary sources. The text includes 160 illustrations.

91. Lewis, Claudia. "A Review of Children's Literature Anthologies and Core Texts." *Children's Literature* 6(1977): 246–54.

This bibliographic essay reviews standard children's literature anthologies and textbooks current in 1977. The author begins with a listing of texts and guides to children's literature, most of which are discussed in the essay. Her interest is in examining approach, coverage, and critical thinking skills. Four anthologies are examined: Sutherland and Arbuthnot's *Children and Books*, Huck and Kuhn's *Children's Literature in the Elementary School*, Hollowell's *A Book of Children's Literature*, and Butler's *Sharing Literature with Children*. The Sutherland-Arbuthnot and Huck-Kuhn anthologies are organized by genre, covering some of the best in poetry, fiction, and fact, with the hope that further reading will follow. Criticism is not a major consideration. The Hollowell book is compared as similar in approach, but with briefer introductions and descriptions. Butler's book, by contrast to the others, offers a thematic arrangement.

A variety of core texts are examined. The two giants are Sutherland and Arbuthnot's *Children and Books* and Huck and Kuhn's *Children's Literature in the Elementary School*. While both texts cover many subjects and current issues, their breadth necessitates little depth. Some of the smaller texts go into more detail. Two that are found wanting in terms of attention to critical thinking: Georgiou's *Children and Their Literature* and Lickteig's *An Introduction to Children's Literature*. A new book by Lonsdale and Macintosh, *Children Experience Literature*, is valued for its original approach and practical application.

Several texts take a more in-depth approach to critical thinking: James Steel Smith's *A Critical Approach to Children's Literature*, Anderson and Groff's *A New Look at Children's Literature*, and Sebesta and Iverson's *Literature for Thursday's Child*. Seven small books are included in a series titled, *Literature for Children*, edited by Pose Lamb. Patricia Cianciolo's *Illustrations in Children's Books* includes a 60-page annotated bibliography. Bernice Cullinan's *Literature for Children: Its Discipline and Content* emphasizes literary criticism in engaging higher level thinking skills. Rebecca Lukens's *A Critical Handbook of Children's Literature* is a valuable supplementary text, particularly for its discussion of literary elements. Masha Rudman's *Children's Literature: An Issues Approach* explores issues of race, gender, siblings, divorce, death, aging, war, and sex. Nancy Larrick's *A Parent's Guide to Children's Reading* is used in some college courses for its current overview of children's reading interests and recommended titles.

92. Lukens, Rebecca J. *A Critical Handbook of Children's Literature.* Fourth edition. Glenview, IL: Scott, Foresman/Little, Brown Higher Education, 1990.

This latest edition of a standard handbook in the field presents children's literature as literature, different only in degree, not in kind, from writing for adults. The book is designed to train students to make critical judgments in evaluating literature and to increase pleasures in literature. The chapters include critical discussions, followed by a summary, reading and evaluating criteria, and a list of recommended books.

Literary elements are emphasized, such as plot, style, setting, point of view, character, and theme. Children's literature should be judged by the same standards as adult literature. Children can benefit over a lifetime by early exposure to good literature.

The fourth edition includes a new chapter on picture books and a revised chapter on the major genres of literature. Separate chapters examine nonfiction and poetry.

The updated appendices highlight award-winning books, magazines, and reviewing publications. A glossary of literary terms is included.

Several children's books are used extensively as examples in the text: *Charlotte's Web*; *Roll of Thunder, Hear My Cry*; *The Borrowers*; *The Witch of Blackbird Pond*; *The Incredible Journey*; *A Wizard of Earthsea*; *The Slave Dancer*; and *Island of the Blue Dolphins*. These books could be assigned as corollary reading.

This is the major textbook to examine children's literature in terms of literary elements.

93. Moss, Anita, and Jon C. Stott. *The Family of Stories: An Anthology of Children's Literature.* New York: Holt, Rinehart and Winston, 1986.

This textbook is based on the structural and generic similarities of literature forming "the family of stories." The editors draw on Northrop Frye's literary theories, particularly his notion of the familial relationship of literature in *The Educated Imagination*, and on Joseph Campbell's principle of heroic journeys, linear and circular, in *The Hero with a Thousand Faces*. Frye and Campbell stress that stories are understood because the characters, settings, and actions represent the human condition.

The editors organize their literary selections to show connections. The first three selections illustrate the traditional genres of folktales, hero tales, and myths. The next three sections on literary fairy tales and legends show how children's writers of the past two centuries have re-created traditional motifs into their own imaginative works. The seventh section contains modern works which are grouped by journey patterns.

Introductions to each section describe genre characteristics, stylistic patterns, thematic motifs, literary origins, publishing history, literary criticism, and curricular use. Annotated bibliographies at the end of each section include related literature. While the reading selections are fairy tales and folklore, picture books and novels are covered to some extent in the appendix, with commentary and discussion of important works.

Methodology for teaching literature and building curriculum is included in the appendix. In teaching interpretive skills to children, the authors stress reader response theories, drawing on the work of Louise Rosenblatt, D. W. Harding, Stephen Dunning and Alan Howes, Hugh and Maureen Crago, Alan Purvis, and Northrop Frye. Their approaches to teaching literature to children are based on numerous workshops and on research in the classroom. An annotated bibliography notes pertinent secondary sources in the field.

The authors are well-known scholars and teachers of children's literature who have practical classroom experience with children. Moss is a specialist in Victorian fairy tales and Stott is the author of *Children's Literature from A to Z.*

94. Nodelman, Perry. *The Pleasures of Children's Literature.* New York: Longman, 1992.

This introduction to children's literature is designed to provide an interdisciplinary approach to the subject. Drawing upon recent research, it places children's literature in the context of children's literary education. The book is divided into two sections: to provide adults with contexts and strategies of comprehension, and to suggest ways of teaching children these contexts and strategies.

Children's literature is described as an "intersection of two different sets of contexts: our ideas about children, and our ideas about literature." Perry Nodelman draws upon reader-response theories to construct an approach to reading children's literature. Using the concept of the implied reader, he suggests a necessary repertoire of skills and a set of strategies by which the characteristics of children's literature are revealed through generic pattern.

Children's literature as a genre is described by the following characteristics: simple and straightforward, action-centered, about childhood, a child's point of view, optimistic, tending toward fantasy, a form of pastoral idyll, innocent viewpoint, didactic, repetitious, and a balance of idyllic and didactic. Ideological issues are discussed, such as gender roles. Various literary theories and approaches are covered, including Jungian, psychoanalytical, structural, and deconstruction. Various genres are discussed: poetry, picture books, fairy tales and myths, nonfiction, and fiction. The author is known for his writing on fairy tales and a theoretical work on picture books, *Words About Pictures*. An extensive bibliography on the literature in the field recommends readings in children's literature as a genre, critical theory, and pedagogy. Index.

95. Norton, Donna E. *Through the Eyes of a Child: An Introduction to Children's Literature*. Third edition. New York: Merrill, 1991.

This book is designed for children's literature classes in English, education, and library science departments. The third edition updates book suggestions and research findings, and includes a section on literary elements and a chapter on multicultural literature.

The book begins with the connections between children and books, the history of children's literature, evaluating and selecting literature for children, illustration, and then follows with chapters on specific genres: picture books, traditional literature, modern fantasy, poetry, contemporary realistic fiction, historical fiction, nonfiction, and multicultural literature.

Most chapters are further divided into two parts: genre and involvement. The author describes the characteristics, history, and titles related to a particular genre and then gives strategies for involving children in that genre. Extensive bibliographies of children's books are provided.

The appendix cites book selection aids, professional reading, book awards, readability charts, and publishers' addresses. Indexes.

96. Paulin, Mary Ann. *More Creative Uses of Children's Literature*. Hamden, CT: Library Professional Publications, 1992.

This book is a sequel and companion to *Creative Uses of Children's Literature* (Library Professional Publications, 1982). The new volume has a goal similar to that of the earlier edition: to introduce as many books as possible to children in as many creative ways as possible. The books seek to incorporate art, music, puppetry, and creative dramatics into language arts or library programs for elementary school children. Many of the same topics and themes are covered, with the addition of material published in the last decade. References exist to the earlier edition, so the two books serve together as a resource to books and activities for children.

The opening chapter covers booktalking, techniques, and themes — such as travel, survival, and the holocaust. Also included in this chapter is a list of books chosen by children, along with annotations on 118 award-winning titles. The second chapter introduces books by their titles, which themselves can show plot, character, setting, and theme. Books can be grouped accordingly for sharing with children. Other chapters present author and genre introductions, the use of media, and whole language instruction. The volume includes extensive indexes by author, title, subject, and multimedia.

This book is one of the few sources that integrate media and literature in terms of activities and suggested titles. The author's experience as a media specialist is invaluable.

97. Purves, Alan, and Dianne L. Monson. *Experiencing Children's Literature*. Glenview, IL: Scott, Foresman, 1984.

This text presents an approach to children's literature based on the transactional theory of Louise Rosenblatt. The book's two main premises are that any piece of writing or pictorial narrative is potentially literature and that the reading of literature involves a transaction between the reader and the text.

Transactional theory has value as a way to integrate various theories related to literature and literary criticism, children and child development, and education and curriculum. Transactional theory presents a coherent approach to accommodating diverse critical methods.

The authors introduce the field with a brief history and a description of research areas: textual editing, bibliographical studies, editing of ancillary materials, biographical studies, and historical studies. Various genres are examined from the perspective of the reader: folklore and myth, prose, poetry, and picture books.

In subsequent chapters Alan Purves and Dianne Monson explore the literary transaction and the nature of children's and adults' responses to literature, criteria for liking and judging books, the place of literature in the schools, and curriculum evaluation.

Numerous booklists, notes, charts, and illustrations are included. Index.

98. Rosenblatt, Louise M. *Literature as Exploration*. Fourth edition. New York: Modern Language Association, 1976.

This classic text of what is now known as "reader response" was first published in 1938. Among the earliest scholars in educational or literary studies to emphasize the importance of reader response, Louise Rosenblatt focused on the importance of experience through literature. She proposed a new approach for teaching literature: a reader-centered methodology that emphasized what real readers thought of the literature they were reading. *Literature as Exploration* is often cited as the first empirically based theoretical statement of the importance of the reader's role.

The author centers on the complex dynamics of personal responses to literature. Part 1 details some of the problems of the teacher of literature and the student in approaching the literary experience. Part 2 presents the necessary background and setting for spontaneous reactions to literature, the effects of the student's personal history in relating to literature, and ways of expanding the student's response to literature. Part 3 examines literary sensitivity as the source of insight and discusses the relationship of literature to basic social concepts, personality, emotion, and reason. A coda reiterates the major theme of the necessity for the reader's active participation in literature.

Reading is a transactional interplay between the reader and the text. Reading for cognitive understanding — efferent reading — and for aesthetic enjoyment — aesthetic reading — are different processes. Schools tend to emphasize the first and neglect the second.

Rosenblatt's ideas are further developed in *The Readers, the Text, the Poem: The Transactional Theory of the Literary Work* (1978).

99. Rothlein, Liz, and Anita Meyer Meinbach. *The Literature Connection: Using Children's Books in the Classroom*. Glenview, IL: Scott, Foresman, 1991.

This textbook is designed for preservice and inservice teachers, preschool through grade eight. The goal is to encourage an appreciation for quality literature and a lifelong love of reading. The approaches, strategies, and activities for using children's literature are organized into four sections: developing interest in literature; genres and elements; literature and the reading program; and connections. The emphasis is clearly pedagogical, with greater attention to methodology than to the literature itself or a survey of authors and illustrators. The authors integrate research into their discussions, and each chapter is well supported by references to the literature. Sample activity sheets and book evaluations are provided. Bibliographies list suggested books for each subject covered. The appendices provide a listing of children's book awards, resources for teaching literature, and publishers' addresses. Index.

100. Rudman, Masha Kabakow. *Children's Literature: An Issues Approach*. Second edition. New York: Longman, 1984.

This book is one of the few subject-centered textbooks in the field. The author arranges books by issues related to child development or cultural values: family, sex, gender roles, heritage, special needs, old age, death, and war. Each chapter includes an introduction to the issue, a discussion of how that issue is addressed in children's literature, suggested reading activities, an annotated reference list, and recommended children's books.

A foreword by Jane Yolen is written from the perspective of an author struggling with issues of the human condition. The introduction by Rudman explores the subject of bibliotherapy and summarizes the chapters that follow.

The last chapter, "Methodology," describes ways of using children's books as materials for a skills approach to the teaching of reading. The author addresses the reading process, activities for enhancing interest in reading, and practical guidelines for the classroom.

The appendix lists publishers' addresses, children's book awards, and professional sources on children's literature. Indexes.

101. Rudman, Masha Kabakow, editor. *Children's Literature: Resources for the Classroom.* Boston: Christopher-Gordon, 1989.

This collection of essays for teachers is organized into three parts: the history and literary genres of children's literature; the selection and evaluation of children's books; and the broader use of children's books in the home, school, and media.

The first four chapters examine literary history and contemporary figures in the field. Jane Yolen surveys the history from the sixteenth century to the present as a reflection of societal concerns. Masha Rudman introduces distinguished authors and illustrators: Eric Carle, Tomie dePaola, John Steptoe, Ed Young, Jean Fritz, Julius Lester, Charlotte Zolotow, Patricia McLachlan, Jane Yolen, Katherine Paterson, and Cynthia Voigt. Donna Norton identifies and analyzes genres.

The section on evaluation and criticism offers perspectives by Anita Silvey on reviewing; by Eileen Tway on dimensions of multicultural literature; by Barbara Feldstein on selection versus censorship; and by Joanne Bernstein on bibliotherapy.

The final section examines the application of children's literature to the reading program by Masha Rudman; children's books on video by Diana Green; and family-school partnerships by Nancy Larrick. Julius Lester's address on literature's moral power, "The Good, the True, and the Beautiful," is included as an afterword, a final word.

102. Russell, David L. *Literature for Children: A Short Introduction.* New York: Longman, 1991.

This introduction to children's literature addresses both the literary aspects and the pedagogy of the field. The book is designed to supplement the reading of the actual literature itself. The book is divided into two parts: the context within which children's books are examined (historical survey, child development, and instructional methods), and the literary genres and critical apparatus to read and evaluate the literature. The genres include picture storybooks; alphabet, counting, and concept books; folk literature; Mother Goose rhymes; poetry; fiction; fantasy; realistic fiction; biography; and informational books.

Children's literature is defined in its broadest possible range, encompassing books for infants as well as teenagers. Each chapter includes a bibliography of critical works and of literary works. The appendix lists children's book awards. Index.

103. Saltman, Judith. *The Riverside Anthology of Children's Literature.* Sixth edition. Boston: Houghton Mifflin, 1985.

Houghton Mifflin has published five editions of *The Anthology of Children's Literature* since 1935. *The Riverside Anthology* continues to emphasize literature known for its literary and artistic quality. The selections are designed to introduce the range of genres, to give an overview of the literature, and to offer a balance among classics, traditional literature, and contemporary writing. The selections are organized to reflect the chronological development of children's reading interests and skills: from nursery rhymes and poetry to picture books, folktales and legends, fiction, and informational books.

The introduction, "Trade and Plumb-Cake Forever," discusses the development of children's literature as a commercial and artistic effort. Two historic strains are still evident: didacticism and escapist fiction. A third position is a more literary approach, based on developing pleasure through the experience of literature.

Each section is preceded with an introduction which discusses the genre as literature and art. The section "Readings on Children's Literature" presents a history of the criticism in the field and excerpts from critical writings. An extensive bibliography at the end includes suggested readings related to each chapter. The appendix lists various children's book awards. Indexes.

104. Sloan, Glenna. *The Child as Critic: Teaching Literature in Elementary and Middle Schools.* New York: Teachers College Press, 1984.

The Child as Critic, first published in 1975, was well received as an original approach to teaching language arts. Glenna Sloan argued that a lifelong literacy — "a love for language and an awareness of its infinite possibilities" — is best developed through a structured study of poetry and stories. Her framework of a unifying theory of literature drew on the work of distinguished critic Northrop Frye, who wrote the foreword. Frye is known for his structural approach to the study of literature at all levels, emphasizing literary patterns from mythology. Sloan builds a primary and middle school literary curriculum based on his literary criticism. Frye describes four basic story forms or plots that shape story content: romance, tragedy, satire and irony, and comedy. The author develops structured learning sequences using this structured framework. Separate chapters examine the study of poetry, fiction, and creative writing.

The revised edition includes the middle school grades. Other additions include in chapter 1, "The Case for Literature," a research base to support literature's critical role in language development; an analysis in chapter 2, "A New Approach to Literature," of the stages in the development of children's literary insights; an expanded overview in chapter 5, "Theory into Practice," of the literary theories of the literature program and suggestions for curricular implementation; and new strategies in chapter 7, "The Study of Story," for teaching literary criticism. New reading lists and examples from contemporary books are added. The bibliography includes selected reference works and children's books and stories.

The book is useful for teachers, particularly of gifted students, and, with its strong commitment to literature as the basis for literature, for librarians.

105. Stewig, John Warren. *Children and Literature.* Second edition. Boston: Houghton Mifflin, 1988.

This survey of both traditional and contemporary children's literature is designed to teach literary analysis of children's books and ways to use literature with children. A major goal is to enable a classroom teacher to be a book evaluator. John Stewig, a noted expert in English education, discusses children's literature as "a literature of variety," with diversity in genre, format, and subject.

The author begins with an analysis of literature and of illustration, and then follows with chapters on specific genres: alphabet books, picture books, wordless books, traditional literature, poetry, historic fiction, biography, contemporary fiction, fantasy, and information books. One chapter explores children's reading interests, particularly animal stories, mystery and detective fiction, sports stories, and science fiction. The final chapter discusses ways of planning a literature program, including integrated units of study.

A particular emphasis is made on observing and evaluating children's responses to literature. Each chapter contains expository information, contemporary examples, a section of classics, strategies for instruction, a summary, suggestions for further study, and a bibliography of children's books and professional readings. Indexes.

106. Sutherland, Zena, and May Hill Arbuthnot. *Children and Books.* Eighth edition. New York: HarperCollins, 1991.

First published nearly 40 years ago, this textbook is well established in the field. The book is designed for children's literature courses in library science, education, and English. The dual emphasis of the book is reflected in the title: children and books. The focus is on understanding children and their needs as well as on literary and bibliographical aspects of children's literature. The discussions are organized around major authors of past and present. The emphasis is primarily on printed books, with some attention to other media.

Part 1 is an overview of books for children, criteria for evaluation, the history of children's books, books for the young, and noted illustrators of the nineteenth and twentieth centuries. Part 2 is a study of genres, subdivided by their major authors. Separate chapters discuss folktales; fables, myths, and epics; modern fantasy; poetry; modern fiction and historical fiction; and biography and informational books. Part 3 approaches methodology in introducing children to literature and in enhancing the curriculum. Part 4 examines issues related to children's books, including censorship, research, internationalism, literary, literature-based curriculum, and children's book awards. Extensive bibliographies end each chapter.

Appendices include book selection aids, adult references, publishers' addresses, children's book awards, and a pronunciation guide. Indexes include subject, author, illustrator, and title.

107. Sutherland, Zena, and Myra Cohn Livingston, editors. *The Scott, Foresman Anthology of Children's Literature.* Glenview, IL: Scott, Foresman, 1984.

This anthology is designed to introduce students to a variety of children's literature and to provide a foundation for future reading in the field. The book includes selections of poetry, folktales, realistic fiction, historical fiction, fantasy, biography, and informational books. Each genre is introduced with background information.

In addition to the literary selections, several essays direct the reader's attention to specific aspects of children's books and their presentation to children. In "What Literature Can Do for Children," Rebecca Lukens discusses genres, literary elements, and the particular pleasures and understandings of quality literature. In "Children's

Literature in the Classroom," Sue Woestehoff Peterson focuses on practical guidelines for the elementary teacher and emphasizes the literary work as art, not as a tool. The closing essays by Patricia Cianciolo explores the role of illustration in picture books, which have a broad audience of readers.

The reference section includes annotated bibliographies of children's book genres and professional readings. Index.

108. Vandergrift, Kay E. *Child and Story: The Literary Connection*. New York: Neal-Schuman, 1980.

The author uses various theories of literary criticism to examine the role of story for children. The connection between child and story is a richly imaginative experience, a personal, public, and critical awareness. Knowledge and respect for the child, children's literature, and literary criticism are all related. Developing critical abilities in children rather than presenting specific classic texts is the emphasis.

Kay Vandergrift builds a foundation on the theory of critical reading, the levels of reading, and the importance of story in children's lives. She then explores specific story elements, such as literary form, story structure, compositional elements, and illustration. Genres and compositional elements are presented in a matrix for guiding consideration of books.

The chapter on presenting literature focuses on interactive discussion rather than on reports. The author relates personal teaching experiences with early elementary grades in analyzing stories and comparing literature. A list of questions for discussing literature is included. Children are encouraged to move beyond analysis to creative writing and multimedia presentations. Critical approaches to literature are based largely on Northrop Frye's cyclical pattern of viewing literature.

The book is geared to teachers and librarians working with an age range from preschool through grade school. Many of her suggestions, such as reading aloud, can be applied to teaching older children. She also includes a list of dubious practices, such as reading literature for phonics instruction, prizes, and bibliotherapy. She reviews the literature in the field and from related disciplines and proposes research topics. Many of the author's recommendations apply to the school and the home. The book is particularly useful for training teachers in language arts.

The author, a professor of children's literature at Rutgers, is well known in the field. Her background includes being a classroom teacher, librarian, and school administrator. She is also the author of *Teaching Role of the School Library Media Specialist* and *Children's Literature: Theory, Research, and Teaching*.

Each chapter in this book includes a list of children's books. A larger bibliography of secondary sources on literary criticism, psychology, and child development conclude the work. Index of authors, titles, and subjects.

Chapter 4

Teaching Children's Literature To Adults

This book had its origins in the survey of the teaching of children's literature done by the Children's Literature Assembly and described by Lynda G. Adamson in 1987 (see number 110 below). The survey indicated that there were great differences in the way children's literature was taught in three different academic departments: education, English, and library science. A search of the professional literature revealed a wealth of articles by professors in all three disciplines describing interesting, creative, and inspiring methods they use for involving their students, at both the graduate and undergraduate levels, with literature for children and young people. They come from the United States, Canada, and Great Britain, with a few from other countries. They describe small, intimate classes, classes with hundreds of students and many assistants, and a course for distance learning. Some attract students who do not plan to work with children, or to work with them in capacities other than as librarians or teachers, such as psychologists. We hope that reading these annotations, and in some cases going to the articles they describe, will be helpful to both inexperienced and experienced teachers of children's literature to adults.

109. Adamson, Lynda G. "And Who Taught You Children's Literature?" *The Horn Book* 61.5 (September–October 1985): 631–32.

Education, librarianship, and English approach children's

literature from unique perspectives. A survey by the Children's Literature Assembly of the National Council of Teachers of English reveals some of these differences.

The survey indicated only one common text taught in all three disciplines: *Charlotte's Web*. Library science and English, but not education, mention *Alice in Wonderland* and *The Wind in the Willows*. Education and library science reflect a greater interest in Newbery Award books, while English is more interested in older classics. Both the library science and English booklists contain a much greater number of titles.

The survey revealed a preponderance of reading in fiction. Other genres — nonfiction, poetry, folklore — are only slightly covered.

The seven authors most widely read are picture-book creators: Maurice Sendak, Ezra Jack Keats, Robert McCloskey, Dr. Seuss, Tomie de Paola, Arnold Lobel, and Beatrix Potter.

In content, library science and education emphasize picture books, illustrators, realistic fiction, historical fiction, biography, and nonfiction. English courses focus more on the history of children's literature. Education and library science emphasize child development and book selection. A combination of these approaches would enhance the quality in each discipline and ensure that students were well prepared in assessing children's books, regardless of the department.

110. Adamson, Lynda G. "Results of the Children's Literature Assembly's Survey of Teaching in U.S. Colleges and Universities." *Bookbird* 25 (September 1987): 11–15.

A survey was sent to teachers of children's literature to determine the differences in courses when taught in English, education, or library science departments. The survey explored varieties of approach, curriculum, teaching techniques, and course content. The major difference was found to be in emphasis: in English, on literary elements; in education, on the literary text as resource; and in library science, on children's interests. The primary text in education was Charlotte Huck's *Children's Literature in the Elementary School*. Library science faculty commonly used Zena Sutherland and Dianne Monson's *Children and Books*. English instructors did not identify a specific text, but instead chose children's books. Other differences were in the use of bibliographies, with library science drawing most upon bibliographies for selection and organization of material, and in the number of books read by the students. The only book read in common by all three disciplines was *Charlotte's Web*. Reading across genres was not consistent, with nonfiction being neglected.

The author argues for a balance between disciplinary concerns in the teaching of children's literature. These three equally valid approaches offer distinctive strengths from each discipline. A combination of the best of each would improve the quality of pedagogy in the field. She concludes, "Library Science's emphasis on the literature's interest to children added to Education's understanding of genre combined with English's concern with literary merit would create an integrated and exciting basic course in Children's Literature."

111. Aitken, David, and Anthony Kearney. "Children's Books in Teacher Education at St. Martin's College Lancaster." *Signal* 49 (May 1986): 44–51.

St. Martin's College Lancaster offers professional training for teachers at the undergraduate and graduate level. A two-year part-time advanced diploma in reading and language offers an in-service program for teachers. All education majors take a one-term course in fiction and extra weeks on poetry and drama. Students majoring in English have other courses available in which children's literature is studied. English department faculty teach the courses in children's literature. A resource library of 7,000 titles supports the program.

The required course for education students covers subjects like children's literature in the classroom, the range of children's fiction, criteria for selection, response surveys, and storytelling. Students are required to complete four assignments: a paper on children's fiction, using educational and literary criteria; read in common 30 books; compile a subject bibliography; and complete a storytelling exercise.

Questionnaires are given at the beginning of their studies to test students' knowledge of traditional stories, acquaintance with older and contemporary children's classics, and response to award-winning titles. These tests, which are also administered to elementary school students, are used as discussion starters and as motivation for reading.

English-education majors take a variety of courses which emphasize connections to children's reading. A course in "Narrative Art in the Novel" asks students to examine classic works for the nature of narrative, readership exploration of genre and theme, contemporary adaptations, and curricular use in the schools. The students examine the literary text as form, ideas, and then status as a children's classic. Considering how texts could be approached at various levels of readership involves a careful analysis and creative approach to literature. Students are encouraged to design activities for learning and creative expression which extend the meaning of the text. The aim is to combine critical and artistic approaches to literature which can be adapted to classroom teaching.

112. Alfonso, Sister Regina. "Modules for Teaching About Young People's Literature—Module 1: Gender Roles." *Journal of Reading* 30.2 (November 1986): 160–63.

Sister Regina Alfonso, who taught elementary school for 27 years, now teaches children's literature at Notre Dame College of Ohio. She suggests synthesizing experiences for use in genre courses. This brief article on gender roles offers techniques that can be used both with teachers and with youngsters to analyze the content of books. There is a list of books for children that involve gender roles. These are marked to indicate grade levels and genre. Also included is a bibliography of journal articles on gender stereotyping.

113. Alfonso, Sister Regina. "Modules for Teaching About Young People's Literature—Module 2: How Do the Elderly Fare in Children's Books?" *Journal of Reading* 30.3 (December 1986): 201–3.

This article is the second in a series of six modules designed to give preservice and in-service teachers a look at various issues across several genres. The author states that "skill in analyzing issues in children's books is essential for preservice teachers." She offers suggestions for presenting the module to both adult and junior high students. Appended are lists of books for children that involve the elderly, and a short list of journal articles.

114. Alfonso, Sister Regina. "Modules for Teaching About Young People's Literature—Module 3: Values Children Can Learn from Picture Books." *Journal of Reading* 30.4 (January 1987): 299–301.

This third article in the series, designed to give beginning teachers an opportunity to become familiar with the styles of authors and illustrators representative of various genres, deals with picture books. Picture books can be used "to instill specific values and provide springboards to conversations leading to positive attitudes." Older children, too, can benefit from analyzing picture books. Suggestions for teaching the module are included, along with a list of picture books and journal articles about values in children's books.

115. Alfonso, Sister Regina. "Modules for Teaching About Young People's Literature—Module 4: Humor." *Journal of Reading* 30.5 (February 1987): 399–401.

Alfonso bemoans the dearth of humorous books written for

children. She found it difficult to find journal articles concerning the subject, or books other than joke and riddle books. Consequently, the lists of these are short. The unit involves analyzing elements of humor and identifying what makes books funny as well as literary.

116. Alfonso, Sister Regina. "Modules for Teaching About Young People's Literature—Module 5: Picture Storybooks vs. Basal Readers." *Journal of Reading* 30.6 (March 1987): 497–99.

The author cites the lack of literary quality in basal readers and encourages reading teachers to be aware of the many interesting storybooks specifically designed to meet the needs of beginning readers. She stresses that the child should be reading as much from quality literature as from the phonics-based primers. Unlike the other modules, this module is for adults only. The students are asked to read basal readers and analyze them for literary quality, and then to do the same for picture storybooks for beginning readers. A list of books to use and related journal articles are included.

117. Alfonso, Sister Regina. "Modules for Teaching About Young People's Literature—Module 6: Informational Books." *Journal of Reading* 30.8 (May 1987): 682–86.

In this final module Alfonso urges teachers to use literature to make the natural and social sciences, mathematics, the fine arts, and other areas of the curriculum come to life. She includes picture books, folktales, biographies, and historical fiction. This module, like module 5, is for adult students only. The list of journal articles accompanying this module is much longer than the lists for the others. The list of informational books also is longer and is divided into picture books, biographies, fine arts, science, and social studies.

118. Allen, Melody Lloyd, and Margaret Bush. "Library Education and Youth Services: A Survey of Faculty, Course Offerings, and Related Activities in Accredited Library Schools." *Library Trends* 35.3 (Winter 1987): 485–508.

The authors note the paucity of applicants for library positions in public libraries' children and youth departments. In order to explore the reasons for this lack and to answer questions about library school preparation for these positions, they surveyed ALA accredited library schools. Respondents were asked to provide information about courses "which prepare a student for work in public library children's services." Usable responses were received from 56.7 percent of all accredited programs.

The article includes data on the number of courses offered, the type of faculty (full-time or adjunct, and rank) teaching the courses, and the size and frequency of the classes. Of special interest is the table listing names of faculty teaching in particular schools and their research interests and projects. The authors conclude that the study did not produce a clearly defined analysis of curriculum, enrollment, and teaching in courses in children's, young adult, and school librarianship, but raised questions for future studies. The present study into the state of library education and youth services creates a "reason for concern, but not despair, about the future of education for youth librarians."

119. Atkinson, Dorothy. "Teaching Teachers About Children's Books: How, Why, and to What Effect." *The School Librarian* 35 (August 1987): 202–8.

This article describes activities of a group of people who have made children's books their special interest. This group includes librarians, teachers, and children. The ideas developed by this group inform the work with teachers-in-training. All techniques center on fostering independent reading development and enjoyment of reading. Planned intervention in reading is discouraged.

Special emphasis is given to making attractive books readily available in the classroom, and giving children opportunities to discuss, in a variety of settings, whole books. This is in contrast to planned intervention techniques that had been employed, such as using a single paragraph for a comprehension test.

Strategies for creating interest in books include fancy-dress parades of book titles, book clubs, and talks with local writers. It is suggested that newer, high-interest books should be presented along with classics. Numerous comments by children are included.

120. Atkinson, Joan L. "Library Education for Young Adult Specialists." In *New Directions for Young Adult Services*, Ellen V. LiBretto, editor. New York: Bowker, 1983. 163–80.

The author, a professor of young adult literature at the University of Alabama, discusses the political environment of preservice education. Young adult specialists are an endangered species, much like library schools themselves. The education of young adult specialists is tied to the destiny of library schools, which are experiencing survival struggles. The use of young adult specialists as adjunct faculty is explored. Librarians could benefit from understanding political systems theory and organizational behavior. Conflicts abound between the field's perceived service agenda and the university's perceived research mission. Competencies of young adult librarians are presented. The young adult course has three major goals: to enhance understanding of adolescent development and needs in relation to current political and social climates; to introduce literature, multimedia materials, and professional publications relevant to the young adult specialty; and to communicate current issues in the materials and services area. A survey of 25 schools indicates no consensus on textbook but, instead, the use of required readings. Suggested titles to cover the literature and service components are given. Content in young adult courses is continually evolving. An open system model of organizational behavior is recommended. Students will need to read in various formats, to confront the dilemma of quality versus popularity, and to learn reader's advisory skills. Knowledge of freedom of speech issues is critical to the field. Notes and bibliography.

121. Barron, Pamela Petrick. "Production of a Telecourse in Library and Information Science: 'Jump Over the Moon: Sharing Literature with Young Children.'" *Journal of Education for Library and Information Science* 27.4 (Spring 1987): 247–56.

Pamela Barron, a professor at the University of South Carolina, describes the development and use of a telecourse for long distance learning in children's literature. The initial proposal to videotape lectures in a traditional setting for broadcast was turned down because this approach is not effective. Barron and Jennifer Burley, the children's literature course teachers, were selected to develop content, coordinate the library research, and function as editors and reviewers of the script. They wrote a study guide to accompany the tapes, field tested, and made modifications.

Discussed in the article are the processes of selecting the host for the series, developing the skills needed for writing television scripts, and related research. Books to support learning objectives had to be located and gathered, and copyright permissions obtained. The result was 15 videos, supplemented by a study guide, an anthology of readings, and a faculty/administrator's guide. The course has been popular with students who are mature and self-directed, but can also work well with others with more guidance.

122. Barron, Pamela Petrick, and Jennifer Q. Burley. *Jump Over the Moon: Selected Professional Readings*. New York: Holt, Rinehart and Winston, 1984.

This collection of readings is designed to accompany a college-level telecourse on the selection and evaluation of picture books for young children, from birth to age nine (see number 13 above). The book can be used separately as a reference source on the literature of early childhood. The readings were selected in order to introduce concepts within a developmental process and to introduce children to the pleasures of reading through an interactive approach. The book's organization is centered on the developmental needs of children. The introduction includes two articles with conflicting perspectives on picture books. Other articles address the complexity of some picture books that enable them to be used with intermediate age children. The subjects covered sequentially include Mother Goose rhymes, poetry, alphabet and counting books, illustrations, informational books, folktales, and storytelling. One section on sharing picture books contains creative ideas for intergenerational reading. The final section covers extended vocabulary books. Each chapter contains a separate bibliography. No index.

123. Bass, Marion. "New Corn from Old Fields: A Study of the Potential Children's Literature to Be Gleaned from English Literature Existing Prior to the Seventeenth Century." *English Quarterly* 17.4 (Winter 1984): 23–29.

Tracing the beginnings of children's literature from the seventeenth and eighteenth centuries, when the prevailing society resulted in didactic and religious mores, Marion Bass urges a return to earlier times when literature sparkled with excitement, adventure, and fascinating characters. Tales such as *Beowulf* are suspenseful and exciting and could inspire wonderful illustrations to accompany a text in modern English. Other suggestions are Chaucer's "House of Fame," "Sir Gawain and the Green Knight," and "Noah's Flood." Also mentioned are a number of Shakespearean plays. Bass asserts that this literature forms the foundation upon which our entire literary heritage is constructed. The only chance many people have to be exposed to this heritage is when they are studying stories as children.

124. Benne, Mae. "Course Development: From a Gleam in the Eye to a Full-Term Product." *Top of the News* 43 (Winter 1987): 177–82.

Mae Benne, a professor of children's literature — from the University of Washington, Graduate School of Library and Information Science — examines the evolution of her course. A good course should be more than a sum of its parts; it should enhance a student's understanding of the field, and skills should be adaptable to other situations.

A course changes each time it is taught. Some of the influential factors include the social and technological environment, the background of the students, the changing perception of the teacher, and the mysterious "chemistry" of the class. Three factors determined course revisions in children's literature: the needs of students in the children's area; the fit of courses taken elsewhere with their own program; and the phenomenal growth of materials about children's literature.

Previously, two courses existed, which were similar in scope. The first course covered the various genres and selection and bibliographical aids. The second course covered other areas, such as illustration and film, translations, current issues, specialized awards, and reading guidance.

A curriculum study brought many changes. An upper division service course was developed which would be offered only to out-of-department students. A two-course sequence for departmental students — "Children's Materials" — covers evaluation and use in one course and bibliography and resources in the other. The first course focuses on various genres and book activities. The second course examines historical foundations, the role of the publisher, selection aids, information uses, social and psychological values, the teaching of children's literature, and professional organizations.

Librarians responsible for children's services must expand their service beyond reading guidance and library skills. Information sources should be emphasized. Subject access must be improved. The evaluation and use of AV and computer software demand attention.

125. Broderick, Dorothy M. "The Newbery Committee That Never Was." *Top of the News* 20 (March 1964): 210–15.

Teachers of children's literature looking for a way to motivate students to read widely and to get involved in discussing and evaluating books would do well to follow the model described in this article. Dorothy Broderick set her class up as a Newbery Committee, reviewing all the books considered for the medal in an entire decade. She describes the entire procedure and the outcomes, both intellectual and practical. She describes the enthusiasm of the students, "who felt they were reading with a purpose rather than simply writing reports." A complete reading list is included.

126. Butler, Francelia. "How to Teach a Mass Class in Children's Literature Year After Year." *ADE Bulletin* 68 (Summer 1981): 21–22.

Francelia Butler, a professor of English at the University of Connecticut, shares the techniques she uses to establish and maintain interest in her children's literature course. The course, which attracts students from all disciplines in the university, is organized around themes such as "Toys and Games", "Sex Roles," and "Fools." Many outside speakers are invited to speak to the class, and these are always individuals with special knowledge or expertise related to the theme under study.

Written assignments are creative, including skip-rope rhymes, games, personal essays, and plays. Students create "Family Folklore Books," which have proven immensely popular and rewarding. Grading and administration of the class are described. In addition to a graduate assistant, Butler is able to offer credit to 14 students selected from "A" students from the previous semester's class. Half do administrative office work and the other half work in the class, which numbers 300 students each semester. These students take a special leadership course and prepare reports. Butler reports success with her methods in other courses as well.

127. Butler, Francelia. "The Role of Children's Literature in Shaping Professional Aspirations." *National Forum: Phi Kappa Phi Journal* 61.4 (Fall 1981): 42–43.

Francelia Butler, professor of English at the University of Connecticut–Storrs and founder of the annual *Children's Literature*, emphasizes the usefulness of children's literature for a variety of professions. These include pediatrics, juvenile justice, psychology, and publishing. Obviously, a large number of the students taking children's literature courses are preparing to be parents and/or teachers of children. Some creative assignments and research projects in such courses are described, including the preparation of a family folklore book. Butler cautions that courses in the field are occasionally canceled because they are not seen as "useful." She mentions the complexity of the subject, the difficulty of teaching it, and the paucity of research.

128. Butts, Dennis, and Tony Watkins. "Children's Books in Teacher Education at Bulmershe College of Higher Education." *Signal* 48 (September 1985): 176–81.

A variety of degree programs at Bulmershe College of Higher Education offer coursework in children's literature. The program offered for training teachers of children ages 7–11 is the major program, comprising a majority of the undergraduate and graduate students in education.

Children's books appear in the curriculum under the section "Language and Literacy." The priorities of classroom application and knowledge of the field are competing concerns which challenge the instructor to meet both needs.

One approach to meeting short-term needs of teachers in training is to discuss a few selected books along with pedagogical strategies. Reading lists broaden the students' experience with literature. Students are expected to be familiar with about 75 books by the end of the course. Attention is also given to use of books in a multicultural society.

A recent innovation to the program was a curricular conference begun in 1985. Part of this conference was devoted to an exploration of children's books as part of human experience. Authors were invited to read from and talk about their books.

Secondary school students majoring in English have opportunities to study children's books as well. The current program approaches notions of text, readers, and society. In the first year students study autobiography, do some creative writing, and read books for children ages 5–8 or 7–11. Students also present papers on particular books. In the second year students can take an elective on nineteenth-century children's books.

Supplementary courses are offered so education students may take more than the minimum requirements in children's literature. Some popular offerings have been a class in modern children's literature and education, and, for honors students, a class in children and literature. This course uses literary and developmental theories within a cultural context.

Some of the most commonly used texts include John Rowe Townsend's *Written for Children*, Dennis Butts's *Good Books for Young Readers*, Margaret Meek's *The Cool Web*, Fred Inglis's *The Promise of Happiness*, Bruno Bettelheim's *The Uses of Enchantment*, Jack Zipes's *Breaking the Magic Spell*, and Wolfgang Iser's *The Act of Reading*. The library has built particular strength in resource books and books for the study of historical children's literature.

Future plans include a two-year master's program leading to an M.A. in children's literature.

129. Chambers, Aidan. "Letter from England: Teaching Children's Literature Part 2." *The Horn Book* 60.6 (December 1979): 707–10.

Aidan Chambers continues his discussion of teaching techniques in training teachers to teach children's literature. He is convinced that students need a strong background in adult literature and requires such reading as a complement to the curriculum. He likes to note similarities between child and adult texts, to reveal the technical limitation of children's fiction, and, above all, to provide a literary context.

Students are also encouraged to write their own children's stories, poems, and plays in order to understand the practical concerns of an author. Such creative writing makes them more sensitive readers of children's literature and more sympathetic teachers — of children and books.

Chambers also considers the environment of teaching, making the classroom conducive to the development of children's reading skills. Besides the aesthetics of the room, the reading environment includes structured time to read and browse.

His final summation states the need for an incorporation of the act of reading and the study of literature into explorations of children's literature. All assignments are directed toward this encompassing of what is often considered to be three separate studies. He designs his course to include a commonality of literature, adult as well as children's texts; an annotated record of what a student reads, privately and professionally; a critical piece as well as some creative writing for children; seminar and group-organized explorations of "the act of reading as a phenomenological event; the act of criticism as a rhetorical study; and the act of mediating literature to children as a pedagogic-critical performance."

130. Chang, Margaret. "Fantasy Literature: Encounters in the Globe of Time." *School Library Journal* (September 1990): 163–64.

The author presented a one-month course on time fantasies to students at Williams College. Inspired by Betty Levin's course and Eleanor Cameron's title essay in *The Green and Burning Tree: On the Writing and Enjoyment of Children's Books*, the course centered on Cameron's notion of "the globe of time," the continuities of past, present, and future.

The liberal arts students were nostalgic about favorite childhood books, revealing the power of children's literature to help shape identity. A popular author was Madeleine L'Engle, whose "unabashed celebration of intellect" spoke to their own talents.

The challenge was to move the students beyond nostalgia to a more analytical understanding of childhood favorites, and to a heightened sense of growth and change which are elements of fantasy literature. The syllabus contained a mix of old and new, past and present. The authors included Edward Eager, C. S. Lewis, Madeleine L'Engle, E. Nesbit, Alison Uttley, Lucy Boston, Philippa Pearce, Ann Schlee, Nancy Bond, Robert Westall, William Mayne, Pauline Clarke, and Penelope Lively.

131. Clark, Beverly Lyon. "Books for Children Deserve to Be Part of Literary Studies." *The Chronicle of Higher Education* (October 17, 1990), B2–B3.

Beverly Clark, who teaches English at Wheaton College in Massachusetts, writes from the perspective of children's literature as literary studies for adults, rather than as preparation for teaching children. She advocates including children's classics in literary survey courses, as well as teaching it as a separate course. "For what we read as children," she says, "has a profound effect on us, more profound than anything we are likely to read as adults." She points out that because women are prominent as authors of children's literature, the course has been able to address women's concerns and issues. Clark's current research centers on school stories. They give us "truths about race, gender, loss, community. Truths that both terrify and clarify."

132. Clements, Frank. "Children's Literature in the Education of Teachers." *Children's Literature in Education* 4 (1971): 24–31.

This article is the first of a series of reports in this journal on approaches to children's literature in teacher education. The survey covers colleges of education, an institute of education, and the education department of a university. These institutions include Milton Keynes College of Education, Worcester College, Bingley College of Education, Nottingham College of Education, University of Liverpool Institute of Education, and Exeter University.

Insufficient information on the various programs made it difficult to derive conclusions. Children's literature is, at the very least, gaining strength as an academic program. High course enrollments demonstrate keen interest in the subject among students.

The survey investigated depth of coverage, course objectives, and assignments. The depth of coverage is contingent on the duration of the courses, which vary from two semesters to half-term units. The author describes how courses are organized and the components emphasized at the various institutions. Some course goals and assignments are listed from syllabi.

In an afterword, Sidney Robbins of Exeter draws several conclusions. The study of children's literature is becoming part of the English curriculum for teachers during their initial training or for advanced work. The information presented showed a wide variety of ways of organizing such coursework. English faculty sense the need to relate to other departments. Robbins draws upon the work of F. R. Leavis to argue for a continuity of creative activity. Students need to experience children's literature studies as linked to experiences with other literary studies and creative work. Coursework in English should express a sense of continuity "across the whole gamut of expressive language activity."

133. Cochrane, Kirsty. "Children's Literature in New Zealand: New Initiatives in Higher Education." *Signal* 64 (January 1991): 25–32.

Children's literature is flourishing in New Zealand. New Zealanders buy more books per capita than do the inhabitants of any other country. The public library system is strong and well supported. The increase in indigenous children's book publishing is marked. The New Zealand Children's Book Foundation has recently been established by the New Zealand Book Council. The National Library of New Zealand sponsored its first national conference on children's books.

Another step forward is the initiation of an honors course in children's literature at the University of Waikato in Hamilton, the first of its kind in New Zealand. The library collection includes 70,000 children's books and 20 periodicals. The course was built on the belief that children's literature has strong literary quality which necessitates a text-based rather than issue-oriented approach. Literature was chosen to reflect classic works as well as New Zealand authors for children.

The course list includes: *The Secret Garden*; *Alice's Adventures in Wonderland*; *Treasure Island*; *Five Children and It*; *Puck of Pook's Hill*; *The Wind in the Willows*; *The Lion, the Witch, and the Wardrobe*; *Ballet Shoes*; *Pigeon Post*; *A Traveller in Time*; *The Owl Service*; *Earthfasts*; *Charlotte's Web*; *The Wolves of Willoughby Chase*; *Motherstone*; and *The Tricksters*. Course requirements include a bibliography, a major research essay, and a seminar presentation.

134. Croxson, Mary. "Children's Books in Teacher Education at Worcester College of Higher Education." *Signal* 45 (September 1984): 173–79.

Worcester College of Higher Education has a long tradition of teaching children's literature. The specialty in children's literature which developed when the school was a teacher training college has formed the basis of study in the English and education departments. A large practice library of 20,000 volumes supplements staff resources.

The English department's involvement in children's literature informs the understanding of children's literature as literature. The value of children's books extends well beyond reading skills to include deep linguistic, psychological, social, and intellectual growth.

Undergraduates study children's literature in their first, third, and fourth years of a primary course. The first year's course, "An Introduction to Language and Literacy," primarily involved with storytelling and selection, is integrated with school experience. The third-year program, "The Language Curriculum," emphasizes learning to read and responses to literature. In the fourth year, "Planning the Language Arts Curriculum" involves school experiences, seminars, and a thesis. The one-year graduate program may include study in children's literature in its secondary English curriculum.

In-service programs are also offered for teachers and librarians. A certification program for school librarians offers study in children's literature as well as in child development, bibliography, and library skills. Worcester also offers teachers a short-term, intensive summer school course, involving seminars, tours of libraries and schools, and author visits. The author visits are involved with the course in children's fiction, offered as part of a degree program, the diploma for professional studies in education. Further graduate programs are planned which will include research into children's literature.

135. Duijx, Toin. "Children and Literature Becoming a Subject of Serious Study in the Netherlands." *Bookbird* 25.4 (December 1987): 6–7.

Duijx relates the current state of children's books in Holland. While the public realizes the importance of juvenile literature for developmental growth and publishers continue to add to their lists for children, the universities have been slow to respond with institutional support.

Some of the current activity is described through the work of two important pioneers. Lea Dasberg, a professor of historical pedagogies at Ulbrecht University and later at Amsterdam University, wrote a standard work, *The Children's Book as Educator*, which was the report of an extensive study, and published in 1981. Ria Bauer van Wechem of Leiden University approached the subject from developmental psychology and pedagogy and coordinated interuniversity research interest.

The author teaches at Leiden a course titled "Child and Media Studies." The book is viewed as an auxiliary means to child development, especially for the acquisition of language and the growth of the imagination. Bibliotherapy is also considered.

A national platform was founded to promote education and research in the broad field of children's books, including universities, publishers, authors, and illustrators. A newsletter is circulated with descriptions of bibliographies, reviews, and research news. Symposia, tours, and research activities are also coordinated. A recent project is investigating the transition from children's to adult literature. Ongoing groups explore historical research, curriculum for teacher education, and criticism.

136. Evans, W. D. Emrys. "Children's Books in Teacher Education — The University of Birmingham." *Signal* 44 (May 1984): 103–11.

At the University of Birmingham no specifically designed courses exist in children's literature, although the subject is integrated into the teacher training program. Much of the graduate program is geared toward preparation of examinations, but modern children's books are introduced. An elective course is offered on literature in education, which presents a variety of genres. The undergraduate program focuses on language development as well as literature. Resources are slight, although the department is building a paperback collection of contemporary children's literature.

The author describes some of the approaches student teachers take in the classroom. The text *Patterns of Language* is used frequently for techniques in teaching fiction. Some students use the public library facilities, such as the Birmingham Central Children's Library's collection of multicultural literature.

The program is informed by reader-response theory, led by Aidan Chambers's writing and including the works of Louise Rosenblatt, Wolfgang Iser, and others.

The author hopes the department can add more on children's literature to the program, perhaps with the cooperation of the English department. Curricular and budgetary pressures restrict expansion of the field.

137. Foster, John. "The Teaching of Children's Literature in Australia." *Bookbird* 1, 2 (1983): 3–7.

Children's literature in Australia is offered largely through the universities in the five large urban areas of Sydney, Melbourne, Brisbane, Adelaide and Perth. Nonurban areas have occasional curricular coverage.

The teaching of children's literature began in Australia in 1956 at Newcastle when it was integrated into regular literature classes. By 1976 the subject was taught in three universities and 43 colleges through the departments of English literature, teacher education, or school librarianship. At present, five universities and about 50 colleges offer children's literature; one autonomous department of children's literature exists. Enrollment is high, particularly since the course is often required of those entering teaching or librarianship.

The emphases vary from scholarly research to professional concerns with reading; some are a blend of each. The majority of courses blend the literary with a practical application. Examples from various institutions illustrate the different approaches. The qualification of instructors is enhanced by more doctorate and specialist degrees in the field. Methods of instruction vary from lectures for large groups to small-group tutorial discussions. Methods of assessment vary from papers to exams, including such projects as writing and illustrating a picture book, preparing bibliographies, storytelling, and book reviews.

Children's literature is popular on Australian campuses. Some students perceive it to be an easier course than other literature options. Gender stereotypes also persist. The subject is treated seriously by a growing number of people who are influencing the professionals who will work with children. The questionable financing of higher education is the major problem for the future.

138. Fox, Geoff. "Children's Books in Teacher Education at the University of Exeter." *Signal* 47 (May 1985): 112-19.

St. Luke's College, which merged with Exeter University School of Education, played an active role in promoting children's literature. Sid Robbins, lecturer at St. Luke's and founding editor of *Children's Literature in Education,* was instrumental in holding conferences in the late 1960s and early 1970s and in building a children's literature curriculum.

A resource library supplements the program with a large collection of novels, poetry, folklore, picture books, media, and books about children's literature. Classroom sets of novels and poetry books can be used for courses or practice teaching.

The undergraduate program aims to instill enthusiasm for reading, supported by knowledge of available resources. Students typically read a book a week and often read aloud from their books. Children's literature is also introduced in the regular second-year English program in a course which meets once a week for a ten-week term. Students read from a list of contemporary classics and meet two hours per week to discuss these texts and various genres of children's literature. Students initiate projects which involve research or creative writing.

English education students in a one-year course have a limited time to study the field before practice teaching in the second term. The aim is to begin something: coming away with teaching ideas, new books to use, and information on professional resources. Advanced courses have been offered in the past on the processes of children's reading.

Practical application is accomplished through practice teaching, storytelling in the schools, and poetry performances. "Poetry Days" and "Touring Poetry Shows" involve children, students, and tutors in the group process and creative expression.

139. Gay, Carol. "The Onus of Teaching Children's Literature: The Need for Some Reappraisals." *ADE Bulletin* 47 (1975): 15–20.

The author argues for the inclusion and serious consideration of children's literature within the curriculum of the English department. Children's literature as a scholarly field is hindered by its traditional alignments with schools of library science, schools of education, and associations with children. Humanists tend to disdain a literature which seems simple and without critical apparatus for analysis.

English departments need to include children's literature for three major reasons: the course is badly needed; it is a new field with immense research possibilities; and the interest level of students creates a critical demand. English departments have a responsibility to staff children's literature courses and to train specialists in the subject. Careful analysis is needed of the cultural, artistic, historical, psychological, and philosophical significance of children's literature. Not until children's literature is approached as "the best art form for something [the artist] has to say" (C. S. Lewis) will the onus be removed from teaching children's literature.

The author was active in the Children's Literature Association and instrumental in building a program in children's literature at Youngstown State University. An annual award is given in her name by the Children's Literature Association for a high school essay analyzing children's literature.

140. Gross, Elizabeth H. "The Teaching of Children's Literature." *Wilson Library Bulletin* 42 (October 1967): 199–205.

A questionnaire was mailed to 130 institutions in which a course in children's literature was given. The questionnaire was designed to elicit information concerning the basic resources needed by an institution about to inaugurate such a course. As a result, basic tools are listed and discussed. Also discussed are textbooks, special materials, budgets, and selection of children's titles for the collection. "[A]n abundance of materials is needed so that students now being trained to work with children can learn to sift the good from the mediocre and to discover for themselves those books that will meet the requirements of a specific child, enabling him to grow mentally and emotionally in a world that will require the best of which he is capable."

141. Hayes, David. "College Students Reading to Preschoolers." *Reading Horizons* 24.4 (Summer 1984): 225–30.

Because David Hayes believes in the importance of adults seeing young children reacting to books, noneducation majors in his children's literature course at the University of Virginia were given the opportunity to interact with preschoolers as an alternative to a term paper. The students told stories and read to children ages two through six weekly over a six-week period. The papers they wrote at the end of the experience demonstrated that they had learned lessons concerning motivation, attention span, related activities, and kinds of books.

Motivating devices used by the students are described, including the method of calling each student individually by name to come to the storytelling session. Recommendations for maintaining attention are creative and include rehearsing the book before sharing. For related activities, one student dressed up stuffed animals to represent characters in the book.

The kinds of books selected by the students to share included rhyme/rhythm books, wordless picture books, predictable books, animal stories, participation books, and familiar character books.

142. Hearne, Betsy. "Problems and Possibilities: U.S. Research in Children's Literature." *School Library Journal* (August 1988), 27–31.

This article is a shortened version of a paper delivered at the International Youth Library Conference in Munich, April 1988. Betsy Hearne surveys the extent of scholarly interest in the field, with particular attention to the distinctions between children's literature as text or as tool. As an interdisciplinary subject, children's literature attracts scholars in literature, librarianship, education, psychology, sociology, anthropology, history, and art. Each discipline offers a different emphasis and critical methodology.

Library science and education are interested in theme and practical use; literature in textual analysis; history in context; psychology and sociology in therapeutic benefits; anthropology in folklore; and art in graphics. The fields seem uncommunicative, with little passage of knowledge from one area to another.

Library science has the longest tradition of involvement in the field, although its influence is limited and its research more in the realm of service than research. Annotated bibliographies, surveys, and collections are the most researched areas in the field. Much slighter attention is given to aesthetics. To Hearne, "The primary sources are rich, the resources fine-tuned, but the critical research is still in an embryonic state."

Children's literature is at an important crossroads of artistry, service, and research. New patterns of broad-based cooperative scholarship are the new challenge. This is a much-cited source that analyzes the contemporary disciplinary interests and their productivity. References.

143. Helbig, Alethea. "Curriculum Planning in Literature for Children: Ways to Go." *ChLA Quarterly* 10.1 (Winter 1986): 197–98.

The English department at Eastern Michigan University offers both an undergraduate minor in children's literature and a graduate master's program. The curriculum was developed to broaden the students' knowledge and appreciation of imaginative literature, particularly of those preparing for teaching, and to increase their familiarity with and critical evaluation of the literature of childhood.

The English department had long offered two children's literature courses: an undergraduate survey in genres and a graduate methods course. In 1970 the curriculum expanded with an undergraduate minor. That program includes two introductory English courses: introduction to children's literature and a course in literary criticism; and a choice of courses, including folklore, mythology, Shakespeare, and the Bible as literature.

The success of that program led to an expansion of graduate coursework. A Master of Arts in English with a concentration on children's literature is now offered. This scholarly approach to the subject is a traditional 30 hours of graduate work, with 12 hours in children's literature. The curriculum consists of the history of children's literature, teaching of children's literature, major genres in children's literature, and a special topics seminar. Some of the seminar subjects include mythology, fantasy, the modern novel, poetry, early childhood literature, writing for children, and children's writing.

144. Hunt, Peter. "'But Don't Go Into Mr. McGregor's Garden': Children's Books in Britain Today." *The New Advocate* 1.3 (Summer 1988): 155–64.

Peter Hunt updates his 1983 report on the state of children's books in England (see *The Advocate* 1983). Changes in educational requirements and evaluation are affecting resources and curriculum. Teachers are beginning to use more noncanonical literature. The publishing of hardback fiction is so small that few unconventional books appear, only surefire sellers.

Reductions in funding for higher education have made children's literature classes, potentially appealing to students, more prominent. The revolution in literary theory which undermined the old canons of the English curriculum have opened the field for further college study. A small number of English departments are now offering degree programs in children's literature. A recent research seminar indicated a high level of interest in the teaching of children's literature.

As the study of children's literature becomes more respectable, controversies arise over the adaptation of classic texts. The recent storm of protest over the Ladybird Press version of *Peter Rabbit* illustrates the factions which exist. A counterbalance is Janet and Allen Ahlberg's *The Jolly Postman* which stimulates other works of creative genius.

The professional literature shows a marked middle ground between the academic and the popular. Writers such as Aidan Chambers, Elaine Moss, Robert Leeson, and Margery Fisher make strong persuasive cases for their own practiced approaches to bringing children and books together. While no major coherent movement in British children's literature seems imminent, isolated individual authors and texts bring hope.

145. Hunt, Peter. "Examining Children's Literature: Children's Books at the University of Wales." *Signal* 62 (May 1990): 147-58.

Children's literature has been expanding into English departments of British universities on the graduate level; children's literature is now offered in an undergraduate program at the University of Wales in Cardiff.

With a merger and reorganization, the English department changed the status of children's literature from a 20-lecture course to a 40-plus lecture course. No longer embedded within a series of lectures called "Language and Society," the course was validated on its own, defended by the author before the faculty as a subject of timely literary, social, educational, and commercial importance. New understandings in critical theory on the role of the reader help to legitimize the interdisciplinary study of children's literature.

The one-year course is organized around four major topics: definitions and critical approaches; the history of children's literature; the twentieth century and contemporary children's books; and special topics like censorship, multimedia books, and international books.

The students read Townsend's *Written for Children* as a text, along with *Puck of Pook's Hill*, *The Wind in the Willows*, *Alice in Wonderland*, *How Tom Beat Captain Najork and His Hired Sportsmen*, and *The Stone Book Quartet*. The great strength of the course lies in the noncanonical status of the literature, which allows students the freedom to think and express on their own.

Samples from a required examination and a course syllabus are included.

146. Jackson, William. "Children's Fiction in a College of Education." *School Librarian* 23 (September 1975): 201-4.

William Jackson, principal lecturer in English at Hamilton College of Education in Scotland, describes the course work available to students training to be teachers. There has been a great deal of pressure on the curriculum, caused by the large amount of material to be covered, and children's fiction has suffered. There also has been a tendency to deemphasize reader response to fiction and aesthetic/literary values in favor of "information" to be gained from the book. Jackson deplores this trend. He hopes that proposals then being brought forward for the alteration of primary training would "allow us to develop more effectively the student's own personal response to literature, for it is on the teacher's own delight in such material and her own sensitivity to it that we would hope to build."

More effective than work with students is the in-service and development work provided by the three lecturers in the program. This is because teachers with some experience and some status are in a position to effect changes in the curriculum, while students and beginning teachers are not. These programs consist of conferences that feature talks by distinguished authors and illustrators. Also featured are seminars within which specific books are discussed, and workshops which "aim at developing specific skills in art, drama, puppetry, story-telling, writing, work with less able children."

The lecturers also visit schools to provide in-service training. Meetings often are held at 4:00 P.M. so that teachers who cannot get release time to attend a daylong seminar can participate. Attendance is good and interest high—teachers do not have to be made interested in the use of books; it is just necessary to help them use them more effectively.

147. Jobe, Ronald. "Children's Literature and Teacher Education in Canada." *Early Child Development and Care* 48 (1989): 59–66.

After listing the increased improvement in the quality and quantity of Canadian children's literature, and the reasons for the attention now being paid to it in the teaching profession, Ronald Jobe discusses the results of a survey of higher education concerning the teaching of children's literature. Courses in departments of English, education, and library education were surveyed. It was found that while objectives focused on evaluation and selection, critical reading and written expression, presenting literature in the classroom, and historical development, methods used in English and education departments differed. English courses focused on essays and examinations. Education courses included participation, book sharing, formal book talks, storytelling, annotated book lists, research papers, reading journals, writing a children's book, and thematic unit plans for using children's books in the classroom. Other teaching strategies, popular Canadian children's books, and textbooks are mentioned.

148. Jobe, Ronald. "Children's Literature as an Academic Pursuit: The University of British Columbia Model." *Bookbird* 23.4 (1985): 12-13.

Children's literature is thriving in academia in Canada. Nearly every college and university offers courses in the field. The University of British Columbia offers studies in children's literature from four perspectives: the faculty of education; the librarianship school; the faculty of arts; and the departments of English and creative writing. Off-campus extension courses are also available.

The department of language education in the faculty of education offers three courses in the teaching of children's and youth literature in schools, in which relations between child, the book, and the curriculum are the essential components. The librarianship program stresses literary heritage as well as publishing practices. The English department approaches the subject from an in-depth historical examination of titles, often using R. G. Moyles's text, *From Instruction to Delight* (Oxford). The creative writing course, taught by a successful author, studies techniques and creative application.

The challenge ahead is to integrate more Canadian authors into the curriculum, which has emphasized largely British and American books.

149. Kaye, Marilyn. "Learning How: Remarks on the Teaching of Children's Literature." In *Celebrating Children's Books*, Betsy Hearne and Marilyn Kaye, editors. New York: Lothrop, Lee and Shepard, 1981. 188-97.

The real test in evaluating a children's literature course cannot be student response, which is generally positive to the subject matter, but, instead, what is being taught and learned. The emphasis is too often on a memorized bibliography of authors and titles rather than on the reasons for their stature in the field, and an understanding of the evaluative process.

Students, fearful of critical analysis, seek the security of classifications and criteria for evaluation. They must be led to evaluate each book individually and on its own terms. While reader identification is a natural first step in revealing character development, the emphasis should go beyond the subjective to an understanding of technique and what the author has done to make the characters believable.

The inquiry process is cumulative, moving from an open-ended question to an understanding of what an individual text might indicate or could signify. The method is one of discovery through the tools of critical thinking. Examples from discussions on Paul Zindel's *The Pigman* and M. E. Kerr's *If I Love You, Am I Trapped Forever?* illustrate the process of discovery.

Course assignments extend the interpretive process on an individual basis. Isolating one aspect of a work or comparing similar elements in two or more novels are suggested approaches for essays or longer papers. Comparing reviews of one specific work helps students appreciate the variables in response and what makes some critics more credible than others.

Students should complete such an introductory course with a sense of how quality literature works. Just as they will assume professional responsibilities in selecting books for children, we must teach what "makes the good books good."

150. Kingore, Bertha W. "Storytelling: A Bridge from the University to the Elementary School to the Home." *Language Arts* 59.1 (January 1982): 28–32.

Bertha Kingore is a professor in the Hardin Simmons University School of Education. She describes what happened when she included storytelling as a part of her literature class for preservice teachers. After learning the techniques of storytelling and telling stories to one another in class, the students went in pairs to elementary classrooms to tell stories. This was such a success that recruiting and training children as storytellers followed. Children who learned and told a story were awarded a certificate. This activity is seen as valuable for both teachers and children in a number of ways, not least of which is a new involvement with literature.

151. Kinnell, Margaret. "Cross-Cultural Futures: Research and Teaching in Comparative Children's Literature." *International Review of Children's Literature and Librarianship* 2.7 (Winter 1987): 161–73.

This article is concerned with research in children's literature, rather than with the teaching of it. The comparative research that has been done is reviewed, and research needs outlined. The need for cross-cultural research comes from our increasingly multicultural society. Teaching programs in children's literature "should be reflecting the concerns of these [culturally mixed] students and the needs of their societies, as well as the demands of scholarship." Margaret Kinnell points out that it is as important to examine illustration and picture books as it is to research literature. Little has been done in this area, and what is available is not well recognized. It is suggested that cross-cultural research projects offer excellent opportunities for collaboration between students or researchers in the various literatures being compared. The difficulties in implementing comparative studies are discussed. These are politics, access, cost, lack of translations/lack of facility in other languages, concept transfer, and choice of research method when researchers are collaborating.

When teaching classes of students from various cultures, Kinnell emphasizes the need to break out of the traditional curriculum. While many foreign students are specifically interested in learning about English language books and literature, if they are to return to their homelands to teach children or be librarians there, they need to explore and become knowledgeable about their own literature. This process can be enriching for the entire class.

152. Kissen, Rita M. "Multicultural Education: The Opening of the American Mind." *English Education* 21.3 (October 1989): 211–18.

Rita Kissen, who teaches in the department of English language and literature of Central Michigan University in Mount Pleasant, describes the growth of her students when she taught "Children's Literature of Emerging Nations" for the first time in several years. At the beginning of the course, she found her 35 students to be biased, ethnocentric, racist, and sexist. Through the study of 12 books selected from the collection at the Information Center on Children's Cultures at UNICEF, the UN Children's Fund, the students developed not only an appreciation of other cultures but also a variety of methods for sharing this appreciation with the children they would soon be teaching.

Methods used in this course included storytelling, experience of ethnic cuisines, and visits to the class by representatives from the cultures being studied. "Students researched materials appropriate for the elementary or middle school, on the history, geography, and culture of the country under discussion, as well as the current state of writing and publishing for children." Students learned to preview materials for children with sensitivity for cultural bias.

It was discovered that the university's library lacked multicultural resources, and a concerted effort was mounted to enrich the collection. The ideas and methods presented in this article could be useful for any multicultural literature course, and could be incorporated as well in a general course.

153. Kutzer, M. Daphne. "Children's Literature in the College Classroom." *College English* 43.7 (November 1981): 716–23.

This article addresses the problems of a professor of English teaching children's literature to a class made up primarily of in-training teachers, or students who are preparing in some way to work with children and books. This creates a tension between a desire to discuss, in literary terms, the books the teacher knows and admires, and a need to discuss popular children's books, many of which cannot be discussed in literary terms.

Much of the material covered in children's literature classes is not children's literature at all, and should be excluded from such courses. These include myth, legend, poetry written for adults, and rhymes written for children. Much of this material should be included in education courses. Prose fiction remains, and from this should be selected classics that children still read, contemporary books of literary merit, and popular books of questionable merit. Such a collection can be used as the basis on which to construct a course that addresses questions of literary merit, audience, purpose, social and educational value, censorship, and the dangers of nostalgia.

Teachers who understand the techniques of literary analysis will find it easier to guide children into critical analysis. Determination of literary merit is particularly problematic with children's books, as it is difficult to judge children's books by adult standards, although literary techniques can be considered. Questions of social value frequently arise, since children's books are often viewed as a way to civilize the young. Adult ideas of what children should read shape the field of children's literature. Censorship and the dangers of nostalgia often result.

Commentary on this article and response by the author appear in *College English* 45 (February 1983): 190–97.

154. LaBonty, Jan. *College Students as Readers*. ERIC 335-631, 1990. 15 pp.

Jan LaBonty reviews research on the reading habits of adults, reports on a survey she conducted, and a project she conducted in one of her classes. The research reveals that teachers do not read for pleasure or for professional knowledge. They have little awareness of children's literature. Those teachers who do read and know children's literature tend to be older teachers. LaBonty's survey showed that undergraduate education students also do not read. Most did not read professional journals, and did not have a favorite children's poet or author.

LaBonty points out that the classroom teacher is the model of reading for the child. The teacher exposes children to books and provides opportunities for recreational reading. Obviously, teachers who do not read and who are unfamiliar with children's literature will be unable to inspire children to read or to guide their selection of reading materials. What is needed is a change in the content of education courses. Students in such courses should be required to read professional literature and children's literature. They should study the subjective and transactional nature of reading.

As a follow-up to the survey, students in reading-related classes were asked to set personal reading goals in three areas: recreational reading, professional reading, and children's literature. At the conclusion of the project, many students reported an enjoyment in reading for pleasure that had nearly been forgotten. A number of their comments are included with the paper.

155. Laughlin, Mildred Knight. "Approaches to Teaching Children's Literature." *Journal of Education for Librarianship* 23 (Summer 1982): 23–28.

A description is given of a survey sent to teachers in schools of library and information science. The author was preparing to take part in a panel on the differences of approach to teaching children's literature by English professors, education professors, and library science professors. They were asked about their overall perspective in teaching the course; four major objectives of the course; whether a textbook was required, and if so, its title; topics introduced as units; instructional methods; methods of determining if students have done required reading; and methods used in deriving final grades. No statistical analysis of the data is offered.

156. Lieberman, Jan. "Planning Programs for Children: A Library School Course." *Emergency Librarian* 13 (November–December 1985): 11–13.

Lieberman describes the incident that led to the development of a new library school course at San Jose State University. The course, unlike others in the curriculum that focus on theories and research, is the practical application and extension of children's literature. It gives students the opportunity to plan theme units and present them to the class. The plans included coordination with other library departments and publicity and promotion of the program. Also included in the course are visiting presentations by working children's librarians. Besides describing the scope of their jobs, and their budgeting and staffing problems, the visitors gave demonstrations of children's programs. These included storytelling, booktalking, puppetry, and reading aloud.

157. Lonsdale, Ray, and John Spink. "Children's Books in the Education of Librarians at the College of Librarianship Wales, Aberystwyth." *Signal* 54 (September 1987): 203–9.

The College of Librarianship Wales is the largest school of library and information science in the United Kingdom and one of the largest in the world. The major children's literature course is "Libraries and Literature for Young People." The emphasis is on library materials in use by young people, viewed within a social and cultural context. Information needs, publishing trends, literary genres, illustration, and nonprint media are considered. Contemporary issues are traced through discussions of characteristics, development, range, and variety of groups of books.

The goal throughout the course is to show not only the range of books and nonprint materials but "to demonstrate how these can contribute to young people's leisure and work through informed and imaginative promotion by librarians, teachers and parents."

Resources include the Horton Collection of historical materials; the Children's Room, a model school library and media center; and the Welsh National Center for Children's Literature.

In-service training is offered teachers and librarians in literature and information sources and the development of an information skills curriculum.

158. Mathews, Virginia H. "WNBA Offers a Plan for a Course in Children's Literature." *Publishers' Weekly* 168 (Oct. 22, 1955): 1802–3.

In this short article Virginia Mathews describes a course that was offered as in-service training for teachers in New York by the Women's National Book Association. It was intended as a refresher course for teachers, "showing them some of the ways of relating books to the life and learning of the classroom, giving it added richness, color and dimension." The course included a study of publishers and the place of the children's book department within the publishing house. Also studied was the work of the children's book editor. Because the course was offered in New York, the opportunity was taken to have authors, illustrators, editors, and publishers visit the class. At the time of writing, plans were being made to affiliate with schools of library science and education, and to expand to other parts of the country.

159. Meek, Margaret. "Symbolic Outlining: The Academic Study of Children's Literature." *Signal* 53 (May 1987): 97–115.

"Symbolic Outlining" is the ninth annual Woodfield Lecture, given on May 20, 1986, at the Department of Library and Information Studies, Loughborough University. A British critic and reading expert, Margaret Meek argues for a theory of literature which includes both books and children; one which conceptualizes emergent readers and their texts. Meek confronts the paradoxes which abound in adult reactions to literature for children. Books for the young cannot be separated from their sources of creation and production. Children's books cannot be studied as discrete texts, but emerge within cultural and historical studies of childhood and children reading. Academic studies should focus on "how children learning to read become those who take to reading, as an activity beyond a social obligation, in a literate society."

The author examined the intersection of children's literature and established academic disciplines. Three conceptual perspectives exist: adults writing books for children, their own first readers; adults writing about children's books, their own interpretive readings and research; and children reading, their own adaptation of social practices as well as literary forms. The first two perspectives are the most common in academia, with biographical and autobiographical studies as well as social history. The child as reader is a complex consideration, largely neglected.

Children's literature transcends disciplinary boundaries and traditional academic institutions. Studies need to begin with children's language development within a cultural context. We need to know how children approach and adapt the process of reading, particularly as they enter into fictional words, in the "traffic in possibilities."

160. Monseau, Virginia R. "The Role of Children's and Adolescent Literature in the Undergraduate Curriculum." *CEA Forum* (1989):3–4, 6–8.

Why are courses in children's and adolescent literature not often taught in English departments, and why are such courses, when they are taught, denigrated by such terms as "kiddie lit"? Virginia Monseau argues for the inclusion of children's and adolescent literature in the college English curriculum. Attitudes toward children's literature need reexamination. Children's literature is the foundation of literary appreciation, an essential part of literary history, an enlightening experience for all students, different from adult literature only in degree, and valuable in its retrospective understanding.

The courses in children's and adolescent literature at Youngstown State University are defined as to audience, purpose, and content.

The children's literature course is taken primarily by elementary education majors, with some students from English and other disciplines. The purpose is to give students a broad background in children's literature; students become knowledgeable by reading children's books. Ten to fifteen children's novels are required, besides numerous fairy tales, rhymes and poems, and picture books. Written requirements include critical papers, journals, quizzes, and exams.

The adolescent literature course attracts a varied audience of parents, prospective English teachers, and students from diverse disciplines interested in adolescents and their literature. Reading requirements are similar to those in the children's literature course, although more emphasis is placed on nonfiction. Students read novels, short stories, poetry, and critical essays.

161. Moon, Cliff. "Teacher Training and Children's Fiction." *The School Librarian* 22 (March 1974): 6–10.

Cliff Moon reports on a two-part survey done in Bristol, England. The first part of the survey involved letters to three colleges of education. Respondents were asked to describe patterns of training in children's fiction existing in the colleges. The second part consisted of a distribution of surveys to recently trained teachers. The aim of the questionnaire was to elicit information about the effectiveness of their training, if any. It was ascertained that teachers felt a need for training, that they felt the use of fiction in teaching is of great importance, and that the great majority of them have a great interest in the literature themselves.

The courses themselves are minimally described, but included reading, discussions, storytelling, conferences, and book events. The book events were well supported by students, where they took advantage of opportunities to see and buy new books, participate in storytelling sessions with children, see films, and hear children's authors speak. The students felt that the most important aspect of training is reading vast quantities of fiction. They expressed a need to know how to judge suitable age levels for individual books.

The courses offered in connection with teacher training and library training were found to be better preparation for teaching than were the courses offered in English programs. This no doubt reflects the focus on research and literary content rather than on children that can be expected in such courses.

162. National Council of Teachers of English. *Teaching Children's Literature in Colleges and Universities*. Elliott D. Landau, editor. New York: NCTE, 1968.

The results of a survey of 573 people who teach children's literature are reported. The data are presented with little comment. The survey covered professional preparation and activities, course content, and materials and techniques. Numerous teaching techniques are listed, as well as the minimum number of books required to be read. Textbooks, indices, periodicals, and other materials considered basic by the teachers are listed. Indications of collection size available can be a useful guide in places where new courses are being established. All information is shown in tables, and summaries of each section are included. Especially valuable is the list of nine recommendations formulated by the committee conducting the study. These recommendations address book collections, required coursework for teachers, research needs, critical reviews, and professionalism.

163. Neumeyer, Peter F. "Children's Literature as It Is Taught in University English Departments in the U.S. in 1985." *Bookbird* 23.4 (1985): 4-11.

English departments are awakening to children's literature. Attacks on the notion of an exclusive canon of classics books, considerations of what constitutes a text, and attention to reader response have all contributed to a higher status for children's literature in the humanities.

While most activity in the past has been confined to education departments, a number of exceptional examples exist. Frances Clarke Sayers taught children's literature in the English department at UCLA more than 30 years ago. A handful of universities have offered courses, particularly through the work of scholars like U. C. Knoepflamcher, Roger Sale, Jack Zipes, and Anne MacLeod. The Center for the Study of Children's Literature at Simmons College (Boston) has been a model program for the disciplined study of children's books as literature. Seminars offered through the National Endowment for the Humanities have furthered scholarly interest.

The battle is not yet won, as some colleagues do tend to look askance at the serious treatment of children's books. But high enrollments, prolific scholarship, new dissertations, and prominence of theories of semiotics and popular culture have enhanced the status of the subject. The author reports on his own descriptive survey of six institutions where children's literature is particularly well served by scholars in the field: Seattle University; Clemson University; University of North Carolina, Charlotte; University of Florida; Eastern Michigan; San Diego State University. The breadth of courses, special programs, and institutional support is examined.

The author explores the works generally taught, despite resistance to establish a canon of children's literature. A sampling of texts and curricular approaches is cited.

164. Neumeyer, Peter F. "Children's Literature in the English Department." *ChLA Quarterly* 12.3 (1987): 146–50.

Peter Neumeyer describes his establishment of a children's literature course in the English department of San Diego State University. He explains the objectives of such a course, defines the relationships of children's literature to other academic fields, and its place within a literature curriculum.

Neumeyer states that children's literature is by definition comparative literature, and he discusses its relationship to courses taught in education and library science programs. Broadening the discussion, he describes interactions with philosophy, anthropology, sociology, ethics, graphic arts, and the craft of bookmaking.

Neumeyer describes some specific assignments, literary devices, and further objectives of the course.

165. Nodelman, Perry. "Teaching a Unit of Fairy Tales." *ChLA Quarterly* 7.2 (Summer 1972): 9–11.

Perry Nodelman, a well-known scholar and teacher of children's literature, advocates the teaching of fairy tales in an introductory course. Fairy tales unsettle complacent readers who feel superior to the subject. The peculiarities of fairy tales reveal important insights into writing for children.

The author begins the course with versions of *Little Red Riding Hood*. Seeing a familiar text with variants demonstrates the persistence and flexibility of the genre. Fairy tales can be told in various ways, but all the versions tell the same story. Students, for example, tell the story cumulatively, each offering a sentence. Nodelman adds historical background to the variations. Contrasting the Perrault and Grimm versions reflects a changed attitude toward what is appropriate for children.

Students are divided into groups to discuss different versions of *Little Red Riding Hood*. What is distinctive to this version? Is it a good version of the story? Is it a good story? What is consistent in the various versions? What makes popular fairy tales so powerful? Since most of these versions are illustrated, the students begin to develop skills at analyzing pictures and text.

The students compile a list of commonly known fairy tales. These are stories the students could tell if asked to do so. Frequently listed are *Little Red Riding Hood, The Three Little Pigs, Goldilocks and the Three Bears, Jack and the Beanstalk, Cinderella, Sleeping Beauty, Snow White,* and *Hansel and Gretel.* Literary elements are explored which are common to all literature, and some that are distinctive to fairy tales.

Contemporary retellings are examined for artistry and for attitudes that alter the texts. Judgments about children's literature and the needs of children raise issues of the uses of literature. Contemporary versions are compared to traditional tales for their storytelling qualities.

The 15 hours or more of class time devoted to fairy tales in a children's literature course is a large investment, but productive in introducing students to literary criticism, comparative literature, ideological issues, and storytelling at the core of children's books.

166. Nodelman, Perry. "Teaching Children's Literature: An Intellectual Snob Confronts Some Generalizers." *Children's Literature in Education* 17.4 (1986): 203–14.

Perry Nodelman, who teaches a course that has its emphasis on the literature rather than on children (he knows nothing about children, he says), was accused of being a snob by a student filling out an evaluation form. This is because he forces students, most of whom have social science or education backgrounds, to confront the literature as literature, and to react to it. He wants them to learn to evaluate the books, poetry, and other literature, and to react to it, while they want to be given facts and things to memorize and give back on tests. Nodelman advises instructors who need to be liked by their students not to use his methods. However, he says, the students learn to think, and learn about literature. He hopes that through that learning they will gain something he can not give them — ways to use literature in creative and meaningful ways with the children they will be teaching or working with. "My approach would be the one usually taken to literature by literary scholars; we would be reading these books not in terms of our guesses about how children might respond to them, but in terms of our own enjoyment and understanding of them ... you cannot hope to understand a work of literature until you allow yourself to respond to it and then explore that response."

One technique used in the course is to read a picture book without the accompanying pictures, or to look at pictures without the accompanying stories. The students comment on these experiences and then are able to generalize about the relationships of words and pictures. Another is to have each student bring to class five poems. The poems are read aloud and their choice defended to the class. The class reaches a consensus about the five best poems of all those brought in, and then tries to determine what makes them good. All tests are based on stories or poems not previously discussed in class.

167. Paul, Lissa. "Teaching Children's Literature in Canada." *Signal* 58 (January 1989): 35-50.

The author reports on a children's literature symposium on teaching children's literature that was a preconference to Kaleidoscope, organized by the Canadian Children's Book Centre. Various disciplines and interest groups spoke about the state of children's books in publishing, academia, and the schools of Canada.

The discussion centered on what to teach, how to teach, and how to evaluate students. Common concerns are the need to familiarize students with a wide range of books, including Canadian literature, and the development of skills in literary discourse. The inexperience of students in reading for pleasure and in talking about literature was frequently attributed to poor pedagogical approaches to literature in the schools. University students need to be exposed to a variety of quality literature that can be used in student teaching.

A variety of curricular approaches are shared. Class sets of books and anthologies are two common means of using literature. With the conviction that students need to read real books, the author requires students to read 16 or 17 books from a course list.

One controversial issue is the use of books by Canadian authors and illustrators. A recent survey indicated only about 20 percent of reading lists include Canadian books. Paul lists various Canadian books which are most popularly used and debates the various perspectives on Canadian content of children's books.

As to pedagogy, there seemed to be agreement that Aidan Chambers's reader-response approach best accomplishes the two goals of encouraging affective pleasure in books and the capacity to engage in literary discourse.

Some of the most common means of evaluating students were shared: formal essays, final exams, and response journals. The need is to engage students in responsive and analytical approaches to children's literature.

168. Pilhjerta, Ritva-Liisa. "The Teaching of Children's Literature in Finland." *Bookbird* 25.4 (December 1987): 5.

Children's literature is taught at the universities of Helsinki, Jyväskylä, Tampere, and Turku. The author describes the program at the University of Helsinki where she conducts a seminar. The course begins with a description of reference works and book selection aids, followed by an historical survey, and then intensive reading of classic works by authors such as Defoe, Carroll, Andersen, Alcott, and Stevenson. After studying international classics, the students read Finnish children's literature.

Other seminars include a year-long course in which students explore research in the field and then write criticism based on critical reading and evaluation. These courses are offered through the department of Finnish literature and education. A related course is taught through the department of comparative literature. The greatest need is for more reseearch in the history of children's literature. Few comprehensive studies exist.

169. Pond, Patricia. "Teaching Children's Literature—With Paperbacks." *Top of the News* 25 (January 1969): 162–70.

A course in the School of Librarianship at the University of Oregon is described. It was found that prospective teachers and librarians taking the children's literature course often had not done much reading themselves. It was decided that rather than require a textbook, the students would purchase, at about the same price, ten paperback books. The selection of the books to be made available, the negotiations with the college bookstore, and the success of the plan are described. The goals of the plan were to encourage the students to buy and own quality children's books and encourage reading aloud and discussion of the books. The goals were met and the program considered successful.

170. Post, Robert M. "Interpreting Literature for Young Children." *Communication Education* 32.3 (July 1983): 285–91.

Citing the relationship between a child's being read to and his or her own reading ability, Robert Post, a professor of speech communication at the University of Washington, urges a course in oral interpretation of literature for young children. This course would acquaint the student with basic principles of oral interpretation, guide in the selection of suitable literature, develop skills of oral interpretation, and introduce ways in which oral interpretation of literature may be used for educational purposes.

Selection of literature to perform is seen as more important than how it is performed. Good poetry and good prose, both fiction and nonfiction, may be used. The selector should be alert for sexism and racism that abound in children's literature. Illustrations should be consistent with good art. Stories should have unified and complete plots, be full of action, and have realistic dialogue, characters, and settings that are vivid and believable. Nonfiction should be factually accurate. Finally, a book is a good book for children only when they enjoy it.

In performance, enjoyment is primary. Generally, exaggerated use of voice and body is demanded. Aesthetic distance is broken when performing for children. The children become participants, and the alert interpreter must be prepared for interruptions. Various props may be used. Suggestions for the nonprofessional are given; for instance, for the parent or relative who is handed an unfamiliar book and asked to read it without having time to prepare.

171. Probst, Robert E. "Response-Based Teaching of Literature." *English Journal* 70.7 (November 1981): 43–47.

In this essay Robert Probst discusses reader-response literature teaching in college and high school classes. He defines response-based teaching as a pattern of thinking and talking that begins with the reader's response to the literary work and moves from there on to other matters. The original response may be emotional, intellectual, or visceral, but in Probst's classes the discussion returned first to the poem itself ("View of a Pig" by Ted Hughes), and then ranged to biographical investigations of the poet, historical questions, and life experiences. This kind of teaching places a great responsibility on the students. They must think and decide, and deal with ambiguity. Probst thinks there is not much point in working for less.

172. Rasmussen, Bonnie. "Children's Books in Teacher Education at Armidale College of Advanced Education." *Signal* 57 (September 1988): 197–205.

Children's literature is the center of the language arts program at this university in New South Wales, Australia. Their curriculum is shaped by the whole language approach to the teaching of literacy skills. Beyond using books for reading instruction, the program offers units in children's literature as a literature and two separate courses. The philosophy is to model the teaching of all the literacy skills through real books. The goals of the children's literature course include developing competence in assessing literary merit and a critical approach to books; to demonstrate literature as a source of pleasure and enlightenment, for personal as well as professional development; and to develop understanding of the characteristics of genres associated with developmental stages of literacy.

Emphasis is placed on Australian authors, illustrators, and critics, with selective readings cited. Teacher trainees are exposed to principles of collection development and the process of publishing, so that they can participate in the selection and ordering of books for the whole-language classroom. Students also experiment with writing and illustrating materials for children. The developmental stages of literacy are taught through literary examples, everyday reading strategies, and an exploration of cultural issues affecting reading.

Effective response to literature is a goal, with the reading and discussing of the importance of literature as part of our lives.

173. Rosenblatt, Louise M. "The Literary Transaction: Evocation and Response." *Theory Into Practice* 21.4 (Fall 1982): 268–77.

As the acknowledged earliest exponent of what is termed reader-response theory, Louise Rosenblatt expresses concern with the diffusiveness of the term. She discusses her view of the reading transaction, which occurs along a continuum between efferent, information gathering reading, and aesthetic, personal response reading. She emphasizes that factual material may be read aesthetically, and literary material may be read efferently, as it must be when used in a basal-text mode. The continuum idea is important, as the stance is predominantly efferent or aesthetic, neither purely one nor the other. Children are naturally oriented toward aesthetic response to literature, but traditional teaching has emphasized efferent reading to the extent that children, in responding to adults' expectations, may lose the aesthetic response ability.

Rosenblatt believes that both stances should be taught, and that children should know what type of response is expected. In teaching literature the primary responsibility of the teacher is to encourage, not get in the way of, the aesthetic stance. She asserts that understanding the transactional nature of reading would correct the tendency of adults to look only at the text and the author's presumed intention, and to ignore as irrelevant the child's response if it is outside this preconceived view. The teacher can reinforce the child's own linguistic processes, provide a receptive, nonpressured atmosphere and, after the reading, deepen the experience. Providing opportunities for nonverbal response may be the safest way to deepen the experience, as requests for verbal response may reveal a testing motive. In answer to proponents of teaching literary conventions, Rosenblatt states that they are "vacuous concepts without recognition of the importance of stance." Students can be given the appropriate terminology when they need it. Rosenblatt ends by recalling that the transactional theory "avoids concentration solely on the reader's contribution or on feeling for its own sake, but centers on the reciprocal interplay of reader and text."

174. Ross, Elinor Parry. "Moving Toward a Whole Language College Classroom." *Journal of Reading* 35.4 (December–January 1991–92): 276–81.

Elinor Ross, a faculty member in curriculum and instruction at Tennessee Technological University, combined her children's literature course and reading methods course after having taught each one separately in the traditional lecture, discussion, textbook, and exam format. Concluding that a holistic approach could be as useful for college students as it is for children, she incorporated reader-response activities, group work, practicums, literature webs, and journals. Activities were purposeful, and the students were involved and grew professionally. This approach to learning has a favorable effect on the ways these in-training teachers manage their own classrooms.

175. Sadler, Glenn Edward, editor. *Teaching Children's Literature: Issues, Pedagogy, Resources*. New York: Modern Language Association, 1992.

Teaching Children's Literature is a volume in the "Options for Teaching" series. It is designed to be an informative resource guide for those interested in the current trends in teaching children's literature and for those constructing coursework. The five divisions reflect its range of material: "Critical Issues and Approaches," "Course Descriptions," "Research Programs," "Selected Collections of Children's Literature," and "Readings and Resources."

The introduction is by consultant editor U. C. Knoepflmacher, an English professor from Princeton University who is an active scholar and teacher in the field. He surveys the current status of children's literature as a legitimate division of English departments and professional scholarship. He compares the heightened interest to the strides made by feminist scholarship in the 1970s and attributes the interest in part to the "process of defamiliarization and refamiliarization" of rereading childhood books as an adult. What is created is a dynamic of response which reflects and reconciles William Blake's sense of "innocence and experience." What is needed is a further integration of children's literature within other coursework, so that children's books can illuminate other traditions within literature, such as folktales, fairy tales, and nonfictional discourses. More attention to the integration of child and adult readers is needed in interpreting texts and the reading process.

The selected bibliography cites reference works, texts and anthologies, and works of history and criticism. Also listed are periodicals and annuals in the field, addresses of special collections, and organizations sponsoring children's literature. The afterword contains an interview by the editor, Glenn Edward Sadler, with Maurice Sendak and Dr. Seuss.

176. Scott, Anne. "Children's Books in Teacher Education at Craigie College of Education, Ayr." *Signal* 52 (January 1987): 24–30.

Craigie College of Education in Ayr, Scotland, offers a four-year undergraduate program and a one-year graduate program. The emphasis is on fiction: literature for moral and social development, aesthetic pleasure, and language development. The author includes selected titles and assignments for various years of the program.

In-service courses assist teachers in the field with the teaching of fiction, poetry, and writing. Emphasis is not on transference to the classroom, but on helping teachers understand the nature of literature and its role in child development.

Their whole language approach views literature as function and form, as pragmatic as well as aesthetic. Children's books exist for children, whatever their use in the classroom may be. While application is important, the value of literature exists for the individual's delight and self-knowledge. Through a process of personal reflection and social interaction, students discover "a way back to childhood, which is revealed as a way forward into teaching young children."

177. Shachter, Jacqueline. "Videotaping Children's Authors: Temple University's Unique Teaching Program." *Library Journal* 97 (April 15, 1972): 1504–8.

Videotapes of interviews with children's authors were produced in a program sponsored by the Free Library of Philadelphia and Temple University's College of Education. At the time the article was written, 12 tapes had been produced. Shachter describes the tapes, their production, their content, and their uses. They are especially useful as motivators — it was found that students were much more interested in the authors' works after viewing tapes. The authors are presented in a much more intimate setting than is possible when they lecture. The students from the literature courses prepare questions and interact with the interviewee in a studio setting. There are spontaneous and honest reaction to questions, and much material for class discussion. Information about obtaining copies for classroom use is given at the end of the article.

178. Shercliff, W. H. "The Manchester Polytechnic Library's Collection of Children's Books." *Signal* 57 (September 1988): 206–11.

Manchester Polytechnic has a substantial collection of children's books, historic books on education, and works on book design. These various collections were merged into one through acquisitions and mergers with Didsbury College of Education and the Manchester Institute of Higher Education. While a tutor-librarian at Didsbury College, the author built a collection to support the study of children's literature and to improve the background to studies in education and social history. The institute's collection included some valuable books connected with the teaching of domestic science (home economics). Collectively, the books and periodicals of well over 5,000 items comprise an important research collection for the history of childhood.

The collection's strengths are the following: popular Victorian authors, including several first editions; late eighteenth- and early nineteenth-century books along with the early compendia which preceded information books on particular subjects; successive editions of the classics; long runs of children's magazines; book arts; and early picture books.

The collection is used by staff and students in connection with the study of art and design, literary criticism, and social history. Teacher training and library science courses study the development of a literature of childhood. Book art students are interested in the development of the physical shape, binding, typography, graphic design, and illustration of children's books.

A catalogue, *Morality to Adventure: Manchester Polytechnic's Collection of Children's Books 1840–1939* (Bracken, 1988), by W. H. Shercliff, has been published to record an area of special strength. For the purpose of the catalogue, a children's book is defined as one which a child could read or hear read without the need of instruction. Books for teachers are excluded. The catalogue follows the arrangement into 21 sections, similar to categories of other histories and compilations, such as the catalogue of the Osborne Collection.

The author urges the collection and preservation of books published since 1939 which chronicle a period of high achievement in children's book publishing.

179. Snow, Miriam. "One Children's Literature Course." *Reading and the School Library* 2 (March–April 1936): 121–23.

Miriam Snow describes one of the earliest children's literature courses for adults, taught in a normal school in Washington, DC. The students were required to do a great deal of reading, to learn to judge the merits of a book, to use books in teaching various subjects, and to learn to read and to advocate reading for pleasure.

180. Spoerl, Dorothy Tilden. "Research and the Newbery and Caldecott Books." *Wilson Library Bulletin* 26 (June 1952): 818–19.

Dorothy Spoerl describes a project for graduate students that is designed to require them to read and study award books. Simply assigning the list for reading, without a purpose attached, results in an assignment that lacks coherence and which may not be honestly carried out. Spoerl asked her students, who do not have a thesis requirement, to outline a thesis topic based on Caldecott and Newbery books. Included would be a justification and a sample based on a few of the books. This assignment resulted in careful readings of the texts and excellent suggestions for research. Some topics suggested were occupations, fear, death, religion, parents, and school.

181. Taxel, Joel. *Sensitizing Students to the Selective Tradition in Children's Literature.* ERIC 213–647, 1982. 27 pp.

The selective tradition refers to a dominating set of perspectives. The term comes from Raymond Williams, who argues that culture is transmitted in a selective way, which excludes certain groups or traditions from the larger universe of knowledge. As a college professor of children's literature, the author explores the meaning of a selective tradition through the study of children's literature. Two courses are offered: a general service course for undergraduate education majors, and a doctoral level course on gender and racial issues.

The concept of a selective tradition is central to the author's attempts to raise student consciousness on ideological issues. The emphasis is on evaluating books by literary analysis as well as social and political factors.

His primary teaching method is to have students consider texts in relationship to their own experience and to critical commentary. An example is given of a picture book text that reveals a stereotypical female image and the class dialogue over the extent and effects of such depiction. Stereotypes are generally imprinted at an unconscious level and through repeated exposure. Another strategy is to compare two books on a similar subject, setting, and theme.

Students show greater sensitivity to issues and to their own values as transmitted to children. Notes and references.

182. Taxel, Joel. "Teaching Children's Literature." *Teaching Education* 1.1 (February 1987): 12–15.

The author, a professor at the University of Georgia, describes his course offered in the early childhood program. His first concern is to convince students of the importance of the subject and the need for critical reflection. He attempts to dispel myths about children's literature through the course itself rather than through direct confrontation with beliefs about the diminutive status of literature for children. His course goals for students include the following: to derive pleasure from reading fine literature; to understand the nature of their own responses; and to articulate their responses in terms of literary elements, such as plot, characterization, theme, style, and illustration.

Class time is spent reflecting on childhood reading experiences and on responding to common texts. In stressing reader response, he insists on explanation and defense. This builds their powers of judgment. He encourages students to struggle with the large issues of the day that influence literature for children. The readings are supplemented by information provided by films, filmstrips, and professional journals. Issues of racism, sexism, and censorship are examined through literary texts and supplementary sources.

The large goal is to enable students to share the joys of literature and to be aware of the role of literature in shaping children's consciousness.

183. Taylor, Mary-Agnes. "Which Way to Castle Yonder?" *ChLA Quarterly* 12.3 (1987): 142–44.

Mary-Agnes Taylor discusses the problems created when one reads a criticism of a work before reading the work itself. Such commentary can completely block creative reading.

Taylor conducted experiments with Maurice Sendak's *Higglety, Pigglety, Pop!* using adult students who had read critiques compared to those who had not. She asked them to respond to allusion and symbolism, and found differences between the two groups.

184. Trin, Mary. "Magic Abroad! Children's Literature at the Catholic College of Education Sydney." *Bookbird* 23.1 (1985): 21–24.

All education students in the College of Education Sydney (Australia) take children's literature. The objectives of the course are to acquire knowledge of children's literature, including oral interpretation of stories and poems, and to plan for the effective use of children's literature in the classroom.

Students prepare an annotated bibliography containing bibliographic information, indication of genre, comments on theme, a brief summary, ideas for classroom use, and age level. Each student includes at least 20 books on the bibliography along with other reading.

The criteria for assessment of bibliographies include: suitability, the quality of the book as literature; level of perception, indicated by response; ease of referral; and presentation, with attention to detail. The course is generally organized into three genres: folklore, modern fantasy, and realism. Along with the study of form and structure, the students explore Maslow's hierarchy of needs. Examples of books matching Maslow's categories are provided and are included in the bibliography.

185. Vandergrift, Kay E. *Children's Literature: Theory, Research, and Teaching.* Englewood, CO: Libraries Unlimited, 1990.

Kay Vandergrift, a noted teacher of children's literature, states in the preface to her book that "teachers, especially beginning teachers, often teach their students the way they were taught." She feels that it is "important for those who teach adults to develop materials and teaching strategies with enough depth to allow real intellectual growth for students of different ages and different levels of experience and knowledge." She then sets forth ideas based on theoretically based critical analyses of works for children and young people, research, and practical teaching strategies.

The heart of the book addresses teaching and children's literature. Many models of university teaching are offered, explicated, and critiqued. Vandergrift then describes and advocates the "literary model" as the best approach for teaching and outlines the states of the teaching composition. She addresses the use of technology in teaching and teaching style.

Following this general description, a history of the development of one course is given, along with examples of syllabi and worksheets for various courses. Finally, Vandergrift reviews the present state of continuing education in children's literature and discusses a short-term focused institute. The book includes extensive bibliographies and a detailed index. This is a valuable contribution from an experienced and respected practitioner in the field.

186. Watson, Jerry J., Patricia Sharp and Bill Snider. "Should Literary Classics Be Part of Children's Literature?" *English Education* 13.4 (December 1981), 217–23.

In considering content for an undergraduate course in children's literature, these professors questioned whether they could assume that students would be familiar with classics and award-winning books. A survey of students to determine their knowledge of 50 authors and their best-known works revealed a low level of knowledge. Only 19 of the 50 were familiar to 50 percent of the students. Highest recognition was for fairy tales. Of twentieth-century writers, only Dr. Seuss was known by the top quartile. While cautioning that lists of classics need constant revision and updating, and that there is never agreement on the authors/titles that all children "should" be exposed to, the authors note that the books most often read by the students are ones that are generally acknowledged to have no literary merit. They concluded that time must be taken in an introductory class for classics and award books so that future teachers will have a foundation for guiding their own students to appreciate literary quality.

187. Watson, Victor. "Children's Books in Teacher Education at the University of Cambridge." *Signal* 46 (January 1985): 27–33.

Homerton College at Cambridge offers undergraduate courses in children's literature in the education department. The emphasis in the department is phasing out secondary education and increasing the education of junior and middle school teachers. This change has included the introduction of a course on literature for children as the first part of a year-long course on language in the primary school. Faculty from the English and drama departments teach the course in groups of 20 students in 10 two-hour classes.

The course begins with stories and picture books for the very young. Then the course moves on to reading schemes, which are question sheets based on criteria such as vocabulary, story content, illustrations, and possible stereotypes. Students then explore short novels, traditional tales, children's poetry, and finally longer novels. Students are required to submit three assignments: the reading scheme or work sheet; an anthology of children's poetry; and annotated cards on books read. A core list of 12 novels is supplemented by a list of recommended authors.

The program is based on the assumption that students must first think as adult readers about children's books before they can teach them to children. The aim is that students will become more discriminating readers. A resource library of about 5,000 children's books supports the program.

More specialized courses are available to students in their third year. A course called "Fiction in Schools" introduces students to a wide range of good books written for children and adolescents. Students are required to submit a record of their reading and an essay outlining possible applications in the classroom. This course will be replaced by a more substantial year-long course, "Literature and School," covering a wider spectrum of literature read in school and at home.

The English department also offers coursework in children's literature. English majors can take a course in the history of children's literature. Part of the English curriculum includes a segment on "Literature and Childhood," which explores books written for children in the eighteenth century, studied in relation to the works of Locke, Richardson, Rousseau, Wordsworth, Blake, and other writers who were concerned about the education of children.

The undergraduate students seem surprised and excited by the range of books available for children's reading. They become adept at practical matters of classroom activities using books. They experience more difficulty in developing individualized reading programs. Also challenging is working with textual matters, directing the attention of a class to words used with subtlety and quality.

188. Weber, Rosemary. "Children's Literature: Books for Teaching It." *Wilson Library Bulletin* 45 (Oct. 1970): 172–79.

Rosemary Weber, who teaches at Drexel Institute School of Library Science, begins by asking a series of questions to be addressed by instructors assigned to teach a course in children's literature. One question is the choice of a textbook, if one is to be used, and the remainder of the article discusses this choice.

Four textbooks are reviewed extensively and recommendations made at the end of the article. The texts are: Sutherland and Arbuthnot, *Children and Books* (1964); Georgiou, *Children and Their Literature* (1969); Huck and Kuhn, *Children's Literature in the Elementary School*, (1968); and Smith, *A Critical Approach to Children's Literature* (1967).

Writing in 1970, Weber emphasized the need to remain current, and some of these books are criticized for being dated at the time of review. However, the approach taken in analyzing the texts can be useful for an instructor considering a more recent text. Moreover, since the reviews are so thorough, an instructor may decide to use one or more of these texts as a resource book for a particular aspect of the course being developed.

Weber first considers each text individually, describing its emphases and approach. She then compares the texts in a number of theme areas — treatment of Mother Goose, poetry, traditional literature, fairy tales and fantasy, animals, picture books, realistic literature, historical fiction, biography, nonfiction, and nonprint. Finally, problems posed by using each text are outlined and the bibliographies are critiqued.

189. Wendelin, Karla Hawkins. "Informal Children's Literature Inventory: Test Yourself." *Reading Horizons* 25.2 (Winter 1985): 141–47.

This inventory of 40 multiple-choice items is designed for teachers to assess their knowledge of children's literature. An answer key and suggestions for maintenance or remediation are included.

190. Williams, Geoff. "Children's Books in Teacher Education at the University of Sydney." *Signal* 56 (May 1988): 133–41.

The author begins with a tribute to two pioneers for children's literature in Australia: Maurice Saxby and Ken Watson. Their examples illustrate the "strength and vulnerability" of courses in children's literature at Sydney University, where individual initiative has had a limited effect on institutional support.

Children's literature is taught in the School of Teaching and Curriculum Studies, University of Sydney, offering coursework for the undergraduate and graduate levels, including a Ph.D. in children's literature.

Beginning courses work toward an enthusiastic reception of children's literature and its role in literacy development. Experiential work with young children with reading difficulties, lectures on contemporary children's books and professional readings, and other fieldwork and observations of reading practices build a strong foundation. Intermediate courses extend children's literature across the curriculum. Discussions of children's literature center on the pedagogy of literary texts, based on the complexity of writing for children.

A seminar emphasizes the integration of critical practice and classroom practice. A guiding principle is the need for children's literature in education to adopt a theory of language which reveals relationships between texts and their contexts of production and interpretation. Examples of texts and professional readings are given. Governmental reorganization of higher education may affect some of the structure in place.

191. Zaharias, Jane Ann. "Implications of State-Wide Survey of Children's Literature Instruction." In *The Best of the Bulletin of the Children's Literature Assembly of the National Council of Teachers of English*, Carolyn J. Bauer, editor. 1987. Volume 1.

The author examines characteristics of exemplary literature-based reading programs and their implications for course design. A study was conducted of children's literature instruction in the state of Ohio to ascertain the extent to which the courses prepare students to carry out literature-based reading programs.

Reading programs which are literature based should have the

following components: read-aloud activity, individualized reading of fiction; in-depth critical study of books read in common; interdisciplinary content; and a wide variety of responses.

The survey queried professors of children's literature at colleges and universities in Ohio, and focused on major course objectives, course content, course structure, instructional materials, and course assignments and activities. The results of the survey indicated that most courses are content centered, emphasizing the explication, interpretation, and evaluation of children's literature. Most course assignments are adult-appropriate rather than child-centered. This course design is viewed as inadequate preparation for literature-based reading programs. The author recommends modifying present courses in structure and in teaching method.

Her recommendations include the following: require development of classroom materials and activities; present interdisciplinary materials; demonstrate effective use of books; emphasize the management of individualized reading; and introduce reader-response theory.

Chapter 5

Teaching
Children's Literature
to Children and
Young People

The professional literature abounds with articles and books describing creative, exciting, and successful experiences with children or young people and books. Many are based on the reader-response theories first advocated by Louise Rosenblatt. Others emphasize the need for students to learn the codes and conventions of literature, and describe methods for this kind of teaching. Some are written by classroom teachers, others by university professors as a result of their classroom research. All have in common the concept that literature is valuable in itself and for itself, that children and young people will respond to it and enjoy it if they are not prevented from doing so, and that reading and sharing stories is one of life's great pleasures. Articles and books that have not been included in this bibliography are ones that "use" literature for some other purpose, worthy as that purpose may be. We have excluded writings that describe methods for using literature to teach reading, science, tolerance, sharing, geography, history, or any of dozens of other ends for which literature serves as a means. The emphasis here is on the past ten years, though some particularly important earlier works are included, along with some that are still useful and inspiring.

Although the annotations are intended to be long enough, in the case of journal articles, to give a good idea of the content, if the

ideas seem interesting and worth considering for one's own classroom, nothing is better than reading the original. Many details,
nuances, and philosophical statements will be missing from annotations. However, classroom teachers may not have access to these
journals, especially back issues, so it is hoped that sufficient information is included in the annotations to provide inspiration and
plans for implementation.

192. Armstrong, Mary K. "Petunia and Beyond: Literature for the
Kindergarten Crowd." *Reading Teacher* 35.2 (November 1981):
192–95.

A kindergarten teacher, Mary Armstrong describes the many activities she uses to help her pupils learn to love and value books and
literature. Her classroom is full of posters and stuffed toys representing
favorite books and characters. Many books are available, and the
children can take a book home each day. Many celebrations are held
throughout the year — celebrations of authors' or characters' birthdays.
Children's Book Week is a special time, with puppet shows and dress-up
parades. At other times the children bring their teddy bears or other
literary character dolls to kindergarten. Finally, they experiment with
making up their own stories, dramatize favorite stories, and visit the
public library. Throughout, the author conveys her love of children and
of literature.

193. Bagnall, Norma. "It Was *Real* Exciting: Adults and Children
Studying Literature Together." *ChLA Quarterly* 12.3 (1987):
144–46.

Inspired by curiosity about the differences in adult response and
child response to children's literature, Norma Bagnall designed a six-
week course at Missouri Western State College that included both
children and adults as students. This course was taught in the department of English.

The class began with a discussion of the Disney version of Snow
White compared to Grimm's Snowdrop. All discovered that there was
more to reading than just finding out what happens. In the following
weeks students read the book to be discussed before the class met. Adults
learned, to their surprise, the depth and literary quality of children's
literature. Children gained in their understanding of literary devices.

194. Barton, Bob, and David Booth. *Stories in the Classroom:
Storytelling, Reading Aloud and Roleplaying with Children.*
Portsmouth, NH: Heinemann, 1990.

This work, originally published in Canada, explores approaches to using books with children. The authors build a case for a "storytelling culture" in which teachers are participants in the exploration of narrative. The authors weave children's literature and the children's own personal stories. The approach reflects reader-response theories in which the students are cocreators of the stories they read and hear. "Story" is used both as a noun and a verb, a dynamic process of learning.

The book begins with a discussion, "The Power of Story," which explores why children need stories, why children need to story, and the story culture of the classroom. The authors integrate passages from scholars, storytellers, teachers, and poets into their discussion of the oral tradition, what they call "the story tribe," the sharing of literature, and a model for storying. Recommended readings from children's literature are included within the discussions of genre or approach.

A "story response repertoire" instructs in the use of story talk, telling and retelling stories, story drama, reading stories aloud, writing our own stories, parallel reading, story visuals, and celebrating stories and authors. Bibliography and index are included.

195. Bauer, Caroline Feller. *Read for the Fun of It: Active Programming with Books for Children*. New York: H. W. Wilson, 1992.

Caroline Feller Bauer is known for her abilities as storyteller and teacher. Her books traditionally present some practical theories on bringing books to children and then offer specific programs and activities of value to teachers and librarians. Not only does she suggest a poem or story to use, but she generally includes it as well. Her books become anthologies of stories, poems, craft ideas, and music — a full range of activities around children and their books.

Caroline Bauer's latest book is another mixture of methods and art forms that work well together with children. She explores read-aloud choices, reading incentive programs, reader's theater, book talks, visual stimuli, creative writing activities, storytelling, poetry, puppets, magic, and games.

The book offers a survey of literature-based promotion ideas on a wide range of topics. Some of the ideas concern strategies for soliciting administrators, grandparents, retirees, and even other children to read aloud in the classroom or library. She suggests several good resource books for selecting read-aloud titles and offers some ideas on scheduling special programs. At the end of the chapter is her own annotated list of workable titles for reading aloud, arranged by grades, including some for mixed-age audiences.

School-wide reading program; author visits; crafts, puppets, signs, and prop-making for visual storytelling; poetry activities; and magic tricks and games are all treated separately, with specific strategies, programs, and booklists.

Read for the Fun of It states not only her title but her approach in this and in her other books. They are practical resources for anyone who plans or performs book activities with children. The emphasis is on fun, on stimulating a lifelong love of reading through active participation of young and old.

196. Blass, Rosanne J., and Nancy E. Allen Jurenka. *Classroom Uses of Children's Literature: A Research Report.* ERIC 291-084, 1987. 13 pp.

In spite of all that has been written about the importance of literature in the classroom, research shows that many teachers do not use the recommended practices, even though many of them are quite simple to implement. Since the third and fourth grades have been identified as particularly opportune times to encourage children to become involved with literature, Blass and Jurenka surveyed third and fourth grade classroom teachers to identify the extent to which they practiced common recommendations. Thirty-nine activities were listed on the survey, and respondents were asked to indicate if they used the activities daily, weekly, monthly, annually, or never. Of the 600 questionnaires mailed 219 were returned. The authors point out that those not returning the questionnaires are more than likely not using literature in the classroom at all. A composite classroom based on results has a collection of books and time to read each day. The children are members of a book-buying club, and they visit the library weekly. The teacher reads aloud to the students weekly. Children prepare book reports, discuss books in class, illustrate books, write new endings. Some annual events include skits and plays, making bookmarks or bookcovers, puppet shows, and storytelling. The authors suggest that teachers should use more varied activities on a more frequent basis to make literature memorable.

197. Bromley, Karen D'Angelo. *Webbing with Literature: Creating Story Maps with Children's Books.* Boston: Allyn and Bacon, 1991.

This handbook explores the use of semantic webbing in classroom literature instruction. Webbing is a strategy by which a graphic representation is created of categories of information and their relationships. The basic structure of a web consists of a core concept or idea at the center, web strands radiating beyond the core, strand supports tying each web strand, and strand ties of supporting details. Research and theory are presented to support the use of semantic webs for enhanced comprehension and learning. Building on schema theory, webbing promotes comprehension as it relates new material to the known and builds personal involvement with text. Webbing is particularly applicable to combining instruction in various content areas and to connecting reading and writing.

Separate chapters explore story elements in various genres, provide selection criteria, offer literary activities, and suggest response activities in writing and reading. An extensive children's literature section includes annotated bibliographies, web illustrations, and classroom suggestions for both picture books and books for older students that are primarily text. The appendix lists award-winning books. Index.

198. Burgan, Mary. "The Question of Work: Adolescent Literature and the Ericksonian Paradigm." *Children's Literature in Education* 19.4 (Winter 1988): 187–98.

Mary Burgan is professor and chair of English at Indiana University–Bloomington, where she has established a graduate specialization in children's literature. She describes here an approach she uses in college classes, one that can be used with success in teaching adolescents as well.

She begins with Erik Erikson's eight stages of development, which identify "competence," or work, as the central experience of the school-age child. The question of work is a significant one in adolescent literature, and it is a theme that readily engages the interests of students.

Some books discussed from this aspect include *The Catcher in the Rye, The Wind in the Willows, Treasure Island, The Lord of the Rings, The Earthsea Trilogy,* and *Harriet the Spy.* Burgan points out that Jim's knowledge of river lore in *Huckleberry Finn* is much more satisfying than Tom Sawyer's ersatz rituals. The detailed descriptions of tasks in Laura Ingalls Wilder's books are mentioned, and the gardening skills used in *The Secret Garden.* Burgan concludes by discussing the limited vocational objectives presented for girls, in contrast to the wealth of opportunities presented for boys.

199. Chambers, Aidan. *Booktalk: Occasional Writing on Literature and Children.* London: Bodley Head, 1985.

Aidan Chambers is a British author and educator whose writings on children's literature are well regarded. This collection of essays brings together recent lectures, articles, and essays on children and their reading, the nature of literature in child development, and teaching literature to teachers and children. The author also addresses his own fiction: *Breaktime* and *Dance on My Grave.*

"The Role of Literature in Children's Lives" reveals the author's belief in the power of literature for children's lives and the role of adults in making this possible. "The Reader in the Book," a reader-response approach to teaching children's literature, won the first award for criticism given by the Children's Literature Association. The life-giving power of literature is affirmed in "The Child's Changing Story." "Letter from England" and "Alive and Flourishing" deal with young adult literature. "Ways of Telling" is a personal exploration of his own fiction. "Teaching Children's Literature" is a reprint of two articles from *The Horn Book* (see numbers 200, 201 below). "Whose Book Is It Anyway?" and "Tell Me: Are Children Critics?" concern our developing understanding between modern critical theory and work with children. In the latter chapter Chambers presents a practical approach for generating response to literature.

The book includes a bibliography of sources and a list of contemporary children's books cited.

200. Chambers, Aidan. "Letter from England: Summerhouse Blues." *The Horn Book* 56.5 (October 1980): 565–69.

This thoughtful essay is indirectly but powerfully about teaching literature in a way that results in children becoming literary readers. Chambers describes author visits he makes to classrooms, conversations he has with children who have read his books, and discussions children have about books. He describes the methods of a poor teacher and of a good one. The poor teacher condescends to her students. The good teacher treats the students as friends while gently maintaining order, reads aloud to the children, and provides time for individual reading and library visits.

201. Chambers, Aidan. "Letter from England: Teaching Children's Literature." *The Horn Book* 60.5 (October 1979): 571–76.

Aidan Chambers, author, editor, and parttime teacher of children's literature, looks back on ten years of teacher education. His goals in his various teaching formats are: to enhance the understanding of literature for children, to foster their own insights into literature and the reading process, and to discover the best ways of bringing books and children together.

Because of his conviction that teachers bring to their work with children the same methods by which and the same books with which they themselves were taught, Chambers tries to model an experiential response to literature. One rule of thumb is to have the students do the same activity that they will ask the child to perform, such as reading a novel a week and reporting on it.

Classroom discussions are problematic, considering the predictable response from a teacher's dominant critical posture. No one correct reading of a text exists. The teacher must remain the leader in the classroom — the one with the greatest experience with literature who can offer one among many legitimate interpretations. As leader, the teacher can, by illuminating literary technique, help the student discover the book read by the individual and the one written by the author. The class then explores the totality of all these experiences with text.

Chambers encourages students to serve as leaders of groups as a way to discover effective strategies for eliciting responses to literature.

202. Cianciolo, Patricia J. *Critical Thinking in the Study of Children's Literature in the Elementary Grades.* ERIC 303-804, 1988. 71 pp.

This report from the Center for the Learning and Teaching of Elementary Subjects, East Lansing, Michigan, explores creative thinking in the study of literature as an art form. The author explores the major factors that have influenced trends in the literature curriculum in the elementary grades within the last 30 years, research focusing on critical thinking about children's literature, and literature programs originating from textbooks, state departments of education, and commercial curricular products.

The paper presents a modern history of the most common approaches to literature study in the elementary school. Drawing on recent research, the author presents some commonly held principles of literature instruction: literature is an art; the purpose of art is to evoke affective response; literature is writing that is valued for its beauty of form, its emotional and imaginative power; literature is one of the humanities; the subject of literature is the human condition; aesthetic responses to literature cannot be directly taught or learned; the study of literature depends on knowing what literature is and how it works; the content of literature relates to the structure and form of the given selections; and students should select their own titles for the study of literature. Extensive references.

203. Cianciolo, Patricia J., and Richard S. Prawat. *Experts Define the Ideal Elementary Literature Program.* ERIC 327-864, 1990. 43 pp.

This report is produced from the Center for the Learning and Teaching of Elementary Subjects in East Lansing, Michigan. It presents the views of six experts in the teaching of literature: three university professors and three elementary school teachers. These experienced teachers offered their perspectives on the ideal curricula in general and the literature curriculum in the elementary grades in particular.

The results demonstrated agreement on the features of an ideal curriculum described in a set of framing questions. They preferred a curriculum in literature that is more focused and coherent than is currently common. Most viewed literature as an opportunity for reaching goals in language arts and across disciplines. Literature was perceived as an instructional tool, with some recognition of its value for self-knowledge. The recognition of literature as an aesthetic in its own right was lacking. The appendix includes the mission statements and objectives of the curriculum improvement study.

204. Conlon, Alice. "Giving Mrs. Jones a Hand: Making Group Storytime More Pleasurable and Meaningful for Young Children." *Young Children* 47.3 (March 1992): 14–18.

Alice Conlon describes an unenjoyable read-aloud session in a kindergarten. The teacher obviously was relieved when it was over, and the children were inattentive. She goes on to describe what can and should be the pleasures of storytime as well as its benefits. Reading aloud to young children models reading to them and allows them to practice making sense of stories. Conlon offers a number of suggestions that could help the teacher described. The first suggestion relates to book selection. A number of helpful bibliographies are listed. Other suggestions relate to the read-aloud environment and ways to value and encourage the children's responses. Other pointers are given for effective reading aloud, guidelines are offered for selecting picture books, and a bibliography of predictable books is appended.

205. Cox, Carole, and Joyce E. Many. "Toward an Understanding of the Aesthetic Response to Literature." *Language Arts* 69.1 (January 1992): 28–33.

Referring to the reader-response theory of Louise Rosenblatt, the authors, both university teachers of children's literature, explore what happens when children in grades five through eight are allowed to choose their own books and respond to them in their own ways. The students portrayed responded with synopses, novel outlines of their own, poems, and links to their own experience and beliefs. This theory of teaching literature raises the question of the teacher's role. Cox and

Many suggest (1) allowing students opportunities to make choices about how they will organize their evocation of a text; (2) allowing adequate time to respond; (3) providing opportunities for students to talk — to themselves, to other students, and to genuinely interested teachers; (4) encouraging students to make personal and intertextual connections; and (5) supporting and encouraging signs that the reader's focus of attention is on the lived-through experience of the literary evocation. References.

206. Cullinan, Bernice E., editor. *Children's Literature in the Reading Program*. Newark, DE: International Reading Association, 1987.

The why and how of integrating children's books into a reading program are the subject of this collection of essays and suggested resources. The early chapters build a case for literature as the motivator for all language experience. Bernice Cullinan shows how stories stimulate reading comprehension and enthusiasm at any age. Bill Martin tells his own story of the power of literature in shaping his life's work. Nancy Larrick shows how to involve students in poetry through suggestions from her in-service students and recommended titles.

The second section describes reading programs that use literature in the elementary grades (K–3). Charlotte Huck and Kristen Kerstetter relate how a kindergarten class uses books with beginning readers. Linda Lamme describes a whole language approach to teaching reading, which draws on book discussions, writing, and reading aloud.

Children's literature in the middle grades (4–6) is the subject of three chapters on expanding reading skills. Rudine Sims Bishop describes books that can enhance multicultural education. Dorothy Strickland suggests strategies of dialogue letters and story structure for the continuity of a language arts program. Sam Sebesta finds children's books to be integral to the arts, stimulating art, dance, drama, and writing.

The upper grades are reached through Dianne Monson's description of teaching characterization through realistic and historical fiction; and M. Jean Greenlaw and Margaret McIntosh explore science fiction and fantasy.

Broader contexts for children's books are described in the final section. Ira E. Aaron supplements a basal program with real books. Roselmina Indrisano and Jeanne Paratore relate their experience with teaching disabled students. Francie Alexander reports on the California Reading Initiative. Arlene Pillar lists resources for selecting and using children's books.

Throughout the text are teaching ideas adapted from classroom experience. The book is an accessible introduction to the practicality and purpose of children's literature in the classroom.

207. Cullum, Carolyn N. *The Storytime Sourcebook: A Compendium of Ideas and Resources for Storytellers.* New York: Neal-Schuman, 1990.

The book serves as a resource to locate ideas for children's book programming in public libraries. It is designed for an audience of children three to seven years old. The programs are designed to broaden the child's experience with literature; to relate to the physical, emotional, and intellectual concerns of the child; and to encourage the sharing of experiences with peers.

One hundred topics for programs are described, including appropriate picture books, filmstrips, films, and videocassettes, with full bibliographic citations to publishers. Word games, physical activities, fingerplays, songs and craft projects are included for most programs.

The appendix includes a directory of book publishers; filmstrips, film and video distributors; information on films and videos; a bibliography of children's books and resource materials; and an index to picture book titles, authors of picture books, and song titles.

208. Eeds, Maryann, and Ralph Peterson. "Teacher as Curator: Learning to Talk About Literature." *Reading Teacher* 45.2 (October 1991): 118-26.

Noting that there is a welcome emphasis on teaching literature for its own sake in elementary school, Maryann Eeds and Ralph Peterson of Arizona State University review the experiences of three teachers leading literature-response discussion groups for the first time. Teachers who are products of traditional literature classes, where one interpretation is correct, may feel tentative and unsure with this type of study. It is suggested that they prepare for the discussions by careful reading of the text, jotting down notes and page numbers as they read. A series of questions about literary elements for teachers to ask themselves as they read is provided. Lengthy transcripts of children's discussions of three books make up the rest of the article. Accompanying interpretations point out where teachers took opportunities to "shoot a literary arrow." Teachers are advised to "trust the books, trust the students, trust yourself."

209. Egawa, Kathy. "Harnessing the Power of Language: First Graders' Literature Engagement with *Owl Moon.*" *Language Arts* 67.6 (October 1990): 582-88.

The author explains her decision to use literature in a first grade class based on the lack of rich, descriptive language in district-adopted texts. She wanted her students to be able to discuss stories rather than merely to decode print. While there are many ways to use literature in a classroom, Kathy Egawa offers guidelines as suggestions. These include choosing the books and introducing the books. She suggests reading a book to the children, reading it again, and discussing the book.

The experience of the class with *Owl Moon* is described in detail, including the spontaneous responses of the children. These include a poster that the children made of some of their favorite words, with illustrations, and letters to the author and illustrator of the book. Egawa is convinced that first graders can stretch their vocabularies and appreciate and respond to rich literary language.

210. Fenwick, Geoff. *Teaching Children's Literature in the Primary School*. London: David Fulton, 1990.

The book is a guide to teaching children's literature on the elementary level. Prepared for British teacher education, the book offers many insights applicable to American language arts programs. British primary schools are analogous to U.S. elementary schools; reading schemes are similar to basal reading programs. Some reference is made to the National Curriculum, a standardized program that targets content and achievement goals. The author's thesis is that children's books need to be taught, not just made available. The teaching will improve children's reading, attitudes toward reading, writing ability, and socializing influence. We teach literature, basically, because it is part of our literary heritage, which should encompass both ancient stories and contemporary popular work.

The author examines children's literature as story. He explores the power of stories, distinguishing between storytelling and story reading. Research is cited to substantiate the value of stories. Preparatory and performance skills for storytelling are presented, with specific suggestions for verbal and nonverbal communication. Children's storytelling is encouraged, beginning with the retelling of traditional tales and proceeding to their own writing. Responding to literature includes oral, written, dramatic, and artistic activities.

Other components of a language program which are explored include sustained silent reading, poetry reading and writing, and popular media. A final chapter examines resources and issues related to children's literature. Each chapter includes references and related readings. Index.

211. Flender, Mary G. "Charting Book Discussions: A Method of Presenting Literature in the Elementary Grades." *Children's Literature in Education* 16.2 (Summer 1985): 84–92.

Various types of charts, all illustrated in the article, are used to teach literature in grades 2–6. The first chart is developed as a result of examining the cover illustration and the title prior to beginning to read a book. The children look for clues to help them predict the plot of the story. Other charts result from class and group discussions of plot, theme, characterization, stylistic details, and connections with other books, both fiction and nonfiction. These "connections" discussions and charts help children see the universality of literature. The charts are recorded with magic marker on construction paper so they can be retained for reference.

The children like seeing their responses and words recorded. The charts thus "provide a record of class experiences and an acknowledgment of individual perceptions."

212. Fox, Carol, and Margery Sauer. *Celebrate Literature! A Spiraling Curriculum for Grades K–6.* ERIC 297-265, 1988. 15 pp.

This paper describes a seven-volume set of guides for teaching literature, using children's books rather than basal readers. Teachers are encouraged to read aloud to their classes each day, both from the suggested titles and from their own favorites, and to give children opportunities to select and read books. The curriculum books were selected on the basis of quality and appropriateness for grade level. The strands chosen for study are folk literature, poetry, picture books and fiction, author study/biography, and nonfiction. The activities provided are examples of thoughtful, evaluative, and creative responses to literature. These include a literature time each day, experiences that allow children to interact with books, gentle instruction in literary terms, sharing thoughts about literature, and playing with language.

The goals are: (1) to introduce children to their literary heritage; (2) to encourage children to read for pleasure and knowledge; (3) to provide children with knowledge of literary elements and structure; (4) to allow for creative response to literature; (5) to develop children's ability to evaluate literature; and (6) to develop independent readers and thinkers. Specific objectives are listed for each goal. A unit format is provided, and a list of terms used is defined. Suggestions for incorporating literature into the basal program are given. These allow more creative response than the usual basal activities.

213. Galda, Lee. "Readers, Texts, and Contexts: A Response-Based View of Literature in the Classroom." *The New Advocate* 1.2 (Spring 1988): 92–102.

Lee Galda, who teaches in the department of language education at the University of Georgia, reviews research related to the transaction between the text and the reader, focusing on the ideas of Louise Rosenblatt. In relating theory to classroom practice, she considers the types of questions that elicit aesthetic rather than efferent response. She also discusses the context readers bring to the transaction as a result of the communities (in the broadest sense) from which they come.

In the second part of the article Galda reviews separately the research related to the reader, the text, and the context. She points out that influences on response include personal style, experience, gender, preferences, and expectations for reading, reading ability, and past literary experience. A lack of experience with a wide variety of literature can be addressed by a program of wide reading in the classroom. While it can be difficult to lead a young girl, for instance, away from exclusive reading of romances, this can be done through read-aloud sessions, class discussions, and other response activities. Certain aspects of text that all readers will agree about are presented, and the author's choices of vocabulary, point of view, and aspects of style and characterization are seen as exercising some control over response. Genre may influence response, with fantasy eliciting responses different from those of realistic fiction. Context includes not only the experience the reader brings to the text but also the group with which it is discussed, the physical environment, and peer influence.

Finally, the classroom environment is discussed in detail. Teachers can limit response by insisting upon one particular mode, or can extend response by providing: (1) an environment filled with opportunities to read and respond; (2) a secure environment; and (3) an environment which provides time to read and respond. References.

214. Hade, Daniel D. "Being Literary in a Literature-Based Classroom." *Children's Literature in Education* 22.1 (March 1991): 1–17.

In literary classrooms reading literature is play. Playing with literature includes taking delight in the sound and rhythms of language and becoming intimately involved with story. Young children play "I Spy" with illustrations, finding hidden pictures and connections. Older children incorporate books they have read into their playground activities. During read-aloud sessions, children experiment with the story, interrupting to discuss events and possibilities. Reading ceases to be play when adults impose forms to meet their own purposes. Some examples are "using" books as moral lessons or counseling aids, for teaching phonics, or formulaic guided reading.

Hade lists and elaborates on the characteristics of the literary classroom: readers share their reading; what is shared is accepted as "honorably reported"; teachers push for rigor; children are provided with opportunities to read and respond; children have personal choices; and there is variety.

Master teachers are urged to share their knowledge, and researchers are urged to go as observers into their classrooms so that their technique in literature-based teaching will not be a passing fad.

215. Hall, Susan. *Using Picture Storybooks to Teach Literary Devices: Recommended Books for Children and Young Adults*. Phoenix, AZ: Oryx, 1990.

This is an excellent book, both for classes of adults studying children's literature and for practitioners working with children and young people. Susan Hall, a librarian, points out that good picture books make use of the full range of literary devices, and because of their focus and simplicity, they can be used to teach the devices more successfully than can often used, more complex stories and books.

The author discusses in chapter 1, "The Picture Storybook Audience," the uses of picture books with various age groups, emphasizing that picture books aren't just for prereaders. Other chapters are "Analyzing the Picture Book," "Picture Storybooks, Illustrated Story Books, and Picture Books," "Literary Quality in Picture Storybook Literature," and "Bibliographical Selection Process."

In part 2 Hall lists 30 literary devices with books that illustrate each device. For instance, under "Inference" a definition of the device is given with an example. Then follows a list of 62 books that illustrate inference, with summaries and examples. Here is one of the entries:

Low, Joseph. *Mice Twice*. New York: Atheneum, 1980.

A devious hungry cat expects to feast on two mice when Mouse asks if she can bring a guest with her to Cat's invitational dinner.

Examples: The reader knows what the cat really means when he says, "I was just thinking, 'How nice to have a friend for supper!'" Cat is pleased when Mouse asks if she can bring along a friend. Cat thinks "Mice Twice!"

Other Devices: Irony; Poetic Justice (page 78).

Finally, Hall lists all books included and the devices they illustrate. The index was compiled by Linda Webster.

216. Hancock, Marjorie R. "Literature Response Journals: Insights Beyond the Printed Page." *Language Arts* 69.1 (January 1992): 36–42.

This article describes a pilot study that investigated the content and process of sixth-grade literature response journals. A student who had completed all the basal reading texts and was engaged in an independent reading program, participated in the study by recording her responses daily as she read. Her entries were read and responded to with encouraging, nonevaluative comments. The entries revealed the student's empathy and sometimes exasperation with the characters. She related the experiences in the books to her own life and speculated about how she would feel and act in similar situations. Marjorie Hancock points out the great difference between the journal and a book report written after the book has been read. Such book reports usually retell the story but do not reveal the emotions aroused by the book. Those emotions may be forgotten if not recorded, but when they are recorded, they can be reviewed by the recorder or shared with another student reading the same book.

217. Hannabuss, Stuart. "Metaphors, Morality, and Children's Books." *The Use of English* 38.3 (Summer 1987): 51–58.

Stuart Hannabus discusses the pervasive use of metaphor, both simple and extended, in literature, including children's literature. He points out that extended metaphor, as when the entire book or story operates on several levels, one of which is metaphor, can enable readers to understand and identify with basic truths. Such use of metaphor can lead children to recognize that their own ideas, dreams, and fantasies are understood and shared by others. As he says, "the metaphorical approach can open up dimensions of meaning, concentrate the essence of meaning in such forms as parable and allegory, and exploit moral and ethical agenda." Eighteen specific titles are explored, as well as Norse legend, fairy tales, folk tales, and myth. Specific questions, such as "How can we know evil?" are suggested for some titles.

218. Hepler, Susan. "The People Behind the Pens." *Learning* 17.7 (March 1989): 38–40.

Pointing out that children often choose to read many or all books by a favorite author, Susan Hepler suggests in-depth study of an author to enhance appreciation and understanding of the books. A specific example, using Donald Crews as the author, demonstrates how the children responded.

219. Hickman, Janet. "Everything Considered: Response to Literature in an Elementary School Setting." *Journal of Research and Development in Education* 16.3 (Spring 1983): 3-13.

This research study uncovered, among other results, a discovery that the teacher is a powerful determiner in children's responses to literature, even when the atmosphere is apparently open and nondirective. Two books, Saul Silverstein's *Where the Sidewalk Ends* and D. McPhail's *The Magical Drawings of Moony B. Finch*, were presented to children ranging from kindergarten to fifth grade. The Silverstein book was more readily available in the classrooms, and teachers solicited, modeled, and accepted a variety of responses to it, including nonverbal response. Children enjoyed the book, often selecting poems from it to read to others, sharing the poems spontaneously, laughing, and acting out responses. The McPhail book was not freely available in the classroom. Teachers did not share in its presentation by the researcher. Verbal responses were solicited, and responses were limited to verbal. No art work, dramatizations, or spontaneous discussions resulted.

220. Hickman, Janet. "Research Currents: Researching Children's Response to Literature." *Language Arts* 61.3 (March 1984): 278-84.

Janet Hickman puts forward the advantages of researching children's response to literature in a natural classroom setting. Such a setting provides a wider context for understanding the responses. An example is given of a seven-year-old's response to *Little Blue and Little Yellow*. Looking at the work without knowing the context reduces the researcher's ability to understand and evaluate it. The researcher in this instance was able to discuss the child's picture with her. Her eagerness, her intonation, and her facial expressions were important parts of her response, and they showed a high degree of involvement with literature.

Hickman goes on to discuss the importance of human context in response to literature. Both the teacher and other children give cues for "acting like a reader." In the classroom studied one of the most frequently observed behaviors was the spontaneous sharing of literature. The most important feature of the classroom is the teacher, who is the number one model reader. The teacher arranges time, provides materials, controls the physical setting, and presents expectations about what is to happen. The teacher is discussion leader. "It is clear that whatever teachers do or fail to do with books has its effect on children's progress as readers of literature."

221. Johnson, Terry D. "Presenting Literature to Children." *Children's Literature in Education* 10.1 (Spring 1979): 35–43.

Terry Johnson is concerned that adults be able to share books with children in ways that increase the child's appreciation without marring the enjoyment of the work. While parents and librarians have opportunities to read to children and discuss books with them, teachers, working with relatively large groups of children, may fall into the trap of teaching about literature the same way they teach math or history. Other teachers, reacting to such travesties, may go too far in the other direction, presenting stories with no guidance. While this is preferable to worksheets or multiple choice questions, there are ways to teach about fiction without being coercive or unpleasant. However, Johnson notes, as each piece of fiction is unique, the teaching opportunities associated with it are unique as well. There are no universally good ideas for teaching literature.

Any planned activity associated with a piece of literatue should result from taking into consideration the story, the nature of the children, and the manner of the story's presentation. Some specific stories and ways to present them are suggested. William Steig's *Sylvester and the Magic Pebble* is a good book to use for appreciation of plot. Acting out *Where the Wild Things Are* helps children understand the psychology of the story, while cumulative rhymes lend themselves to choral speaking. Anticipatory questions can be used when clues have been given in the text, but they are useless if no clues are offered. Learning new vocabulary is best done naturally, by hearing and seeing words used in context. Vocabulary lessons should be avoided unless a definition of a particular word is crucial to understanding and the context does not provide meaning.

222. Johnson, Terry D., and Daphne R. Louis. *Literacy Through Literature.* Portsmouth, NH: Heinemann, 1987.

An education professor and a classroom teacher share ideas and concepts for including literature in the classroom as the basis of a whole language program. The authors present the underlying assumptions and practical teaching considerations, initial instruction in literacy, and developing sequential literacy activities. Activities are described with a theory, practical suggestions, and illustrations. The emphasis throughout is on training students to be self-learners. The underlying philosophy is that children learn language, not through reading programs and instructional manuals, but from "writers, dreamers, and poets." Resource bibliography.

223. Kelly, Patricia R. "Guiding Young Students' Response to Literature." *Reading Teacher* 43.7 (March 1990): 464-70.

Teaching third grade while taking a graduate course in children's literature provided Patricia Kelly with a perfect opportunity to combine her roles as teacher and researcher. Although she had been accustomed to sharing literature with children in a more integrated than basal approach, and had encouraged lively literature discussions and other responses, she decided to extend this approach by introducing the prompts advocated by D. Bleich in *Subjective Criticism* (1978). These prompts ask: (1) what the reader noticed in the book, (2) how the reader felt about the book, and (3) how the book is related to the reader's experience.

Because the students' reading levels varied, responding to literature was introduced by the teacher reading aloud. The prompts also were responded to orally at first. In the second phase the stories were read aloud, with responses being written. All students, regardless of reading level, were able to respond both orally and in writing to the stories read, although differences in the sophistication of the responses were evident. Students reading at a higher level made more summary-like descriptions. As the year progressed, written responses increased in length. Students began to notice and comment on style and use of fantasy. "The research showed that responding to literature fostered comprehension, discussion, and writing skills, and promoted emotional involvement with and appreciation of literature."

224. Kiefer, Barbara Z. "The Child and the Picture Book: Creating Live Circuits." *ChLA Quarterly* 11.2 (Summer 1986): 63-68.

While the theories advanced by Louise Rosenblatt have been widely applied to the teaching of literature, they have not been used as much with picture books. In this study the author spent 40 weeks in three classrooms with children ages 7-10 observing how they reacted to picture books. She describes how children varied in the ways they chose books, looked at books, and talked about books, and in the behaviors they exhibited in response to books.

In talking about the books, the children used the vocabulary of experts, and in some cases they made up words they needed. Their verbal responses were (1) informative — reporting, retelling, or comparing the contents of the pictures; (2) heuristic — discovering, making inferences, or predicting; (3) imaginative — creating new forms, or making the unfamiliar familiar through the use of metaphors or similes; and (4) personal — associating personal experiences, expressing emotion, or giving opinions.

The children's comments showed them developing critical thinking about cognitive factors and aesthetic factors. They appreciated the artist as a real person and were aware of stylistic elements and technical choices.

Some techniques used by teachers who worked with these children are described. All the classrooms were ones where literature was valued. The teachers read to the children and talked with the children about the books. They helped the children understand the author/illustrator's role in the creation of the book. The teachers listened to the children and gave them time.

225. Kiefer, Barbara Z. "Picture Books as Contexts for Literary, Aesthetic, and Real World Understandings." *Language Arts* 65.3 (March 1988): 260–71.

The author describes responses of third- and fourth-grade children, in literature-based classes, to picture books. While some researchers have asserted that pictures interfere with reading, Barbara Kiefer at the College of Education, University of Houston, concluded that picture books provide the opportunity for deepening literary and aesthetic responses. She also found that children in literature-based classrooms provided richer and deeper responses than did children in traditional classrooms. The time provided for literature study and response is an important feature in literature-based classrooms. Teachers read to the children, often for extended periods, and convey their love of books when they do. Children are given time to think before they respond — periods of silence sometimes last as long as a minute. Time is allowed for independent reading, reading conversations, buddy reading, and student-initiated activities in response to reading. There is time to return to books as experience grows and insight changes. Another feature is the abundant availability of good books attractively displayed. Teachers are of utmost importance, of course, and the approach of one especially good one is described. The piece concludes with some examples of student response to picture books. References.

226. Koeller, Shirley A. "The Child's Voice: Literature Conversations." *Children's Literature in Education* 19.1 (Spring 1988): 3–16.

Describing children's interest in and need for talking about the literature they read, the author describes four aesthetic teacher stances which inspire pupil/literature conversations. Each stance encourages curiosity, original response, and excitement about literature. Adopting these stances can be difficult for teachers. If the children have been accustomed to structured, factual questions with "right" answers, they will not readily adapt to an environment that provides opportunities for spontaneous response to a literary work. In addition, aesthetic stances require abundant literature sources and repeated trial and error in matching child and text.

In the "mentor stance" the teacher suggests and models ways to select, read, study, and discuss literature. Teachers who initially lead discussions can search for ways to transfer this role to the students themselves so that the teacher's role diminishes.

The "peer-fellowship stance" focuses on student interaction. If the teacher participates, it is not as leader but as peer. Active disagreement and controversy are accepted in this stance.

The "director-editor-manager-coach stance" conveys that the key factor in pupil learning is what the pupil already knows. The teacher determines what models will best meet each pupil's needs and plans activities based on the individual's potential. Children are encouraged to provide answers to their own questions.

The "proud-parent stance" is appropriate for literary works that speak directly to the reader. Teacher intervention is inappropriate, but a group of students working together can explore meaning in various ways. Teachers can give the students the literary work but assign no specific problem. The assignment is to find a problem and work on it. In the example given, four sixth grade students read Paul Fleischman's *I Am Phoenix*. Discussion among the four centered on rereading, with individuals expressing preferences for passages or poems. Uncertainty about the phoenix legend led them to further reading in encyclopedias.

In aesthetic teacher stances a playful attitude toward literature is adopted. Sometimes models, frameworks, ideas, guidance, and encouragement are provided. In other instances, literature is lavished on children and they are given the freedom to find their own way with it.

227. Koeller, Shirley A. *Literary Experience, A Neglected Essential*. ERIC 216-306, 1981. 19 pp.

Shirley Koeller reviews professional literature about reading and literature. The position that abundant experience with literature encourages and improves reading is overwhelmingly supported. Strategies used by successful teachers are listed; they include: (1) making their own enthusiasm evident as they read aloud and discuss books; (2) valuing each pupil as a reader and responder to books; (3) making many books available; and (4) planning for children to discuss and respond to books. The theories of Louise Rosenblatt and others who emphasize reader response are discussed at length. Included are a chart suggesting observations and high-level questions to stimulate response, and references.

228. Landes, Sonia. "Picture Books as Literature." *ChLA Quarterly* 10.2 (Summer 1985): 51–54.

Sonia Landes discusses the ways illustrators enhance and expand text, and in the case of some nursery rhymes, even making sense out of nonsense. She describes some techniques used by Randolph Caldecott and goes on to discuss the work of modern illustrators, who use the cover to "wrap" the book. She describes a mini-study she did with four first-grade children and the book *Stanley and Rhoda* by Rosemary Wells. She showed the children the first and last pages of the book only and then asked them "What do you see?" The remarks of the children as they discuss the book are recorded, revealing great attention to detail and the ability to make subtle inferences. The author continues by discussing ways that children can begin to understand imagery, and how the size of illustrations and the shapes in them become metaphors. With the wise use of good picture books, teachers can lead children to become readers before they can read.

229. Langer, Judith A. "Understanding Literature." *Language Arts* 67.8 (December 1990): 812–16.

Judith Langer, professor of education at the State University of New York, Albany, and codirector of the Center for the Learning and Teaching of Literature, has developed a reader-based theory for the teaching of literature that she calls *envisionment*, where understanding grows and changes over time. Examining how students think when they read for literary purposes, she identified four relationships between the reader and the text. These are: (1) being out and stepping in, (2) being in and moving through, (3) being in and stepping out, and (4) stepping out and objectifying the experience. These four stances are described by examples from seventh-grade students' literary conversations.

The differences in literary reading and informational reading are discussed, followed by possibilities for instruction. Types of questions are suggested to tap initial understandings, developing interpretations, reflecting on personal experiences, and elaborating and extending.

230. Lehman, Barbara A., and Patricia R. Crook. "Effective Schools Research and Excellence in Reading: A Rationale for Children's Literature in the Curriculum." *Childhood Education* 64.4 (April 1988): 235-36, 238, 240-41.

The authors review the research that establishes the need to use children's literature to teach reading. Recent research supports the view that: (1) more school time should be devoted to reading literature that stimulates the imagination; and (2) more than basal materials are required for effective instruction. Drawing on this research, the authors explain why children's literature enhances effectiveness and describe effective use of children's books.

The following research findings on learning are applied to the use of children's literature: children will learn better if they understand what they are to learn and why; children will learn what they are taught; teacher expectations affect students' level of performance; using appropriate and varied materials helps to ensure a high rate of success and promotes achievement; effective teachers do not rely on materials to teach or to provide a formula to be followed unquestionably; and effective teachers allocate classroom time judiciously.

The following research findings on reading are applied to the use of children's literature: a reading program that is literature-based should not neglect basic skills; teachers who ask more higher-order questions have students who achieve more; and teachers who effectively use children's literature as the content of their reading programs know and love children's books.

Children's books have the potential to change reading instruction from skill acquisition to learning and knowledge. Children's literature in the curriculum can increase teacher effectiveness. References to research studies in the field.

231. Lindauer, Shelley L. Knudsen. "Wordless Books: An Approach to Visual Literacy." *Children's Literature in Education* 19.3 (1988): 136-41.

Many teachers avoid the use of wordless books with children, feeling that reading them would be difficult and not as enriching as reading a picture book with text. The teachers may not feel creative enough to make up the words themselves, but the children will do that. Shelley Lindauer, who teaches at Utah State University, advances a number of advantages of using wordless picture books with young children. Looking at and talking about the books enhance appreciation of the illustrations and the acquisition of new vocabulary. The children learn sequential thinking, the development of a sense of story, visual discrimination, inferential thinking, and predicting conclusions. Both prereading and reading children can tell stories with the prompts provided by the books. Suggestions are offered for sharing wordless books with young children, and for associated activities. Children may like to tape record their interpretation of the story or have it written down. A transcript is given of a cooperative group story as narrated by three- and four-year-old children. References and selected bibliography of wordless books are included.

232. Logan, John W. "ERIC/RCS Report: Developing Children's Appreciation of Literature." *Language Arts* 60.4 (April 1983): 518-21.

John Logan discusses the need to motivate children to enjoy literature and to prepare them to have a positive attitude toward it before introducing the literature itself. He describes a number of methods for accomplishing this aim, including teacher modeling, reading aloud, providing plenty of books, and teaching children to read easily and well. In addition, the use of book fairs and music to stimulate interest in literature is suggested.

233. Lowery-Moore, Hollis, and Lesta Burt. "Children's Literature Courses." *Internationalizing Library and Information Science Education: A Handbook of Policies and Procedures in Administration and Curriculum.* New York: Greenwood, 1987.

In 1953 the International Board on Books for Young People was established for the purpose of promoting international understanding, encouraging literacy, promoting wide distribution of literature to children, establishing libraries, encouraging continuing education for those involved with children's literature, and encouraging publication of good books. Other organizations promoting international understanding through children's books are mentioned. The authors analyze current course offerings for international content, using the findings of the Children's Literature Association of the U.S. National Council of Teachers of English survey (see chapter 5, number 54) and other information.

Finally, suggestions are made for infusing children's literature curriculum with a sense of the international. Traditional literature is the vehicle now most often used. Poetry can be a world language. Science fiction "reveals a nation's conscience as no other genre being produced today." Biography is useful, as is current realistic fiction.

Although the authors would like to see courses in international children's literature established, they realize that incorporating international literature into currently existing courses is more feasible. Not many children's books are translated, but award-winning books are often chosen for translation, and these awards are increasing.

Suggestions are made for specific assignments involving the literature of other countries.

234. Matte, Gerard. "Jack and Jill No Longer Go Up the Hill: Primary Education in Australia 1986 and Children's Literature." *Quadrant* 30.1-2 (January–February 1986): 99–101.

Gerard Matte criticizes the use of such books as *When the Wind Blows* and *The Tin-Pot Foreign General and the Old Iron Woman* on the basis of their psychological inappropriateness for children. They are, he says, pure propaganda, and children do not have the resources or experience to deal with them. The first title presents nuclear war as inevitable and individuals as powerless. The second presents a distorted and biased view of the Falklands War. In it "we have the interrelated motifs of Poor and Sad people being overtaken by Cruel, Horrible people. This to the child is not about the Falklands War, but about nasty versus good; where rulers are school bullies and everyone else is nice and kind." Both books are by Raymond Briggs and are published by Hamish Hamilton.

235. May, Jill P. "Creating a School-Wide Literature Program: A Case Study." *ChLA Quarterly* 12.3 (1987): 135–37.

May, who teaches children's literature at Purdue University, describes a program that transferred the language arts curriculum in a private school from textbooks to literature. Objectives included literature appreciation, writing improvement, literary criticism, and "more creative children in all areas of the curriculum." Besides reading and discussing books, the children heard books read aloud by their teachers. "At the end of the year [Principal] Van Wieren asked the teachers if they wanted their language arts textbooks back. All said no." The program, still functioning at the time of writing, resulted in improvements in students' attitudes toward reading and writing. They were reading more library books, talking about literature, borrowing favorite authors' styles in their own writing, and even learning grammar.

236. Mikkelsen, Nina, and Vincent Mikkelsen. *Beyond the ABC: Toward a Rhetoric of Children's Literature and Reading.* ERIC 294-154, 1987. 19 pp.

The Mikkelsens raise the questions "Would scholars examining our present literature for children be able to learn how authors teach children? Or must adults teach an author's text? What happens when children are left to discover meaning for themselves?" A survey of 16 teachers of reading revealed that those teachers felt their role is directive. They described using a text of *Cinderella* as a means to ends — a way to teach other things. None of them suggested letting the children explore the book at their own pace, relating pictures to story, and responding freely. The last part of this paper describes two children doing just that — their reactions to the cover, the remainder of the illustrations, and the text are recorded at length, with interpretation. The authors conclude that these two children, interacting with the book and with one another, dealt with abstract concepts of time and growth, self indulgence and self control, magic power and human responsibility, and ways pictures can advance the story. They discussed possible events for blank space. The authors call for more studies of children responding to literature. As a result, they hope that more teachers will move beyond present practices that lead to convergent thinking and emphasis on isolated skills, and "allow children more often to read — as authors teach."

237. Miles, Betty, and Avi Miles. "School Visits: The Author's Viewpoint." *School Library Journal* 33.5 (January 1987): 21–26.

This very thorough article by two children's authors who make school visits covers the subject from first contact through follow-up after the visit. Topics covered include selecting and contacting the author, fees, publicity, travel and lodging, and scheduling. Preparation for the visit includes reading the author's books and making them available in the library and for purchase. Autographing is discussed, and various types of sessions with groups of children. Of special importance is planning the entire visit collaboratively. Not forgotten are the visiting author's personal needs. Such visits, when properly planned and managed, are enriching experiences for children, and exciting and enjoyable for all involved.

238. Monseau, Virginia R. "The Adolescent as 'Mock Reader': Some Thoughts for the Teacher of Literature." *ChLA Quarterly* 12.3 (1987): 140–42.

Virginia Monseau explores what typically happens when adolescents are expected to read and become intellectually and emotionally involved with such "adult" classics as *Great Expectations* or *The Man Without a Country*. She advocates selecting from the wealth of contemporary adolescent literature now available. Students can and do respond to these books, which demonstrate the same literary devices that are found and taught in the classics.

Monseau describes Walker Gibson's "mock reader" ("Authors, Speakers, Readers, and Mock Readers." In *Reader-Response Criticism: From Formalism to Post Structuralism*, Jane P. Tompkins, editor. Baltimore: Johns Hopkins University Press, 1980) as an explanation for the adolescent's lack of interest in the classics:

> Young adult literature can coexist with the classics in the classroom. Common sense tells us that students need a choice if they are to become discriminating readers. Some students might choose *Killing Mr. Griffin* over *Great Expectations* not because they are intellectually inferior or too lazy to read a more demanding work but because they are ready and willing, at this stage in their reading development, to take on the 'mask and costume' that the book requires. This doesn't mean that they will not eventually read and enjoy a book like *Great Expectations*.

239. Nix, Kemie. "On Producing Brand-New Book Lovers." *ChLA Quarterly* 12.3 (1987): 131–34.

Kemie Nix describes a program she instituted for teaching literature to elementary school children over a span of three years. She emphasizes the importance of continuity and the chilling effect textbook teaching has on any latent interest in reading. When she began her program, in a private school, she always found a few children who were readers. These children were little affected by the program. With the others, however, there were gratifying results.

Nix then tried her program in a low-income urban public school. At the time the article was written, results of this experiment were inconclusive, although some individual successes were achieved.

Nix describes homework assignments, the diary she designed, and the cooperation and support needed from school administrators and faculty colleagues.

240. Nodelman, Perry. "Editor's Comments: Teaching Children, or Teaching Subjects." *ChLA Quarterly* 10.2 (Summer 1985): 50.

Perry Nodelman reprints an excerpt from a symposium held by the Children's Literature Association. The symposium dealt with the development of a curriculum of literary study for the primary grades. The guidelines excerpted advocate the study of literature as a transaction, not the use of literature to promote other forms of learning. The aim is to communicate the pleasure of literature, using different approaches with different children at different times.

241. O'Brien, Kathy L. "A Look at One Successful Literature Program." *The New Advocate* 4.2 (Winter 1991): 113–23.

"A literature program requires very different ways of thinking about books than a basal reader program does." This is what Kathy L. O'Brien, who teaches at California State University, San Bernardino, discovered when she spent a year doing research in a third- and fourth-grade classroom. As a result of this experience, she described successful practices that minimize basalization and maximize analysis of and dialogue about literature.

(1) Students were not required to look up definitions of vocabulary words before reading the chapter or book. Vocabulary is discussed naturally when children talk about a book and why they like certain passages.

(2) No comprehension worksheets that required students to fill in the blank or write one- or two-line answers to questions based on their reading were used. Such worksheets elicit static responses and discourage dynamic dialogue needed for understanding literature.

(3) The practice of using excerpts or breaking the book up into a chapter-by-chapter reading format was avoided. Literature study involves reading whole books. Excerpts actually discourage reading the book.

(4) Class sets of books were not used exclusively. Students had choices about what they read. This is an integral part of literature study.

(5) A broad definition of grade level was applied when considering books to use with students. There is no such thing as a book that is appropriate for one and only one grade level.

(6) Individual interpretations of and response to the book were emphasized. Differences in interpretation were accepted and encouraged. Students went back to the text to explain and support their thinking.

(7) Discussions about the elements of the book were encouraged. Crucial aspects of story were addressed when appropriate.

(8) Students led the discussion. Students learned how to talk about books with leadership and modeling on the part of the teacher.

(9) Themes, authors, and genres were studied in depth. This in-depth study helped students see relationships among books and recognize authors' styles. This does not interfere with choice — students may choose authors or genres to investigate.

(10) There was strong focus on the ideas of the book. This is one of the most important points of a literature program. Discussion focused on what the author reveals about the human condition.

(11) Students drew connections between what they read and their own lives. Students will naturally discuss parallels between their lives and the books they read.

(12) Literature from various cultures and ethnic groups was included. Children sought books about people like themselves; they could identify with the characters. They also were given opportunities to be exposed to characters from diverse backgrounds to broaden their experience and understanding. Successful literature programs maintain the integrity of the text and of the reader. They help students develop an understanding of and love for literature.

242. O'Hara, Michael. "'Anything Goes' . . . Connecting Children to Literature: A Personal View." *Children's Literature in Education* 21.2 (June 1990): 119–27.

Michael O'Hara, who teaches children's literature in Ireland, responds to an article attacking the use of publishers' kits and packages for teaching literature. Rather than trivializing literature, the kits and packages often make literature accessible to pupils who could not otherwise enjoy it. O'Hara argues for an "anything goes" approach — anything that can involve and excite children about literature and encourage them to become more involved with it. He mentions dramatizations, the use of music, excerpts, and condensations. If some children will never be able to read Dickens, Shakespeare, or Conrad, let them at least know the stories and some of the authors' wonderful language. He suggests that the purists back away from their extreme position of "literature *qua* literature" and trust English teachers to love literature, know their students, and use publishers' materials and anthologies in creative ways to bring great literature to as many children as possible.

243. Peck, David. *Novels of Initiation: A Guidebook for Teaching Literature to Adolescents.* New York: Teachers College Press, 1989.

This guidebook for teachers contains analyses of 12 American novels most commonly read in junior high or high school English classes. Included are adult classics that have been adopted by youth, as well as novels written for the young adult audience. The selections are linked by the theme of initiation, tracing the passage of young protagonists from childhood to adulthood.

The novels are arranged according to level of difficulty, with the most challenging texts appearing first. The arrangement also connects the books' thematic resonance. The discussions have a similar format: opening with a compressed list of information about the book, followed by a literary analysis, and concluding with a guide to teaching the novel and suggestions for related reading. Discussion questions center on affective as well as analytical topics.

The novels covered are: *The Catcher in the Rye*, *Adventures of Huckleberry Finn*, *The Chocolate War*, *Ordinary People*, *The Bell Jar*, *The Great Gatsby*, *The Red Badge of Courage*, *To Kill a Mockingbird*, *The Member of the Wedding*, *The Red Pony*, *A Day No Pigs Would Die*, and *Roll of Thunder, Hear My Cry*.

Sample thematic units, a selected reading list, and a glossary comprise the appendix.

244. Prest, Peter, and Julie Prest. "Theory Into Practice: Clarifying Our Intentions: Some Thoughts on the Application of Rosenblatt's Transactional Theory of Reading in the Classroom." *English Quarterly* 21.2 (1988): 127-33.

Establishing the theory of literature as a "way of reading, one which includes the writer, the text, and the reader," the authors discuss Louise Rosenblatt's theory of the reading transaction. Rosenblatt provides a useful reader-response theory through her concept of efferent and aesthetic modes of response. Teachers, however, in attempting to implement a Rosenblatt-style reader-response stance in the classroom, often send mixed messages by the questions they ask. After further discussion of efferent reading, the authors offer guidance for promoting aesthetic responses. Questions for literary texts that elicit efferent response are seen as much of the cause for student apathy toward literature.

245. Probst, Robert E. "Dialogue with a Text." *English Journal* 77.1 (January 1988): 32-38.

Robert Probst begins by describing a scene in a suburban junior high school. The students had read the story "So Much Unfairness of Things" by C. D. B. Bryan, were obviously heavily engaged by the story, and were prepared to discuss their responses. The teacher, however, was intent on teaching literary devices and was unable to lead or participate in the discussion the students wanted to have, or even to allow it to occur. Probst follows by describing how that scene could have differed if the approach advocated by Louise Rosenblatt had been followed. Rosenblatt's principles assert that students must be free to deal with their reactions and to find links between the story and their own experience. Some open-ended questions are suggested for students to use in discussing a literary work with one other student, or in a small group. Guidance is offered for creating the kind of classroom atmosphere that encourages this type of exploration of literature, which Probst admits can be difficult at first. But, he concludes, "if meaning is a human act rather than a footlocker full of dusty facts, then we must focus attention on the act of making meaning rather than simply on the accumulation of data."

246. Probst, Robert E. *Five Kinds of Literary Knowing.* ERIC 333-446, 1990. 23 pp.

Drawing upon Louise Rosenblatt's theories, the author explores five different kinds of literary knowing: (1) knowing about self, (2) knowing about others, (3) knowing about texts, (4) knowing about contexts, and (5) knowing about processes of making meaning.

Literature encourages readers to reflect on aspects of their lives. Attention to individual responses among readers allows students to gain insight into their lives. Students discover their own similarities to and differences from other readers. A text offers an opportunity for aesthetic pleasure. Meaning is determined by the context in which the reader and the text meet. Students can learn about their own processes of making meaning from texts. Journals and reading logs help to initiate exchanges among students as to differing responses.

The emphasis on reader response changes the structure of a course. The expository, analytical essay should not be taught exclusively. Other genres can be adapted to classroom use. Classroom instruction and the overall curriculum should be organized along developmental lines, in line with the thematic interests and responses of adolescence.

247. Probst, Robert E. *Response and Analysis: Teaching Literature in Junior and Senior High School.* Portsmouth, NH: Heinemann, 1988.

This resource book is based on response-based teaching of literature. The author, grounded in the writings of Louise Rosenblatt (*Literature as Exploration*), argues that "literature is experience, not information," inviting the reader to participate.

The first part of the book presents the logic and application of response-based teaching. Focusing on the uniqueness of the act of

TEACHING YOUNG PEOPLE (248)

reading, he gives various readings of texts which offer students the opportunity to respond, in private and in relation to others. The second part deals with literary genres, adolescent literature, and visual literacy. Finally, the author presents the program: the literature curriculum, evaluation, and current literary theories. The author approaches adolescent literature by major themes, with an extensive bibliography of readings. The theoretical discussion of reader response covers several current approaches to interpreting literature and ends with a long bibliography of professional literature.

248. Raphael, Taffy E., et al. "Research Directions: Literature and Discussion in the Reading Program." *Language Arts* 69.1 (January 1992): 54–61.

Teachers at the Center for the Learning and Teaching of Elementary Subjects at Michigan State University established book clubs in order to answer the question "How might literature-based instruction be created to encompass instruction in both comprehension and literature response?" Through pilot work, two areas of knowledge were identified that were important: knowledge about *what* to discuss and *how* to discuss it. Book clubs are small student-led discussion groups. Reading, of course, was a central component. In this research the readings were assigned and were related to units designed to teach theme or genre. A second component was writing, with each student keeping a reading log. The third component, discussion, took place both in the small book clubs and in larger groups. This provided an opportunity to learn from each other, and for teachers to identify gaps in knowledge. Instruction, the fourth component of the research, included modeling, comprehension, and synthesis activities.

The researchers sought to answer a number of questions related to the main research question. A major question was "What is the nature of classroom talk about text?" It was found that in their discussions, students (1) shared written responses from reading logs; (2) clarified points of confusion; (3) discussed the main theme; (4) related to other texts; (5) critiqued the author's success; (6) identified the author's purposes; (7) discussed the process of response; (8) related ideas from the text to personal experiences or feelings; and (9) related to prior knowledge.

In order to investigate how book clubs can be extended to non-traditional learners, programs were started with groups of learning-disabled students and remedial readers. Within a three-month period the effects were evident in the ability of younger students to discuss the books in meaningful ways. Their discussions reflected many of the same purposes as those of the regular education students. Older students, however, showed great resistance, preferring to "fill in the blanks" or select "the correct answer." Overall, however, the authors felt rewarded by the students' understandings about literacy. References.

249. Salvner, Gary M. "Readers as Performers: The Literature Game." *ChLA Quarterly* 12.3 (1987): 137–39.

Literature games, described here, could be used as an activity with any age group to explore the entire ambiance of a particular book. Salvner describes events at the annual English Festival sponsored by the English department at Youngstown State University. Students (2,500 each year) who attend the festival read in advance seven books that will be the focus of the festival.

> In ... the Festival literature games, students from different schools are organized into teams of five or six and work under strict time limits. Once organized, the teams are invited through printed instructions to investigate and solve a problem which derives from a scenario they are asked to imagine. As they begin to work through that scenario, they come in contact with one or more elements of a novel or novels they have all read ... and shortly discover that the resolution of the game's problem can only be accomplished by discussing their shared reading and collaboratively writing about it.

The games remove the students from the rules of the classroom to the rules of the games, lead them to generalize and see analogies, and foster energetic and involved discussion of literary works.

250. Sandel, Lenore. *Another Look at Mother Goose: Prior Knowledge or Endangered Species.* ERIC 311-412, 1987. 11 pp.

Following the precepts of schema theory, with its emphasis on prior knowledge and experience, the author surveyed the familiarity of students in children's literature classes with Mother Goose rhymes. While the survey findings are not indicated as such, the author analyzes the responses and their application for teaching poetry and building on disparate learning experiences with language. When testing students' recall of 30 couplet endings, Sandel noted that responses were based on auditory awareness of rhyming, on use of context, or some familiarity with auditory form and an attempt to represent the corresponding visual form.

The author offers suggestions to classroom teachers to help "preserve the endangered Mother Goose species of our literary heritage." As part of early reading activities, the teacher could explain meanings of unfamiliar words, share rhyming words with different meanings, distinguish between the rhythms of poems, associate visual representation of words read orally, check understanding of word meaning based on auditory familiarity, examine spelling errors for semantic and graphemic confusion, listen to children repeating words learned orally to clarify meanings, use Mother Goose rhymes as an early read-to-peers experience, introduce the historical background of Mother Goose rhymes, and distinguish the poetic qualities found in Mother Goose verse.

251. Sarland, Charles. *Young People Reading: Culture and Response.* Philadelphia: Milton Keynes, 1991.

This book is part of the English, Language, and Education Series, published by Open University Press. One of the earliest titles in this British series was Donald Fry's *Children Talk About Books*, which is considered a foundation to this present study. Charles Sarland is interested in the cultural, ideological, and experiential factors in the interaction of young people with books. The author reports on his own research into the response of young adults to popular literature, a response that is related to "wider cultural meaning making."

Sarland conducted a pilot study to survey current reading choices of children and young adults and the reasons behind teachers' choices of texts for classroom use. These reasons are structured within a framework of five elements, which are often in conflict within the English curriculum and the larger political context. Through group discussions and interviews, he explored the responses to popular reading of male and female students from diverse age and ability levels. The responses of the students are explored as to issues of violence and paranormal, gender differences, cultural order, identification, and cognition and prediction.

The author presents a model of response which incorporates insights from the research findings. The model stresses that reading is an active process of meaning making and that readers and texts both have ideological and cultural assumptions, what he calls "repertoires." He raises issues that are stimulated through the research, such as the treatment of controversial topics, use of videos, values education, and the inclusion of popular reading materials. The author argues that students can demonstrate analytical skills with texts they particularly enjoy. Accessible literature can reveal narrative techniques and the study of character as role rather than as psychology. Of most importance is treating young people and their reading choices seriously. The teachers' role is to help them understand what they do know already and what they want to learn.

A final chapter includes recommended readings and an extensively annotated list of interdisciplinary readings from the fields of literary criticism, folklore, sociology, and education. The author focuses on how each of these theoretical books in this series has affected his own thinking into the dialectic relationship of young people and their literature. A lengthy bibliography of primary and secondary works and an index are included.

252. Sawyer, Wayne, and Ken Watson. "American Children's Literature Down Under." *English Journal* 75.3 (March 1986): 35-37.

Literature is widely studied in Australian schools. While many novels are Australian, British and American novels are introduced as well. The schools are increasingly adopting practices which involve students in active response to and the exploration of literature. These activities are briefly described. The authors note that Australian literature is little used in the United States. They suggest that such use is a means of broadening students' general experience of literature and of providing another perspective for viewing one's own literature. Specific titles are suggested.

253. Schwartz, Sheila. *Teaching Adolescent Literature: A Humanistic Approach*. Rochelle Park, NJ: Hayden, 1979.

The author approaches young adult literature by subject areas or theme. Her approach is to choose contemporary works that reflect the human condition in all its diversity. Louise Rosenblatt's *Literature as Exploration* is cited as a foundational work in her approach.

The categories include: the outside/the other; minorities; regions and locales; teenagers and sex; violence, real and vicarious; family life and lifestyles; and science fiction as prophecy.

As a teaching guide, the book offers book selection criteria, sample teaching guides, and lists of activities. Selected readings accompany each subject chapter, with professional resources included at the end.

254. Sierra, Judy, and Robert Kaminski. *Multi-Cultural Folktales: Stories to Tell Young Children*. Phoenix, AZ: Oryx, 1991.

This storytelling guide to multicultural stories is particularly suited for young audiences. In the introduction the authors characterize these folktales by their structure: repetitious episodes, poetic language, rhythmic refrains, and memorable characters with unusual names and exaggerated traits. These tales often convey important insight into social behavior and values. Countries of origin are cited for each story, which merely indicates the place in which one version of the story was collected. Groups of stories with similar core plot and characters are known as tale type, with individual stories as variants. Exploring tale types and variants helps to introduce comparative literature. The author advises against applying the stories too directly to the social studies curriculum since the tales are often fantasy. Knowing other cultures' stories helps to extend knowledge and sensitivity of the global community. Twenty-five stories and rhymes are arranged in youngest-to-oldest order, for age ranges from two to seven. The first 13 stories are accompanied by patterns for flannel-board figures. Several chapters explore techniques for storytelling and using flannel boards and puppets. The final section focuses on resources for storytelling, including listing of folktales for picture book storytelling, resource guides, indexes, and bibliographic sources.

255. Silvey, Anita. "The Basalization of Trade Books." *The Horn Book* 65 (September–October 1989): 549–50.

   In a brief editorial Anita Silvey warns of the dangers of misusing books by subjecting them to the practices of basal readers. She mentions lengthy study guides for Eric Carle's *The Very Hungry Caterpillar* and Ted Clymer's *Frog and Toad Are Friends* that she calls inane. Creating work sheets and drills for great novels does great harm.

256. Slattery, Carole. "Thinking About Folklore: Lessons for Grades K–4." *Journal of Youth Services in Libraries* 4.3 (Spring 1991): 249–58.

   Carole Slattery advocates a more structured approach to folklore than is usual in elementary classrooms. She presents three increasingly complex levels for the study of folklore. The first of these is cultural literacy. The media is full of allusions to fairy tales, nursery rhymes, and stories. Every literate person should recognize these allusions. The second is literary structure: romance, tragedy, satire and irony, and comedy. All nursery tales will fit into one of these categories, and children can understand this concept. The third is metaphor. The archetypes found in ancient tales still have meaning today. These levels are sequential, and the remainder of the article gives specific ideas for teaching nursery rhymes to grades K–1, literary structure (repetitive and cumulative tales) to grades K–2, and archetypes (Cinderella) to grades 2–3. The origin of the modern superhero and the remarkable servants pattern is taught to grades 3–4. The author notes that the study of folklore in elementary school provides a structure for thinking about literature, and it prepares students for the more complicated stories encountered later.

257. Sloan, Glenna. *Helping Children to Grow as Critics of Literature.* ERIC 293-160, 1988. 16 pp.

Pointing out that children are critics before they can read — rejecting one book and identifying another as a favorite to hear again and again — and that older children are familiar with subliterary forms (comics, television, and advertising), Glenna Sloan asserts that to become *knowledgeable* critics of literature, they first have to become familiar with a great deal of literature. They then can be guided toward insights into the significance of individual literary works and toward an understanding of literature as a coherent body of interrelated works.

Getting children to read can be difficult. Sloan outlines strategies her graduate students used to entice elementary schoolchildren to broaden their selections. These included reading inventories, which resulted in lists of books to interest individual children; modeling; readers theater; children's book talks; displays; and talks by authors.

Sloan continues with methods for teaching literary criticism at the elementary level. These include group discussions by small groups in front of the class. This provides an opportunity for all to learn to keep on-topic, to amend one another's ideas, to offer concrete evidence for opinions, to hear others out, and to reach conclusions and make judgments. Sample questions are offered for approaching stories. Finally, a unit for fifth graders, based on heroes, is described in some detail. Books to constitute a nucleus for the unit are listed, along with suggested activities.

258. Smith, Edna K. "Teaching Theme to Elementary Students." *Reading Teacher* 43.9 (May 1990): 699–701.

Edna Smith, a reading consultant, briefly outlines a method for teaching the concept of theme to elementary school children. The children are given a story to read and are asked to say in one word what it is about. They discuss this problem first with a partner, and then in the group. A second story with the same theme is assigned, and the children should quickly identify the theme. Charts developed as a result of the discussions are illustrated and other activities described.

259. Spears-Bunton, Linda A. "Welcome to My House: African American and European American Students' Responses to Virginia Hamilton's *House of Dies Drear.*" *Journal of Negro Education* 59.4 (Fall 1990): 566–76.

The article describes an experiment conducted by the author and a high school English teacher that involved introducing African American literature into the established canon of an honors course. Based on the reader-response theory of Louise Rosenblatt, it is demonstrated that the transaction between the reader and the text depends greatly on the previous experience, the interest, and the culture of the reader. In this racially mixed class, African American literature at first revealed latent racism and tended to create tension. With the introduction of *House of Dies Drear*, however, the entire class became engrossed and engaged. The author confirms that "response to literature occurs within a triad — reader, text, and context — and that facilitating active response takes time and multiple and diverse literary experiences."

260. Stewig, John Warren. *Literature: Basic in the Language Arts Curriculum.* ERIC 232-188, 1983. 28 pp.

Asserting that literature can be a victim of the hype that forces a "return to the basics" in the school curriculum, John Stewig addresses the many important functions that literature serves, with the first and most important being enjoyment. Other reasons for reading are escape, stimulation of the imagination, understanding ourselves and others, understanding others who are unlike ourselves, understanding the nature of language, learning about other times and places, and obtaining information.

Stewig advances seven characteristics of excellence to look for when selecting books for children. These are: (1) characterization — believable; (2) dialogue — sounds like real people talking; (3) setting — vivid descriptions; (4) plot — good sequence of events; (5) conflict — carefully constructed; (6) resolution — can be negative, positive, or neutral, but should be successful; and (7) theme — an element of literary evaluation. Examples of books that deal effectively with these characteristics are offered.

Finally, Stewig discusses responses to literature. After pointing out that sometimes the best response to a book is no response at all, he suggests various activities based on verbal, physical, visual, musical, and written responses.

261. Stott, Jon C. "'It's Not What You Expect': Teaching Irony to Third Graders." *Children's Literature in Education* 13.4 (Winter 1982): 153-63.

This is a detailed description of one lesson in the Spiralled Sequence Story Curriculum described by the author in a later article (see number 262 below). Irony is taught to third grade children using Lynd Ward's Caldecott Medal–winning book *The Biggest Bear*. After defining irony, Jon Stott describes its many instances in the book. He then discusses how the teacher can lead children to see and discuss the incongruities in the story, both in a first reading and in later readings. After these discussions, the children are given a definition for irony and a chart illustrating it. They can then be led to discover ironies in other stories they have read. Follow-up activities are described, and the continuing study of irony in other books selected for the year's study. Students who have been through this process often discuss irony at home when reading stories or watching television.

Stott points out the crucial relationship between the teaching and research done at the university level, and the teaching of literature to children. Any adult who expects to teach irony to children must have an adult understanding of the nature and function of literary irony as well as a good background in children's literature.

262. Stott, Jon C. "The Spiralled Sequence Story Curriculum: A Structuralist Approach to Teaching Fiction in the Elementary Grades." *Children's Literature in Education* 18.3 (1987): 148–62.

Jon Stott outlines theoretical ideas that embody a structuralist approach to the study and teaching of literature. Based on these ideas, he developed an approach for teaching literature to children with the object of helping children to become better readers of the stories they encounter. The stories are presented in an order which permits students to perceive significant elements first in less complicated stories.

Four criteria are used in choosing books for a specific class: the potential learning level of the class, the literary background of the children, the literary quality and teachability of specific stories, and the learning objectives for the particular year of the literary program.

In the Spiralled Sequence Story Curriculum, there is not only an order for studying works in each grade, but one encompassing works from kindergarten through grade six. Specific objectives are defined for each grade level; for instance, conflict in grade two and heroes in grade six. While this sounds rigid, the curriculum is, in fact, a flexible structure, with neither the selection of books nor their order being inviolable.

It is important for adults presenting the program to have a thorough understanding of the concepts being presented and of the stories necessary to present them clearly and convincingly. Moreover, the presentation should be pleasurable for both teacher and children.

In order to illustrate the concepts discussed, the curriculum for grade three is described. Major objectives are developing awareness of irony, the journey motif, and setting. These elements are combined in the books used, which include *Blueberries for Sal* (Robert McCloskey), *The Lion, the Witch, and the Wardrobe* (C. S. Lewis), *The Wind in the Willows* (Kenneth Grahame), and *The Little House in the Big Woods* (Laura Ingalls Wilder). Ways to discuss the books in relation to the objectives are outlined, although this is not a basis for implementing such a program.

Critics have objected that the approach is too ambitious for young children, but Stott has found that this is not the case—children's abilities and interests are more likely to be underestimated than overestimated. The approach has been criticized for being too intellectual and for ignoring the emotional response to literature. While Stott concedes the importance of the emotional response, he argues that stories use language to communicate, and readers must know the codes in order to respond emotionally. This stance underlies the entire article—children can better understand and respond to literature if they have been trained in its conventions.

263. Stott, Jon C. "A Structuralist Approach to Teaching Novels in the Elementary Grades." *Reading Teacher* 36.2 (November 1982): 136–43.

In order to teach sixth-grade students some of the "grammar of literature," the structure of story, Jon Stott, who teaches at the University of Alberta, details lessons constructed around Tolkien's *The Hobbit*. The primary focus in these lessons is the growth of Bilbo Baggins's character.

Preparation consists of giving the students enough literary training and background to approach the work. This is done through presentation and study of short stories that show character development, and through study of the creatures from folklore used by Tolkien. The entire book is read aloud to the class over a three-week period before individual copies are distributed.

Discussion centers around the changes in Bilbo, invisibility, qualities of heroism, unlikely heroes, and reunion scenes. The use of charts and maps is discussed, but not specific methods of presentation, as these will depend on the teacher's own preferences and the responses and abilities of the children. Follow-up activities include essays and exploration of music, film, and illustrated editions of *The Hobbit*, and related fantasies for further reading.

264. Stott, Jon C. "Teaching Literary Criticism in the Elementary Grades: A Symposium." *Children's Literature in Education* 12.4 (Winter 1981): 192–206.

The symposium took place at the Children's Literature Association Conference in 1981 at Minneapolis. The panel was composed of professors of English who also teach children in elementary grades: Sonia Landes, Jon Stott, Anita Moss, and Norma Bagnall. The purpose of the session was to attempt to bridge the gap between "book people" and "child people," a distinction that John Rowe Townsend made in his Arbuthnot Lecture, "Standards of Criticism for Children's Literature."

Sonia Landes related how she moved second graders beyond literacy into literature through Beatrix Potter's *The Tale of Peter Rabbit*. The students learned to read the text and pictures, to discover relations between the two, and to notice the shape of a story, the development of character, and the use of language. They were able to use the same literary elements in their own stories, in the work of others, and in life. When students were shown another version of *Peter Rabbit*, they were able to make comparisons between this adaptation and the classic.

Jon Stott presented his Spiralled Sequence Story Curriculum, developed through his work with second graders. His aim is to teach students the relationships between "the family of stories" — common techniques, settings, character types, and conflicts. Stories are categorized and compared to other works belonging in many categories. The object of the spiral is to arrange a work so that it is linked to stories preceding and following it. Stott lists his specific objectives and a sequenced order of readings.

Anita Moss spoke about how she taught principles of literary criticism to fourth graders: structural patterns, use of setting, the nature of conflict, irony, and point of view. The theoretical base was the work of critic Northrop Frye, whose theories have been made accessible to language arts through Glenna Sloan's book, *The Child as Critic*. Beginning with traditional folktales, Moss introduced notions of story structure, which were applied to the reading of other fiction and the children's own writing. She listed the sequence of writing assignments and readings which led to the students' incorporation of literary criticism and functional skills of narrative in their own writing and reading.

Norma Bagnall related her approach to teaching Newbery Medal books to fifth graders. The book *Bridge to Terabithia* is read aloud with attention to vocabulary. Author Katherine Paterson's use of language is intricately tied to her theme. Board games, puzzles, and creative writing are developed based on speech variation between characters and important language from the story. Literary devices like foreshadowing are taught to help students learn the craft of storytelling.

265. Stott, Jon C. "'Will the Real Dragon Please Stand Up?' Convention and Parody in Children's Stories." *Children's Literature in Education* 21.4 (December 1990): 219–28.

Literary language makes use of various conventions — its vocabulary. Until the conventions are internalized, the interaction between the text and the reader is incomplete. Children who grow up with books learn this language naturally, as they do any language. Children without a literary background, however, must be consciously taught the conventions.

Jon Stott uses as an example a series of lessons based on dragon lore that teach parody to fourth- and fifth-grade students. First, dragon stories are studied and characteristics of dragons and the conventions of the stories identified. Following this, dragon parodies are introduced. Other activities associated with the lessons are described.

266. Thomas, Jane Rest. "Books in the Classroom: Unweaving the Rainbow." *The Horn Book* 63.6 (November–December 1987): 782–87.

Using a line from a poem by John Keats, Jane Thomas explores the way educators attempt to "unweave the rainbow" by dissecting literature in order to decode. Thomas expounds from student response to teaching assignments which divide a work rather than see it whole, which use literature for instruction in language.

Thomas attacks the practice of basalizing literature, of reducing its text to more palatable terms according to the perceptions of a textbook editor. This reduction strips the work of its integrity, diminishing the power of particular words and symbols. Editors tend to minimize the intelligence of young readers who can approach literature with abstraction.

The fragmented and evaluative method of teaching literature and writing produces the illiteracy and alliteracy so common in the United States. Literature is an art which students need to experience as art, as in the love of words which communicate information, thoughts, and feelings in the reader.

267. Tomlinson, Carl M., and Carol Lynch-Brown. "Adventuring with International Literature: One Teacher's Experience." *The New Advocate* 2.3 (Summer 1989): 169–78.

The authors, who teach adults (Carl Tomlinson at Northern Illinois University and Carol Lynch-Brown at Florida State University), describe a case study involving the use of translated literature with third and fourth graders. The children, rural and poor, whose parents have limited educational backgrounds, might be expected to have little interest in such literature. The authors, however, expected that they would respond positively to a good story and that the exposure would increase their cultural sensitivity. The challenges presented to teacher and students by international literature are described, including foreign names and terms, little commonality of experience, and stylistic differences. The book used, *The Leopard*, by Cecil Bødker, was first carefully read by the teacher, Tina Frese. Her presentation to the class divided itself into four parts. The first, orientation, lasted just one day. They included looking at the cover and title, and discussing what the children knew about Ethiopia. The second phase, exposition, lasted four days. The first part of the book is slow, and the children felt bored. The teacher was able to help them through this phase, a time when many teachers give up on international books. As the conflict began to develop, the integration phase began. This lasted 17 days, the time it took to complete the reading. During this phase, the students' interest and attentiveness grew daily. Other, related activities were introduced, including film strips, group writing, and a reading center display of materials including other books about Africa. The final phase, completion, lasted one day. Affective responses of the children are described. Many children chose to reread the book independently. Others wrote journals and continued related reading. The authors advocate using international books as well as realistic fiction written by American authors about children of different cultures.

268. Vandergrift, Kay E. "Meaning-Making and the Dragons of Pern." *ChLA Quarterly* 15.1 (Spring 1990): 27–32.

In order to demonstrate how young readers make meaning, Kay Vandergrift discussed the Pern novels of Anne McCaffrey with seven high school students who were familiar with the novels and who were articulate in discussing plot, characterization, language, and other literary elements. The discussions began with students writing brief personal responses to six questions intended to elicit general responses that capture personal experiences. They also were used to refer readers back to the books throughout the discussions. The questions related to content, feelings, beliefs, memory, sharing, and different readings. The dragon lore in the books and the students' responses to the books, which took place in three two-hour sessions, are described in some detail. Near the end of the time the group returned to the original questions. These helped the group summarize and reflect upon what had taken place. They agreed on what the novels are about and what the meaning of them is. Vandergrift identifies the starting point for this discussion as the primary difference from the way literary analysis is frequently done. Rather than assuming that meaning is inherent in the structure of the text, reader-response criticism attends first to particular and private meanings made by readers, and then goes back to the printed page to clarify interpretations and share meanings with others. Although there was little disagreement about the books in this group, the discussions enabled each reader to gain perceptions and nuances from others. This type of investigation values both the literary work and the reader.

269. Watson, Jerry J. *Literary Gaps Invite Creative Interaction.* ERIC 271-730, 1985. 10 pp.

This paper draws upon the theoretical work of Wolfgang Iser and Arthur Applebee. Iser, a leading theorist of reader response, initiated the concept of "literary gaps" as the "vacant pages" which invite the reader to enter into a text and, through reflection, create configurative meaning of what is being read. Applebee's research focuses on children's response to stories. Applebee has identified three categories to distinguish children's types of interactions with stories: the complexity of literary and personal experience, a mastery of techniques and conventions of literary forms, and the relationship between the experience of the work and the reader's own life.

The author reports on his own classroom research into determining the types of interaction of children to modern fantasy. A picture story book, *Louis the Fish*, was read to children in grades 1, 4, and 6. Students were asked to rewrite the story and fill in the narrative blanks with their own re-creations.

The examples of student writing support the theories of Iser and Applebee. Children draw upon their own experiences with literature and life to interact with a literary work. Modern fantasy, in particular, stimulates children's creative thinking and writing.

Connecting reading and writing activities can produce the most creative imaginative responses in children. Suggestions are offered: select reading that is rich in meaning; select works that can be read aloud to a group or read independently; educate children about "literary gaps" and their own involvement in making meaning; ask students after the first reading about what they would like to know; provide time for rewriting and editing; and make the writing available for others to read. Booklist and references.

270. Weiss, Adele B. "Using Picture Storybooks to Teach Literary Elements to the Disabled Reader." *Pointer* 27.1 (Fall 1982): 8-10.

Adele Weiss, who teaches learning-disabled middle schoolers, did not find the necessary complexity and subtleties to teach literary elements in the reading materials supplied for her class. Turning to picture books, she found appropriate materials. The reading level ranged from first to sixth grade, and author and artist worked together to create a particular mood that took into consideration both plot and characterization. A list of picture storybooks for older readers and suggested activities for developing theme, setting, plot, and characterization are provided.

271. Zaharias, Jane Ann. "Literature Anthologies in the U.S.: Impediments to Good Teaching Practice." *English Journal* 78.6 (October 1989): 22–27.

The reader, not the text, holds the key to any literary work, asserts Jane Zaharias. This refers to the prior knowledge the reader brings to the experience. In this review of three U.S. and three Canadian anthology series, she attacks anthologies, not for the literature they include but for the questions and activities they suggest. These questions contribute to the idea that reading is passive and that the real meaning resides in the text. Zaharias provides specific examples of questions from various anthologies that demonstrate both this formalistic approach and reader-response approaches. Appropriate questions and preparation activities were found in the Canadian textbooks. This review is useful, either for selecting one of the series reviews, or for aiding in examination and selection of other literature anthologies.

272. Zarrillo, James. "Theory Becomes Practice: Aesthetic Teaching with Literature." *The New Advocate* 4.4 (Fall 1991): 221–34.

A professor in the Graduate School of Education at California State University, Long Beach, who formerly taught elementary school, James Zarrillo applied Louise Rosenblatt's ideas about reading when he visited a classroom for two weeks to teach reader-response literature. Zarrillo developed five principles of aesthetic teaching: (1) the goal of the aesthetic teacher is to encourage children to adopt an aesthetic stance toward literature; (2) the setting for aesthetic teaching has four characteristics: time, choice, trust, and freedom; (3) the questions and prompts teachers pose determine whether or not aesthetic reading will occur; (4) aesthetic teaching is response-centered; and (5) evidence of aesthetic reading can be found in the behavior of students.

In the fourth-grade classroom he visited, Zarrillo read aloud to the class and conducted individual conferences while the children read and wrote in response journals. Two book groups were formed for small group discussions of a book read in common. And finally, two chapters of *Stuart Little*, the read-aloud book, were presented by readers' theater groups.

Zarrillo includes transcripts of some of his individual conferences and group discussions. He points out instances when he became too controlling of the discussion, illustrating how difficult it can be for a teacher to adopt an aesthetic stance when accustomed to formulaic teaching. Excerpts from students' written responses also are included.

An argument is made for restricting literature to aesthetic response and using nonfiction for teaching efferent skills. While special materials can be used for teaching reading skills, Zarrillo points out that the best way to learn reading is to read, and he points to research that shows that vocabulary building takes place during silent reading. He laments the use of literature as reading textbooks, with study guides, exercises, and projects. "Aesthetic teaching," he asserts, "elevates the role of the reader, celebrates the joy of reading, and realizes the full potential of literature in the lives of our students."

PART II

Eight Representative Syllabi

Children's literature is traditionally offered in three different academic departments: education, English, and library science. The following condensed syllabi are samples gathered from professors teaching courses in these respective departments.

The syllabi are contributed by Jan Susina, Department of English, Illinois State University, Normal; Jill May and Darwin Henderson, School of Education, Purdue University, West Lafayette, Indiana; and Joan Atkinson, School of Library and Information Studies, University of Alabama, Tuscaloosa.

A variety of coursework in the subject is represented: children's literature; young adult literature; foundations in literature for children; nineteenth-century children's literature; folktales and fairy tales; and studies in the history of literature for young people. The syllabi include goals, texts, suggested readings, and assignments.

Other sources for course descriptions are Kay Vandergrift's *Children's Literature: Theory, Research, and Teaching* (Libraries Unlimited, 1990) and Glenn Edward Sadler's *Teaching Children's Literature: Issues, Pedagogy, Resources* (Modern Language Association, 1992).

Education

"Media for Children"
Purdue University

Jill P. May
Darwin L. Henderson

OBJECTIVES OF THE COURSE

1. To understand the basic elements found in good children's literature.
2. To develop the ability to evaluate and share a wide variety of printed and non-printed materials with children and young people for their personal and educational development.
3. To define how literature fits into the world of the child.
4. To understand the role of the critic as an interpreter of literature who defines its role within society.
5. To understand the difference between popular culture and classical materials.

WEEK ONE—AN OVERVIEW

During this week, the course objectives, grading system, and semester assignments will be discussed. Time will be spent discussing the basic elements found in good literature. Literary definitions will be explored, and the role of the critic will be introduced.

Reading Assignments

—Beginning pages in class syllabus and literary terms.

—Perry Nodelman. *The Pleasures of Children's Literature*, Chapters 1 and 2. Longman, Inc.

—Susan Tchudi and Stephen Tchudi. *The Young Writer's Handbook: A Practical Guide for the Beginner Who Is Serious About Writing.* Aladdin.

WEEK TWO—FOLKLORE

Attention will be given to the history of oral literature and to the folktale as children's literature. The plots, characters, styles and themes of oral literature will be shared. Together the class will explore the values of folk literature, discussing how it can help children understand themselves, the form of literature, the patterns which are found in traditional story, and the cultural values in the tales. Finally, the interpretations of professional critics will be explored, as well as the roles of the picture book and film in story interpretation.

Reading Assignments

—Andrew Lang, editor. "The Tale of the Youth Who Set Out to Learn What Fear Was," "The Forty Thieves," "Prince Darling," "East of the Sun and West of the Moon," "Little Red Riding Hood," "The Sleeping Beauty in the Wood," "Beauty and the Beast," "The Story of Pretty Goldilocks," and "Hansel and Gretel," in *Blue Fairy Book.* Dover Publications, Inc.

—Nodelman, Chapter 11.

Media Presentation

—*Little Red Riding Hood* (filmstrip).

WEEK THREE—
LITERATURE'S ADAPTATIONS
IN MODERN CULTURE

Popular culture's use and misuse of oral tales will be discussed. The process of reinterpreting oral tales in visual forms will be introduced and explored. As a class, we will discuss the strengths and weaknesses of updating old tales in modern interpretations. Rationale for the adaptation of story in children's literature will be discussed, and the possibilities of writing a literary fantasy with folkloric roots will be shared.

Reading Assignments

— Natalie Babbitt. *The Search for Delicious.* Sunburst Books.

— Nodelman, Chapter 8.

Media Presentation

— *The Frog King or Faithful Henry* (film).

WEEK FOUR —
ILLUSTRATING BOOKS

Reading Assignments

— Crescent Dragonwagon. *Half a Moon and One Whole Star.* Illustrated by Jerry Pinkney. Aladdin.

— Nodelman, Chapter 10.

Media Presentation

— *Evolution of a Graphic Concept: The Stonecutter* (filmstrip).

Written Assignment

— Choose one of the tales in Andrew Lang which was new to you and in a four to six page paper (typed, double spaced) compare it to a Walt Disney version of a traditional fairy tale (i.e., *Sleeping Beauty, Snow White, Robin Hood, Cinderella, The Three Little Pigs*). If you remember the Disney tale from your childhood, try to recall how you reacted to it when you first saw or heard it. What are the values of sharing Lang and or Disney with children? Which belongs in the school? Why?

WEEK FIVE — MYTHIC PATTERNS

Myths contain story patterns which help the stories hold together as cultural and religious teachings. The mythic hero is a traveler who shows others how to live. Mythic patterns will be explored, using various archetypes which have been restructured in modern fantasy.

Reading Assignments

— Verna Aardema. *Bringing the Rain to Kapiti Plain*. Dial/Pied Piper.

— Tomie dePaola. *The Clown of God*. Voyager Books.

— Isaac Bashevis Singer. *Power of Light*. Sunburst Books.

— John Steptoe. *The Story of the Jumping Mouse*. Mulberry Books.

WEEK SIX — CHILDREN'S HEROES

This week we will consider what heroes really are, why we identify with them, and what makes any hero "real" rather than a stereotype.

Reading Assignments

— June Jordan. *Kimako's Story*. Sandpiper Paperbacks.

— Nodelman, Chapter 13.

— Beatrix Potter. *The Tale of Benjamin Bunny*. Dover Publications, Inc.

— Beatrix Potter. *The Tale of Flopsy Bunnies.* Frederick Warne and Company, Inc.

— Beatrix Potter. *The Tale of Peter Rabbit.* Dover Publications, Inc.

WEEK SEVEN — BIOGRAPHY: REALITY OR MYTH?

Archetypal books point the way for other books that follow their patterns. Just as there is an Arthurian pattern, so there is a pattern of literature for biography. How does the author use the story's events to set the story's mood? Help the reader become involved? How can they be conventionalized?

Reading Assignments

— Allen Say. *The Lost Lake.* Sandpiper Paperbacks.

— Mildred Taylor. *The Friendship* and *The Gold Cadillac.* Skylark.

Written Assignment

— Reader response journal for term paper books.

WEEK EIGHT — NONFICTION AS LITERATURE

In spite of the fact that the study of literature within our society focuses upon fiction, libraries report that nonfiction circulates at a higher rate than fiction in their children's departments. This week the class will take a closer look at the craftsmanship found in writing nonfiction, will explore the differences between illustration for fiction and for nonfiction, and will try to determine what makes a good nonfiction book.

Reading Assignments

— David Macaulay. *Mill.* Sandpiper Paperbacks.
— Nodelman, Chapter 12.

WEEK NINE —
SOCIETY IN LITERATURE

The twentieth century has brought great changes in American literary materials which have been created for children. The modern author is creating honest books which relate directly to the modern child. We will explore how this modern realism is different from the earlier more romanticized pictures of family life, and how heroes have changed in these modern stories. We will also determine why earlier heroes may have been historically accurate, honestly portrayed.

Reading Assignment

— Nodelman, Chapter 5.

Written Assignment

— Paper thesis and summary of research.

WEEK TEN —
THE CREATIVE PROCESS

A good writer must carefully combine characters and setting within the story line if he is going to maintain the reader's interest. His descriptions must draw the reader into the events; his conversation must appear natural and must support the characters' personalities. The story will only be successful when the reader becomes involved. How does the author create a book that can involve the child reader?

Reading Assignments

—Robert Lawson. *The Fabulous Flight.* Little, Brown and Company.

—Jill Paton Walsh. *Birdy and the Ghosties.* Farrar, Straus and Giroux, Inc.

WEEK ELEVEN— TIME IN LITERATURE

In stories which are realistic, the idea of a period in history is extremely important. The author tries to impose a feeling for that period within his/her story, and in doing so s/he relies upon factual information about a certain place, a certain chain of events. Even when the author is writing romantic stories or fantastic stories, a feeling for the passing of time is involved. In this sense, time is as important an element in writing as is character development or plot structure.

Reading Assignment

—Betty Vander Els. *Bombers Moon.* Farrar, Straus and Giroux, Inc.

Media Presentation

—*Where the Buffaloes Begin* (VHS).

WEEK TWELVE— ADOLESCENT LITERATURE

What is adolescent literature? How does it differ from children's literature? Where does it fit in the schools? These questions will be discussed during this week.

Reading Assignment

— Cynthia Voigt. *Tree by Leaf.* Juniper.

Media Presentations

— *The Fable of He and She* (film).
— *The Swineherd.*

WEEK THIRTEEN —
PICTURE BOOK LITERATURE

Reading Assignments

— Robert McCloskey. *Blueberries for Sal.* Puffin Books.
— A. A. Milne. *When We Were Very Young.* Yearling Books.
— Uri Shulevitz. *One Monday Morning.* Aladdin.

Media Presentations

— *Where the Wild Things Are.*
— *Maurice Sendak.*

Written Assignment

— Paper due.

WEEK FOURTEEN — POETRY

What is poetry and how does it encourage creative response? How can children be guided in their poetry appreciation? What poetry appeals to the child? Why? Using Mother Goose, poetry of the child's everyday world, and adult poetry, the class will explore and attempt to answer these questions.

Reading Assignments

— Nodelman, Chapter 9.

— Bobbye S. Goldstein, compiler. *Bear in Mind: A Book of Bear Poems.* Illustrated by William Pene du Bois. Puffin Books.

— Arnold Adoff. *Sports Pages.* Illustrated by Steve Kuzma.

— Clyde Watson. *Catch Me and Kiss Me and Say It Again.* Illustrated by Wendy Watson. Philomel Books.

WEEK FIFTEEN —
CHILDREN AND LITERARY CRITICISM

What do children's literature experts say about children and their understanding of literature? What new ways of sharing literature are being suggested? What is the state of the art in the schools? This week will include some answers to these questions and will suggest some areas yet to be explored.

Reading Assignment

— Nodelman, Chapter 14.

WEEK SIXTEEN —
TOWARD AN ENLIGHTENED
IMAGINATION

Test Week

Surveying the growth and development of children's literature can help us to understand what children's literature really is, how it fits into the lives of children, how it can be shared. This week will summarize the trends, touchstones, and archetypal patterns found within children's literature.

English

"Foundations in Literature for Children"
Illinois State University

Jan Susina

TENTATIVE SYLLABUS

Introduction

The Discovery of Childhood and the Development of Children's Literature

Image and Text: Beatrix Potter — *The Tale of Peter Rabbit* and *The Tale of Squirrel Nutkin*

Edith Hamilton — *Mythology*

Charles Perrault — "Sleeping Beauty" and "Cinderella"

Charles Perrault — "Little Red Riding Hood," "Bluebeard," and "Master Cat"

Mme. de Beaumont — "Beauty and the Beast"

Jacob and Wilhelm Grimm — *Household Tales*

Hans Christian Andersen — *Tales Told for Children*

John Ruskin — *The King of the Golden River*

John Newbery — *Mother Goose's Melody*

Edward Lear

Heinrich Hoffmann — *Struwwelpeter*

Lewis Carroll — *Alice's Adventures in Wonderland*

Louisa May Alcott — *Little Women*

Robert Louis Stevenson — *Treasure Island*

James Barrie — *Peter Pan*

Kenneth Grahame — *The Wind in the Willows*

L. Frank Baum — *The Marvelous Land of Oz*

Laura Ingalls Wilder — *Little House on the Prairie*

E. B. White — *Charlotte's Web*

Maurice Sendak — *Where the Wild Things Are*

William Steig — *Sylvester and the Magic Pebble*

Chris van Allsburg — *Jumanji*

Beverly Cleary — *Dear Mr. Henshaw*

Trends in Contemporary Children's Literature

GOALS OF THE COURSE

This course is a historical study of the development of children's literature in English. We will read and discuss mythology, folklore, some poetry written or appropriate for children, some classic children's texts as well as some contemporary picture books, and historical fiction. We will consider various interpretations of the stories, poems and pictures created for or presented to children, what we know about how children understand them, and how children's books express and confirm certain attitudes and beliefs about childhood.

TEXTS

Beverly Cleary — *Dear Mr. Henshaw* (Dell/Yearling)

John W. Griffith and Charles H. Frey — *Classics of Children's Literature* (Macmillan, 3rd ed.)

Edith Hamilton — *Mythology* (Mentor)

Virginia Hamilton — *The House of Dies Drear* (Collier)

E. B. White — *Charlotte's Web* (Harper/Trophy)

"Literature for Young Children"
Illinois State University

Jan Susina

TENTATIVE SYLLABUS

Introduction

Children's Literature and the Young Child

Nodelman — Chapter 1

Frog Prince

Perrault's Fairy Tales

Hans Andersen's Fairy Tales

Walt Disney's Adaptation of Fairy Tales

Carl Sandburg — *Rootabaga Stories*

The Sense of Place: Regionalism in Children's Literature

Aesop's Fables

Mother Goose's Melodies

Contemporary Poetry for Children

ABC and Counting Books

Magazines and Informational Books

Censorship and Children's Literature

Reading the Picture Book: Image and Text

Nodelman — Chapter 7

Beatrix Potter — *The Tale of Peter Rabbit*

Nodelman — Chapter 4

Dr. Seuss

Nodelman — Chapter 3

Presentations on Caldecott Books

Margaret Wise Brown — *Goodnight Moon*

Nodelman — Chapter 9

First Books

Nodelman — Chapter 1

Wordless Picture Books

Nodelman — Chapter 6

Crockett Johnson — *Harold and the Purple Crayon*

Multicultural World of Children's Literature

Contemporary Children's Music: Raffi and Others

Paper on Contemporary Picturebook Due

Children's Video

Maurice Sendak — *Where the Wild Things Are*
                  — *In the Night Kitchen*
                  — *Outside Over There*

Nodelman — Chapter 5

Chris Van Allsburg — *Jumanji*
                     — *The Garden of Abdul Gasazi*

Nodelman — Chapter 2

The Dumbing Down of Children's Literature

Beverly Cleary — *Ramona the Brave*

Trends in Contemporary Children's Literature

GOALS OF THE COURSE

This is a course in children's literature which will concentrate on texts appropriate for children from ages five to nine. We will consider various interpretations of the stories, poems, pictures, informational material and video created for, or presented to, children, what we know about how children understand them, and how children's books express and confirm certain attitudes and beliefs about childhood.

TEXTS

E. F. Bleiler (ed.)—*Mother Goose's Melodies* (Dover)

Margaret Wise Brown—*Goodnight Moon* (Harper/Trophy)

Beverly Cleary—*Ramona the Brave* (Dell/Yearling)

Alfred David and Mary Elizabeth Meek (eds.)—*The Frog King and Other Tales of the Brothers Grimm* (Signet)

S. A. Handford (ed.)—*Aesop's Fables* (Penguin)

Crockett Johnson—*Harold and the Purple Crayon* (Harper/Trophy)

L. W. Kingsland (trans.)—*Hans Andersen's Fairy Tales: A Selection* (Oxford)

A. A. Milne—*Winnie-the-Pooh* (Dell/Yearling)

Perry Nodelman—*Words About Pictures: The Narrative Art of Children's Picture Books* (University of Georgia Press)

Charles Perrault—*Perrault's Fairy Tales* (Dover)

Beatrix Potter—*The Tale of Peter Rabbit* (Dover)

Carl Sandburg—*Rootabaga Stories, Part I* (HBJ)

Maurice Sendak—*Where the Wild Things Are* (Harper/Trophy)

PRESENTATIONS ON CONTEMPORARY PICTUREBOOKS

1. *The Amazing Bone*—William Steig

2. *Owl Moon*—Jane Yolen, ill. John Schoenherr

3. *A Visit to William Blake's Inn*—Nancy Willard, ill. Alice and Martin Provensen

4. *The Little House*—Virginia Lee Burton

5. *Paddle-to-the Sea*—Holling Clancy Holling

6. *Snow White and the Seven Dwarfs*—Jacob and Wilhelm Grimm, trans. Randall Jarrell, ill. Nancy Ekholm Burkert

7. *Mirette on the Highwire*—Emily Arnold McCully

8. *Sam, Bangs and the Moonshine*—Evaline Ness

9. *The Giving Tree*—Shel Silverstein

10. *The Magic School Bus*—Joanna Cole, ill. Bruce Degan

11. *The Tunnel*—Anthony Browne

12. *Alexander and the Terrible, Horrible, No Good, Very Bad Day*—Judith Viorst, ill. Ray Cruz

13. *Black and White*—David Macaulay

14. *The Jolly Postman*—Janet and Allan Ahlberg

15. *The Stinky Cheese Man and Other Fairy Stupid Tales*—Jon Sciezka, ill. Lane Smith

16. *The Very Hungry Caterpillar*—Eric Carle

17. *Tuesday*—David Wiesner

18. *The Snowman*—Raymond Briggs

19. *The Snowy Day*—Ezra Jack Keats

20. *Lon Po Po*—Ed Young

21. *Why Mosquitoes Buzz in People's Ears*—Verna Aardema, ill. Leo and Diane Dillon

22. *Arrow to the Sun*—Gerald McDermott

23. *Tar Beach*—Faith Ringgold

24. *Sayonora, Mrs. Kackleman*—Maria Kalman

25. *Flossie and the Fox*—Patricia McKissack, ill. Rachel Isadora

"Studies in the History of Literature for Young People"

Illinois State University

Jan Susina

TENTATIVE SCHEDULE

Introduction to the course

Assignment of class presentations

John Rowe Townsend — "Standards of Criticism for Children's Literature"; Felicity Hughes — "Children's Literature: Theory and Practice"; Aidan Chambers — "The Reader in the Book"; Lissa Paul — "Enigma Variations: What Feminist Theory Knows About Children's Literature"; Margaret Meek — "What Counts as Evidence in Theories of Children's Literature," in Peter Hunt's *Children's Literature*

"The Yellow Dwarf," "Beauty and the Beast," "Sleeping Beauty," "The Three Wishes," "Little Red Riding Hood," "Diamonds and Toads," "Bluebeard," "Puss in Boots," "Cinderella," "Hop o' My Thumb," in Iona and Peter Opie's *The Classic Fairy Tales*

G. K. Chesterton — "Ethics of Elfland," in Hunt's *Children's Literature*

Oral Report 1: Madame d'Aulnoy and Madame de Beaumont and the French Fairy Court Tradition

Oral Report 2: Charles Perrault and the Fairy Tale

"The Frog Prince," "The Twelve Dancing Princesses," "Rumpelstiltskin," "Hansel and Gretel," "The Tinder Box," "The Princess and the Pea," "Thumbelina," "The Swineherd," in Iona and Peter Opie's *The Classic Fairy Tales*

Oral Report 1: The Brothers Grimm and the Fairy Tale

Oral Report 2: Hans Christian Andersen and the Fairy Tale

Patricia Demers and Gordon Moyles — *From Instruction to Delight*, Sections 1, 2, 4 and 5

Oral Report 1: John Locke and his theories of education

Oral Report 2: John Newbery and children's book publishing

Patricia Demers and Gordon Moyles — *From Instruction to Delight*, Sections 6, 7 and Edward Lear and Heinrich Hoffmann

Oral Report 1: Jean-Jacques Rousseau and his theories of education

Oral Report 2: Edward Lear's nonsense literature

"History of Tom Thumb," "Jack the Giant Killer," "Goldilocks and the Three Bears," "Three Heads in the Well," in Iona and Peter Opie's *The Classic Fairy Tales*

John Ruskin — *King of the Golden River*

Eleanor Mure's "Story of the Three Bears"; Catherine Sinclair's *Holiday House*; and Francis Paget's *Hope of the Katzekopfs*, in Demers and Moyles' *From Instruction to Delight*

Charles Dickens — "Fraud on the Fairies"; John Ruskin — "Fairy Stories"; and Roger L. Green — "The Golden Age of Children's Books," in Hunt's *Children's Literature*

Oral Report 1: The Dickens/Cruikshank Fairy Tale Debate

Oral Report 2: Ruskin's Defense of Fairy Tales

Thomas Hughes — *Tom Brown's School Days*

Oral Report 1: Boys will be boys: Victorian notion of maleness

Oral Report 2: Victorian school stories

Lewis Carroll — *Alice in Wonderland* and *Through the Looking-Glass*

Section 3 of Demers and Moyles' *From Instruction to Delight*

Oral Report 1: Carroll's *Underground*

Oral Report 2: *Looking-Glass* as sequel to *Wonderland*

Louisa May Alcott — *Little Women*

Oral Report 1: The Angel in the House: Victorian ideal woman

Oral Report 2: A. M. Barnard's sensational fiction

Christina Rossetti — *Sing-Song: A Nursery Rhyme Book*

Christopher Smart, William Blake, Ann Taylor Gilbert and Jane Taylor, Elizabeth Turner, William Roscoe, Catherine Ann Dorset, Charles and Mary Lamb, Peter Piper, Thomas Love Peacock, Clement Moore, Mary Hale, Mary Howitt and Eliza Follen, in Demers and Moyles' *From Instruction to Delight*

Oral Report 1: Rossetti's *Speaking Likenesses*

Anna Sewell — *Black Beauty*

Oral Report 1: Animal Stories for Children: sentimentality and naturalism

Robert Louis Stevenson — *Treasure Island*

Oral Report 1: Children's periodicals

Rudyard Kipling — *The Jungle Book*

Oral Report 1: Kipling and imperialism for children

Oral Report 2: Kipling, Lord Baden-Powell and the Boy Scouts movement

Beatrix Potter — *The Tale of Peter Rabbit*

William Moebius — "Introduction to Picturebook Codes," in Hunt's *Children's Literature*

Oral Report 1: Potter's Rabbit Saga: Peter, Benjamin Bunny, Flopsy Bunnies and Mr. Todd

Oral Report 2: Randolph Caldecott's picturebooks

L. Frank Baum — *The Wonderful Wizard of Oz*

Oral Report 1: Baum and the creation of American fairy tales

Oral Report 2: *Wizard of Oz*: Book into Film Classic

GOALS OF THE COURSE

This course is intended to introduce students to historical development of British and American children's literature from its beginning in folklore to 1900. The focus of the course will be on the ways in which children's literature either reinforces or subverts the values and standards of the period in which it is written. The course will examine the changing concept of childhood and how children's texts reveal a society's deep-seated concerns about gender roles and ideological beliefs concerning race and class. The course will focus primarily on significant texts from the 17th, 18th, and 19th centuries which were either written specifically for children or were widely read by children. The course will also introduce students to a variety of critical approaches to children's literature and examine the development of the criticism of children's literature as an academic field.

TEXTS

Louisa May Alcott—*Little Women* (Bantam)

L. Frank Baum—*The Wonderful Wizard of Oz* (Dover)

Lewis Carroll—*Alice's Adventures in Wonderland* and *Alice's Adventures Through the Looking-Glass* (Puffin)

Patricia Demers and Gordon Moyles, eds.—*From Instruction to Delight: An Anthology of Children's Literature to 1859* (Oxford)

Thomas Hughes—*Tom Brown's School Days* (Puffin)

Peter Hunt—*Children's Literature: The Development of Criticism* (Routledge)

Rudyard Kipling—*The Jungle Books* (Signet)

Iona and Peter Opie, eds.—*The Classic Fairy Tale* (Oxford)

Beatrix Potter—*The Tale of Peter Rabbit* (Dover)

Christina Rossetti—*Sing-Song: A Nursery Rhyme Book* (Dover)

John Ruskin—*The King of the Golden River* (Dover)

Anna Sewell—*Black Beauty* (Signet)

Robert Louis Stevenson—*Treasure Island* (Puffin)

FORMAT OF THE COURSE

This course will be conducted as a seminar which means students are expected to do the reading prior to class and come prepared for active discussion of the texts during the session. Undergraduates will be required to write two short papers (8–10 pages) while graduate students will write one short paper and one longer research paper (15-20 pages). All students will give a 15-minute oral presentation.

CLASS PRESENTATIONS

Oral Report 1: Madame d'Aulnoy and Madame de Beaumont and the French Fairy Court Tradition

Oral Report 2: Charles Perrault and the Fairy Tale

Oral Report 1: The Brothers Grimm and the Fairy Tale

Oral Report 2: Hans Christian Andersen and the Fairy Tale

Oral Report 1: John Locke and his theories of education

Oral Report 2: John Newbery and children's book publishing

Oral Report 1: Jean-Jacques Rousseau and his theories of education

Oral Report 2: Edward Lear's nonsense literature

Oral Report 1: The Dickens/Cruikshank Fairy Tale Debate

Oral Report 2: Ruskin's Defense of Fairy Tales

Oral Report 1: Boys will be boys: Victorian notion of maleness

Oral Report 2: Victorian school stories

Oral Report 1: Carroll's *Underground*

Oral Report 2: *Looking-Glass* as sequel to *Wonderland*

Oral Report 1: The Angel in the House: Victorian ideal woman

Oral Report 2: A. M. Barnard's sensational fiction

Oral Report 1: Rossetti's *Speaking Likenesses*

Oral Report 1: Animal stories for children: sentimentality and naturalism

Oral Report 1: Children's periodicals

Oral Report 1: Kipling and imperialism for children

Oral Report 2: Kipling, Lord Baden-Powell and the Boy Scouts movement

Beatrix Potter — *The Tale of Peter Rabbit*

Oral Report 1: Potter's Rabbit Saga: Peter, Benjamin Bunny, Flopsy Bunnies and Mr. Todd

Oral Report 2: Randolph Caldecott's picturebooks
Oral Report 1: Baum and the creation of American fairy tales
Oral Report 2: *Wizard of Oz*: Book into Film Classic

RECOMMENDED READINGS

Louisa May Alcott/A. M. Barnard

— Nina Auerbach. "Austen and Alcott on Matriarchy: New Women or New Wives," in *Community of Women*.

— Humphrey Carpenter. *Secret Gardens.* (chapter 4).

— Judith Fetterley. "Little Women: Alcott's Civil War." *Feminist Studies* 5 (1979): 367–83.

— Madeline Stern. *Behind a Mask: The Unknown Thrillers of Louisa May Alcott*.

— Madeline Stern. *Plots and Counterplots: More Unkonwn Thrillers*.

Hans Christian Andersen

— Reginald Spink. *Hans Christian Andersen and His World*.

— Jack Zipes. "H. C. Andersen and the Discourse of the Dominated," in *Fairy Tales and the Art of Subversion*.

L. Frank Baum

— Michael Patrick Hearn. "L. Frank Baum and the Modernized Fairy Tale," in Michael Patrick Hearn, ed., *The Wizard of Oz: Critical Heritage Series*.

— Selma Lanes. "America as Fairy Tale," in *Down the Rabbit Hole*.

Lewis Carroll

— Humphrey Carpenter. *Secret Gardens.* (chapter 2).

—Michael Hancher. *Tenniel's Illustrations to the "Alice" Books.*

—Derek Hudson. *Lewis Carroll.*

Children's Periodicals

—Kristin Drotern. *English Children and Their Magazines, 1751-1945.*

—Mary Thwaite. *From Primer to Pleasure in Reading.* (4: chapter 10).

Marie-Catherine d'Aulnoy and Jeanne-Marie de Beaumont

—Jack Zipes. "Rise of the French Fairy Tale and the Decline of Fairy in *Beauties, Beasts and Enchantment.*

Development of Children's Literature

—Philipe Ariès. *Centuries of Childhood.* (1962).

—F. J. Harvey Darton. *Children's Books in England.* 3rd ed. (chapters 1-3).

—Percy Muir. *English Children's Books, 1600-1900.* (chapter 1).

Charles Dickens/George Cruikshank

—Charles Dickens. "Fraud on the Fairies," in Lance Salway's *A Peculiar Gift.*

—William Roscoe. "Children's Fairy Tales and George Cruikshank," in Lance Salway's *A Peculiar Gift.*

—Nicholas Tucker. *Suitable for Children: Controversies in Children's Literature.* Part 1.

Wilhelm and Jacob Grimm

—John M. Ellis. *One Fairy Story Too Many.*

— Jack Zipes. *The Brothers Grimm.*

— Jack Zipes. "Who's Afraid of the Brothers Grimm?" in *Fairy Tales and the Art of Subversion.*

Thomas Hughes/School Stories

— Dominic Hibberd. "Where There Are No Spectators: A Rereading of *Tom Brown's Schooldays.*" *Children's Literature in Education* 21 (1976): 64–73.

— P. W. Musgrave. *From Brown to Bunter.*

— Isabel Quigley. *The Heirs of Tom Brown: The English School Story.*

Rudyard Kipling/Boy Scouts

— *Children's Literature.* Kipling Issue 20 (1992).

— Michael Rosenthal. *The Character Factory: Baden-Powell's Boy Scouts and the Imperatives of Empire.*

— Angus Wilson. *The Strange Ride of Rudyard Kipling.* (1977).

Edward Lear

— Ina Hark. *Edward Lear.*

— Alison White. "With Birds in His Beard," in Sheila Egoff's *Only Connect.*

John Locke

— Mary Jackson. *Engines of Instruction.* (chapter 4).

— Geoffrey Summerfield. *Fantasy and Reason.* (chapter 3).

— Mary Thwaite. *From Primer to Pleasure in Reading.* (2: chapter 2).

— John Rowe Townsend. *Written for Children.* (chapter 2).

Nineteenth-Century Children's Book Illustration: Potter and Caldecott

— Percy Muir. *English Children's Books*. (chapter 7).
— Maurice Sendak. *Caldecott and Co.*
— John Rowe Townsend. *Written for Children*. (chapter 12).

Charles Perrault

— Jack Zipes. "Setting Standards for Civilization through Fairy Tales," in *Fairy Tales and the Art of Subversion*.

Beatrix Potter

— Humphrey Carpenter. *Secret Gardens*. (Part II, chapter 4).
— Margaret Lane. *The Tale of Beatrix Potter*.

Christina Rossetti

— Barbara Garlitz. "Christina Rossetti's *Sing-Song* and Nineteenth-Century Children's Poetry." *PMLA* 70 (1955): 539–43.
— U. C. Knoepflmacher. "Avenging Alice: Christina Rossetti and Lewis Carroll." *Nineteenth Century Literature* 41 (1986): 299–328.
— Thomas Burnett Swann. *Wonder and Whimsy: The Fantastic World of Christina Rossetti*.

Jean-Jacques Rousseau

— Mary Jackson. *Engines of Instruction*. (chapter 7).
— Mary Thwaite. *From Primer to Pleasure Reading*. (2: chapter 4).
— John Rowe Townsend. *Written for Children*. (chapter 3).

John Ruskin

— Jane Fillstrup. "Thirst for Enchanted Views in Ruskin's *The King of the Golden River.*" *Children's Literature* 8 (1980).

— U. C. Knoepflmacher. "Resisting Growth through Fairy Tale in Ruskin's *The King of the Golden River.*" *Children's Literature* 13 (1985).

— John Ruskin. "Modern Fairy Stories," in Lance Salway's *A Peculiar Gift.*

Anna Sewell

— Margaret Blount. *Animal Land: The Creatures of Children's Fiction.*

— Susan Chitty. *The Lady Who Wrote "Black Beauty."*

— Mary Thwaite. *From Primer to Pleasure in Reading.* (4: chapter 7).

Robert Louis Stevenson

— Robert Kiely. *Robert Louis Stevenson and the Fiction of Adventure.*

Victorian Boys and Girls

— J. S. Bratton. *The Impact of Victorian Children's Fiction.*

— Deborah Gorham. *The Victorian Girl and the Feminine Ideal.*

— Judith Rowbotham. *Good Girls Make Good Wives: Guidance for Girls in Victorian Fiction.*

BOOKS ON RESERVE

Auerbach, Nina, and U. C. Knoepflmacher, eds. *Forbidden Journeys: Fairy Tales and Fantasies by Victorian Women Writers.* (1992).

Bettelheim, Bruno. *The Uses of Enchantment: The Meaning and Importance of Fairy Tales.* (1976).

Carpenter, Humphrey. *Secret Gardens: The Golden Age of Children's Literature*. (1985).

Carroll, Lewis. *Alice's Adventures Underground*. (1863).

Darton, F. J. Harvey. *Children's Books in England*. 3rd ed. (1982).

Demer, Patricia, ed. *A Garland from the Golden Age: An Anthology of Children's Literature from 1850 to 1900*. (1983).

Demer, Patricia, and Gordon Moyles, eds. *From Instruction to Delight: An Anthology of Children's Literature to 1850*. (1982).

Egoff, Sheila, ed. *Only Connect: Readings on Children's Literature*. (1969).

Hazard, Paul. *Books, Children, and Men* (1944).

Hunt, Peter. *Children's Literature*. (1990).

Jackson, Mary. *Engines of Instruction, Mischief, and Magic: Children's Literature in England from Its Beginnings to 1839*. (1989).

Lanes, Selma. *Down the Rabbit Hole: Adventures and Misadventures in the Realms of Children's Literature*. (1971).

MacLeod, Anne Scott. *A Moral Tale: Children's Fiction and American Culture, 1820–1860*. (1975).

Muir, Percy. *English Children's Books from 1600 to 1900*. (1954).

Opie, Peter, and Iona Opie, eds. *Classic Fairy Tales*. (1974).

Phillips, Robert, ed. *Aspects of Alice*. (1971).

Salway, Lance. *A Peculiar Gift: Nineteenth Century Writings on Books for Children*. (1976).

Summerfield, Geoffrey. *Fantasy and Reason: Children's Literature in the Eighteenth Century*. (1984).

Thwaite, Mary. *From Primer to Pleasure in Reading*. (1963).

Townsend, John Rowe. *Written for Children*. (1965).

Zipes, Jack. *Beauties, Beasts and Enchantment: Classic French Fairy Tales*. (1989).

Zipes, Jack. *Breaking the Magic Spell: Radical Theories of Folk and Fairy Tales*. (1979).

JOURNALS

Children's Literature
Children's Literature Association Quarterly
Children's Literature in Education
The Horn Book
Journal of Popular Culture
The Lion and the Unicorn
Nineteenth-Century Literature

"Literature for Children"
Illinois State University

Jan Susina

SYLLABUS

Introduction: The Discovery of Childhood and the Development of Children's Literature

Image and Text: Beatrix Potter — *The Tale of Peter Rabbit* and *The Tale of Squirrel Nutkin*

Maurice Sendak — *Where the Wild Things Are*

Charles Perrault — Selection

Mme. de Beaumont — "Beauty and the Beast"

Jacob and Wilhelm Grimm — *Household Tales*

Hans Christian Andersen — *Wonderful Stories for Children*

John Ruskin — *The King of the Golden River*

John Newbery — *Mother Goose's Melody*

Robert Louis Stevenson — *A Child's Garden of Verses*

Edward Lear — Selection

Lewis Carroll — *Alice's Adventures in Wonderland*

Louisa May Alcott — *Little Women*

Robert Louis Stevenson — *Treasure Island*

L. Frank Baum — *The Wonderful Wizard of Oz*

Laura Ingalls Wilder — *Little House on the Prairie*

Robert McCloskey — *Homer Price*

E. B. White — *Charlotte's Web*

Scott O'Dell — *The Island of the Blue Dolphins*

Virginia Hamilton — *The House of Dies Drear*

Louise Fitzhugh — *Harriet the Spy*

Judy Blume—*Are You There God? It's Me, Margaret*
Beverly Cleary—*Dear Mr. Henshaw*

THE COURSE

This course is a historical study of the development of children's literature in English. We will read and discuss fairy tales, some poetry written or appropriate for children, and some classic children's texts. We will also examine some recent picture books for children and fiction for older children. We will consider how we understand the stories, poems and pictures created for or presented to children, what we know about how children understand them and how children's books express and confirm certain attitudes and beliefs.

TEXTS

Judy Blume—*Are You There God? It's Me, Margaret* (Dell/Yearling)

Beverly Cleary—*Dear Mr. Henshaw* (Dell/Yearling)

Louise Fitzhugh—*Harriet the Spy* (Dell/Laurel-Leaf)

John Griffith and Charles Frey—*Classics of Children's Literature* (Macmillan, 3rd ed.)

Virginia Hamilton—*The House of Dies Drear* (Collier)

Robert McCloskey—*Homer Price* (Puffin)

Scott O'Dell—*Island of the Blue Dolphins* (Dell/Yearling)

E. B. White—*Charlotte's Web* (Harper/Trophy)

"Literature for Adolescents"
Illinois State University

Jan Susina

TENTATIVE SYLLABUS

Introduction

The Development of Adolescent Literature

Little Women

Catcher in the Rye

Chocolate War

Censorship

Walden

Civil Disobedience

Island of the Blue Dolphins

Planet of Junior Brown

To Kill a Mockingbird

Diary of Anne Frank

Born to Run

Sherlock Holmes

Frankenstein

THE COURSE

This course will emphasize extensive reading of contemporary young adult novels with special attention to the analysis of literary representation of the developmental stage of adolescence. The course will discuss the development of the genre and will investigate thematic and stylistic changes in the literature.

TEXTS

Louisa May Alcott — *Little Women* (Bantam)

Arthur Conan Doyle — *The Adventures of Sherlock Holmes* (Penguin)

Robert Cormier — *The Chocolate War* (Dell)

Anne Frank — *The Diary of a Young Girl* (Pocket)

Virginia Hamilton — *The Planet of Junior Brown* (Collier)

Harper Lee — *To Kill a Mockingbird* (Warner Books)

Dave Marsh — *Born to Run: The Bruce Springsteen Story* (Dell)

Scott O'Dell — *Island of the Blue Dolphins* (Dell/Yearling)

J. D. Salinger — *The Catcher in the Rye* (Bantam)

Mary Shelley — *Frankenstein* (Penguin)

Henry David Thoreau — *Walden* and *Civil Disobedience* (Signet)

"Advanced Topics in Literature for the Young"

Illinois State University

Jan Susina

SYLLABUS

Introduction

Charles Perrault — "Sleeping Beauty," "Little Red Riding Hood," "Bluebeard," "Cinderella," "The Fairies," "The Master Cat," "Ricky of the Tuft," "Little Tom Thumb"

Jacob and Wilhelm Grimm — "Cinderella," "Little Red Cap," "Brier Rose," "Snow White," "Rumpelstiltskin," "Frog Prince," "The Wolf and the Seven Young Kids"

Jacob and Wilhelm Grimm — "Rapunzel," "The Three Spinners," "Hansel and Gretel," "The Fisherman and His Wife," "The Bremen Town Musicians," "The Robber Bridegroom," "The Juniper Tree," "The Golden Goose," "All Fur"

H. C. Andersen — "The Little Mermaid," "The Steadfast Tin Soldier," "The Ugly Duckling," "The Emperor's New Clothes"

H. C. Andersen — "The Princess and the Pea," "Thumbelina," "The Nightingale," "The Shepherdess and the Chimney Sweep," "The Happy Family," "The Goblin at the Grocer's," "Dance, Dolly, Dance"

Catherine Sinclair — "Uncle David's Nonsensical Story about Giants and Fairies"

George Cruikshank — "Cinderella"

Anne Ritchie — "Cinderella"

Harriet Childe-Pemberton — "All My Doing"

John Ruskin — *The King of the Golden River*

Grimm — "The Water of Life"

Charles Kingsley — *The Water Babies*

Nineteenth-Century Children's Book Illustration

Lewis Carroll — *Alice's Adventures in Wonderland*

Charles Dickens — "The Magic Fishbone"; Dickens' "Fraud on the Fairies" (handout)

George MacDonald — "The Day Boy and the Night Girl," "The Golden Key"

Mark Lemon — *Tinykin's Transformations*

Christina Rossetti — "Goblin Market," *Speaking Likenesses* (handout)

Lewis Carroll — "Bruno's Revenge"

Edward Knatchbull-Hugessen — "Charlie Among the Elves"

Juliana Ewing — "The Ogre Courting"

Jean Ingelow — "The Prince's Dream"

Tom Hood — *Petsetilla's Posy*

Lewis Carroll — *Through the Looking-Glass*

Maggie Browne — *Wanted — A King*

Lucy Clifford — "Wooden Tony," "The New Mother" (handout)

Alfred Crowquill — "Heinrich"

Mary de Morgan — "A Toy Princess," "Through the Fire," "The Wanderings of Arasmon"

Mary Molesworth — "The Story of a King's Daughter"

Andrew Lang — "Princess Nobody"

Oscar Wilde — "The Happy Prince"

Rudyard Kipling — "The Potted Princess"

Laurence Housman — "The Rooted Lover"

Kenneth Grahame — "The Reluctant Dragon"

Edith Nesbit — "The Last Dragon"

J. M. Barrie — *Peter Pan*

Oral presentations

THE COURSE

This course will focus on the "golden age of children's literature" and primarily on the genre of the literary fairy as it developed in Victorian Britain. Initially an adult literary form, the folk tale and its companion, the literary fairy tale, were transformed during the nineteenth century to become the most popular forms of children's literature.

The first half of the course will concentrate on the standard European collections of Charles Perrault, Wilhelm and Jacob Grimm, and Hans Christian Andersen. The second half of the course will be concerned with the literature adaptations of the form produced by British authors including Lewis Carroll, Jean Ingelow, Charles Kingsley, Christina Rossetti, George MacDonald, Juliana Ewing, John Ruskin, Mary De Morgan, and J. M. Barrie.

In addition to the primary reading, there will be assignments of related critical works, most of which will be on reserve. The course will deal with the issues of popular culture and social history, the dual audience of children and adult found in children's literature, and the importance of illustrations in nineteenth-century children's literature.

TEXTS

Hans Christian Andersen — *Hans Andersen's Fairy Tales.* ed. Naomi Lewis (Puffin)

J. M. Barrie — *Peter Pan* (Puffin)

Lewis Carroll — *Alice in Wonderland* and *Through the Looking-Glass* (Puffin)

Jonathan Cott, ed. — *Beyond the Looking-Glass: Extraordinary Works of Fairy Tale and Fantasy* (Overlook Press)

Wilhelm and Jacob Grimm — *The Complete Fairy Tales of the Brothers Grimm: Vol. I.* ed. Jack Zipes (Bantam)

Charles Kingsley — *The Water Babies* (Puffin)

Charles Perrault — *Perrault's Fairy Tales* (Dover)

Jack Zipes, ed. *Victorian Fairy Tales: The Revolt of the Fairies and Elves.* (Routledge and Kegan Paul)

BOOKS ON RESERVE

Primary Works

Andersen, H. C. *Fairy Tales.* (1960).

Browne, Frances. *Granny's Wonderful Chair.* (1856).

Carroll, Lewis. *Alice's Adventures Under Ground.* (1863, rpt. 1964).

Carroll, Lewis. *Annotated Alice.* Martin Gardner, ed. (1960).

Cott, Jonathan, ed. *Beyond the Looking-Glass: Extraordinary Works of Fairy Tale and Fantasy.* (1971).

Cruikshank, George. *Cruikshank Fairy-Book.* (1853, rpt. 1963).

Dickens, Charles. "A Holiday Romance."

Green, Roger Lancelyn, ed. *Modern Fairy Stories.* (1955).

Grimm, Jacob, and Wilhelm Grimm. *The Complete Fairy Tales of the Brothers Grimm.* Jack Zipes, ed. (1987).

Hood, Tom. *Petsetilla's Posy.* Diane Johnson, ed. (1851, 1868, 1870, rpt. 1977).

Ingelow, Jean. *Mopsa the Fairy.* (1869).

Kingsley, Charles. *The Water-Babies.* (1863).

Lang, Andrew. *Prince Prioio and Prince Ricardo.* Peter Neumeyer, ed. (1889, 1893, rpt. 1977).

Minard, Rosemary, ed. *Womenfolk and Fairy Tales.* (1975).

Rossetti, Christina. *Sing-Song, Speaking Likenesses, Goblin Market.* R. Lorring Taylor, ed. (1872, 1874, 1893, rpt. 1977).

Ruskin, John. *The King of the Golden River.*

Wilde, Oscar. *Complete Fairy Stories of Oscar Wilde.* (1973).

Zipes, Jack, ed. *Victorian Fairy Tales. The Revolt of the Fairies and Elves.* (1987).

Secondary Works

Avery, Gillian. *Childhood's Pattern: A Study of Heroes and Heroines of Children's Fiction, 1770–1950.* (1975).

Avery, Gillian. *Nineteenth-Century Children: Heroes and Heroines in Children's Stories, 1780–1900.* (1965).

Bettelheim, Bruno. *The Uses of Enchantment: The Meaning and Importance of Fairy Tales.* (1976).

Bottigheimer, Ruth B. *Fairy Tales and Society: Illusion, Allusion, and Paradigm.* (1986).

Bottigheimer, Ruth B. *Grimms' Bad Girls and Bold Boys: The Moral and Social Vision of the Tales.* (1987).

Darton, F. J. Harvey. *Children's Books in England.* 3rd ed. (1982).

Egoff, Sheila. *Only Connect: Readings on Children's Literature.* (1969).

Ellis, John M. *One Fairy Story Too Many: The Brothers Grimm and Their Tales.* (1983).

Green, Roger Lancelyn. *Teller of Tales.* (1946).

Hunt, Peter. *Criticism, Theory and Children's Literature.* (1991).

Luthi, Max. *The European Folk Tale: Form and Nature.* (1982).

McGlathery, James M. *The Brothers Grimm and Folktale.* (1988).

Opie, Peter, and Iona Opie. *Classic Fairy Tales.* (1974).

Phillips, Robert, ed. *Aspects of Alice.* (1971).

Prickett, Stephen. *Victorian Fantasy.* (1979).

Rose, Jacqueline. *The Case of Peter Pan: Or the Impossibility of Children's Fiction.* (1984).

Sale, Roger. *Fairy Tales and After: From Snow White to E. B. White.* (1978).

Tatar, Maria. *The Hard Facts of the Grimms' Fairy Tale.* (1987).

Zipes, Jack. *Breaking the Magic Spell: Radical Theories of Folk and Fairy Tales.* (1979).

Zipes, Jack. *Don't Bet on the Prince: Contemporary Feminist Fairy Tales in North America and England.* (1986).

Zipes, Jack. *Fairy Tales and the Art of Subversion: The Classical Genre for Children and the Process of Civilization.* (1983).

Zipes, Jack. *The Trials and Tribulations of Little Red Riding Hood.* (1983).

JOURNALS

Children's Literature
Children's Literature Association Quarterly
Children's Literature in Education
The Horn Book
Journal of Popular Culture
The Lion and the Unicorn
Nineteenth-Century Literature

SUGGESTED READING

H. C. Andersen

—Reginald Spink. *Hans Christian Andersen and His World.* (1972).

J. M. Barrie

—Harry Geduld. *James Barrie.* (1971).

—Jacqueline Rose. *The Case of Peter Pan.* (1984).

Lewis Carroll

—Michael Hancher. *Tenniel's Illustrations to the "Alice" Books.* (1986).

—Derek Hudson. *Lewis Carroll.* (1977).

—Richard Kelly. *Lewis Carroll.* (1977).

Lucy Clifford

—Anita Moss. "Mothers, Monsters, and Morals in Victorian Fairy Tales." *Lion and Unicorn* 12:2 (1988).

Development of Children's Literature

— Ariès Philipe. *Centuries of Childhood.* (1962).

— F. J. Harvey Darton. *Children's Books in England.* 3rd ed. (1982). (chapters 1–3).

— Percy Muir. *English Children's Books, 1600–1900.* (1954). (chapter 1).

Charles Dickens

— Michael Kotzin. *Dickens and the Fairy Tale.* (1972).

— Harry Stone. *Dickens and the Invisible World.* (1979).

Juliana Ewing

— Gillian Avery. *Mrs. Ewing.* (1964).

— Marghanaita Laski. *Mrs. Ewing, Mrs. Molesworth and Mrs. Hodgson Burnett.* (1951).

Folk Tales

— Bruno Bettelheim. *The Uses of Enchantment.* (1976).

— Max Luthi. *Once Upon a Time: On the Nature of Fairy Tales.* (1970).

— Peter and Iona Opie. *Classic Fairy Tales.* (1974).

— J.R.R. Tolkien. "On Fairy-stories," in *Tree and Leaf.* (1965).

Kenneth Grahame

— Margaret Blount. *Animal Land.* (1974). (chapter 7).

— Peter Green. *Kenneth Grahame.* (1959).

— Lois Kuznets. *Kenneth Grahame.* (1987).

Wilhelm and Jacob Grimm

— Ruth B. Bottigheimer. *Fairy Tales and Society. Grimms' Bad Girls and Bold Boys.* (1987).

— John M. Ellis. *One Fairy Story Too Many.* (1983).

— James M. McGlathery. *The Brothers Grimm and Folktale.* (1988).

— Maria Tatar. *The Hard Facts of the Grimms' Fairy Tale.* (1987).

Charles Kingsley

— Humphrey Carpenter. *Secret Gardens.* (1985). (Part 1, chapter 1).

Rudyard Kipling

— James Harrison. *Rudyard Kipling.* (1982).

— Angus Wilson. *The Strange Ride of Rudyard Kipling.* (1977).

Andrew Lang

— Roger Lancelyn Green. *Andrew Lang.* (1946).

— Eleanor De Selms Langstaff. *Andrew Lang.* (1978).

George MacDonald

— Richard H. Rees. *George MacDonald.* (1972).

— Robert Lee Wolff. *The Golden Key: A Study of the Fiction of George MacDonald.* (1961).

Mary Moleworth

— Sanjay Sircar. "The Victorian Auntly Narrative Voice and Mrs. Moleworth's *Cuckoo Clock.*" *Children's Literature* 17 (1889).

Nineteenth-Century
Children's Book Illustration

— Jonathan Cott, ed. *Victorian Color Picture Books*. Vol. 7, *Masterworks of Children's Literature*. (1983).

— William Feaver. *When We Were Young: Two Centuries of Children's Book Illustration*. (1977).

— Percy Muir. *English Children's Books*. (1953). (chapter 7).

— John Rowe Townsend. *Written for Children*. (1965). (chapter 12).

— Joyce Whalley. *Cobwebs to Catch Flies: Illustrated Books for the Nursery and School Room, 1700–1900*. (1975).

Charles Perrault

— Roger Sale. *Fairy Tales and After*. (1978). (chapter 3).

— Jack Zipes. *Fairy Tales and the Art of Subversion*. (1983). (chapter 2).

Christina Rossetti

— Georgian Battiscombe. *Christina Rossetti*. (1981).

— U. C. Knoepflmacher. "Avenging Alice: Christina Rossetti and Lewis Carroll." *Nineteenth Century Literature*. (1986).

— Thomas Burnett Swann. *Wonder and Whimsy: The Fantastic World of Christina Rossetti*. (1960).

John Ruskin

— Jane Fillstrup. "Thirst for Enchanted Views" in Ruskin's *The King of the Golden River*." *Children's Literature* 8 (1980).

— U. C. Knoepflmacher. "Resisting Growth through Fairy Tale in Ruskin's *The King of the Golden River*." *Children's Literature* 13 (1985).

Victorian Fairy Tales

— Brian Alderson. "Tracts, Rewards and Fairies: The Victorian Contribution to Children's Literature," in Asa Briggs, ed., *Essays in the History of Publishing.* (1977).

— Gillian Avery. *Nineteenth-Century Children.* (1965). (chapters 2 and 6).

— Roger Lancelyn Green. *Tellers of Tales.* (1946). (chapters 5-8).

— Edith Honig. *Breaking the Angelic Image: Woman Power in Victorian Children's Fantasy.* (1988).

— Stephen Prickett. *Victorian Fantasy.* (1979).

— Lance Salway. *A Peculiar Gift: Nineteenth Century Writings on Books for Children.* (1976).

Oscar Wilde

— Michael Kotzin. "'Selfish Giant' as Literary Fairy Tale." *Studies in Short Fiction.* (1979).

— Robert Martin. "Oscar Wilde and the Fairy Tale: 'The Happy Prince' as Self-dramatization." *Studies in Short Fiction.* (1969).

Library Science

"Literature for Children"
The University of Alabama

Joan Atkinson

I. *Catalog Course Description:* Three hours. Deals with major developments in literature for preschool, primary, and intermediate grade children (ages birth to twelve), the areas of children's literature, and effective methods of helping children to enjoy and use literature.

II. *Course Goals:*

1. Introduction to a wide range of types of literature for children and techniques of artists who illustrate children's books.

   Educational Objectives: The student will read as wide a variety of books as possible by as many recognized authors and illustrators as is feasible. The student will participate in class discussions of many examples, both exemplary and flawed. The student will do reasearch on one illustrator and demonstrate practice of evaluation of illustrators.

2. Cultivation of the ability to view a book, film, filmstrip, videotape, etc., from the child's perspective and thus evaluate its appeal to children and at the same time evaluate it critically, showing insight into its themes and techniques of construction, as professional expertise demands.

   Educational objective: The student will evaluate the effectiveness and usefulness of a variety of materials produced for children based on the following criteria: literary merit, quality of illustrations, uses in meeting children's learning and developmental needs, and treatment of social issues.

3. Opportunity to further develop personal characteristics such as self-assurance, creativity, good communication skills, warmth and enthusiasm by sharing literature and materials with a group.

   Educational objective: The student will participate in class activities sharing techniques for using books with children, including reading aloud, booktalking, drama and reader's theater.

4. Knowledge and use of professional publications and review media to guide in selection and use of materials.

   Educational objective: The student will use professional publications to complete the following assignments: illustrator assignment, content analysis assignment, controversial book assignment and curriculum-related project.

5. Identification of some of the issues in children's literature today: dealing with controversial materials, the place of book awards, parent involvement in children's reading, encouraging literacy, selecting multicultural materials and materials suited to the needs of special learners.

   Educational objectives: The student will complete an assignment dealing with controversial materials. The student will read and discuss award-winning books and will participate in a "notable books committee" debate.

6. Appreciation of the potential of good literature to enhance and interrelate every area of the curriculum.

   Educational objective: The student will complete a project which demonstrates appropriate use of children's trade literature to enhance the teaching of a curriculum area.

7. Knowledge and skills that enhance the student's potential to practice reflective decision-making.

   Educational objective: The student will complete all assignments to increase the breadth and depth of knowledge of what is available in literature and how each type contributes to children's learning and development.

III. *Required Textbooks and Readings:*

Glazer, Joan I. *Literature for Young Children.* 3rd edition. Columbus: Charles Merrill, 1991.

Larrick, Nancy. "Illiteracy Starts Too Soon." *Phi Delta Kappan,* Nov. 1987, 184–89. Letters of response in "Backtalk," *Phi Delta Kappan,* March 1988. (On Reserve)

Sutherland, Zena. *Children and Books.* 8th edition. Glenview, IL: Scott, Foresman and Co., 1991.

Trelease, Jim. *The New Read-Aloud Handbook.* New York: Penguin, 1989.

IV. *Assignments:*

The assignments are given to help achieve the course goals.

A. *Reading, Listening, Viewing*

Students will read as wide a variety of books as possible by as many recognized authors as is feasible. They will watch children's television shows, videos, and plays and will visit children's bookstores, museums, toy stores, etc., as there is opportunity. They will observe children's responses to media in the situations mentioned. They will share media with children whenever possible. They will read professional publications and *keep a journal* based on the above activities. Entries should be made at least twice a week. Not every experience of the student needs to be recorded, but responses or ideas generated by the reading should show reflection on the course content. The instructor will inspect the journal at mid-term and conclusion of the course.

The categories into which children's books are divided, according to Sutherland, are:

> picture story books
> other books for the very young
> folk literature and fables, myths and epics
> modern fantasy
> poetry
> modern realistic fiction
> historical fiction

biography
informational books

If there is a question about the categorization of a particular book, please consult the bibliographies provided in Sutherland, *Children and Books*.

Students will bring to class meetings books to share with the class on the topic or activity for study, as appropriate.

B. *Content analysis*

Typed bibliography is to be photocopied for all class members. Please use the standard form for bibliographic citation included on the assignment sheet.

C. *Booktalk on award winners*

D. *Controversial book assignment*

E. *Traditional literature assignment*

F. *Illustrator assignment*

G. *Emphasis on reading assignment*

H. *Curriculum-related project*

I. *Notable books committee*

COURSE OUTLINE

Introduction
Evaluation of children's books
Read Glazer, Chapters 1, 2

Evaluation continued
Read appropriate chapters in Sutherland

Illustration assignment due

Reading aloud
Read Jim Trelease, *The Read-Aloud Handbook*

Literature to support language development. Read article by Nancy Larrick and Glazer, Chapter 5; in Sutherland, alphabet, nursery rhymes and wordless books.

Literature to support intellectual development, Glazer, Chapter 6 and Sutherland on beginning reading, concept, informational (especially science) books. Technique: book discussion.

Literature to support aesthetic and creative development, Glazer, Chapter 9; Sutherland on poetry and traditional literature. Traditional literature assignment due.

Literature to support moral and social development, Glazer, Chapter 8; Sutherland on modern fiction. Content analysis due.

Literature to support personality development, Glazer, Chapter 7; Sutherland on modern fantasy. Technique: reader's theater/drama.

Dealing with controversial materials. Controversial book assignment due.

Booktalking award winners
(Assignments will be made)
Magazines

COURSE BIBLIOGRAPHY

— Bauer, Caroline Feller. *Handbook for Storytellers*. American Library Association, 1977.

— Bauer, Caroline Feller. *Presenting Readers Theatre*. Wilson, 1987.

— Bauer, Caroline Feller. *This Way to Books*. Wilson, 1983.

— Carlson, Ruth Kearney. *Enrichment Ideas*. Brown, 1970.

— Champlin, Connie, and Nancy Renfro. *Storytelling with Puppets*. American Library Association, 1985.

— Cullinan, Bernice E., and Carolyn W. Carmichael, eds. *Literature and Young Children*. National Council of Teachers of English, 1977.

— Hearne, Betsy. *Choosing Books for Children*. Delacorte, 1981.

—Huck, Charlotte, et al. *Children's Literature in the Elementary School.* 4th ed. Holt, Rinehart and Winston, 1987.

—Kimmel, Mary Margaret, and Elizabeth Segel. *For Reading Out Loud!* Rev. ed. Delacorte, 1988.

—Lukens, Rebecca J. *A Critical Handbook of Children's Literature.* 3rd ed. Scott, Foresman, 1986.

—New York Public Library. *The Black Experience in Children's Books.* NYPL, 1984.

—Polette, Nancy. *E Is for Everybody.* 2nd ed. Scarecrow, 1982.

—Roberts, Patricia. *Alphabet: A Handbook of ABC Books and Activities for the Elementary Classroom.* Scarecrow, 1984.

—Rountree, Barbara, et al. *Creative Teaching with Puppets.* The Learning Line, Inc., 1981.

—Rudman, Masha Kabakow. *Children's Literature: An Issues Approach.* 2nd ed. Longman, 1984.

—Sloyer, Shirlee. *Readers Theatre: Story Dramatization in the Classroom.* National Council of Teachers of English, 1982.

CURRICULUM-RELATED PROJECT

Choose whether you prefer to work on a project appropriate for primary grades or for upper elementary students and follow the appropriate directions below.

Prepare materials on a topic for study or a curriculum-related topic of interest to children. The Alabama State Department of Education's *Skills/Concepts Handbook K-6* outlines the skills and concepts children are expected to master grade level by grade level. You may use this to see where your topic might fit into a teacher's planning.

For Primary Grades (K-3):

Select approximately 15 trade books, that is, works of literature as opposed to materials produced overtly for instruction on the selected topic. Include both new and older books, with emphasis on books published in the '80s and '90s. Evaluate the books. Prepare a unit guide or program guide on the topic as indicated below.

For Upper Elementary Grades (4-8):

Select one or two key books, based on length and grade level, that you might use with a class studying this topic or in the public library with parents who are homeschooling their children. Evaluate the books. Prepare a unit guide or program guide on the topic as indicated below.

The guide should include:

— unit or program title

— unit or program theme

— objective(s) or summary (whichever is more appropriate)

— annotated booklist of works that will be used to develop the theme and reach the objective(s), with evaluative comments

— topics for discussion

— activities, which may relate the topic to art, music, folklore, social studies, science, etc. or to developmental areas such as language development, social or moral development, personality development, etc.

— supplementary booklist, where appropriate

Prepare to present your topic to the class by sharing one or more of the key books in detail in a creative way and others briefly. Prepare a handout of not more than three pages for each class member, placing the topic and your name at the top and listing books and/or activities to supplement the teaching or enjoyment of this topic.

CONTROVERSIAL BOOK ASSIGNMENT

There are several objectives for this assignment. One is to raise awareness of the number and diversity of issues that make children's books potentially controversial. Another is to provide an opportunity for in-depth study of one title to which objections have been made. Finally the assignment challenges students to examine or reexamine their beliefs in intellectual freedom for children or freedom of access to ideas for children.

1. On reserve is a folder called Controversial Book Assignment, in which are placed lists of books challenged somewhere in the United States during 1986–90. Please scan those lists and read several of the complaints about children's books.

2. Select one of the titles for your personal study. Please put your name by the title you have selected so that we can get as wide a variety of titles studied as possible.

3. After reading the book, look up as much information as you can find about it. This may include reviews, listings in professional sources and stated objections. Photocopy a few of the most pertinent of these. (Look for material in the reference books category, Ref Z1037. Also consult *Children's Literature Review,* Ref Z 1037 .A1 C52 and *Children's Book Review Index.*) Synthesize the information in a one-page or shorter summary that follows the model below.

Bishop, Claire. *The Five Chinese Brothers.* Illus. by Kurt Wiese. Coward McCann, 1938.

An Asian American elementary teacher has expressed concern that the library's picture book collection contains this book. She states that several Asian American groups consider the book to be racist. The illustrations convey the impression that all Chinese look alike, a circumstance that is degrading as well as inaccurate. She also questions the authenticity of the folktale and recommends that a newer title, *Six Chinese Brothers* (Cheng, Hou-Tien, Holt, 1979) be substituted.

Summary of documentation: The book was recommended for children at the time it was published (*Library Journal,* Nov. 15, 1938; *Horn Book,* September 1938, vol. 14, no. 5) and was called a modern classic by *Publisher's Weekly* in 1960 (178: 12–16, Nov. 14, 1960). During the mid–1970s it was the object of several articles and letters to the editor, some castigating it ("The Five Chinese Brothers: Time to Retire," *Interracial Books for Children Bulletin,* vol. 8, no. 3, 1977) and some in its defense ("A Case for the Five Chinese Brothers," *School Library Journal* 24:90–91, October 1977, with letters following in the December 1977, February 1978 and April 1978 issues). Critics who attacked the book deplored the stereotyped pictures and the lack of human compassion shown by the townspeople, who they said were portrayed as a bloodthirsty mob. They claimed also that the book fosters racial bias and insensitivity on the part of non-Asian American children and a bad self-image on the part of Asian Americans. Critics who defended the book argued that its cartoon-like illustrations were appropriate for the folktale genre and that it was not intended to be pictorially or ethnographically accurate; they felt that the story engenders positive feelings toward Asians.

In the 1980s the book is listed in the standard collection tool for children, *Children's Catalog,* 15th edition, 1986, but not in the equally recognized selection tool, *The Elementary School Library Collection.* It is also listed in *Best Books for Children: Preschool Through the Middle Grades,* 3rd edition, 1985, edited by John Gillespie and Christine Gilbert.

Decision: Should the library keep the *Five Chinese Brothers?* Add *Six Chinese Brothers,* which was recommended in all three selection tools mentioned for the 1980s? Be ready to justify your decision in class, giving points to be made in response to the complaint.

On the date the assignment is due, bring to class your one-page typed summary and photocopies of the most pertinent articles and/ or reviews related to your title.

WEB ASSIGNMENT

Definition and Uses of Webs

The web is a diagram that charts the possible ways of developing a single topic through use of a variety of types of literature. Webs are a form of brainstorming. They suggest many more ideas than will actually be used with any one group on the selected topic. Use of the activities and books suggested in webs will enrich the curricular study of a particular topic. Bringing the books suggested in a web from the library to the classroom during the study of a topic will give students opportunities to browse among materials that will reinforce concepts/skills being studied. Reading aloud stories or poems whose themes, characters, settings, etc. deal with the curricular topic allows students to experience personally, though vicariously, the situation under consideration. Students thus make practical application of concepts in an enjoyable setting.

Assignment

Each student is to prepare a web on a particular curricular topic. Topics will be selected from the Alabama State Department of Education publication *Skills/Concepts Handbook K-6,* 1986. Students will interview a teacher about a particular topic on which the teacher would like to have a web constructed. The topic must be identified by grade level in the *Skills/Concepts Handbook.*

On the due date students will bring photocopies of their webs for each class member:

(1) a diagram of the topic

(2) activities either incorporated into the diagram or listed on a separate sheet

(3) a bibliography which includes complete bibliographic information on the books suggested.

See Glazer, pp. 67-73, for discussion and a completed example of a web on Rain. Also see folder on reserve for other examples of webs.

ILLUSTRATOR ASSIGNMENT

Illustrator's name, location, and date of birth: (Start your search on your illustrator in *Something about the Author,* in Reference collection on main floor.)

Information on the illustrator can be found: (Browse the Reference shelves and consult catalog.)

Major books by this illustrator are:

The kind of books this illustrator creates include:

What children would probably enjoy about the work of this illustrator includes: (See Children's Preferences, Sutherland, pp. 133-34, and use whatever experience you have had in observing children in their use of illustrated books.)

Select one of the elements in artistic design (color, line, shape, texture, arrangement) mentioned in Sutherland, pp. 130–32, that you think is notable in the work of your illustrator and prepare to share with your group examples of the illustrator's use of that element.

READING ALOUD

Please read Jim Trelease's *The New Read-Aloud Handbook* for discussion. Read as many of the books suggested in the picture books and short novels sections of the bibliography (pages 157–217) as you find feasible. (Students in CEE will probably read from the short novels section predominantly and will read fewer titles than those reading heavily from the picture books section. Students in CEC will probably read predominantly from the picture books section. Everyone should read something from both levels, however.)

Directions: For each book you read, do one of the following:

A. Read it aloud to an individual child or a group of children and write briefly their responses in such a way that it is clear what they enjoyed about the book or which parts were their favorites.

B. After reading the book, write briefly what you think children would enjoy about the experience of hearing that book read aloud. Use principles suggested by Trelease if you feel unsure of yourself.

Turn in the read aloud record you have accumulated by that date. You are invited to continue to add to it as the semester progresses.

Reading Aloud in Class

In class we will spend part of the class period reading aloud in small groups. In preparation please select and have in hand during the next week a book recommended in Trelease's short novels or novels section of the bibliography (pp. 202–49). Turn in the title you will read to the instructor next week. You will be divided into groups that will provide the greatest possible diversity of types of literature in the read-aloud experience.

Please follow these steps in preparing to read: Read the entire book and select a passage that can be read in 7–10 minutes. The passage should be interesting and indicative of what the book has to offer. Practice. Prepare an introduction that will give your group enough information so that they will be able to understand where your particular reading fits into the rest of the book (the context, in other words). On the date of the reading, please place in your folder a sheet with the title you read and the exact page numbers you used. Include the sentence with which you began your reading and the sentence with which you concluded it.

EVALUATION ASSIGNMENT

Directions: For the following titles, apply the principles of evaluation we have discussed in class. On a scale of one to five, with a book like *Pamela Learns to Ride* being a one and a book like *Where the Wild Things Are* being a five, rank the six books below. Jot down a few notes about the literary elements, the illustrations and the needs of children that the book is intended to meet. Your notes will become the basis for class discussion.

1. Christian, Mary Blount. *Swamp Monsters.* Illus. by Marc Brown. New York: Dial, 1983.

2. dePaola, Tomie. *The Clown of God.* New York: Harcourt, Brace, Jovanovich, 1978.

3. McKee, David. *Snow Woman.* New York: Lothrop, Lee and Shepard, 1988.

4. McKissack, Patricia C. *Flossie and the Fox.* Illus. by Rachel Isadora. New York: Dial, 1986.

5. MacLachlan, Patricia. *Through Grandpa's Eyes.* Illus. by Deborah Kogan Ray. New York: Harper, 1980.

6. Varga, Judy. *Circus Cannonball.* New York: Morrow, 1975.

TRADITIONAL LITERATURE ASSIGNMENT

Find examples of different authors' and illustrators' interpretations of the work of traditional literature that you are assigned. Prepare to talk about the comparisons and contrasts in the following ways:

1. How do the texts vary? Are the variations because of different ages of audiences, different regions of the country or world, different views toward presentation of violence to children, creative writing experiments, etc.?

2. How do the illustrations vary? Choose a scene that is common to all versions and mark the various examples so that you can show those contrasts to your group members quickly.

1. Little Red Riding Hood
2. Jack tales
3. Aesop's fables
4. Cinderella
5. Beauty and the Beast
6. The Twelve Dancing Princesses
7. The Frog Prince (Princess)
8. The Three Bears
9. The Bremen-Town Musicians
10. Puss in Boots
11. Anansi tales
12. Three Billy Goats Gruff
13. The Fisherman and His Wife
14. Jack and the Beanstalk
15. Hansel and Gretel
16. Rumpelstiltskin
17. St. George and the Dragon
18. Sleeping Beauty
19. Snow White
20. East 'o the Sun and West 'o the Moon
21. The Old Woman and Her Pig
22. Henny Penny
23. B'rer Rabbit tales
24. Noah's Ark

25. Paul Bunyan tales

26. Johnny Appleseed

27. Lion and the Mouse tales

28. The Gingerbread Boy (or the pancake or johnny-cake)

CONTENT ANALYSIS ASSIGNMENT

Content analysis is a method of doing research that is analytical, objective, systematic and quantitative. Using this method the researcher identifies variables for study and identifies a population of pertinent communications that potentially includes those variables.

In this course the population of communications for study is children's books. Our class will not be selecting all pertinent books that present a certain topic, theme or characteristic, but each student will examine several titles and systematically analyze their treatment of selected variables.

If a student is interested in children's books that present the topic of divorce, for example, variables to look for might be how long ago the divorce took place, which parent the child protagonist lives with, frequency of the child's visits with the other parent, whom the child blames for the divorce (especially to see whether the child blames himself), the degree to which the child has accepted the situation, what factors have helped the child to maintain a sense of self-worth, whether religion has contributed to the child's life, etc. These variables will differ from study to study, as each researcher's interests differ.

The assignment for this course is to select a topic or characteristic that you wish to study, to read and analyze from five to twenty-five books (depending on length and difficulty) that treat the topic and to present your findings in a typed paper of approximately one thousand words. A bibliography of books studied should be briefly annotated and copies provided for all members of the class.

An example of a bibliographic citation and annotation follows:
Gerstein, Mordicai. *The Seal Mother*. New York: Dial, 1986. Gr. 2-4

A boy helps his forlorn mother, a selkie, return to her beloved undersea kingdom in this haunting but lively retelling of a centuries-old Scottish folktalk.

Preparation for Content Analysis Assignment

For next class meeting please read the following article:
— Smith, H. W. (1988). "Missing and Wanted: Black Women in Encyclopedias," *School Library Journal,* February, pp. 25-29.

Also read *one* of the following:

— Busbin, O. M., and S. Steinfirst (1989). "Criticism of Artwork in Children's Picture Books: A Content Analysis," *Journal of Youth Services in Libraries,* Spring, pp. 256-66.

— Davis, G. L. (1986). "A Content Analysis of Fifty-seven Children's Books with Death Themes," *Child Study Journal* 16 (1): 39-54.

— Kirk, K. A. (1986). "Environmental Content in Award-Winning Literature: 1960-1982," *The Journal of Environmental Education* 17 (3): 1-7.

— Shannon, P. (1986). "Hidden within the Pages: A Study of Social Perspective in Young Children's Favorite Books," *The Reading Teacher* 39 (7): 656-63.

REQUIRED READING TALLY SHEET

Please read works of as diverse a group of authors and illustrators as possible. Concentrate on the recognized authors listed in your textbooks and strike a balance between older, classic books and newer, modern books. At least half of your reading should be of books published in the 1980s and 1990s. You want to demonstrate through your tally of reading that you are both up-to-date in your knowledge of children's literature (K–6) and aware of older books and authors whose works continue to contribute to the minds and imaginations of modern day children.

For each book, list title, author, illustrator (if different from author), date, number of pages, and grade level.

Flossie and the Fox. By Patricia McKissack. Illus. by Rachel Isadora, 1986, unpaged, K–4.

Categories

Five winners of the Caldecott Award for illustration.

Three winners of the Newbery Award or Newbery Honor books (at least two published since 1980).

Ten books from Trelease's read-aloud recommendations for predictable, wordless, and picture books (pp. 153–202).

Three read-alouds from the novels sections in Trelease (pp. 202–49).

Five books of poetry (recommendations in Trelease and Sutherland; other titles by recommended authors may be used).

Five illustrated folk or traditional tales.

Three books of modern fantasy for older readers (grades 4–6).

Three books of modern realistic fiction for older readers (grades 4–6).

Three books of historical fiction for middle grade or older readers. Read one book by Jean Fritz for this or the next two categories.

Three biographies, one for younger, one for middle grade, and one for older readers.

Ten informational books on a variety of topics and at different audience levels.

Five books by black authors or illustrators. Especially note authors who have won the Coretta Scott King Award (Sutherland, p. 716).

Three books by international authors. Some examples are listed (Sutherland, pp. 718–20).

Familiarize yourself with authors who have won various awards other than the Newbery and Caldecott. These are listed on pp. 714–20 of Sutherland and might be used for selection of reading in several of the categories.

READER'S THEATRE ASSIGNMENT

Reader's theatre is an activity that combines elements of reading aloud, storytelling, acting, and listening to create an integrated language arts experience that is genuinely fun for all participants. It provides reading motivation and opportunities for creative expression that build self-esteem in students.

Reader's theatre begins with a literary work that lends itself to dramatic adaptation. Characteristics of this kind of work, according to Bernice Cullinan, are

— tight plots with suspense and clear endings,

— convincing characters who can be visualized in speech and action,

— vivid themes which add cohesion to a text, and

— sprightly dialogue that brings a story to life.

To present reader's theatre, teachers, librarians and students read to select a story, write to adapt it to a script, speak expressively as they read their lines, and listen to their peers as coparticipants or audience.

ASSIGNMENT: Each group will develop a reader's theatre program that could be used with students of varying ages and reading abilities. The program should develop one theme and should use at least three literary works, preferably of different genre or types. Themes that students have used effectively in the past include boyhood, twins, Christmas creatures, and humorous deception. On the date the assignment is due, students should bring scripts marked appropriately for other students to read. After an organizational time spent in group work, as many of the scripts as possible will be presented and videotaped.

MATERIALS AND SERVICES
FOR YOUNG ADULTS

I. *Course Description:* Introduction to the field of adolescent media (print and non-print formats) with emphasis on the understanding (1) of the physiological, cognitive, psychological and moral development of adolescents, (2) of changing social and political attitudes that affect the content of materials for adolescents and (3) of the impact of adolescent media on learning and behavioral change. Selection and use of adolescent media reflect application of this understanding to regular and special user groups: adolescents with reading difficulties, the gifted, and other minorities.

II. *Texts:*

Carlsen, Robert. *Books and the Teenage Reader.* Second edition revised. Harper and Row, 1980.

Donelson, Kenneth L., and Alleen Pace Nilsen. *Literature for Today's Young Adults.* Scott, Foresman, 1989.

Edwards, Margaret. *The Fair Garden and the Swarm of Beasts.* Hawthorn, 1974.

Konopka, Gisela. "Requirements for the Healthy Development of Adolescent Youth." Reprint from *Adolescence,* Fall 1973.

Young Adult Services Division, American Library Association. *Directions for Library Service to Young Adults.* American Library Association, 1977.

III. *Goals:*

A. Understanding of the physiological, cognitive, psychological and moral development of adolescents as these relate to literature and services provided for them.

B. Understanding of the political and social climate as it affects integration of adolescents into adult roles.

C. Knowledge of the characteristics of various media (hardbound books, paperbound books, magazines, films and filmstrips, videodiscs, cassettes, etc.) and their effect on the learning and behavior of adolescents as reported in research literature.

D. Application of professional principles in selection of materials, recognizing the role of review media, the role of professional standards, and the role of the environment.

E. Ability to perform functions necessary to service effectiveness: doing effective floor work, booktalking, providing reader's advisory service and youth advocacy service, annotating booklists, compiling bibliographies, etc.

IV. *Assignments:*

1. Reading

Students will read a minimum of 30 young adult books, two professional books, and 10 professional articles or pamphlets on young adult literature, teaching issues, services, or development. Some reading is assigned and other reading is selected at the student's discretion. Students will turn in a reading report each week as discussed in class and will annotate 15 of the books read.

2. Viewing, listening

Students will spend a minimum of two hours per week viewing or listening to young adult or professional films, filmstrips, cassettes, records, videocassettes, etc.

3. Observations/Interviews
a. Observations

Students will observe teenagers in two locations, a public hangout and a library, and will write a two-page report of findings.

b. Interviews

Students will interview five young adults about their reading preferences.

4. Term project

Each student will complete a term project that will be shared with other class members. Instructions will be provided.

5. Effective talk
a. Informal (though prepared) class talk

For each of the topics for the course, students should read the assigned book by the day for class discussion of that topic and should come prepared to talk about the book in the following two ways:

1. Give a 30–60 second description that would convey to young adults enough information to let them know whether they would like that kind of book. This is a preparation for doing effective floor work and reader's advisory service with young adults.

2. Give a 2–4 minute evaluation of the book considering its theme, tone, style, readability, length, appeals, weaknesses, etc. This is a preparation for reviewing and for sitting on committees that evaluate young adult titles and produce recommended lists.

b. Formal booktalking

Students will prepare booktalks to present before the class and to be videotaped. A typed, double-spaced copy, two to three pages long, should be turned in.

6. Reviews/Annotations

Students will read three new titles published for young adults, fill out an evaluation form, and write a 75–100 word review and a one-sentence annotation of each title.

7. Final examination: a synthesis of the work done during the semester, with sharing of group projects. Groups of three or four will select an author of significance to young adults and do an author study with oral presentation and appropriate handouts for all class members.

V. *Course Outline:*

Introduction
Definition and scope of young adult services
Professional organizations

Reading preferences of young adults
Assessing readability
High interest/low vocabulary materials
Two-page paper due reporting observations of young adults
    at a hangout and library

The young adult novel
Two-page paper due on personal experience of adolescence
    and role of reading

Growth/Identity/Coming of Age

Materials selection and professional publications
Read Konopka article

Separation/Belonging

Short stories, plays, poetry, humor

Preparation for formal booktalking
Peers/Power Relationships

Sexual relationships/Body and Self

Romance
Coping with censorship

Booktalks
(From Fantasy..., Mystery..., Survival... lists)

Panel on services to young adults
Historical fiction and biography

Term projects due

Annotations due

Final examination

TERM PROJECT

Students will select an issue or topic that pertains to young adults. Topics completed successfully in the past include body image and self esteem, adolescents in stepfamilies, messages rap music sends, physically disabled adolescents, moving, homeless teenagers, YAs of alcoholic parents, literature preferences of black, adolescent boys, effects of unprotected sex and adolescents, including AIDS. Scanning professional literature, including the periodical *Adolescence,* may provide you more ideas. The topic will be treated in the following ways:

(1) do a bibliographic search of related research and select the five items most recommended for colleagues to read;

(2) select five recommended items that are written or produced for a young adult audience;

(3) evaluate the extent to which the materials produced for young adults took into account the research findings on the topic;

(4) discuss implications of your findings for teaching or performing library service to young adults.

Write a paper reporting your results in the four areas indicated. These should be duplicated for each class member. In doing part one, you may either annotate items separately or write a bibliographic essay. The point, however, is to make it clear why each of the five items is important and what it contributes that is unique. (If two items do exactly the same thing, one would be dropped in favor of another that adds to the body of knowledge.) In part two, annotations for each item will make clear what perspective it offers to the young adult reader, viewer or listener. Part three is asking you to synthesize your findings from parts one and two. Part four is asking you to apply findings to the areas of library service and education for young adults, broadly defined.

MATERIALS AND SERVICES FOR YOUNG ADULTS
ADOLESCENT LITERATURE— READING LIST

Growth/Identity/Coming of Age

Blue Heron. Avi.

Red Sky at Morning. Richard Bradford.

Permanent Connections. Sue Ellen Bridgers.

Growing Season. Alden Carter.

Wolf. Gillian Cross.

The Cat Ate My Gymsuit. Paula Danziger.

White Peak Farm. Berlie Doherty.

M. C. Higgins the Great. Virginia Hamilton.

Sister. Ellen Howard.

Cat, Herself. Mollie Hunter.

Sound of Chariots. Mollie Hunter.

Gentlehands. M. E. Kerr.

Pageant. Kathryn Lasky.

Ring of Endless Light. Madeleine L'Engle.

The Brave. Robert Lipsyte.

The Impact Zone. Ray Maloney.

Looking On. Betty Miles.

Somewhere in the Darkness. Walter Dean Myers.

The Island. Gary Paulsen.

A Day No Pigs Would Die. Robert Newton Peck.

Angel Dust Blues. Todd Strasser.

Child of the Owl. Laurence Yep.

The Pigman's Legacy. Paul Zindel.

Alabama/Southeast Regional Materials

All Together Now. Sue Ellen Bridgers.

Sara Will. Sue Ellen Bridgers.

Leroy and the Old Man. W. E. Butterworth.

Tender. Mark Childress.

Trial Valley. Vera Cleaver.

Lizard. Dennis Covington.

Walking Across Egypt. Clyde Edgerton.

Ellen Foster. Kaye Gibbons.

Father's Melancholy Daughter. Gail Godwin.

Summer of My German Soldier. Bette Greene.

Don't Forget to Call Your Mother: I Wish I Could Call Mine. Lewis Grizzard.

Old Dogs and Children. Robert Inman.

Motherwit. Onnie Lee Logan.

Boy's Life. Robert R. McCammon.

Thirsty City. Phillip Q. Morris.

Mama Day. Gloria Naylor.

Dixie Storms. Barbara Park.

Missing May. Cynthia Rylant.

And Nobody Knew They Were There. Otto Salassi.

Growing Up Gay in the South. James T. Sears.

The Redneck Preacher's Son. Luke Wallin.

Separation/Belonging

Steffie Can't Come Out to Play. Fran Arrick.

Tunnel Vision. Fran Arrick.

Tiger Eyes. Judy Blume.

Home Before Dark. Sue Ellen Bridgers.

Midnight Hour Encores. Bruce Brooks.

What Hearts. Bruce Brooks.

Dance on My Grave. Aidan Chambers.

Rainbow Jordan. Alice Childress.

Anything for a Friend. Ellen Conford.

A Tangle of Roots. Barbara Girion.

The Leaving. Lynn Hall.

Man Without a Face. Isabelle Holland.

The Island Keeper. Harry Mazer.

After the Rain. Norma Fox Mazer.

A Formal Feeling. Zibby O'Neal.

Hatchet. Gary Paulsen.

Father Figure. Richard Peck.

The Best of Friends. Margaret I. Rostkowsky.

Welcome Home, Jellybean. Marlene Shyer.

Friends 'Til the End. Todd Strasser.

Star for the Latecomer. Paul Zindel.

Short Stories, Plays, Poetry, Humor

Life Doesn't Frighten Me at All. John Agard, comp.

The Faithless Lollybird. Joan Aiken.

Young Monsters or Young Mutants. Isaac Asimov.

Paradise Cafe and Other Stories. Martha Brooks.

Athletic Shorts. Cris Crutcher.

Center Stage. Don Gallo.

Class Dismissed. Mel Glenn.

I Heard a Scream in the Street. Nancy Larrick.

The Compass Rose. Ursula LeGuin.

Alchemy and Academe. Anne McCaffrey.

Dear Bill, Remember Me? Norma Fox Mazer.

Heartbeats and Other Stories. Peter D. Sieruta.

Baseball in April and Other Stories. Gary Soto.

Gathering of Flowers. Joyce Carol Thomas.

Rachel the Angel and Other Stories. Robert Westall.

2041. Jane Yolen, ed.

Things That Go Bump in the Night. Yolen and Greenberg, eds.

Vampires. Yolen and Greenberg, eds.

Early Sorrow: Ten Stories of Youth. Charlotte Zolotow.

An Overpraised Season. Charlotte Zolotow.

Peers/Power Relationships

Fly Free. C. S. Adler.

No Kidding. Bruce Brooks.

After the First Death. Robert Cormier.

Beyond the Chocolate War. Robert Cormier.

The Chocolate War. Robert Cormier.

I Am the Cheese. Robert Cormier.

The Healer. Peter Dickinson.

Daughters of Eve. Lois Duncan.

Killing Mr. Griffin. Lois Duncan.

The Day They Came to Arrest the Book. Nat Hentoff.

I Wear the Morning Star. Jamake Highwater.

Fell Back. M. E. Kerr.

Alan and Naomi. Myron Levoy.

The Love Bombers. Gloria Miklowitz.

Princess Ashley. Richard Peck.

My Name Is Asher Lev. Chaim Potok.

The Wave. Morton Rhue.

A Fine White Dust. Cynthia Rylant.

Run, Shelley, Run. Gertrude Samuels.

A Hand Full of Stars. Rafik Schami.

House of Stairs. William Sleator.

The Magician. Sol Stein.

The Road to Memphis. Mildred Taylor.

Sexual Relationships/Body and Self

Steffie Can't Come Out to Play. Fran Arrick.

Are You There God? It's Me, Margaret. Judy Blume.

Deenie. Judy Blume.

Forever.... Judy Blume.

Then Again, Maybe I Won't. Judy Blume.

Winning. Robin Brancato.

Hard Feelings. Don Bredes.

A Hero Ain't Nothin' But a Sandwich. Alice Childress.

Crazy Horse Electric Game. Chris Crutcher.

Sex Education: A Novel. Jenny Davis.

Vision Quest. Terry Davis.

He's My Baby Now. Jeannettte Eyerly.

Annie on My Mind. Nancy Garden.

Edith Jackson. Rosa Guy.

The Quartzite Trip. William Hogan.

Little, Little. M. E. Kerr.

Night Kites. M. E. Kerr.

Love Is One of the Choices. Norma Klein.

Mom, the Wolf Man and Me. Norma Klein.

The Best Little Girl in the World. Steven Levenkron.

One Fat Summer. Robert Lipsyte.

Teacup Full of Roses. Sharon Mathis.

I Love You, Stupid! Harry Mazer.

Up in Seth's Room. Norma Fox Mazer.

Did You Hear What Happened to Andrea? Gloria Miklowitz.

Fast Sam, Cool Clyde, and Snuff. Walter Dean Myers.

For All the Wrong Reasons. John Neufeld.

Are You in the House Alone? Richard Peck.

The Alfred Summer. Jan Slepian.

Downstream. John Rowe Townsend.

The Dear Ones. Jacqueline Woodson.

My Darling, My Hamburger. Paul Zindel.

Romance

Constance. Patricia Clapp.

The Clown. Barbara Corcoran.

Seventeenth Summer. Maureen Daly.

The Giver. Lynn Hall.

What About Grandma? Hadley Irwin.

Him She Loves? M. E. Kerr.

If I Love You, Am I Trapped Forever? M. E. Kerr.

Love Is a Missing Person. M. E. Kerr.

The Silver Kiss. Annette Klause.

I Will Go Barefoot All Summer for You. Katie Letcher Lyle.

Disappearing Acts. Terry McMillan.

The Distant Summer. Sarah Patterson.

The Cheese Stands Alone. Marjorie Prince.

Circles. Marilyn Sachs.

He Noticed I'm Alive.... Marjorie Sharmat.

How to Meet a Gorgeous Girl. Marjorie Sharmat.

Love's Dream Remembered. Dorothea Snow.

Last Lovers. William Wharton.

Ludell and Willie. Brenda Wilkinson.

Song of the Shaggy Canary. Phyllis Anderson Wood.

Girl Who Wanted a Boy. Paul Zindel.

The Undertaker's Gone Bananas. Paul Zindel.

Fantasy, Science Fiction, Folklore

Azazel. Isaac Asimov.

Ratha's Creatures. Clare Bell.

The Dark Is Rising. Susan Cooper.

This Place Has No Atmosphere. Paula Danziger.

Chess with a Dragon. David Gerrold.

The Dawn Palace. H. M. Hoover.

The Guardian of Isis. Monica Hughes.

A Stranger Came Ashore. Mollie Hunter.

Days of the Dragon's Seed. Norma Johnston.

Castle in the Air. Diana Wynne Jones.

Eight Days of Luke. Diana Wynne Jones.

The Fledgling. Jane Langton.

Tehanu: The Last Book of Earthsea. Ursula LeGuin.

Dragonsong or *Dragonsinger.* Anne McCaffrey.

Dreamsnake. Vonda McIntyre.

Beauty. Robin McKinley.

Outlaws of Sherwood. Robin McKinley.

The Changeover. Margaret Mahy.

Z for Zachariah. Robert O'Brien.

The Duplicate. William Sleator.

Singularity. William Sleator.

The Book of the Dun Cow. Walter Wangerin.

Dealing with Dragons. Patricia Wrede.

Dragon Steel. Laurence Yep.

Mystery, Suspense, Adventure

Westmark. Lloyd Alexander.

The Dangling Witness. Jay Bennett.

The Pigeon. Jay Bennett.

Doris Fein, Phantom of the Casino. T. Ernesto Bethancourt.

Where Are the Children? Mary Higgins Clark.

There's a Bat in Bunk Five. Paula Danziger.

Summer of Fear. Lois Duncan.

One-Eyed Cat. Paula Fox.

Straight or Edge, or Hot Money. Dick Francis.

The Ghost of Flight 401. John Fuller.

Sweet Whispers, Brother Rush. Virginia Hamilton.

An Unsuitable Job for a Woman. P. D. James.

Fell Down. M. E. Kerr.

The Last Mission. Harry Mazer.

The Stalker. Jean Lowery Nixon.

Liars. P. J. Petersen.

Journey. Joyce Carol Thomas.

Discontinued. Julian Thompson.

Deathwatch. Robb White.

Survival/Risk-Taking/Mastery

Bridle the Wind. Joan Aiken.

Daughters of the Law. Sandy Asher.

Gimme an H...E...L...P. Frank Bonham.

The Girl. Robbie Branscum.

Notes for Another Life. Sue Ellen Bridgers.

The Moves Make the Man. Bruce Brooks.

Journey of the Sparrows. Fran Leeper Buss.

Where the Lilies Bloom. Vera Cleaver.

I Know What You Did Last Summer. Lois Duncan.

The Survivor. James D. Forman.

The Throwing Season. Michael French.

Ordinary People. Judith Guest.

Hold Fast. Kevin Major.

Cave Under the City. Harry Mazer.

Mayday! Mayday! Hilary Milton.

Fallen Angels. Walter Dean Myers.

Dogsong. Gary Paulsen.

Woodsong. Gary Paulsen.

Wolf of Shadows. Whitley Streiber.

Center Line. Joyce Sweeney.

Homecoming. Cynthia Voigt.

Fiction for the Social Studies and History/Biography

Steal Away. Jennifer Armstrong.

True Confessions of Charlotte Doyle. Avi.

Be Ever Hopeful, Hannalee. Patricia Beatty.

Jayhawker. Patricia Beatty.

Ajeemah and His Son. James Berry.

Captives of Time. Malcolm Bosse.

As the Waltz Was Ending. Emma Butterworth.

My Brother Sam Is Dead. Christopher Collier and James Collier.

Duke Ellington. James Lincoln Collier.

Traitor. Jean Fritz.

The Endless Steppe. Esther Hautzig.

Voyages of Captain Cook. Dorothy and Thomas Hoobler.

Halfway Down Paddy Lane. Jean Marzollo.

Columbus and the World Around Him. Milton Meltzer.

Underground Man. Milton Meltzer.

The Serpent Never Sleeps. Scott O'Dell.

Lyddie. Katherine Paterson.

The Shining Company. Rosemary Sutcliff.

Taste of Salt. Frances Temple.

Blitzcat. Robert Westall.

The Serpent's Children. Laurence Yep.

Author Biographies/Autobiographies

Presenting Walter Dean Myers. Rudine Sims Bishop.

Presenting Robert Cormier. Patricia Campbell.

A Girl from Yamhill. Beverly Cleary.

Presenting S. E. Hinton. Jay Daly.

Chapters: My Growth as a Writer. Lois Duncan.

Presenting Paul Zindel. Jack Forman.

Presenting Richard Peck. Donald Gallo.

Presenting Sue Ellen Bridgers. Ted Hipple.

Presenting Norma Fox Mazer. Sally Holtze.

Me, Me, Me, Me, Me: Not a Novel. M. E. Kerr.

Judy Blume's Story. Betsy Lee.

Summer of the Great-Grandmother. Madeleine L'Engle.

Starting from Home. Milton Meltzer.

My Discovery of America. Farley Mowat.

Presenting M. E. Kerr. Alleen Pace Nilsen.

Presenting Rosa Guy. Jerrie Norris.

Presenting Norma Klein. Allene Phy.

Presenting Judy Blume. Maryann Weidt.

PART III

Directory of Courses

Children's literature is traditionally situated in departments of education, English, and library science. Some assumptions exist about the differences in these approaches. Courses in English are considered to be more literary, emphasizing historical children's literature and the quality of writing and illustration, while ignoring the readership of the children themselves. Education is assumed to be more focused on the child as student, on the use of literature to teach reading or to assist in problem solving. Library science courses are perceived to take a middle ground between these two positions, with an emphasis on bibliography and book selection.

How do these departments characterize their own courses? Catalogs of colleges and universities across the country have been examined for evidence of the emphases of the various disciplinary approaches. These course descriptions also reveal the extent of children's literature courses across the landscape of higher education.

Some observations can be drawn from this research. Children's literature is commonly taught throughout the country, but in a diversity of departments. A wide range of courses exist that are known as "children's literature." Many colleges and universities offer just one, but others offer several, and a few offer certificates or degrees.

Frequently, a course in children's literature is listed in the education department and a course in adolescent literature in the English department. In other instances, courses are cross-listed under education and English. Sometimes enrollment is limited to education majors, or it is stated that the course does not count toward the English major, which indicates that these are service courses for the education department. Most courses offered by English departments seem aware of their constituency in education and express the use and selection of books for children.

While "children's literature" and "adolescent literature" are the most commonly offered courses, some programs identify the literature for upper elementary school children or preschoolers in a separate course.

Catalogs of four-year institutions offering a bachelor's and/or graduate degree were examined for curricular activity in children's literature in education, English, or library science. The catalogs examined were on microfiche, "The College Catalog Collection," 1989–90, produced by the National Microfilm Library. The course descriptions are summarized here.

For a survey of graduate programs in the field, see the *Directory of Graduate Studies in Children's Literature*, edited by Karen Patricia Smith, published by the Children's Literature Association, 1992. This report of 200 institutions represents an update of the organization's 1986 booklet *Graduate Studies in Children's Literature*.

ALABAMA

Alabama Agricultural and Mechanical University. Courses are offered in Education. CHILDREN'S LITERATURE and LITERATURE FOR YOUTH emphasize selection of books based on reading levels, age, needs and interests. Books are selected both for pleasure and for information.

Alabama State University. Courses here are offered by Library Science. They are CHILDREN'S LITERATURE and MATERIALS FOR YOUNG ADULTS. Preparing students for work in school and public libraries, these courses cover tools for selection, and the interests and needs of children and young adults. Storytelling is included in the first course.

Athens State College. Education offers a survey course in CHILDREN'S LITERATURE that includes field experience.

Auburn University. Three courses are offered by Education. MEDIA FOR CHILDREN offers examination and evaluation of print and other types of materials, SELECTION AND USAGE OF MEDIA FOR YOUTH includes multicultural materials and materials for special and gifted children,

AND TEACHING READING WITH CHILDREN'S BOOKS approaches the teaching of reading through literature, with field experience provided.

Birmingham-Southern College. Education offers LITERATURE AND CREATIVE DRAMATICS FOR CHILDREN, in which the selection and integration of literature and creative dramatics into the total curriculum are examined.

Huntingdon College. Education. CHILDREN'S LITERATURE is a course for elementary school teachers.

Jacksonville State University. Library Science. The two courses offered are CHILDREN'S LITERATURE and BOOKS AND RELATED MATERIALS FOR CHILDREN. The first covers needs and interests of children and selection aids; the second includes materials other than books.

Judson College. Education and English. CHILDREN'S LITERATURE includes both classics and modern literature and is required for elementary education.

Livingston University. Education. LITERACY THROUGH LITERATURE evaluates major types of literature with relation to reading improvement and pleasure. Library Science. Reading interests and needs of children and young adults are studied in LITERATURE FOR CHILDREN AND YOUNG ADULTS. A variety of formats are read, viewed, and evaluated.

Mobile College. Education. In BOOKS FOR CHILDREN AND YOUTH characteristics of good literature and the place of literature in the school program are considerations.

Oakwood College. Education. Extensive reading and sharing are required in CHILDREN'S LITERATURE.

Stillman College. Education. A course designed for teachers and librarians, LITERATURE FOR CHILDREN, emphasizes a practical approach and a 10 hour practicum.

Troy State University. English. LITERATURE FOR CHILDREN, LITERATURE FOR YOUNG ADOLESCENTS and LITERATURE FOR YOUNG ADULTS are teacher preparation courses, with attention given to multicultural literature.

Tuskegee Institute. Education. CHILDREN'S LITERATURE, a survey of various genres, includes lecture and laboratory.

University of Alabama–Birmingham. Education. Five courses are offered. LITERATURE AND STORYTELLING FOR THE YOUNG CHILD includes reading aloud, storytelling, and laboratory experiences. In YOUNG CHILDREN AND THEIR LITERATURE, LITERATURE FOR ELEMENTARY AND MIDDLE SCHOOLS, and BOOKS FOR YOUNG PEOPLE, emphasis is on the needs of the children/adolescents/young people, and the use of literature in the curriculum. Education and English. Students taking LITERATURE FOR ADOLESCENTS study literary works for or about adolescents.

University of Alabama–Huntsville. Education. LITERATURE FOR CHILDREN AND ADOLESCENTS examines the relationship between developmental stages and literature, and the use of library resources in teaching reading.

University of Alabama–Tuscaloosa. Education. FOLKLORE AND LITERATURE is an examination of major verbal genres of American folklore, with attention to black and Native American material. LITERATURE FOR CHILDREN (N–6) offers guidance in the selection and teaching of literature. Library Science. MATERIALS AND SERVICES FOR CHILDREN and MATERIALS AND SERVICES FOR YOUNG ADULTS cover print, non-print, and programming.

University of Montevallo. English. LITERATURE FOR ADOLESCENTS and SEMINAR IN LITERATURE FOR ADOLESCENTS cover classics and modern literature of all genres. SEMINAR IN LITERATURE FOR CHILDREN covers historical and contemporary books. CHILDREN'S LITERATURE includes studies of critics and illustrators.

University of North Alabama. Education. Integration of children's literature with the content areas is the focus of CREATIVE GROWTH THROUGH LITERATURE FOR CHILDREN AND ADOLESCENTS. BOOKS AND RELATED MATERIALS FOR CHILDREN is for teachers of boys and girls from preschool through elementary school age.

University of South Alabama. Education. LITERATURE FOR CHILDREN AND ADOLESCENTS provides a survey of books, periodicals, and media. Library Science. CURRICULUM MEDIA FOR CHILDREN and CURRICULUM MEDIA FOR YOUNG ADULTS emphasize the selection of materials that meet the needs of children and young adults. Appreciation of literature and storytelling are included.

ALASKA

Alaska Pacific University. Education. LITERATURE FOR CHILDREN AND ADOLESCENTS includes wide reading, study of history and trends, and techniques for stimulating growth in independent reading.

University of Alaska–Anchorage. Education. In CHILDREN'S LITERATURE, focus is on reading many books and on selection of books. TEACHING LANGUAGE ARTS AND LITERATURE gives attention to teaching language arts through the use of literature, and the integration of literature, reading, and writing. Students in ISSUES IN CHILDREN'S LITERATURE study current issues and continue study of integration of literature into the curriculum. English. A repeatable course, INTRODUCTION TO CREATIVE WRITING: CHILDREN'S STORIES, offers various approaches to writing children's stories.

University of Alaska–Fairbanks. Education. CHILDREN'S LITERATURE is a survey course of world literature. Students may specialize in a specific age group. LITERATURE FOR CHILDREN allows the student to select the books to study.

University of Alaska–Southeast. Education. Both LANGUAGE AND LITERATURE ACTIVITIES FOR YOUNG CHILDREN and CHILDREN'S LITERATURE emphasize the use of literature in the language arts and total curriculum, and the selection and analysis of books.

ARIZONA

Arizona State University. Education. LEARNING TO READ WITH LITERATURE, for classroom and reading teachers, offers suggestions for helping children learn to read using literature. English. LITERATURE FOR ADOLESCENTS addresses recent literature for junior high and high school students. ADVANCED STUDY IN LITERATURE FOR ADOLESCENTS is a historical and critical survey. Library Science. In CHILDREN'S LITERATURE and EVALUATION OF LITERATURE FOR YOUNG READERS a critical approach is taken to modern and classic literature. In LIBRARY MATERIALS FOR CHILDREN and LIBRARY MATERIALS FOR ADOLESCENTS students select and use print and non-print materials to support the curriculum. Selecting, analyzing, and utilizing literature for Hispanic and Spanish speaking children and adolescents are the purposes of LITERATURE FOR HISPANIC YOUTH/LITERATURA PARA JOVENES HISPANOPERIANTES.

Grand Canyon College. Humanities. ADOLESCENT LITERATURE is a course for students who wish to read and examine the literature being written for adolescents. Teaching methods will be emphasized. CHILDREN's LITERATURE AND STORYTELLING covers all types of literature from outstanding authors. Storytelling and methods of teaching are included.

Northern Arizona University. Education. Both CHILDREN's LITERATURE and ADVANCED CHILDREN's LITERATURE offer practical uses of literature within the classroom. The first offers lab experience, and the second a historical perspective. English. LITERATURE FOR ADOLESCENTS is a preparatory course for junior and senior high school teaching.

University of Arizona. Education. CHILDREN's LITERATURE IN THE CLASSROOM, offered at both the undergraduate and graduate levels, offers analysis of classic and contemporary children's literature of all genres. English and Library Science. HISTORY OF CHILDREN's LITERATURE is a survey to the close of the 19th century. Library Science. CHILDREN's LITERATURE IN SPANISH gives special attention to the needs of schools and libraries. LITERATURE FOR CHILDREN's LIBRARIANS covers literature for younger children. LITERATURE FOR ADOLESCENTS, also for librarians, covers reviewing and book talks. ORAL PRESENTATION OF CHILDREN's LITERATURE covers reading aloud, storytelling, and programming.

ARKANSAS

Arkansas College. Education. Emphasis is on integrating children's literature across the curriculum with a particular multicultural focus in CHILDREN's LITERATURE.

Arkansas State University. Education. LITERATURE IN THE ELEMENTARY SCHOOL helps future teachers gain competence in the utilization of library materials. English. LITERATURE FOR ADOLESCENTS is a genre survey course for teachers. TEACHING LITERATURE IN THE SCHOOLS is a course in methods of presenting literature in the public schools and two-year colleges.

Harding University. English. CHILDREN's LITERATURE is a course of extensive reading for prospective teachers. LITERATURE FOR ADOLESCENTS is a similar course focusing on young adult literature. MYTHOLOGY, FOLK TALES, AND ETHNIC LITERATURE is designed primarily for teachers in secondary schools.

Henderson State University. Education. LITERATURE FOR CHILDREN acquaints students with the evaluation and selection of literature and its presentation to children. METHODS OF TEACHING LITERATURE FOR ADOLESCENTS is a methods course designed for the prospective teacher and is offered at the graduate and undergraduate levels. In ADVANCED CHILDREN'S LITERATURE, emphasis is on analysis of children's literature and its use with children. English. CHILDREN'S LITERATURE is a study of the educational and entertainment values in all genres.

University of Arkansas–Fayetteville. Education. Two courses in CHILDREN'S LITERATURE are offered. One is a comprehensive study, and one is a current survey. ADVANCED COURSE IN CHILDREN'S LITERATURE is for teachers with a good background in the field. Revising, editing, and preparing manuscripts are covered in WRITING FOR CHILDREN.

University of Arkansas–Little Rock. Education. LITERATURE FOR URBAN CHILDREN offers an overview of urban children's needs and includes development of a curriculum.

University of Arkansas–Pine Bluff. Education. A historical approach is taken in CHILDREN'S LITERATURE.

University of Central Arkansas. Education. Bibliotherapy and use of children's literature in an instruction program are studied in CHILDREN'S READING AND BOOK SELECTION. English. Two courses are offered for teacher preparation. LITERATURE FOR ADOLESCENTS explores motivational approaches to teaching literature in secondary schools. CHILDREN'S LITERATURE requires extensive reading and planning of reading lists for children.

University of the Ozarks. Education. LITERATURE FOR CHILDREN deals with the history and development of children's literature and its selection.

CALIFORNIA

California State Polytechnic University–Pomona. English. Two courses are offered, CHILDREN'S LITERATURE and ADOLESCENT LITERATURE. Course descriptions mention readings in myth, folklore, and classics. In the adolescent course, study of the adolescent's reading development and methods of classroom presentation are included.

California Polytechnic State University–San Luis Obispo. English. Three courses, CHILDREN'S LITERATURE, LITERATURE FOR ADOLESCENTS, and CLASSICS FOR CHILDREN AND YOUTH are offered. The first two are teacher preparation courses, while the third is a survey course.

California State University–Bakersfield. Education. Courses offered are CHILDREN'S LITERATURE and ADOLESCENT LITERATURE. Methods of teaching are included.

California State University–Chico. Education. Four courses are offered. LITERATURE FOR YOUNG CHILDREN is an introductory survey of literature for pre-school and primary grade children. LITERATURE FOR CHILDREN covers literature for elementary school children, while LITERATURE FOR ADOLESCENTS is a "critical examination of traditional and modern literature" for secondary school, including selected literary works. SEMINAR IN LITERATURE FOR CHILDREN is a research course for advanced students.

California State University–Dominguez Hills. Education and English. The English department offers CRITICAL APPROACHES TO CHILDREN'S LITERATURE, while Education offers a language arts course, TEACHING WHOLE LANGUAGE READING/LANGUAGE ARTS IN ELEMENTARY SCHOOL, that includes appropriate strategies for implementing a literature-based curriculum.

California State University–Fresno. Education. One course, LITERATURE FOR CHILDREN AND YOUTH, combines literature for all ages.

California State University–Fullerton. English. The CHILDREN'S LITERATURE course covers world literature, including the oral tradition.

California State University–Hayward. Education. A Certificate Program in Children's Literature is offered. Required courses are HISTORY OF CHILDREN'S LITERATURE (English department), CHILDREN'S LITERATURE IN ELEMENTARY EDUCATION, CRITICAL ANALYSIS OF CHILDREN'S LITERATURE, and either LITERATURE FOR THE YOUNG CHILD or LITERATURE FOR ADOLESCENTS. Required units total 13–14 credit hours. Three or four credit hours are selected from the following electives: MYTHOLOGY (English department), TEACHING MULTI-ETHNIC LITERATURE TO CHILDREN, LITERATURE FOR THE YOUNG CHILD, or

LITERATURE FOR ADOLESCENTS. The multi-ethnic course focuses on black, California-Mexican, and Indian literature.

California State University–Long Beach. English. Two survey courses are offered: CHILDREN'S LITERATURE and LITERATURE FOR ADOLESCENTS.

California State University–Los Angeles. English. Besides the CHILDREN'S LITERATURE and LITERATURE FOR ADOLESCENTS courses, a SEMINAR IN CHILDREN'S LITERATURE AND FOLK LITERATURE is offered. The subject matter varies, and the course can be repeated for credit.

California State University–Northridge. Education offers a seminar, THE PROGRAM IN LITERATURE FOR GRADES 7–12: ISSUES, designed for experienced English teachers, curriculum consultants, and secondary credential candidates. English offers survey courses in CHILDREN'S LITERATURE and LITERATURE FOR ADOLESCENTS, both intended for teachers. The English Department also offers a yearly prize to a student who is the author of the best piece of writing, critical or creative, on the subject of children's literature.

California State University–Sacramento. Education. LITERATURE FOR CHILDREN surveys historical and modern children's literature; CHILDREN'S LITERATURE: MODELS AND TEACHING STRATEGIES IN THE ELEMENTARY CLASSROOM is concerned with teaching literature to elementary students.

California State University–San Bernardino. English. One course, CHILDREN'S LITERATURE, is offered.

California State University–Stanislaus. Education offers READING: LITERATURE-BASED INSTRUCTION FOR CHILDREN, intended to revitalize the language arts curriculum. English offers survey courses in CHILDREN'S LITERATURE and ADOLESCENT LITERATURE, both intended for teachers.

Chapman College. Education's offering, TEACHING OF READING IN ELEMENTARY SCHOOL: LITERACY IN THE 20TH CENTURY, emphasizes student-centered instruction and needs of multicultural learners. Students are required to tutor. English offers LITERATURE FOR CHILDREN AND YOUNG ADULTS, which covers history, selection, and evaluation. The course is intended for teachers and writers.

College of Notre Dame. English. The CHILDREN'S LITERATURE course is a historical survey course useful for prospective teachers.

Dominican College of San Rafael. Education's CHILDREN'S LITERATURE, which looks at important authors and illustrators, is for teachers and others working with children. English offers WRITING CHILDREN'S LITERATURE, which ranges from picture books to the novel.

Humboldt State University. English. Two survey courses, CHILDREN'S LITERATURE and ADOLESCENT LITERATURE, are offered, both intended for teachers.

La Sierra University. English. LITERATURE FOR CHILDREN is for teacher certification in kindergarten through grade six.

Loma Linda University. The English department offers LITERATURE FOR CHILDREN for teacher certification.

Loyola Marymount University. Education. IMAGES OF MINORITY CULTURES IN BOOKS FOR CHILDREN (K–12) is designed as an in-depth analysis of literature for children that portrays cultural patterns of various ethnic groups in America. Teaching suggestions are included.

Mills College. Education. A wide variety of literature for children is explored in TEACHING LANGUAGE ARTS AND LITERATURE IN THE PRIMARY GRADES.

Mount St. Mary's College. English. Two courses, LITERATURE FOR THE YOUNG CHILD and CHILDREN'S LITERATURE, are offered. The first is a survey course and includes experiences in storytelling. The second requires wide reading of children's books, study of criticism, and illustrators.

National University. Education. LITERATURE BASED INTEGRATED LANGUAGE ARTS prepares teaching candidates for a literature-based integrated English-language arts program.

Occidental College. Education. LANGUAGE AND LITERATURE IN ELEMENTARY AND SECONDARY SCHOOLS is a language arts course that includes study of literature and participation in a literacy center.

Pacific Union College. English. LITERATURE FOR CHILDREN is a survey course for teachers.

Pepperdine University. English. A survey course, CHILDREN'S LITERATURE, is offered for those preparing to teach. Illustration is included.

Saint Mary's College of California. English. CHILDREN'S LITERATURE focuses on imaginative literature starting in the 19th century. Relationship to adult literature is studied.

San Diego State University. Education and English. The departments offer a Children's Literature Certificate that attests that the student has successfully completed 18 units of study, with a minimum GPA of 3.0, in the field of literature for children. The certificate is offered to upper division and graduate students with a specialization either in Education or in English and Comparative Literature. The English department offers courses in FICTION, SELECTED TOPICS, TOPICS IN AMERICAN LITERATURE, GENRE STUDIES IN AMERICAN LITERATURE, INDIVIDUAL AMERICAN AUTHORS, and TOPICS IN ENGLISH LITERATURE. Any of these count toward the certificate when the subject is children's literature. The department also offers LITERATURE FOR CHILDREN, ADOLESCENCE IN LITERATURE, and CHILDREN'S LITERATURE AND ADVANCED COMPOSITION. The first is a critical analysis course; the second concentrates on works centrally concerned with an adolescent protagonist; the third includes both critical reading and writing for children. The Education department offers CHILDREN'S/ADOLESCENTS' LITERATURE, a survey course; STORYTELLING; and CHILDREN'S LITERATURE IN ELEMENTARY EDUCATION. All these are geared toward preparing teachers.

San Francisco State University. The Education department's course, CHILD DEVELOPMENT THROUGH LITERATURE FOR CHILDREN, combines principles of child development with a study of literature for teachers. Offerings of the English department are COMING OF AGE IN AMERICA, an examination of experiences of adolescents, and STUDIES IN LITERATURE FOR ADOLESCENTS.

San Jose State University. English. Two courses are offered to prepare teachers, CHILDREN'S LITERATURE and LITERATURE FOR YOUNG ADULTS.

Sonoma State University. The English department offers two courses intended for the preparation of teachers, CHILDREN'S LITERATURE and YOUTH AND LITERATURE. SEMINAR: LITERATURE FOR CHILDREN AND ADOLESCENTS is offered by the education department, and also includes study of ways of using literature in the classroom.

Southern California College. English. The CHILDREN'S LITERATURE course examines classics and current writers.

University of California-Berkeley. English offers a survey course, CHILDREN'S LITERATURE. Two courses are offered by Library Science: SURVEY OF CHILDREN'S LITERATURE and CHILDREN'S LITERATURE. Both offer historical background and current trends.

University of California-Davis. English. A survey course covering historical backgrounds and all genres is offered as CHILDREN'S LITERATURE.

University of California-Irvine. English. CHILDREN'S LITERATURE explores the nature of children's literature and the critical problems raised by it.

University of California-Los Angeles. English offers two survey courses, CHILDREN'S LITERATURE and LITERATURE FOR ADOLESCENTS AND YOUNG ADULTS. Courses in CONTEMPORARY CHILDREN'S LITERATURE and STORYTELLING TO CHILDREN AND ADULTS, ORAL INTERPRETATION OF LITERATURE are offered by Library Science. The first emphasizes reading guidance by the librarian; the second offers practice as well as function of folklore and fantasy and library programming.

University of California-Riverside. Education. TEACHING LITERATURE TO CHILDREN AND ADOLESCENTS examines methods of literary study as well as study of the literature.

University of California-San Diego. English. CHILDREN'S LITERATURE is a study of literature written for children in various cultures and periods. ADOLESCENT LITERATURE is a study of fiction, with consideration of the young adult hero. Both may be repeated for credit as topics vary.

University of California–Santa Barbara. Education. The CHILDREN'S LITERATURE course includes bibliotherapy, interrelationships with the total curriculum, and experimenting with children's literature.

University of California–Santa Cruz. English. Emphasis on issues of sexism and racism in children's literature is part of HIGHLIGHTS OF CHILDREN'S LITERATURE SINCE 1960.

University of San Diego. Library Science. READING FOR CHILDREN AND YOUNG ADULTS gives a historical background and discussion of criteria for selection of books for children and adolescents.

University of San Francisco. Education. The applicability of children's literature to linguistic, cognitive, and aesthetic growth is studied in CHILDREN'S LITERATURE.

University of Southern California. Education offers a survey course for teachers, CHILDREN'S LITERATURE IN THE ELEMENTARY SCHOOL. The English department's LITERATURE FOR CHILDREN AND YOUNG ADULTS surveys literature for middle and secondary school students.

University of the Pacific. CHILDREN'S LITERATURE IN THE CURRICULUM, offered by Education, gives an overview of children's literature in content fields and examines research regarding how books may affect the growing child. CHILDREN'S LITERATURE, the English department offering, is a survey of good literature for children. Genres studied include picture books. Also studied are bookmaking and internal design.

COLORADO

Adams State College. English. ADOLESCENT LITERATURE is a course to acquaint prospective English teachers with representative literature. Library Science. LITERATURE FOR CHILDREN is a survey course for teachers, librarians, and others for use of the literature with children. ADVANCED LITERATURE FOR CHILDREN explores issues in literature for children and youth.

Colorado State University. English. ADOLESCENTS' LITERATURE is a survey of the literature and its use.

Fort Lewis College. Education. A sound literature program in the elementary school is a feature of CHILDREN'S LITERATURE. English. There is an emphasis on minority and ethnic literature in LITERATURE FOR THE ADOLESCENT, a teacher preparation course.

Mesa State College. English. Both CHILDREN'S LITERATURE, a history survey, and ADOLESCENT LITERATURE, a genre survey with emphasis on contemporary issues and trends, are offered.

Metropolitan State College of Denver. English. CHILDREN'S LITERATURE, a survey of all levels and types of children's literature, is for prospective teachers and for students interested in the topic *per se*. Recommended for reading, English and secondary majors, LITERATURE FOR ADOLESCENTS is a critical survey.

University of Colorado-Boulder. Education. In CHILDREN'S LITERATURE, students read and evaluate books and trends. In INTEGRATING THE LANGUAGE ARTS WITH CHILDREN'S LITERATURE they are introduced to methods of teaching through children's literature. Education and English. LITERATURE FOR ADOLESCENTS emphasizes modern literature for junior and senior high school students.

University of Colorado-Colorado Springs. Education. CHILDREN'S LITERATURE and CURRENT LITERATURE FOR CHILDREN focus on the books, media, and literature, while ELEMENTARY LANGUAGE ARTS METHODS acquaints students with strategies that include use of literature in the curriculum. ADOLESCENT LITERATURE emphasizes modern literature. READING AND LANGUAGE ARTS FOR THE GIFTED includes a study of children's and adolescent literature among its topics.

University of Northern Colorado. Education. LITERATURE FOR CHILDREN, ADOLESCENTS, AND YOUNG ADULTS includes field experience or a mini-research study. English. SEMINAR IN LITERATURE FOR YOUNG ADULTS emphasizes junior novels and biographies and reading guidance.

University of Southern Colorado. English. Classic and contemporary children's literature, with emphasis on selection and evaluation, is the subject matter of CHILDREN'S LITERATURE.

Western State College of Colorado. English. Both CHILDREN'S LITERATURE and LITERATURE FOR YOUNG ADULTS are teacher preparation courses, emphasizing the varied uses of books in education.

CONNECTICUT

Central Connecticut State University. Education. TEACHING CHILDREN'S LITERATURE is an investigation of the appreciation for literature with children. BIBLIOTHERAPY focuses on the use of books to address problems confronting young people. In FOLKTELLING ART AND TECHNIQUE, techniques of storytelling are studied. English. Extensive reading is required in LITERATURE FOR YOUNG ADULTS, a teacher preparation course.

Connecticut College. Education. Two courses offer study of the literature and its use in the classroom: LITERATURE IN THE SECONDARY SCHOOL and CHILDREN'S LITERATURE.

Eastern Connecticut State University. Education. Both READING AND LANGUAGE ARTS I and READING AND LANGUAGE ARTS II develop theory and instructional implications of literacy development and the integration of the language arts, including literature. English. Two courses requiring critical reading are offered: CHILDREN'S LITERATURE and ADOLESCENT LITERATURE.

Fairfield University. English. WRITING FOR CHILDREN AND ADOLESCENTS is a workshop course and includes the preparation and submission of a manuscript. THE ADOLESCENT IN LITERATURE (COMING OF AGE IN LITERATURE) involves a study of the subject from an interdisciplinary perspective and is useful for those preparing to teach high school English. THE QUEST FOR MEANING IN CHILDREN'S LITERATURE is an indepth study of the search for existential meaning in some old and modern works which reflect views of childhood.

Sacred Heart University. Education. Young adult literature is studied from the perspective of the developmental psychology of adolescents in ADOLESCENT LITERATURE. CHILDREN'S LITERATURE includes development of methods for incorporating literature into classroom experiences. English. CHILDREN'S LITERATURE, required of secondary English education students, is a survey course.

Saint Joseph College. Education. TEACHING OF LITERATURE FOR

CHILDREN includes ways to encourage children to read. TEACHING OF ADOLESCENT LITERATURE addresses the use of literature as it applies to social and emotional development. English. LITERATURE FOR CHILDREN is a critical approach to literature for children.

Southern Connecticut State University. Education. Appreciation and knowledge of children's books is part of the course work of LANGUAGE ARTS AND CHILDREN'S LITERATURE. Library Science. LITERATURE FOR CHILDREN is a critical study of literature for children.

Teikyo Post University. Education. LANGUAGE ARTS includes the study of all language arts in relation to children's literature.

University of Bridgeport. Education. Both LITERATURE FOR YOUNG PEOPLE and YOUNG PEOPLE'S LITERATURE are offered at the "children's" and "adolescent" levels. The first includes procedures for establishing a program in the classroom. The second is a similar course.

University of Connecticut. Education. Four courses are offered to help prospective teachers understand the theory and approaches to teaching language arts through the use of literature. They are APPLICATIONS OF CHILDREN'S LITERATURE TO THE ELEMENTARY SCHOOL CURRICULUM, TEACHING THE LANGUAGE ARTS IN THE ELEMENTARY SCHOOL, TEACHING LITERATURE TO ADOLESCENTS, and PROBLEMS IN THE TEACHING OF CHILDREN'S LITERATURE. English. One course called CHILDREN'S LITERATURE is a survey of the best literature and includes writing of children's literature. The other is a study of major themes and genres. LITERATURE FOR HIGH SCHOOL STUDENTS is an introduction to the guidance of high school reading in literature.

University of Hartford. Education. CHILDREN'S LITERATURE includes techniques for stimulating appreciation and reading of children's books. CHILDREN'S BOOKS: USES AND ASSESSMENTS emphasizes English and American sources and literary elements. English. Various genres are studied in LITERATURE FOR THE ADOLESCENT READER.

Wesleyan University. Education. LITERATURE FOR CHILDREN: ELEMENTARY is a general survey, including ways to use literature with children. Education and English. LITERATURE FOR ADOLESCENTS addresses the problems of what adolescents read and what they should read.

Western Connecticut State University. Education. CONTENT AND METHOD IN CHILDREN'S LITERATURE blends the content of the field with teaching methods and student activities. CREATIVE ARTS IN EARLY CHILDHOOD EDUCATION includes exploration of literature and response to literature. English. A study of the history of children's literature and its presentation to children is the focus of CHILDREN'S LITERATURE. LITERATURE FOR ADOLESCENTS is a similar course.

Yale University. English. LITERATURE FOR YOUNG PEOPLE is an eclectic approach to literature written for or popular with children, with special emphasis on American literature.

DELAWARE

Delaware State College. Education. Field experience with children is required in CHILDREN'S LITERATURE.

University of Delaware. Education. Both CHILDREN'S LITERATURE and CHILDHOOD LITERATURE survey literature for children and its application to the curriculum. TEACHING LANGUAGE AND LITERATURE focuses on integration of the language arts areas, including the use of literature. LITERATURE FOR ADOLESCENTS is an evaluation of classic and contemporary reading materials and their application to the curriculum.

Wesley College. Education. Considerations for selecting literature for children are addressed in LITERATURE FOR CHILDREN.

Wilmington College. Education. Criteria for appropriate selection of children's books is one aspect of LANGUAGE ARTS IN EARLY CHILDHOOD PROGRAMS.

DISTRICT OF COLUMBIA

American University. Education. CHILDREN'S LITERATURE: MULTICULTURAL AND INTERNATIONAL APPROACHES surveys genres of children's literature and the reflection of contemporary issues in children's books.

Catholic University of America. Library Science. SURVEY OF THE DEVELOPMENT OF CHILDREN'S LITERATURE is a historical survey to the turn of the century.

Gallaudet University. English. CHILDREN'S LITERATURE considers the literature in relation to reading readiness.

George Washington University. Education. Landmark works and integration of literature into the curriculum are studied in CHILDREN'S LITERATURE.

Howard University. Education. TEACHING ORAL COMMUNICATION SKILLS THROUGH CHILDREN'S LITERATURE includes the study of children's books and other print material.

Mount Vernon College. Education. The use of classic and trade books in the language arts curriculum is included in CHILDREN'S LITERATURE.

Trinity College. Education. Ways of sharing books in the home and in the school are explored in CHILDREN'S LITERATURE.

University of the District of Columbia. Education. In CHILDREN'S LITERATURE, the history of children's books and the work of illustrators are studied. ADVANCED CHILDREN'S LITERATURE offers guidance to the reading specialist in using literature in the reading program. Library Science. MEDIA FOR CHILDREN is a survey of print and non-print materials.

FLORIDA

Barry University. Education and English. CHILDREN'S LITERATURE is a survey course.

Bethune-Cookman. Education. Classroom and field experience in planning literature programs is offered in CHILDREN'S LITERATURE.

Clearwater Christian College. Education and English. Teaching techniques and the use of literature in the classroom are addressed in CHILDREN'S LITERATURE. English. Christian principles are considered in ADOLESCENT LITERATURE.

College of Boca Raton. Education. LITERATURE — ELEMENTARY SCHOOL includes writing for children and storytelling.

Eckerd College. Education. LITERATURE FOR CHILDREN includes language arts methods. English. Students do either a creative or scholarly project in (DIRECTED STUDY) CHILDREN'S LITERATURE. WRITING WORKSHOP: CHILDREN'S LITERATURE includes both reading and writing.

Flagler College. Education. METHODS OF TEACHING ENGLISH includes a historical survey of literature.

Florida Agricultural and Mechanical University. Education. CHILDREN'S LITERATURE is a survey course designed for the pre-service teacher.

Florida Atlantic University. Education. CHILDREN'S LITERATURE: ELEMENTARY SCHOOL includes storytelling and creative writing.

Florida International University. Education. Strategies for teaching are included in CHILDREN'S LITERATURE. English. CLASSICS OF CHILDREN'S LITERATURE offers an examination of literary texts.

Florida Southern College. Education. TEACHING CHILDREN'S LITERATURE IN ELEMENTARY SCHOOL, K–6 is an integrated approach to the teaching and sharing of literature.

Florida State University. Education. Two courses, TEACHING LITERATURE AND DRAMA IN HIGH SCHOOLS and LITERATURE IN THE ELEMENTARY SCHOOL address approaches to building a literature program.

Hobe Sound Bible College. Education. CHILDREN'S LITERATURE is an interpretive and critical study of literature and its use in the classroom.

Jacksonville University. Education. The use of literature in the classroom setting is included in CHILDREN'S LITERATURE.

Nova University. Education. Text selection, presentation, and history of the literature are part of CHILDREN'S LITERATURE and ADOLESCENT LITERATURE.

Rollins College. Education. CHILDREN'S LITERATURE is an examination of literature appropriate for use in elementary grades. It includes a study of research, major authors and illustrators. The course is offered at the graduate level as LITERATURE FOR THE ELEMENTARY SCHOOL CHILD.

Saint Leo College. Education. The study of literature in all genres is the focus of CHILDREN'S LITERATURE IN THE ELEMENTARY SCHOOL. Special emphasis is given to books commonly used in high schools in ADOLESCENT LITERATURE.

Saint Thomas University. Education. In CHILDREN'S LITERATURE, the emphasis is on planning, designing, and implementing a reading-for-pleasure program.

Southeastern College. Education. Strategies for motivating students to interact with literature are demonstrated in CHILDREN'S LITERATURE.

Stetson University. Education. CHILDREN'S LITERATURE offers experience in matching books to children's interests and needs.

University of Central Florida. Education. LITERATURE FOR ADOLESCENTS stresses the use of literature in the development of young people. STUDIES IN ADOLESCENT LITERATURE examines research in teaching adolescent literature, along with study of major works in the genre. INVESTIGATION IN CHILDREN'S LITERATURE includes literature analysis and evaluation.

University of Florida. Education. Three courses cover use of literature for instructional, informational, and recreational purposes from birth through grade 12: EARLY CHILDHOOD CHILDREN'S LITERATURE, CHILDREN'S LITERATURE IN THE CHILDHOOD CURRICULUM, and TEACHING ADOLESCENT LITERATURE IN THE SECONDARY SCHOOL. English. Emphasis is on the study of literature and the development of a critical knowledge in LITERATURE FOR YOUNG CHILDREN, CHILDREN'S LITERATURE, and LITERATURE FOR THE ADOLESCENT.

University of Miami. Education. Students are required to read a large number of books in CHILDREN'S LITERATURE, a historical survey. HISTORY AND TRENDS IN CHILDREN'S AND ADOLESCENTS' LITERATURE is an exploration of trends as viewed through the issues and problems facing authors, illustrators, and publishers from the 1700s to the present.

University of North Florida. Education. LITERATURE FOR THE ELEMENTARY CHILD is a survey for various grade and interest levels. English. CHILDREN'S LITERATURE considers children's literature for the enjoyment of adults.

University of South Florida. Education. LITERATURE IN CHILDHOOD EDUCATION deals with the selection, evaluation, and use of fiction, nonfiction, and poetry. ADOLESCENT LITERATURE FOR MIDDLE AND SECONDARY STUDENTS is a study of the types of literature read by adolescents. METHODS OF TEACHING ENGLISH—MIDDLE SCHOOL offers methods of integrating the language arts into a literature-based program. NEW PERSPECTIVES ON THE TEACHING OF LITERATURE IN SECONDARY SCHOOL surveys recent research into reader response. Library Science. HISTORY OF CHILDREN'S LITERATURE offers a historical bibliographical survey. STORYTELLING offers guidance for building storytelling programs for libraries. Selection aids and examination of materials for all library types are part of BOOKS AND RELATED MATERIALS FOR YOUNG ADULTS and MATERIALS FOR CHILDREN.

University of Tampa. LITERATURE FOR CHILDREN includes a historical survey and simulated teaching experiences.

University of West Florida. Education. Children's literature is related to the total language arts program in LANGUAGE ARTS IN ENGLISH EDUCATION. English. CHILDREN'S LITERATURE and YOUNG ADULT LITERATURE are designed primarily for education majors.

Warner Southern College. Education. Emphasis is on well-known materials in LITERATURE FOR THE ELEMENTARY SCHOOL. Library Science. MATERIALS FOR CHILDREN and BOOKS AND RELATED MATERIALS FOR YOUNG ADULTS stress selection aids, reviewing techniques, and use of literature.

GEORGIA

Albany State College. Education. The use of books and materials in educational development, with emphasis upon traditional literature, is the study in CHILDREN'S LITERATURE. Techniques for effective use of literature in the classroom for grades K–8 are presented in PREADOLESCENT LITERATURE. SELECTION AND USE OF LIBRARY MATERIALS looks at criteria for selection of books and non-book materials for the school library.

Armstrong State College. Education. Three courses are offered to aid teachers in selection of books for children and adolescents, and their use in the curriculum: LITERATURE FOR CHILDREN, LITERATURE FOR THE MIDDLE SCHOOL LEARNER, and ADOLESCENT LITERATURE.

Augusta College. English. Three courses designed for teacher preparation offer surveys: CHILDREN'S LITERATURE, a survey of genres; LITERATURE FOR CHILDREN, a historical survey, with problems in teaching literature; and LITERATURE FOR PRE-ADOLESCENTS AND ADOLESCENTS, a survey of literature types read by these age groups.

Berry College. Education. CHILDREN'S LITERATURE places emphasis on content and discipline of children's literature. ADVANCED CHILDREN'S LITERATURE includes techniques for integration of literature with content area subjects.

Brenaw Women's College. Education. CHILDREN'S LITERATURE is a study of literary style in children's books in the different genre. ADVANCED CHILDREN'S LITERATURE is a comprehensive study with methods of reading guidance.

Brewton-Parker College. Education and English. CHILDREN'S LITERATURE gives special attention to classics.

Clark Atlanta University. Education. CHILDREN'S LITERATURE includes the use of literature for enhancing cultural pluralism and strategies for presenting literature in creative ways.

Columbia College. Education. LITERATURE FOR EARLY CHILDHOOD EDUCATION, LITERATURE IN THE MIDDLE GRADES, and LITERATURE FOR ADOLESCENTS provide prospective teachers with criteria for selecting literature and for guiding literary experience. CHILDREN'S LITERATURE offers teaching strategies and integration of literature with content areas. TRENDS IN ADOLESCENT LITERATURE focuses on recent publications and prominent writers.

Georgia College. Education. LITERATURE AND WRITING FOR YOUNG CHILDREN presents literature and writing as interactive processes. English. LITERATURE FOR ADOLESCENTS is a survey course.

Georgia Southern University. Education. INTEGRATING CHILDREN'S LITERATURE INTO THE EARLY CHILDHOOD CURRICULUM is designed as a first course in children's literature. It includes a survey, and study of guiding children's reading. LITERATURE FOR THE EARLY ADOLESCENT is an in-depth study of literature and teaching techniques. Both LITERATURE AND WRITING FOR THE MIDDLE GRADES and INTEGRATED LANGUAGE ARTS FOR THE MIDDLE GRADES offer methods of planning and using literature-based programs, and both include field experiences. METHODS FOR TEACHING SECONDARY LANGUAGE ARTS is a similar course at the high school level. MULTIMEDIA APPROACH TO CHILDREN'S LITERATURE is a graduate course for students with a background in children's literature, and it focuses on the development of literacy for the classroom. English. CHILDREN'S LITERATURE is a survey, as is LITERATURE FOR ADOLESCENTS. Both are teacher preparation courses. Another

CHILDREN'S LITERATURE course is an advanced study of the historical development of children's literature.

Georgia State University. Education. READING AND LANGUAGE ARTS IN EARLY CHILDHOOD EDUCATION is a field-based course with a literature component. LITERATURE FOR MIDDLE CHILDHOOD EDUCATION introduces students to the body of literature for children. ADVANCED LITERATURE FOR MIDDLE CHILDHOOD EDUCATION places emphasis on reading motivation and reader response. COMPOSITION AND LITERATURE FOR MIDDLE CHILDHOOD EDUCATION examines developmental and theoretical foundations for teaching literature. ADOLESCENT LITERATURE examines literary instruction and selected literary works. English. THE TRADITION OF CHILDREN'S LITERATURE offers study of the origin and history of children's literature.

Kennesaw State College. Education. CHILDREN'S LITERATURE is a survey that includes approaches for teaching literature. MIDDLE GRADES AND ADOLESCENT LITERATURE reviews current and traditional works in several genres.

LaGrange College. Education. In CHILDREN'S LITERATURE students read widely and report on research. In CHILDREN'S LITERATURE AND LANGUAGE ARTS they deal with competence in the teaching of children's literature with language arts. English. LITERATURE FOR THE MIDDLE SCHOOL focuses on ways to use particular pieces of literature in the classroom.

Mercer University. Education. Two courses in CHILDREN'S LITERATURE are offered. One is a survey that includes knowledge of sources and use of books in the classroom. The other includes contemporary criticism of the literature from various fields, with a transactional approach for teaching children's literature. English. YOUNG ADULT LITERATURE places emphasis on using young adult literature as a bridge to traditional literature.

Morehouse College. Education. CHILDREN'S LITERATURE devises ways of bringing children and books together in a way that makes reading a life-long habit.

North Georgia College. Education. CHILDREN'S LITERATURE and JUVENILE LITERATURE include study of appropriate reading programs for young people and the work of important authors and illustrators.

Oglethorpe University. Education. Two CHILDREN'S LITERATURE courses are offered, both emphasizing use of children's literature in grades one through eight. LITERATURE FOR THE YOUNG CHILD is designed for teachers of ages four through nine.

Piedmont College. Education. Two courses, LANGUAGE ARTS, K–4 and LANGUAGE ARTS, 4–8 include study of the use of literature in the language arts program.

Shorter College. Education. Focus is on the interrelatedness of the language arts, including use of literature, in LANGUAGE ARTS AND LITERATURE: EARLY CHILDHOOD and LANGUAGE ARTS AND LITERATURE: MIDDLE GRADES.

Southwestern. English. Two CHILDREN'S LITERATURE courses offer teacher preparation.

Spelman College. Education. Both child development and use of books to meet childrens' needs are studied in CHILDREN'S LITERATURE. TEACHING LANGUAGE ARTS AND SOCIAL STUDIES IN THE ELEMENTARY/ MIDDLE GRADES includes use of literature in the curriculum.

University of Georgia. Education. CHILDREN'S LITERATURE addresses stimulation of children's reading. CHILDREN'S LITERATURE FOR THE MIDDLE SCHOOL surveys the literature and its use in the classroom.

Valdosta State College. Education. LITERATURE FOR MIDDLE CHILDHOOD EDUCATION is a genre survey, with emphasis on methods of presentation.

Wesleyan College. English. The goal of LITERATURE FOR CHILDREN AND ADOLESCENTS is to teach the literature and help teachers establish libraries.

West Georgia College. Education. LITERATURE FOR THE YOUNG CHILD places emphasis on the integration of literature in all curriculum areas. Education and English. LITERATURE FOR ADOLESCENTS is a study of literature appropriate for the curriculum.

HAWAII

Brigham Young University–Hawaii Campus. Education. Students examine literature for children from an educator's point of view in

CHILDREN'S LITERATURE IN THE ELEMENTARY SCHOOL. English. LITERATURE FOR ADOLESCENTS offers consideration of methods of teaching literature.

Chaminade University of Honolulu. Education. CHILDREN'S LITERATURE focuses attention on the child and teaching in a literature based program.

University of Hawaii–Hilo. Education. Both CHILDREN'S LITERATURE and ADOLESCENT LITERATURE focus on the study of recent materials in literature and their use in the curriculum. Education and English. CHILDREN AND LITERATURE relates the use of literature to social, emotional, and intellectual development.

University of Hawaii–Manoa. Education. CHILDREN'S LITERATURE and LITERATURE FOR ADOLESCENTS address using literature in the classroom. English. CHILDREN'S CLASSICS surveys literature from the seventeenth century to contemporary poetry and fiction. Library Science. MATERIALS AND SERVICES FOR CHILDREN and MATERIALS AND SERVICES FOR YOUNG ADULTS include historical surveys, research, and library services.

IDAHO

Boise State University. Education. CHILDREN'S LITERATURE provides a survey of literature, with emphasis on excellence. LITERATURE FOR YOUNG ADULTS includes a multicultural component. ADVANCED STUDY OF CHILDREN'S LITERATURE promotes development of literature activities for the classroom. English. LITERATURE FOR USE IN JUNIOR AND SENIOR HIGH SCHOOLS is a literary content course designed for teachers.

College of Idaho. Education. Criteria for selection and a genre survey are included in LITERATURE FOR CHILDREN AND ADOLESCENTS.

Idaho State University. Education. LITERATURE FOR CHILDREN includes emphasis on strategies for implementing literature study.

Lewis-Clark State College. English. YOUNG ADULT LITERATURE emphasizes techniques for developing an interest in reading that will continue into adult life.

Northwest Nazarene College. English. Suggestions for stimulating creative activities through literature are included in CHILDREN'S LITERATURE.

University of Idaho. Education. Both CHILDREN'S LITERATURE and CHILDREN'S LITERATURE AND THE CURRICULUM stress use of literature in the classroom. English. LITERATURE FOR ADOLESCENTS offers reading and appraisal of literature for students working for teacher or library certification.

ILLINOIS

Augustana College. English. CHILDREN'S LITERATURE emphasizes poetry, folk tales, and the novel. ADOLESCENT LITERATURE includes theoretical issues relevant to the teaching profession.

Aurora University. Education and English. CHILDREN'S LITERATURE is a survey course that includes bibliotherapy.

Blackburn College. Education. Extensive reading and analysis are required in LITERATURE FOR CHILDREN AND ADOLESCENTS.

Bradley University. Education. CHILDREN'S LITERATURE surveys prose and poetry for kindergarten through junior high. In ANALYSIS AND EVALUATION OF CHILDREN'S LITERATURE emphasis is on recent materials and includes current trends, controversies, and problems.

Chicago State University. Education. Teachers study the many uses of literature in the classroom in LITERATURE FOR YOUNG CHILDREN. Library Science. Selection of materials for school media centers and public libraries is part of the study in LITERATURE AND RELATED MEDIA FOR CHILDREN AND YOUNG ADULTS. STORYTELLING AND FOLK LITERATURE relates literature to storytelling and school curricula.

College of Saint Francis. Library Science. CHILDREN'S AND JUNIOR HIGH LITERATURE prepares the student to handle literature with children.

Columbia College. English. In YOUNG ADULT FICTION published novels are analyzed, but emphasis is on writing novels.

Concordia University. Education. CHILDREN'S LITERATURE: FANTASY includes reading and analysis of major works and techniques for classroom use. Education and English. CHILDREN'S LITERATURE is a general survey with consideration of the school library.

DePaul University. Education. LITERATURE FOR THE YOUNG CHILD focuses on good literature for toddlers through age seven. CHILDREN'S LITERATURE is an introduction to the various types of literature for children of different ages.

Eastern Illinois University. English. CHILDREN'S LITERATURE emphasizes wide acquaintance with the great books of world literature. THE LITERATURE OF ADOLESCENCE is a study of literature written for and about adolescents. STUDIES IN CHILDREN'S LITERATURE is a study in depth of some aspect of children's literature. Topics are announced. Library Science. National and international developments are included in STUDIES IN CHILDREN'S MATERIALS and STUDIES IN ADOLESCENT AND YOUNG ADULT MATERIALS, survey courses of library materials.

Elmhurst College. English. Emphasis is on extensive reading and evaluation of titles appropriate to children at various age levels in CHILDREN'S LITERATURE.

Eureka College. Education. A genre approach is taken to a survey in CHILDREN'S LITERATURE. TEACHING ADOLESCENT LITERATURE is an exploration in popular and classical literature for adolescents.

Governors State University. English. Psychological, cultural, and social issues related to children and literature are introduced in LITERATURE FOR CHILDREN AND ADOLESCENTS. LITERATURE OF IMMIGRANT CHILDREN is set in context with mainstream American writers and American black literature. DEVELOPING WRITING MODELS FROM CHILDREN'S LITERATURE develops models for using literature as the center of classroom oral and written composition activities.

Greenville College. English. Both CHILDREN'S LITERATURE and LITERATURE FOR ADOLESCENTS are comprehensive surveys. The first devotes attention to the historical and folklore backgrounds, and the second to contemporary literature.

Illinois Benedictine College. Education. CHILDREN'S LITERATURE stresses the importance of literature as a basis for a life-long enrichment.

Illinois College. Education. JUVENILE AND CHILDREN'S LITERATURE is an analysis of the scope and nature of literature written for children.

Illinois State University. English. Nine courses are offered. Courses that emphasize teaching the literature to children are LITERATURE FOR YOUNG CHILDREN, LITERATURE FOR PRE-ADOLESCENTS, and LITERATURE IN THE SECONDARY SCHOOL. Two courses offer study of classics and historical development: FOUNDATIONS IN LITERATURE FOR CHILDREN and STUDIES IN THE HISTORY OF LITERATURE FOR YOUNG PEOPLE. A genre course is offered in VERSE FOR CHILDREN and experience in oral transmission in STORYTELLING. Two courses vary in content and may be repeated for credit. STUDIES IN CONTEMPORARY LITERATURE FOR YOUNG PEOPLE is a problem-centered course, emphasizing trends and research. STUDIES IN LITERATURE FOR ADOLESCENTS is an advanced critical examination of the literature.

Illinois Wesleyan University. English. CHILDREN'S LITERATURE is a teacher preparation course required of elementary education majors. LITERATURE FOR ADOLESCENTS is an introduction to literature taught in the intermediate grades and high school.

Kishwaukee College. English. CHILDREN'S LITERATURE introduces students to various forms of children's literature and emphasizes investigation of motivations for reading.

Lewis University. Education. Methods for incorporating and teaching literature in the school curriculum are covered in CHILD AND ADOLESCENT LITERATURE.

Loyola University. Education. ADOLESCENT LITERATURE explores the history of adolescent literature and criteria for selection. Education and English. CHILDREN'S LITERATURE explores the history of children's literature and criteria for evaluation.

McKendree College. Education. CHILDREN'S LITERATURE is a study of the use of literature in the classroom, with inclusion of culturally and ethnically diverse materials.

National Louis University. English. Major emphasis is on content and quality of literature in a teacher preparation course, LITERATURE FOR CHILDREN.

North Central College. English. Methods of teaching and experience in writing are provided in CHILDREN'S LITERATURE.

North Park College. English. CHILDREN'S LITERATURE is a teacher preparation course with guidelines for selecting books for children.

Northeastern Illinois University. Education. LITERATURE FOR YOUNG CHILDREN prepares students for effective teaching of literature in preschool, kindergarten, and primary grades through a wide variety of activities. English. YOUNG ADULT NOVEL provides advanced study in the history of children's literature and recent publication for grades 7–10. CHILDREN'S LITERATURE is preparation for effective teaching of literature in elementary school.

Northern Illinois University. Education. The use of literature to advance language arts and social development is the focus of LITERATURE FOR THE YOUNG CHILD. EVALUATING CHILDREN'S LITERATURE gives attention to literary merit and classroom use of children's books. CHILDREN'S LITERATURE IN A MULTICULTURAL SOCIETY gives a historical and current perspective. English. Approaches to teaching literature in the secondary school are included in THE TEACHING OF LITERATURE. Education and Library Science. LIBRARY MATERIALS FOR CHILDREN includes evaluation and selection of books and audiovisual materials.

Olivet Nazarene University. Education and Library Science. CHILDREN'S LITERATURE is a survey and critical analysis.

Principia College. Education and English. The course in CHILDREN'S LITERATURE explores ethnically and culturally diverse literature and the use of literature in libraries, the classroom, and the home.

Quincy College. Education. CHILDREN'S LITERATURE addresses the enjoyment of literature and its use for curriculum enrichment. In YOUNG PEOPLE'S LITERATURE students learn methods of increasing interest in the written word.

Rockford College. Education. LITERATURE FOR CHILDREN surveys a variety of materials for children through the sixth grade.

Roosevelt University. Education. LITERATURE FOR CHILDREN AND ADOLESCENTS is an advanced course that introduces literature as reflecting literary heritage of a multicultural and ethnic society.

Rosary College. Library Science. LIBRARY MATERIALS FOR CHILDREN and LIBRARY MATERIALS FOR YOUNG ADULTS introduce the selection, evaluation, and uses of books and other materials in the curriculum and with individuals. SERVICES FOR CHILDREN AND YOUNG ADULTS places emphasis on techniques, such as workshops and storytelling, for literature sharing services.

Saint Xavier College. Education. Methods of presenting literature, bibliotherapy, and multiethnic/multicultural literature are included in LITERATURE FOR CHILDREN AND ADOLESCENTS.

Sangamon State University. Education and Library Science. CHILDREN'S LITERATURE is a survey course to aid in selecting materials for children through the elementary grades. English. CLASSICS OF CHILDREN'S LITERATURE is both a literature course and a social history of children and the family. Library Science. BOOKS FOR YOUNG PEOPLE is a survey of the adolescent literature genre.

Southern Illinois University-Carbondale. English. LITERATURE FOR THE ADOLESCENT emphasizes selection of literature for secondary school students. Library Science. LITERATURE FOR CHILDREN is a study of types of literature and the integration of literature in school settings. LIBRARY MEDIA FOR YOUNG ADULTS involves the selection and use of books and other media in junior and senior high school.

Southern Illinois University at Edwardsville. Education. CHILDREN'S LITERATURE prepares teachers to present literature to children.

Trinity Christian College. Education and English. CHILDREN'S LITERATURE relates children's reading to language arts skills.

University of Chicago. Education. SEMINAR: STORYTELLING is a seminar discussion course on issues related to narrative. READING AND ADOLESCENTS is a survey of reading patterns of adolescents and the use of materials in reading guidance. Education and English. CHILDREN, LITERATURE AND CULTURE explores many issues related to children's books, including comparison to adult literature. STORY IN THE ORAL TRADITION is a study of narrative with emphasis on theoretical background. Education and Library Science. CHILDREN'S LITERATURE is a general survey of the literature and its use with children. STORYTELLING emphasizes theoretical background and provides presentation and program planning.

University of Illinois-Urbana-Champaign. Education. CHILDREN'S LITERATURE offers a survey of the literature and its use in the school. CHILDREN'S LITERATURE IN THE CONTENT AREAS stresses effective use of literature to enrich instruction.

Western Illinois University. Library Science. CHILDREN'S LITERATURE and INTRODUCTION TO LITERATURE FOR YOUNG ADULTS are survey courses with emphasis on critical analysis and evaluation of books in various genres. CREATIVE USES OF LITERATURE FOR CHILDREN AND YOUNG ADULTS places emphasis on program development using literature. ADVANCED CHILDREN'S LITERATURE and ADVANCED LITERATURE FOR YOUNG ADULTS include historical development, problems, and trends in literature for children and young adults.

Wheaton College. English. CHILDREN'S LITERATURE is a historical survey and includes critical study in novels for children and young adults.

INDIANA

Anderson University. Education. Wide reading in a variety of children's literature is included in TEACHING THE LANGUAGE ARTS AND CHILDREN'S LITERATURE.

Ball State University. English. Four courses are offered for prospective and practicing teachers. LITERATURE FOR YOUNG CHILDREN is an introductory course. CHILDREN'S LITERATURE offers an overview and intensive study of various types. LITERATURE FOR ADOLESCENTS reviews recent literature and READING LITERATURE IN THE ENGLISH CLASSROOM emphasizes current and research bases for effective reading in the classroom. Some courses are offered at both the graduate and undergraduate levels.

Butler University. Education. SURVEY OF LITERATURE FOR CHILDREN AND YOUTH reviews the literature as well as recent research. Children's Literature includes uses of literature and field experience.

Calumet College of Saint Joseph. Education. CHILDREN'S LITERATURE is a survey of traditional and contemporary literature for kindergarten through junior high.

DePauw University. Education and English. CHILDREN'S LITERATURE is a survey of children's literature attending to its history, canon, and audience.

Franklin College of Indiana. English. CHILDREN'S LITERATURE is required for elementary education majors and includes books about other cultures and reader response.

Goshen College. Education. Extensive reading and writing a children's book are included in CHILDREN'S LITERATURE.

Grace College. Education. Intended for elementary education majors, CHILDREN'S LITERATURE requires wide reading of children's books, both traditional and modern.

Hanover College. Education. CHILDREN'S LITERATURE is a history and survey of children's literature stressing use in the elementary classroom.

Huntington College. Education. LITERATURE FOR CHILDREN AND ADOLESCENTS is designed to acquaint the student with literature available in trade books.

Indiana State University. Education. BOOKS FOR ELEMENTARY GRADES offers study of recent books and their use in the curriculum. English. CHILDREN'S LITERATURE is a teacher preparation course. Library Science. LIBRARY MATERIALS FOR CHILDREN and LIBRARY MATERIALS FOR ADOLESCENTS, offered at graduate and undergraduate levels, review history of the literature and relate its use to the needs, abilities, and interests of children and adolescents. HONORS SUMMER SEMINAR FOR HIGH SCHOOL STUDENTS is open to high school students on the completion of their junior year; the course offers topics in language, literature, and writing.

Indiana University–Bloomington. Education. BOOKS FOR READING INSTRUCTION emphasizes use of young adult literature, trade books, and non-text materials for teaching language arts in grades 5–12. TRADE BOOKS IN ELEMENTARY CLASSROOMS is a similar course for lower grades. TEACHING ADOLESCENT LITERATURE is designed to provide the secondary classroom teacher with training in incorporating literature into instructional programs. Various genres are surveyed in TRADE BOOKS AND THE TEACHER to assist teachers and others in selecting literature and using it for bibliotherapy. English. CHILDREN'S LITERATURE is a survey of historical and modern children's books. LITERATURE FOR YOUNG ADULTS is a study of books suitable for junior and senior high school use, with special emphasis on fiction dealing with problems. TEACHING CHILDREN'S LITERATURE AT THE POST-SECONDARY LEVEL covers classroom teaching in light of current approaches. SURVEY OF CHILDREN'S LITERATURE covers literature from medieval time to the present, while CHILDREN'S LITERATURE addresses issues in the critical and historical study of literature. Library Science. LIBRARY MATERIALS FOR CHILDREN AND YOUNG ADULTS covers evaluation and use of all media sources of informational and recreational reading. LIBRARY SERVICES FOR CHILDREN AND YOUNG ADULTS includes techniques in storytelling and book talks. A CRITICAL ANALYSIS OF LIBRARY MATERIALS FOR CHILDREN AND YOUNG ADULTS gives the historical development of materials and their influence on current trends. SEMINAR IN LIBRARY MATERIALS FOR CHILDREN AND YOUNG ADULTS covers research studies and problems related to library materials.

Indiana University-East. Education. TRADE BOOKS AND THE CLASSROOM TEACHER places emphasis on the use of trade books for teaching language arts and reading with children. BOOKS FOR READING INSTRUCTION examines use of young adult literature for teaching language arts. English. CHILDREN'S LITERATURE assists teachers in selecting historical and modern children's literature. Library Science. LIBRARY MATERIALS FOR CHILDREN AND YOUNG ADULTS provides evaluation and use of books and other media.

Indiana University-Kokomo. English. A study of historical and modern children's books, CHILDREN'S LITERATURE is designed to assist future teachers in selecting the best books for children.

Indiana University-Northwest. Education. BOOKS FOR READING INSTRUCTION examines the use of literature and trade books for reading instruction. English. CHILDREN'S LITERATURE is designed to assist future teachers in selecting the best books for children. Library Science. LIBRARY MATERIALS FOR CHILDREN AND YOUNG ADULTS provides evaluation and use of books and other media.

Indiana University-Purdue University at Fort Wayne. English. CHILDREN'S LITERATURE is a genre and historical survey treated from the literary-critical perspective from which pedagogical conclusions follow. LITERATURE FOR YOUNG ADULTS surveys representative literary works and is intended for any students who plan to work with young people. Library Science. LIBRARY MATERIALS FOR CHILDREN AND YOUNG ADULTS covers evaluation and use of all media, including books.

Indiana Wesleyan University. Education. CHILDREN'S LITERATURE is a study of the type of literature suitable for use in classroom teaching, and it includes field experience.

Marian College. Education. CHILDREN'S LITERATURE is the study of a variety of genres for use in and out of the classroom.

Oakland City College. English. CHILDREN'S LITERATURE includes criteria for the selection of literature for children in elementary school.

Purdue University–Lafayette. Education. CHILDREN'S BOOK ARTISTS is a historical survey of traditional and contemporary illustration techniques used in children's books. CHILDREN'S LITERATURE is a survey of modern and traditional literature for children, with emphasis on selection. ADVANCED STUDIES IN CHILDREN'S LITERATURE is a critical approach to literature and its place in the curriculum. MEDIA FOR CHILDREN is a review of books and other media for media centers. English. LITERATURE IN THE SECONDARY SCHOOLS offers an in-depth study of selected materials. THE FOLKLORE OF CHILDREN in an introduction to oral literature and games of children in America and other cultures.

Saint Francis College. Education. CHILDREN'S LITERATURE is a survey of all categories of books and their use in a literature program.

Saint Joseph's College. Education. CHILDREN'S LITERATURE places emphasis on types of literature and techniques of introducing children to literature.

Saint Mary's College. English. CHILDREN'S LITERATURE explores the various narrative forms of the classic literature for children.

Taylor University. English. CHILDREN'S LITERATURE is a study of the reading interests of children in a multicultural society, with storytelling lab.

Tri-State University. English. CHILDREN'S LITERATURE, designed to deepen the appreciation for such literature, offers opportunity for story telling and reading.

University of Evansville. Education. LITERATURE FOR THE ELEMENTARY AND ADOLESCENT CHILD covers literature, issues, and language materials for kindergarten through young adult. COMMUNICATING VALUES OF LITERATURE gives guidance in selecting materials to further the interests, tastes, and values of literature.

University of Indianapolis. Education. CHILDREN'S LITERATURE IN THE CLASSROOM stresses methods of selection and utilization. English. LITERATURE IN THE JUNIOR HIGH/MIDDLE SCHOOL covers early and modern works.

University of Notre Dame. English. CHILDREN'S LITERATURE is a study of the classics of children's literature and their relation to adult readers.

University of Southern Indiana. Library Science. LIBRARY MATERIALS FOR CHILDREN includes a history of children's books, their selection, and evaluation. LIBRARY MATERIALS FOR ADOLESCENTS includes techniques in reading guidance and attention to the gifted child and retarded reader.

Valparaiso University. English. LITERATURE FOR CHILDREN is a survey, by types, of distinguished literature. LITERATURE FOR ADOLESCENTS places emphasis on reading selected representative books.

IOWA

Briar Cliff College. English. CHILDREN'S LITERATURE covers history and types of children's literature.

Buena Vista College. Education. CHILDREN'S LITERATURE includes methods of presentation of children's poetry, drama, and prose.

Central College. English. LITERATURE FOR CHILDREN furnishes a background through wide reading of both classic and modern materials. LITERATURE FOR YOUNG ADULTS includes principles of selection, evaluation, and presentation of literature.

Coe College. Education. CHILDREN'S LITERATURE includes study of literary criticism and the survey and analysis of various forms.

Cornell College. Education. TEACHING CHILDREN'S AND ADOLESCENT LITERATURE IN THE SCHOOLS includes instructional planning and the teaching of reading.

Dordt College. Education. CHILDREN'S LITERATURE offers study of literature for use in enriching the subject areas of the curriculum and in providing good reading habits. ADOLESCENT READING INTERESTS examines the development of adolescent literature as a genre, with appreciation for enduring literature that promotes Christian perspectives.

Drake University. Education. LITERATURE FOR CHILDHOOD AND YOUTH surveys literature in various media and its use by children and youth. IMPROVING THE TEACHING OF LITERATURE places emphasis on contemporary materials with concern for literary and artistic quality.

Graceland College. English. Literature for Children is designed to increase appreciation of literature and suggest ways to use books with children.

Grand View College. English. Literature for Children and Adolescents is a genre survey and includes reader-response theory.

Iowa State University. English. The History of Children's Literature places emphasis on fantasy literature through the nineteenth century. Literature of Adolescence includes selection of literature for and about adolescents for use in school programs.

Iowa Wesleyan College. Education. Reading Children's Literature includes methods of teaching literature for grades K through 6 and practice in storytelling and reading aloud. English. Readings in Literature for Adolescents familiarizes students with the individualized reading program in the public schools and provides an opportunity for extensive reading.

Loras College. Education. Children's Literature is a survey and critical analysis of books for children.

Luther College. Education. Children's Literature is the study of the literature and its use in the elementary school classroom. English. Adolescent Literature is a course designed for teaching majors.

Maharishi International University. Literature for Children offers study of children's classics using the qualities of the unified field as a means of analysis. Writing ideal literature for children is included.

Marycrest College. Education. Children's Literature offers wide reading and study of the components of a well-balanced literature program. Literature for the Adolescent and Young Adults covers junior novels and adult literature of interest to young adults. Literature for Children and Young Adults relates literary pieces to curriculum areas, with strategies for promoting life-long reading habits.

Mount Mercy College. Education. Children's Literature exposes students to literature through wide reading, with emphasis on implementation of a literature program in the elementary school. Adolescent Literature emphasizes the role of the teacher in the selection of appropriate literature.

Northwestern College. Education. CHILDREN'S LITERATURE is an introduction to the selection of literature for elementary school students.

Saint Ambrose University. Education. CHILD AND ADOLESCENT LITERATURE is a lecture/laboratory course to prepare teachers to present literature to adolescents and children.

Simpson College. Education. JUVENILE LITERATURE is an intensive study of literature for children with reference to their needs and interests.

Teikyo Westmar University. Education. CHILDREN'S LITERATURE is a critical study of varied types of literature available to children. English. ADOLESCENT LITERATURE is a study of the literature of adolescence with emphasis on recent publications.

University of Iowa. Education. LITERATURE FOR CHILDREN I is a general survey course, including recent trends and issues. LITERATURE FOR CHILDREN II includes multimedia approaches to promote pleasure and insight. LITERATURE FOR ADOLESCENTS offers reading and evaluation of literature for junior and senior high school students. READING CHILDREN'S CLASSICS AND AWARD BOOKS includes research pertaining to children's responses to these books. Education and Library Science. LITERATURE AND STORYTELLING FOR CHILDREN offers experience in planning and presenting story programs. Library Science. HISTORY OF BOOKS FOR YOUNG PEOPLE surveys oral tradition through the mid-twentieth century and includes a research project. LIBRARY MATERIALS FOR CHILDREN surveys fiction and nonfiction books and audiovisual formats for preadolescents. LIBRARY MATERIALS FOR ADOLESCENTS is a similar course.

University of Northern Iowa. Education. CHILDREN'S LITERATURE emphasizes ability to evaluate library materials. LITERATURE FOR ELEMENTARY CHILDREN is an advanced course. English. LITERATURE FOR YOUNG ADULTS offers reading and evaluation of literature. Library Science. LIBRARY MATERIALS FOR CHILDREN is a survey of school media, with use of books in the curriculum. LIBRARY MATERIALS FOR YOUNG ADULTS covers selection and evaluation of curricular-related materials. HISTORY OF CHILDREN'S LITERATURE places emphasis on significant authors and illustrators.

Upper Iowa University. English. LITERATURE FOR CHILDREN AND ADOLESCENTS is a survey of literature and its use in the classroom.

Wartburg College. English. LITERATURE AND COMPOSITION FOR JUNIOR AND SENIOR HIGH SCHOOLS is a writing intensive course that prepares secondary English teachers. CHILDREN'S LITERATURE is a concentrated study of genres with criteria for evaluation.

William Penn College. English. CHILDREN AND BOOKS gives attention to the selection of good literature and the technique of story telling. ADOLESCENT LITERATURE is a survey of books that highlight coming-of-age dilemmas.

KANSAS

Baker University. Education. CHILDREN'S LITERATURE surveys history and genres in a course designed for future teachers.

Benedictine College. Education. CHILDREN'S LITERATURE is a study of traditional and modern literature and its presentation to children.

Bethany College. Education. CHILDREN'S LITERATURE gives attention to literary value and structure in a survey of genres. English. ADOLESCENT LITERATURE is an introduction to literature written about and for adolescents; the course emphasizes formal literary analysis.

Bethel College. English. CHILDREN'S LITERATURE introduces a wide variety of literature, emphasizing its selection and presentation to children.

Emporia State University. English. YOUNG ADULT LITERATURE emphasizes the use of literature in the English/Language Arts classroom. Library Science. CHILDREN'S LITERATURE is an introduction that includes use in the classroom.

Fort Hays State University. Education. CHILDREN'S LITERATURE offers opportunity to participate in storytelling and book selection. CHILDREN'S LITERATURE AND READING IN EARLY CHILDHOOOD gives the student a wide background in literature with emphasis on reading skills. ADVANCED LITERATURE FOR CHILDREN AND ADOLESCENTS is designed for those who have some background in literature for these ages. English. YOUNG ADULT LITERATURE is a study of literature suitable for secondary school classrooms.

Friends University. Education. CHILDREN'S LITERATURE enables students to choose material for the school library and to enjoy books.

Kansas Newman College. Education. LITERATURE FOR CHILDREN AND ADOLESCENTS gives special attention to literature of different cultural and ethnic groups.

Kansas State University. English. WRITING CHILDREN'S LITERATURE gives practice in writing book-length or magazine-length prose. LITERATURE FOR CHILDREN provides an opportunity for reading and evaluating books for children. LITERATURE FOR ADOLESCENTS includes selecting, reading, and evaluating books for adolescents.

Kansas Wesleyan College. Education. In CHILD AND ADOLESCENT LITERATURE, reading sensitively is the major emphasis, with attention to issues related to teaching literature.

McPherson College. English. CHILDREN'S LITERATURE is a historical review and a study of selection criteria for each genre. ADOLESCENT LITERATURE reviews themes appealing to adolescents.

Mid-America Nazarene College. Education. CHILDREN'S LITERATURE is a survey and evaluation of different types of literature.

Ottawa University. Education. ADOLESCENT LITERATURE is an examination of a wide range of literary works and their use in school programs. CHILDREN'S LITERATURE places emphasis on ways to make reading a lifetime involvement.

Saint Mary of the Plains College. English and Library Science. LITERATURE FOR YOUNG ADULTS includes consideration of modern issues and selection of books for young people. Education and Library Science. CHILDREN'S LITERATURE introduces current trends and the evaluation of selection tools.

Southwestern College. Education. READING IN THE ELEMENTARY SCHOOL includes children's literature and its interrelation in the language arts program. Education and English. CHILDREN'S LITERATURE explores contemporary issues relevant to use of literature in the classroom.

Sterling College. English. CHILD AND ADOLESCENT LITERATURE is a study of traditional and modern literature.

Tabor College. Education. CHILDREN'S LITERATURE involves reading, discussing, and evaluating stories, poems, and factual material. English. YOUNG ADULT LITERATURE is an analysis and evaluation of literature.

University of Kansas. Education. Both TEACHING YOUNG ADULT LITERATURE and TEACHING LITERATURE FOR YOUNG ADULTS offer students opportunities to read and evaluate the literature and to learn methods for presenting it effectively. LANGUAGE AND LITERATURE IN THE READING PROGRAM includes strategies for promoting the enjoyment of reading with children's literature.

Washburn University of Topeka. Education. TEACHING LANGUAGE ARTS AND JUVENILE LITERATURE IN THE ELEMENTARY/MIDDLE SCHOOL gives emphasis to interrelationship between literature and the language arts skills. ADVANCED CHILDREN'S LITERATURE explores a variety of literary forms with emphasis on evaluation and incorporating literature across the curriculum. English. LITERATURE FOR YOUNG ADULTS covers the history of young adult literature and its use in language arts. TEACHING LITERATURE TO CHILDREN surveys trade books, selection, and the role of literature in the curriculum. LITERATURE FOR CHILDREN offers wide reading in the great literature of the past and present.

Wichita State University. Education. CHILDREN'S LITERATURE allows students to examine books and activities suitable for use with children in preschool and elementary grades. LITERATURE FOR ADOLESCENTS calls for wide reading of all genres and studies of readers' responses. LITERATURE-BASED READING PROGRAMS emphasizes extending literature and media through the reading environment, language arts, and the arts.

KENTUCKY

Alice Lloyd College. Education. In both courses, CHILDREN'S LITERATURE and LITERATURE FOR THE MIDDLE SCHOOL STUDENT, books and other materials are surveyed, and prospective teachers develop creative methods for presentation.

Asbury College. English. CHILDREN'S LITERATURE and EARLY ADOLESCENT LITERATURE are designed for prospective teachers. They are survey courses.

Bellarmine College. Education. A historical survey course, LITERATURE FOR CHILDREN AND YOUTH, is offered.

Berea College. Education. English. Two courses, CHILDREN'S LITERATURE and ADOLESCENT LITERATURE, offered through both Education and English, are designed for teacher education. They emphasize incorporating literature into the curriculum as well as recreational reading.

Brescia College. Education. CHILDREN'S LITERATURE provides an overview of literature appropriate for elementary grades. ADOLESCENT LITERATURE fulfills a requirement for the Provisional Certificate for Teaching in the Middle Grades.

Centre College. English. Literary considerations are emphasized in CHILDREN'S LITERATURE, a course for teachers.

Cumberland College. Education. CHILDREN'S LITERATURE offers laboratory experience in storytelling, puppetry, and other dramatic aids. English. ADOLESCENT LITERATURE is designed for teachers at the middle school level.

Eastern Kentucky University. Library Science. Four courses are offered. Together, three courses, CHILDREN'S LITERATURE AND RELATED MATERIALS, LITERATURE AND RELATED MATERIALS FOR TRANSESCENTS, and LITERATURE AND RELATED MATERIALS FOR YOUNG ADULTS, present literature and media to support the curriculum from ages one to 15 and older. They are intended for teachers and school librarians. ADVANCED CHILDREN'S LITERATURE, for librarians and teachers, explores the characteristics of good reading.

Georgetown College. Education. Laboratory experience in schools is provided as part of LITERATURE FOR CHILDREN AND YOUTH. Many types of literature-based activities are explored.

Kentucky Christian College. Education. CHILDREN'S LITERATURE is a historical survey course. All types of literature except textbooks are studied. ADOLESCENT LITERATURE is a similar course.

Kentucky State University. English. The courses offered, CHILDREN'S LITERATURE and ADOLESCENT LITERATURE, are intended for teacher preparation.

Lindsey Wilson College. Education. CHILDREN'S LITERATURE offers training and experience in ways to share books with children in grades K–4. LITERATURE FOR GRADES 5–8 is a similar course.

Midway College. Education. LITERATURE AND LANGUAGE FOR YOUNG

CHILDREN is an in-depth study of the development of language in young children; the course includes study of literature.

Morehead State University. Education. Two courses offer historical surveys of literature and methods for using books with children and preadolescents: LITERATURE AND MATERIALS FOR YOUNG READERS and LITERATURE AND MATERIALS FOR THE PREADOLESCENT. Library Science. A course similar to those offered by Education, LITERATURE AND MATERIALS FOR YOUNG PEOPLE, offers study of literature for and reading interests and needs of young people grades 7 through 12.

Murray State University. Education. Three courses are offered. CHILDREN'S LITERATURE is for students seeking the elementary certificate. An intensive study of poetry is offered in POETRY FOR CHILDREN, and READINGS AND RESEARCH IN CHILDREN'S LITERATURE offers in-depth study in chosen areas, using an individualized approach. English. LITERATURE FOR ADOLESCENTS is for teachers preparing to teach in junior or senior high school. Library Science. CHILDREN'S LITERATURE covers book and non-book materials, selection aids, trends in publishing, and special emphasis on picture books. HISTORY OF CHILDREN'S LITERATURE traces the development of the children's literary movement and current use of children's classics.

Northern Kentucky University. English. CHILDREN'S LITERATURE is for students seeking the provisional elementary certificate.

Pikeville College. English. A survey of children's literature and its effective use in the classroom is offered in CHILDREN'S LITERATURE.

Thomas More College. Education. Students acquire a knowledge base of authors and books and the role of literature in teaching in CHILDREN'S LITERATURE and ADOLESCENT LITERATURE.

Transylvania University. Education. CHILDREN'S LITERATURE is a course that surveys the history of children's literature, genres, and field experience in introducing literature to children. Students write a children's book.

University of Kentucky. Education. CHILDREN'S LITERATURE is offered at two levels. Both courses are designed to acquaint teachers with children's books and their use in the curriculum. Library Science. Five courses are offered. Books and media are studied in CHILDREN'S LITERATURE AND RELATED MATERIALS, LITERATURE AND RELATED

MATERIALS FOR EARLY ADOLESCENCE, and INFORMATION RESOURCES AND SERVICES FOR YOUNG ADULTS. These three courses cover the literature from preschool through age 20. CRITICAL ANALYSIS OF CHILDREN'S LITERATURE offers advanced study, with a project requiring extensive critical reading. In CREATIVE LIBRARY PROGRAMS FOR CHILDREN, the emphasis is on the oral tradition.

University of Louisville. Education. ADOLESCENT LITERATURE prepares teachers for middle and senior high schools.

Western Kentucky University. Education. LITERATURE FOR YOUNG ADULTS and CHILDREN'S LITERATURE prepare teachers for high school, middle school, and elementary school. ADVANCED CHILDREN'S LITERATURE, also for teachers, includes book reviewing.

LOUISIANA

Centenary College of Louisiana. Education. CHILDREN'S LITERATURE helps teachers learn to use literature throughout the curriculum and to develop and foster a love of reading.

Grambling State University. Education. Five courses are offered, all focused on librarian or teacher education. BOOKS AND RELATED MATERIALS FOR CHILDREN and BOOKS AND RELATED MATERIALS FOR ADOLESCENTS give opportunities for wide reading of books and examination of print and non-print materials. CHILDREN'S LITERATURE gives emphasis to the study of literature as a cultural expression of a people. LITERATURE IN EARLY CHILDHOOD EDUCATION is designed for teachers of preschool and primary-aged children. Laboratory activities are included. LITERATURE FOR CHILDREN AND YOUTH covers historical development and current trends. Practicum experiences and study of bibliotherapy are included.

Louisiana College. Education. CHILDREN'S LITERARY EXPERIENCE requires five hours of weekly observation and participation.

Louisiana State University and Agricultural and Mechanical College. Education. TEACHING LITERATURE IN THE ELEMENTARY SCHOOL covers integration of literature in the total curriculum. Library Science. Three courses address print and non-print for needs of special age groups— MEDIA AND SERVICES FOR CHILDREN, MEDIA AND SERVICES FOR YOUNG ADOLESCENTS, and MEDIA AND SERVICES FOR YOUNG ADULTS.

Psychological development and techniques for communication with parents and teachers are included. THE ART AND PRACTICE OF STORY-TELLING includes planning story programs for libraries and television.

Louisiana State University–Shreveport. Library Science. Two courses, LIBRARY MATERIALS FOR ADOLESCENTS and LIBRARY MATERIALS FOR CHILDREN, provide surveys of the literature and media and uses of materials with children and young adults.

Loyola University. Education. Students taking CHILDREN'S LITERA-TURE study the literature and its uses in the elementary school, with dramatization, storytelling, and field experience included.

McNeese State University. Library Science. CHILDREN'S LITERATURE AND RELATED MATERIALS is a survey of books and related materials. CHILDREN'S AND ADOLESCENT LITERATURE offers critical evaluation of library resources.

Nicholls State University. Library Science. Evaluation and selection of materials for particular age levels is addressed in BOOKS AND MATERIALS FOR CHILDREN'S LITERATURE.

Northeast Louisiana University. Library Science. Three courses, CHILDREN'S LITERATURE, YOUNG ADULT LITERATURE, and LITERATURE FOR CHILDREN AND YOUNG ADULTS survey the literature for all age groups as related to curriculum.

Northwestern State University. Education. Curriculum support and recreational reading are studied in LIBRARY MATERIALS FOR CHILDREN and LIBRARY MATERIALS FOR YOUNG ADULTS. Library Science. Selec-tion and evaluation of print and non-print materials, as well as sources and uses of the materials are addressed in BOOKS AND MATERIALS FOR CHILDREN and BOOKS AND MATERIALS FOR YOUNG ADULTS.

Our Lady of Holy Cross College. Education and Library Science. LITERATURE FOR CHILDREN AND YOUTH helps students identify factors in using and interpreting library materials, including reference books, in relation to the school curriculum. Library Science. Books and materials for the secondary school library are studied in ADOLESCENT LITERATURE.

Southeastern Louisiana University. Library Science. BOOKS AND RELATED MATERIALS FOR CHILDREN and BOOKS AND RELATED

MATERIALS FOR YOUNG PEOPLE are comprehensive courses that include extensive reading and evaluation of the library in relation to the educational program. CHILDREN'S LITERATURE is a research course and includes consideration of bibliotherapy. French. Hungarian. Italian. Spanish. Each of these departments offers a study of the cultural heritage of the literature and culture as reflected in stories, songs, rhymes, and games.

Southern University and Agricultural and Mechanical College. Education. CHILDREN'S LITERATURE prepares teachers to teach children's literature and to use literature with children in the elementary school. Library Science. Books and other materials to enrich the school curriculum are studied in BOOKS AND RELATED MATERIALS FOR YOUNG PEOPLE.

Tulane University. Education. CHILDREN'S LITERATURE is a study and evaluation of selections in verse, story, and drama. CHILDREN'S FOLKLORE places emphasis on preparation of individuals to work with children from non–United States linguistic and cultural communities.

University of New Orleans. Library Science. CHILDREN'S LITERATURE and ADOLESCENT LITERATURE deal with the selection, evaluation, and use of books and materials. Also covered is the role of literature in curriculum supplementation. HISTORY OF CHILDREN'S LITERATURE is a historical survey of text and illustration. Selection and use of literature with gifted youngsters, along with a review of research relating to their reading behavior, are the subject matter of LITERATURE FOR THE GIFTED CHILD.

University of Southwestern Louisiana. English. Historically significant British and American literature is the subject of critical study in HISTORY OF CHILDREN'S LITERATURE and THEMES AND ISSUES IN CHILDREN'S LITERATURE. Library Science. The use of literature in relation to the interests, needs, and curriculum of children and youth is studied in CHILDREN'S LITERATURE and LITERATURE FOR YOUNG ADULTS.

MAINE

Saint Joseph's College. Education. Emphasis in a survey course, CHILDREN'S LITERATURE WITH PRE-PROFESSIONAL FIELD EXPERIENCE, is on establishing literary criteria and thoughtful evaluation of literature.

University of Maine-Farmington. Education. CHILDREN'S LITERATURE and LITERATURE FOR CHILDREN offer an overview of the historical development of children's literature with an emphasis on developing criteria for selecting and evaluating books for the school and public library. LITERATURE FOR YOUNG ADULTS is the study of the development of literature as it is used in the junior high and secondary school and public library. STORYTELLING is designed for teachers, librarians, or individuals interested in this art.

University of Maine-Fort Kent. Education. CHILDREN'S LITERATURE offers techniques for teachers to use in encouraging children to read.

University of Maine-Machias. Education. JUVENILE LITERATURE is a course which encourages extensive reading of literature for young people, while developing standards and criteria for discriminating between works of good and poor quality.

University of New England. Education. In LANGUAGE ARTS AND CHILDREN'S LITERATURE the rich world of children's literature is explored and emphasized as the force that binds the language arts together.

MARYLAND

Baltimore Hebrew University. Education. In TEACHING HEBREW READING AND LITERATURE, materials from Hebrew sources are used to build a developmental reading program. Students use a variety of methods for teaching Bible stories, including arts and crafts and drama, in TEACHING BIBLE STORIES TO YOUNG CHILDREN.

Bowie State University. Education. A study of literature and its use in the classroom is covered in LITERATURE FOR CHILDREN, PROCESS SEMINAR IN EARLY CHILDHOOD EDUCATION – CHILDREN'S LITERATURE, LEVEL I, and LITERATURE FOR CHILDREN. The first course is an orientation to the history, trends, value, and content of the literature, and the last provides field work and projects. English. LITERATURE FOR ADOLESCENTS is a survey of genres, both current and classic, for teacher preparation.

College of Notre Dame of Maryland. Education. CHILDREN'S LITERATURE offers critical analysis of selected books and trends in modern books.

Columbia Union College. English. Two courses, CHILDREN'S LITERATURE and ADOLESCENT LITERATURE, are designed to prepare teachers to choose quality literature.

Coppin State College. English. Teachers learn to help children and adolescents approach quality literature in CHILDREN'S LITERATURE and ADOLESCENT LITERATURE.

Frostburg State University. Education. The use of literary materials in teaching is studied in CHILDREN'S LITERATURE. English. ADOLESCENT LITERATURE offers contemporary and classical works appropriate for or written especially for adolescents.

Hood College. Education. Three courses in CHILDREN'S LITERATURE are offered. All are survey courses for teacher preparation. Development of a classroom library, storytelling, and motivational techniques are some topics addressed. English. LITERATURE FOR ADOLESCENTS is an overview that focuses on authors and themes, with emphasis on contemporary material.

Loyola College. Education. Three courses are offered. CHILDREN'S LITERATURE is an introduction to the literature and how it contributes to child development. THE USE OF LITERATURE IN THE READING PROGRAM incorporates the latest research and methods of teaching reading through children's literature. LITERATURE FOR ADOLESCENTS emphasizes teaching of the novel, short story, poetry, and drama. English. ADOLESCENT LITERATURE: LEWIS AND TOLKIEN gives students an opportunity to concentrate on reading the works of J.R.R. Tolkien and C.S. Lewis. ENCHANTED WORLDS: WRITING CHILDREN'S LITERATURE considers what makes a children's book a classic as well as the current trends in children's publishing.

Montgomery College–Rockville Campus. Education. CHILDREN'S LITERATURE is a survey course for teachers of children in preschool through elementary grades.

Morgan State University. English. LITERATURE FOR ADOLESCENTS is designed for prospective teachers of secondary English.

Mount Saint Mary's College. Education. The integration of children's literature and media techniques is stressed for application in the classroom in CHILDREN'S LITERATURE.

Towson State University. Education. The importance of literature in the curriculum is studied in CHILDREN'S LITERATURE and YOUNG ADULT LITERATURE. The selection and presentation of stories for children are the focus of STORYTELLING.

University of Maryland–Baltimore County College. Education. The literature for age groups from preschool through 18 years is studied in ADOLESCENT LITERATURE and CHILDREN'S LITERATURE. Teaching strategies, development of critical skills, and many genres are covered. Emphases vary in different presentations of SEMINAR IN CHILDREN'S AND ADOLESCENT LITERATURE, and the course may be taken twice for credit.

University of Maryland–College Park. Education. LITERATURE FOR CHILDREN AND YOUTH offers analysis of literary materials for children and youth, both historical and contemporary. ISSUES AND TRENDS IN CHILDREN'S LITERATURE is the study of trends in publishing, advertising, censorship, media adaptation, and reading habits. TEACHING LANGUAGE, READING, DRAMA AND LITERATURE WITH YOUNG CHILDREN is the introduction to the teaching of reading in the context of the language arts. LITERATURE FOR ADOLESCENTS covers fiction and nonfiction, and current theory and methods of instruction. Library Science. CHILDREN'S LITERATURE AND MATERIALS is a survey of literature and other materials as they relate to the needs, interests, and capabilities of young readers. Literary sources and instruction and practice in oral techniques are offered in STORYTELLING: MATERIALS AND TECHNIQUES. ADVANCED SEMINAR IN CHILDREN'S LITERATURE includes historical aspects, individual authors, and major themes and trends in literature.

Villa Julie College. Education. Methods of teaching a variety of genres are addressed in CHILDREN'S LITERATURE and LITERATURE FOR ADOLESCENTS.

MASSACHUSETTS

American International College. Education. TEACHING LANGUAGE ARTS AND CHILDREN'S LITERATURE is a general study of the field of literature for children and ways to encourage its reading by children. Integration of literature with language arts is also addressed.

Anna Maria College. Education. LANGUAGE ARTS AND CHILDREN'S LITERATURE provides an appreciation of traditional and modern literature for children, and use in the teaching of language arts studied.

Boston College. Education. In CHILDREN'S LITERATURE special emphasis is given to understanding the use of children's literature in preschool and elementary classrooms. English. STUDIES IN CHILDREN'S LITERATURE covers some of the major texts in children's literature, with the reading varying from one semester to another. Students taking 19TH-CENTURY CHILDREN'S LITERATURE will explore the relations between the traditional fairy tale and the children's book in the nineteenth century.

Boston University. Education. CHILDREN'S LITERATURE: OVERVIEW is a survey course for teachers and people preparing to become media specialists.

Bradford College. Education. CHILDREN'S LITERATURE: OVERVIEW is a survey of print and non-print for prospective teachers. English. YOUNG ADULT LITERATURE provides an introduction to stylistics and ways to enhance the teaching of language arts.

Curry College. Education. TEACHING READING, WRITING AND CHILDREN'S LITERATURE, PARTS I AND II covers literature and language arts for all elementary grades.

Eastern Nazarene College. Education. The use of literature in the reading program is explored in THE TEACHING OF READING AND CHILDREN'S LITERATURE.

Elms College. Education. A broad overview of the field of young adult literature, including reading guidance, is offered in SURVEY OF YOUNG ADULT LITERATURE. ISSUES IN CHILDREN'S LITERATURE, a survey of literature for nursery through grade six, offers field experiences and requires a research paper.

Endicott College. Education. In LITERATURE FOR CHILDREN historical and current literature is examined, with attention to introduction of children to literature and enhancement of reading appreciation.

Fitchburg State College. Education. Improvement of reading skills and motivating reading are considered in TEACHING READING THROUGH CHILDREN'S LITERATURE. English. CHILDREN'S LITERATURE and LITERATURE FOR YOUNG ADULTS are historical and genre surveys studied in the context of childhood and society. CHILDREN'S LITERATURE emphasizes myth and folktales, social problems, and multiethnic concerns of current literature. The place of literature in the classroom for middle and secondary school levels is the focus of LITERATURE IN THE CLASSROOM: READERS, TEXTS, AND TEACHERS. LITERATURE FOR YOUNG ADULTS introduces recent books suitable for use in middle, junior high, and senior high school. THE ROBERT CORMIER COLLECTION makes use of the special manuscript collection to study the works of this author.

Framingham State College. Education. READING, LANGUAGE ARTS, CHILDREN'S LITERATURE, AN INTERDISCIPLINARY APPROACH includes the philosophy, methodology and materials for a balanced diagnostic reading program. English. Three courses for prospective teachers, LITERATURE FOR CHILDREN, LITERATURE FOR YOUNG ADULTS, and CONTEMPORARY TRENDS IN LITERATURE FOR CHILDREN, offer historical and genre surveys, introduction to bibliographic tools, problems of censorship, social concerns, and reviewing.

Gordon College. Education. Field experience is required for CHILDREN'S LITERATURE and ADOLESCENT LITERATURE, courses that offer techniques for introducing literature across the curriculum.

Lesley College. Education. Wide reading is required in LITERATURE FOR CHILDREN AND YOUNG ADULTS, a course that prepares teachers to use literature across the curriculum.

Merrimack College. Education. ELEMENTARY SCHOOL TEACHING: CHILDREN'S LITERATURE, LANGUAGE ARTS AND SOCIAL STUDIES is a course in which each component of the language arts and social studies is studied separately in relation to literature.

North Adams State College. Education. Prospective teachers develop knowledge of the literature, sensitivity in selecting books, and skill in utilizing them within the class setting in LITERATURE FOR CHILDREN AND YOUNG ADULTS.

Pine Manor College. Education. Emphasis is placed on the classroom teacher's use of books to teach subject matter in THE USE OF CHILDREN'S BOOKS IN PRESCHOOL AND ELEMENTARY EDUCATION. English. CHILDREN'S LITERATURE, FEMALE IMAGES AND GENDER ROLES offers the opportunity to study principles of literary analysis and to trace changing social attitudes toward women through the study of children's literature.

Salem State College. Education. LITERATURE FOR EARLY CHILDHOOD and LITERATURE IN THE ELEMENTARY GRADES require wide reading and prepare teachers to present literature in a creative and imaginative manner. MYTH, FOLKLORE, AND LEGENDS IN CHILDREN'S LITERATURE, while useful for those preparing to work with children, is directed at a wider audience. Includes some study of comparative literature. INTERNSHIP IN CHILDREN'S LITERATURE provides an opportunity to work in areas of the individual's academic interests. English. LITERATURE FOR YOUNG ADULTS is a teacher preparation course at the junior high level.

Simmons College. CHILDREN'S LITERATURE is a genre and historical survey.

Springfield College. Education. In CHILDREN'S LITERATURE, students learn to appreciate and present literature in a variety of ways and to relate it to other arts. In LITERATURE FOR YOUNG PEOPLE, young people's classics are studied for their universal appeal.

Stonehill College. Education. READING THROUGH CHILDREN'S LITERATURE emphasizes children's literature as the foundation of a developmental reading program.

University of Lowell. Education. Development of a literature program is addressed in LITERATURE FOR CHILDREN and LITERATURE FOR YOUNG ADULTS. In LITERATURE FOR CHILDREN literature across the curriculum in a multi-ethnic, multi-cultural environment is addressed. Students explore various topics as they relate to children's literature in SEMINAR: ISSUES, THEMES AND RESEARCH IN CHILDREN'S AND YOUNG ADULT LITERATURE.

University of Massachusetts–Amherst. Education. SURVEY OF CHILDREN'S LITERATURE surveys traditional and recent examples. Approaches for classroom use are included in CHILDREN'S LITERATURE. ISSUES IN CHILDREN'S LITERATURE is an advanced seminar dealing with issues of social significance, while ETHNIC LITERATURE AND THE ADOLESCENT EXPERIENCE examines how adolescent members of minority groups respond to problems stemming from acculturation and discrimination. English. MYTH, FOLK TALE, AND CHILDREN'S LITERATURE examines both the relationship of traditional fairy tales to contemporary children's literature, and the relationship of the literature to the development of the child. CHILDREN'S LITERATURE EAST AND WEST is a study of Far Eastern children's literature. CHILDREN'S LITERATURE is an exploration of books published over the past two hundred years, with attention to changing conceptions of child development. Theoretical questions of genre, audience relationship, and cultural setting are addressed in Seminar: Aspects of Children's Literature.

University of Massachusetts–Boston. English. In both Children's Literature and The History of Children's Literature a critical and historical approach is taken, with the works considered in the context of their historical and cultural settings. Three courses, two of them genre-specific, are aimed at graduate students interested in pedagogical theory and strategies for teaching high school and college students. They are The Teaching of Literature, The Teaching of Poetry, and The Teaching of Fantasy and Science Fiction.

University of Massachusetts–Dartmouth. Education. Children's Literature in the Elementary School is a survey of reading materials available for children. Writing for children is included.

Westfield State College. Education. Children's Literature provides teachers with a background of the major objectives and purposes for children's literature in today's classroom. Literature and the Language Arts provides the prospective teacher with an introduction to literature/language arts programs. English. Literature and the Adolescent offers guidance to teachers who wish to improve the way they teach literature to their students.

Wheaton College. English. Children's Literature provides an in-depth survey focused on appreciating the texts as literature while addressing their responsiveness to children's needs and interests.

Wheelock College. Education. Children's Literature helps students develop a sensitivity to qualities in literature which are meaningful to children. Also addressed are major areas of controversy in the field.

Worcester State College. Education. Literature for Young Children, Children's Literature, and Literature in the Classroom all offer surveys of quality literature and its use in the classroom.

MICHIGAN

Adrian College. Education. Field experience and the laboratory study of the structure of learning are part of Clinical Experience. Literature Appreciation. English. A genre and historical survey designed for students preparing for elementary teaching of library work.

Andrews University. English. LITERATURE FOR YOUNG ADULTS is designed for parents and for the preparation of secondary English teachers and librarians.

Aquinas College. Education. The selection, evaluation, and promotion of literature are addressed in CHILDREN'S LITERATURE and LITERATURE FOR YOUNG ADULTS.

Calvin College. Education. Several courses are offered. LITERATURE FOR THE ADOLESCENT and STUDIES IN ANALYTICAL APPROACHES TO THE TEACHING OF LITERATURE offer a survey and evaluation of adolescent literature, along with theoretical considerations underlying approaches to teaching literature at the secondary level. RECENT LITERATURE FOR CHILDREN is a survey and evaluation course with approaches to the teaching of children's literature. TEACHING READING THROUGH LITERATURE is an investigation of the development of reading skills in elementary school children through the use of literary materials. English. Students apply literary standards and read intensively in CHILDREN'S LITERATURE and ADOLESCENT LITERATURE.

Central Michigan University. English. THE HISTORY OF CHILDREN'S LITERATURE examines major trends as they emerged in England, America, and Europe. Emphasis is on literary analysis. AMERICAN MINORITIES REFLECTED IN ADOLESCENT AND CHILDREN'S LITERATURE focuses on the exploration of the literary and cultural heritage of American minorities. THE HEROIC TRADITION IN CHILDREN'S LITERATURE is a study of the hero and includes modern examples. CHILDREN'S LITERATURE OF THE EMERGING NATIONS looks at modern and folk literature suitable for youth. FANTASY FOR YOUTH puts emphasis on contemporary types. CHILDREN'S LITERATURE and READING GUIDANCE FOR ADOLESCENTS include use of literature with children and adolescents as well as study of the literature. Special problems in children's literature are studied in SEMINAR IN CHILDREN'S LITERATURE.

Concordia College. Education. Two general surveys are offered that include teaching methods: CHILDREN'S LITERATURE and LITERATURE FOR YOUNG ADULTS.

Eastern Michigan University. Education. LITERATURE FOR YOUNG ADULTS includes techniques of reading guidance as well as study of the literature. English. The Master of Arts in English with Concentration in Children's Literature is offered. It provides an opportunity for advanced studies in all major areas of children's literature, folklore, mythology and writing for children. According to the catalog, "Candidates usually begin with an introduction to the major genres of children's literature. ... A second course is devoted to methods of teaching literature to children. ... A third course traces the historical development of children's literature. ... In addition, there is a special topics course that varies from semester to semester and can be repeated for credit."

Courses offered by the department include INTRODUCTION TO CHILDREN'S LITERATURE, CHILDREN'S LITERATURE: CRITICISM AND RESPONSE, CONTROVERSY IN CHILDREN'S LITERATURE, MAJOR GENRES IN CHILDREN'S LITERATURE, TEACHING CHILDREN'S LITERATURE, HISTORY OF CHILDREN'S LITERATURE, CRITICAL APPROACHES TO MYTHOLOGY, WISDOM OF THE PEOPLE: BALLADS, LEGENDS AND TALES, LITERATURE FOR EARLY CHILDHOOD, SPECIAL TOPICS. Some recent topics in SPECIAL TOPICS have included Literature for Younger Children, Recent Fiction, Poetry for Children, The Golden Age of Children's Literature, Fantasy for Children and Young People.

Ferris State University. English. In CHILDREN'S LITERATURE AND ADOLESCENT LITERATURE emphasis is on the selection and evaluation of literature and its use in the classroom.

Grand Valley State University. Education. LITERATURE FOR CHILDREN AND ADOLESCENTS is a teacher preparation course. English. Classic and contemporary materials of importance, teaching strategies, issues, and research are introduced in TEACHING LITERATURE TO CHILDREN and TEACHING LITERATURE TO ADOLESCENTS.

Hillsdale College. English. An examination of literature for children from preschool age through the elementary grades is provided in CHILDREN'S LITERATURE.

Lake Superior State University. Education. Readings are for use with children from birth through kindergarten in EARLY CHILDHOOD LITERATURE.

Marygrove College. Education. A historical and categorical survey of books for children and adolescents is provided in CHILDREN'S LITERATURE.

Northern Michigan University. Education. In CHILDREN'S LITERATURE students are introduced to a study of the literature program in the school. DIRECTED STUDY IN CHILDREN'S LITERATURE provides individual study of a significant topic. The literature for children, ideas about the literature, and ideas about teaching the literature are studied in RECENT CHILDREN'S LITERATURE. English. FOLKLORE/SCIENCE FICTION FOR YOUNG ADULTS is a course for teachers. Library Science. LITERATURE FOR YOUNG ADULTS is a comprehensive study of books for young adults designed for secondary school teachers and librarians.

Oakland University. Education. Seven courses are offered. In LITERATURE FOR CHILDREN, students learn to evaluate literature and use it effectively with children. PERSPECTIVES IN LITERATURE focuses on literature as an art. STORYTELLING AND CREATIVE DRAMATICS focuses on imaginative and dramatic interpretation of literature. The use of trade books in content areas, trends in literature and publishing, and methods of presenting books are studied in ADOLESCENT LITERATURE IN MIDDLE SCHOOLS, JUNIOR AND SENIOR HIGH SCHOOLS. Use of appropriate materials with preschool and early elementary school children is the subject matter presented in LITERATURE FOR THE YOUNG CHILD. THE AUTHOR'S AND ILLUSTRATOR'S ART AND CRAFT provides concentrated study of selected authors' and illustrators' works. Specific ways of incorporating worthwhile literature into the school curriculum are examined in FOUNDATIONS OF LITERATURE FOR CHILDREN AND YOUNG ADULTS.

Olivet College. English. CHILDREN'S LITERATURE is a study of European and American literature for children, with attention paid to the use of literature in teaching.

Saginaw Valley State University. Education. Recent research is discussed in ADVANCED STUDY IN CHILDREN'S LITERATURE, a course for experienced teachers.

Suomi College. English. CHILDREN'S LITERATURE is a historical survey.

University of Detroit-Mercy. Education. This CHILDREN'S LITERATURE course is a study of recent trends, with an examination of books currently being read by children. English. CHILDREN'S LITERATURE, which prepares teachers to use literature in the classroom, is an exploration of values inherent in the major genres of children's books.

University of Michigan. Library Science. Two courses, LITERATURE FOR CHILDREN and LITERATURE FOR YOUNG ADULTS, focus on selecting and presenting books and media to these groups. STORYTELLING emphasizes folk literature. Students become familiar with scholarship, research, and literary criticism in SEMINAR ON LITERATURE FOR CHILDREN.

University of Michigan-Dearborn Campus. Education. The curriculum and the needs and interests of children and young people are considered in LITERATURE FOR CHILDREN and LITERATURE FOR YOUNG PEOPLE, courses intended for librarians, supervisors, and teachers.

University of Michigan-Flint Campus. Education. FOLKLORE AND STORYTELLING emphasizes techniques of preparing and telling stories, and the course involves attendance at a storytelling festival. Education and English. CHILDREN'S LITERATURE surveys the content and literary merit of books read by children.

Wayne State University. Education and Library Science. The use of books with children and the ways they experience literature are covered in SURVEY AND ANALYSIS OF LITERATURE FOR YOUNGER CHILDREN, SURVEY AND ANALYSIS OF LITERATURE FOR OLDER CHILDREN, and LITERATURE FOR ADOLESCENTS. STORYTELLING offers practice in storytelling and reading aloud.

Western Michigan University. English. The focus is on literary values in CHILDREN'S LITERATURE and LITERATURE FOR ADOLESCENTS. STUDIES IN CHILDREN'S LITERATURE is an in-depth study of significant themes, movements, and types.

MINNESOTA

Angsburg College. Education. While emphasis is on the preparation of lesson and unit plans in ENGLISH METHODS, study of adolescent literature is included. KINDERGARTEN-ELEMENTARY CURRICULUM: CHILDREN'S LITERATURE includes laboratory experiences for preparation of materials and resources for children's literature.

Bethel College and Seminary. Education. Motivating children to read and appreciate good literature is addressed in CHILDREN'S LITERATURE. English. A course intended for teachers, JUVENILE LITERATURE includes reading of a wide range of juvenile literature.

Bemidji State University. Education. CHILDREN'S LITERATURE is a survey and reading course. English. Teachers learn to correlate free reading with classroom assignments in LITERATURE FOR ADOLESCENTS, while they gain field experience in teaching literature in DIRECTED CLASSROOM INSTRUCTION STUDIES. MYTHOLOGY, LEGENDS, AND FOLKTALES is a survey of world mythologies as a content in the elementary language arts.

College of Saint Benedict. Education. CHILDREN'S LITERATURE is a readings and analysis course. ADOLESCENT LITERATURE, a course for English majors, relates books and media to classroom settings.

College of Saint Catherine. Education. Study of literature based on developmental needs is the focus of LITERATURE FOR CHILDREN and LITERATURE FOR YOUNG ADULTS.

College of Saint Scholastica. Education. READING, LISTENING AND VIEWING GUIDANCE FOR CHILDREN is a comprehensive study of children's literature with an appraisal of print and nonprint materials to meet the curriculum in elementary school.

Dr. Martin Luther College. Education. Students learn methods of selecting and presenting literature for enjoyment and enrichment in CHILDREN'S LITERATURE.

Hamline University. Education. A goal of LITERARY DEVELOPMENT IN THE ELEMENTARY SCHOOL is to foster literacy development in young children through a child-centered, literature-based approach. English. The goal in TEACHING OF ENGLISH AND ADOLESCENT LITERATURE is to instruct prospective teachers about procedures, materials, and problems in teaching English courses in secondary schools.

Macalester College. English. READING CHILDREN'S LITERATURE is a survey and critical analysis of literature for children and its use in teaching reading.

Moorhead State University. Education. CHILDREN'S LITERATURE: CONTENT AND METHODS is a study of trade books for use with the curriculum. ADVANCED CHILDREN'S LITERATURE is a study of theories of literary criticism and their relation to curriculum decisions.

Saint Cloud State University. Education. Five courses are offered. LITERATURE FOR CHILDREN seeks to foster wide reading and appreciation of fine literature. Coping with change as reflected in literature for children is addressed in READING IN A PLURALISTIC SOCIETY: USING CHILDREN'S BOOKS. Two courses are research-based: READING AND CHILDREN'S LITERATURE: CURRENT RESEARCH and READING: RESEARCH IN CHILDREN'S LITERATURE. READING AND CHILDREN'S LITERATURE: CURRENT ISSUES relates the literature program in the curriculum to the aims of reading instruction. English. SEMINAR IN TEACHING LITERATURE is for junior and senior high school teachers.

Topics vary, and the course may be repeated for credit. TOPICS IN TEACHING ENGLISH sometimes deals with teaching literature to adolescents. Library Science. CHILDREN'S SERVICES/MATERIALS IN PUBLIC LIBRARIES explores programs and materials, print and nonprint, for children ages 0–14.

Saint Mary's College of Minnesota. Education. Ideas for use in the classroom of contemporary and classical literature are presented in CHILDREN'S LITERATURE and ADOLESCENT LITERATURE.

University of Minnesota. Education. Reading interests and use of literature in the curriculum are addressed in LITERATURE FOR THE ELEMENTARY SCHOOL, TEACHING LITERATURE IN SECONDARY SCHOOLS and LITERATURE FOR ADOLESCENTS. Collections of children's literature, their content, accessibility, and research are some areas studied in SURVEY OF SPECIAL COLLECTIONS IN CHILDREN'S LITERATURE and RESEARCH IN SPECIAL COLLECTIONS OF CHILDREN'S LITERATURE. Children's literature is one of the topics of study in CREATIVE WRITING FOR AND BY CHILDREN, a language arts course, and TEACHING SECOND LANGUAGES AND CULTURES IN ELEMENTARY SCHOOLS.

University of Minnesota–Duluth. Education. Many aspects of children's literature, including its use in the classroom, trends, and selection, are presented in CHILDREN'S LITERATURE and CHILDREN'S LITERATURE II. Students study a selected area of literature for in-depth study in LITERATURE IN EARLY CHILDHOOD EDUCATION. LITERATURE FOR ADOLESCENTS provides background for pupil guidance in extensive reading, including vocational interests. STORYTELLING presents needs for storytelling and experience.

University of Saint Thomas. Education. CHILDREN'S LITERATURE provides a survey of classical and recent contributions to the field. Both this course and ADOLESCENT LITERATURE, which is a survey of contemporary literature, present methods and programs to extend and stimulate reading by children and adolescents.

MISSISSIPPI

Alcorn State University. Education. Students learn to present literature to small groups in nursery through junior high school in CHILDREN'S LITERATURE.

Belhaven College. Education. LITERATURE FOR CHILDREN may be offered presenting subject matter and methods for teaching to grades K–3 or for grades 4–8.

Delta State University. Education. BOOKS AND RELATED MATERIALS FOR KINDERGARTEN THROUGH GRADE 8 is a survey of literature and other library materials.

Jackson State University. Education. Pre-reading skills and activities, as well as the use of literature to teach reading are addressed in PRE-READING SKILLS FOR PRESCHOOLERS AND EARLY PRIMARY GRADES and USING LITERATURE TO TEACH READING SKILLS. Education and Library Science. CHILDREN'S LITERATURE provides a comprehensive study of children's literary selections and ways to use books with children. Library Science. Two courses are offered, BOOKS AND RELATED MATERIALS FOR ADOLESCENTS and STORYTELLING, which offers training in the art of presentation to all age groups.

Mississippi College. Education. CHILDREN'S LITERATURE is designed to help future teachers know the importance of books and reading in the life of the young child. English. LITERATURE FOR ADOLESCENTS is a course designed for those preparing to teach in grades 7–12.

Mississippi State University. Education. Preparation of teachers to use literature in the curriculum is provided in TEACHING CHILDREN'S LITERATURE and TEACHING ADOLESCENT LITERATURE. READINGS AND RESEARCH IN CHILDREN'S LITERATURE provides semi-independent study of the literature and its place in the school.

Mississippi University for Women. Education. LITERATURE FOR CHILDREN provides a study of book service to children, with emphasis on preschool and elementary grades.

Mississippi Valley State University. Education. LANGUAGE ARTS AND LITERATURE FOR ELEMENTARY GRADES offers a survey of modern and folk literature and integration into the language arts curriculum.

Rust College. Education. LITERATURE FOR CHILDREN presents a variety of genres for a range of age groups. Library Science. Two courses, BOOKS AND RELATED MATERIALS FOR CHILDREN and BOOKS AND RELATED MATERIALS FOR YOUTH, relate the selection of materials to needs and interests of the reader and to the support and enrichment of the curriculum.

University of Mississippi. Education. In LANGUAGE CONCEPTS AND LITERATURE IN EARLY CHILDHOOD EDUCATION, childhood literature is studied as a stimulus for language and conceptual growth. LITERATURE FOR TODAY'S TEENAGERS addresses the selection and evaluation of current appropriate titles. Library Science. The use and evaluation of print and non-print materials is studied, with emphasis on contemporary titles in SELECTION OF MEDIA FOR CHILDREN.

University of Southern Mississippi. Education. The college offers CHILDREN'S LITERATURE, an introduction and study of use in the curriculum; LITERATURE FOR THE MIDDLE SCHOOL, a study of literature and its use in grades 4-8; and CHILDREN'S LITERATURE IN THE CURRICULUM FOR THE EARLY YEARS: AN AWARENESS, CRITERIA, EVALUATION. Library Science. LITERATURE AND RELATED MATERIALS FOR CHILDREN and LITERATURE AND RELATED MATERIALS FOR ADOLESCENTS are survey courses. STORYTELLING provides practice in storytelling as well as a study of the oral tradition. Advanced study and evaluation are provided in STUDIES IN CHILDREN'S LITERATURE. The summer program in England offers two courses focusing on British children's literature: BRITISH STUDIES: SEMINAR IN CHILDREN'S AND YOUNG ADULT LITERATURE, an intensive study of specific topics, and BRITISH STUDIES: HISTORICAL STUDIES IN CHILDREN'S LITERATURE.

William Carey College. Education. LITERATURE FOR CHILDREN is the study and use of print and non-print, classic and current literature in the curriculum.

MISSOURI

Central Missouri State University. Education. CHILDREN'S LITERATURE offers methods for integrating children's literature into the total curriculum.

East Central College. Education. LITERATURE FOR CHILDREN helps prospective elementary school teachers develop standards for selecting reading materials for children.

Fontbonne College. Education. LITERATURE FOR CHILDREN is a study of major genres in classic and contemporary literature, with their use in the classroom.

Hannibal-LaGrange College. Education. LITERATURE FOR CHILDREN is a study of suitable reading materials for young children. English. YOUNG ADULT LITERATURE focuses on contemporary books and their use in the curriculum.

Lincoln University. Education. BOOKS TO BEGIN ON presents materials for the preschool child and is not intended for degree-seeking students. CHILDREN'S LITERATURE includes criteria for book selection and presentation of literature to children. This course also is offered as an honors course, which includes an honors project.

Maryville College. Education. CHILDREN'S LITERATURE, offered as an undergraduate and as a graduate course, includes principles of selection and adaptation to the needs of the child. In EXPANDING READING SKILLS THROUGH LITERATURE methods and materials are emphasized. There are two courses named ADOLESCENT LITERATURE; both focus on reading and discussion of literature and its use with adolescents.

Northeast Missouri State University. English. Various genres for K-7 are studied in LITERATURE FOR CHILDREN. LITERATURE FOR YOUNG ADULTS also is a teacher preparation course which relates the literature to the needs, abilities, and interests of adolescents.

Northwest Missouri State University. Education. PROBLEMS TEACHING CHILDREN'S LITERATURE TO THE EXCEPTIONAL LEARNER presents methods and materials. Education and Library Science. LITERATURE FOR THE ELEMENTARY SCHOOL includes selection and presentation of literature. Library Science. LITERATURE FOR THE YOUNG ADULT is a study of current and popular materials suitable for high school students.

Park College. Education. LITERATURE FOR ELEMENTARY TEACHERS is a survey of traditional and modern literature for use in the classroom.

Saint Louis University. Education. A study of the literary elements that make literature interesting and meaningful to young children is part of EARLY CHILDHOOD CHILDREN'S LITERATURE. ELEMENTARY SCHOOL METHODS OF TEACHING CHILDREN'S LITERATURE is a survey of award winning literature, with methods of teaching good literature to children. SEMINAR: CHILDREN'S LITERATURE is a review of the various approaches to teaching literature to children.

Southeast Missouri State University. Education. Using literature to promote literature is the focus of TECHNIQUES OF TEACHING CHILDREN'S LITERATURE. English. Three courses are offered for teacher preparation: LITERATURE FOR THE YOUNG ADULT, a survey course; DRAMATIC LITERATURE FOR CHILDREN, a study of prose and poetry, traditional and modern, appropriate for use as bases for dramatic activities in the elementary classroom; and LITERATURE FOR CHILDREN, an advanced study for graduate students that includes in-depth study of selected areas of interest.

Southwest Missouri State University. English. CHILDREN'S LITERATURE and ADOLESCENT LITERATURE offer surveys of literature suitable for classroom use. Particular themes or genres are studied in STUDIES IN CHILDREN'S LITERATURE and YOUNG ADULT NOVEL. HISTORICAL PERSPECTIVES IN CHILDREN'S LITERATURE focuses on one or more periods in the historical development of children's literature.

University of Missouri–Columbia. Education. All three courses focus on surveys of the field and selection of materials for use in the classroom. They are LITERATURE FOR CHILDREN AND YOUTH, LITERATURE IN THE ELEMENTARY SCHOOL, and LITERATURE FOR ADOLESCENTS. Library Science. LIBRARY MATERIALS FOR CHILDREN AND YOUTH focuses on materials, trends, and storytelling.

University of Missouri–Kansas City. Education. LITERATURE FOR CHILDREN and LITERATURE FOR ADOLESCENTS are survey courses that include methods for classroom use. ADVANCED LITERATURE FOR CHILDREN is a historical survey and includes world literature.

University of Missouri–St. Louis. Education. CHILDREN'S LITERATURE I: SURVEY AND ANALYSIS reviews books published in the past ten years and the relationship between literature and societal issues. CHILDREN'S LITERATURE II: SELECTION AND FUNCTIONS includes study of literary elements and the use of trade books in the curriculum. CHILDREN'S LITERATURE AND READING also addresses use of materials in the classroom, reading for enjoyment and information, and bibliotherapy.

Washington University. Education. LITERATURE IN THE ELEMENTARY SCHOOL is a teacher preparation course.

Webster University. Education. Use of literature in the curriculum and multicultural and contemporary issues are part of the study in CHILDREN'S LITERATURE.

William Jewell College. Education. CHILDREN'S LITERATURE AND IN-STRUCTION IN INDIVIDUALIZED READING TECHNIQUES acquaints the student with the best literature for elementary school children.

MONTANA

Carroll College. Education. CHILDREN'S LITERATURE is a review of the literature produced for and enjoyed by children.

College of Great Falls. Education. CHILDREN'S LITERATURE and LITERATURE FOR YOUNG ADULTS are surveys of literature, with selection and evaluation methods.

Dull Knife Memorial College. English. CHILDREN'S LITERATURE is a review of current children's literature and its application to early childhood education.

Eastern Montana College. Education. While TEACHING LANGUAGE ARTS AND CHILDREN'S LITERATURE focuses on an integrated program, use of children's literature for promoting literacy events in the classroom is included. STORYTELLING provides students with a background in the development of oral literature and practice in its use. Methods of promoting books through classroom activities in secondary schools are presented in ADOLESCENT LITERATURE.

Montana State University. Education. Emphasis is upon combining basal readers with children's literature and reading instruction in TEACHING READING AND LANGUAGE ARTS. English. Both SURVEY CHILDREN'S LITERATURE and READING CHILDREN'S LITERATURE address the literature in relation to its use in the classroom.

Northern Montana College. English. CHILDREN'S LITERATURE and LITERATURE FOR ADOLESCENTS are studies of literature important in the curriculum.

Rocky Mountain College. English. CHILDREN'S LITERATURE is a study of classic and contemporary children's literature.

University of Montana. Education. Effective integration of literature within the curriculum and instruction strategies are included in TEACHING ELEMENTARY SCHOOL LITERATURE and SUPERVISION AND TEACHING OF LITERATURE IN THE ELEMENTARY SCHOOL.

Western Montana College. Education. CHILDREN'S LITERATURE is a historical survey and includes extensive reading. LITERATURE FOR SECONDARY STUDENTS relates literature to the needs, interests, and abilities of students.

NEBRASKA

Chadron State College. Education. Students preparing to work with preschool children learn to use appropriate literature and language arts activities in LITERATURE AND LANGUAGE ARTS PROGRAM FOR PRESCHOOL CHILDREN. English. CHILDREN'S LITERATURE offers opportunity for acquiring skills in presenting literature to children. CHILD AND ADOLESCENT LITERATURE suggests teaching techniques effecting desirable reading responses.

College of Saint Mary. Education. Techniques for promoting life-long reading habits are explored in CHILDREN'S LITERATURE. English. LITERATURE FOR YOUNG ADULTS includes the study of traditional and contemporary works written for young adults.

Concordia Teachers College. Education. Specific components on children's literature are included in TEACHING READING IN THE ELEMENTARY SCHOOL. English. Methods of presenting literature to children and insights of using literature in the classroom are studied in CHILDREN'S LITERATURE and READING INTERESTS OF ADOLESCENTS. ISSUES IN LITERATURE FOR CHILDREN AND YOUTH includes study of critical issues as presented in literature and study of censorship.

Creighton University. Education. LITERATURE FOR CHILDREN is a survey of literature for preschool through junior high.

Dana College. Education. CHILDREN'S LITERATURE is designed to give guidance in children's reading for teachers in elementary grades. English. LITERATURE FOR YOUNG ADULTS is a survey course for teachers.

Doane College. Education. In LANGUAGE ARTS AND READING I students are acquainted with literature for children and its application for teaching language arts skills.

Midland Lutheran College. Education. Award books and field experience with children and literature are part of the course work in CHILDREN'S LITERATURE.

Nebraska Wesleyan University. Education. CHILDREN'S LITERATURE examines the place of children's literature in the curriculum. LEARNING RESOURCES FOR YOUNG ADULTS is a survey study of materials for junior and senior high age.

Peru State College. English. The principles of evaluation are applied to selected books in a survey course, CHILDREN'S LITERATURE.

University of Nebraska-Kearney. Education. Teachers set up criteria for choosing and evaluating books in CHILDREN'S LITERATURE, and they evaluate books appropriate for study in secondary schools in LITERATURE FOR ADOLESCENTS.

University of Nebraska-Lincoln. Education. Four courses are offered in which students read widely, survey genres and historical and contemporary books, and study methods for using literature in the classroom. They are CHILDREN'S LITERATURE, CONTEMPORARY CHILDREN'S LITERATURE, LITERATURE FOR ADOLESCENTS, and LITERATURE FOR SECONDARY SCHOOL ADOLESCENTS. English. One CHILDREN'S LITERATURE course is a study of selected works which have attracted adult attention to their artistry and themes. Another with the same title is advanced study in specialized topics related to literature for children, such as criticism or history. HISTORY OF CHILDREN'S LITERATURE emphasizes the evolution of the most prominent types of contemporary children's books.

University of Nebraska-Omaha. Education. LITERATURE FOR CHILDREN AND YOUTH provides emphasis upon developing a broad acquaintance with authors and works and on the use of literature in the classroom. Another course with the same title is a graduate-level course dealing with the utilization of literary materials for children. Library Science. LITERATURE FOR THE ADOLESCENT is designed to assist educators in gaining information about adolescents and their reading and viewing habits.

Wayne State College. Education. Students in CHILDREN'S LITERATURE participate in special projects and activities that explore ways to motivate and enrich literature study with children. ADVANCED CHILDREN'S LITERATURE is a study of children's books, their authors, and their illustrators.

NEVADA

Sierra Nevada College-Lake Tahoe. English. In CHILDREN'S LITERATURE various classics are analyzed for their values, style, and enduring themes. Final project is writing a children's story.

University of Nevada–Reno. Education. BOOK SELECTION FOR CHILDREN and BOOK SELECTION FOR ADOLESCENTS/YOUNG ADULTS are survey courses that include consideration of pupils' reading interests and needs. In TEACHING OF ELEMENTARY LANGUAGE ARTS AND LITERATURE consideration is given to integrating literature of all groups in the total elementary school curriculum. English. CHILDREN'S LITERATURE covers history, genres, traditions, and illustrations of children's books in England and America from 1697 to the present.

University of Nevada–Las Vegas. Education. HISTORICAL DEVELOPMENT OF LITERATURE FOR CHILDREN and CONTEMPORARY LITERATURE FOR CHILDREN AND YOUNG ADULTS survey the books available for use with children and young adults in the classroom. SEMINAR IN CURRENT LITERATURE FOR CHILDREN AND YOUNG ADULTS is limited to the last five years in publishing. Emphasis is on the use of literature in the curriculum and for reading instruction in LITERATURE-BASED INSTRUCTION IN READING/LANGUAGE ARTS, LITERATURE SELECTIONS FOR CHILDREN, and SELECTION AND EVALUATION OF LIBRARY MATERIALS FOR YOUNG ADULTS. LITERATURE FOR CHILDREN AND YOUTH is a graduate-level course dealing with the utilization of literary materials for children from preschool through grade six reading level.

NEW HAMPSHIRE

Franklin Pierce College. Education. CHILDREN'S LITERATURE examines the relationship of children's literature to curriculum areas, and the values of children's literature to both child and adult.

Keene State College. English. CHILDREN'S LITERATURE, an overview of the field, includes evaluation and selection from a literary standpoint. ADOLESCENT LITERATURE examines the problem novel, historical fiction, fantasy and other genres.

New England College. Education. READING IN THE ELEMENTARY SCHOOL includes the integration of reading, writing, and literature.

Plymouth State College. Education. In LITERATURE FOR CHILDREN, special emphasis is given to the use of children's literature in the pre-K through eighth grade curriculum. ADVANCED CHILDREN'S/YOUNG

ADULT LITERATURE helps the educator select literature to develop literature-based language arts programs.

Rivier College. Education. Included in CHILDREN'S LITERATURE is a study of the relationship of trade books to school subjects. Another CHILDREN'S LITERATURE course examines quality prose and poetry to provide for the needs of children. EMERGING LITERACY FOR YOUNG CHILDREN provides methods for teaching children to read through literature. English. THE CHILD IN LITERATURE includes historical and current literature and examines the presentation of the child in literature. Two courses in TEACHING LITERATURE TO ADOLESCENTS are offered. One is a study of fiction and its presentation to a teenage audience. The other deals with the development of adolescent students as readers and interpreters of literature.

University of New Hampshire. Education. Methods of using literature with children are presented in CHILDREN'S LITERATURE.

NEW JERSEY

Centenary College. English. In CHILDREN'S LITERATURE, students learn how to select, evaluate, and use literature for children effectively.

Kean College of New Jersey. Education. THE LITERATURE OF CHILDREN AND YOUTH is a survey course of literature and informational materials. CHILDREN'S LITERATURE IN EDUCATION is a critical study of books and their use in classrooms. EXPLORING BOOKS WITH YOUNG CHILDREN includes techniques for storytelling and writing for children. English. CHILDREN'S LITERATURE and LITERATURE FOR THE ADOLESCENT are historical surveys and studies, to modern times, of the literature.

Princeton University. English. CHILDREN'S LITERATURE is a study of fairy tales and fantasies from a literary, cultural, and psychological aspect.

Rider College. English. LITERATURE OF ADOLESCENTS examines adolescence as a generative force in fiction, poetry, and drama.

Rutgers, The State University of New Jersey. English. LITERATURE FOR CHILDHOOD focuses on folklore, fantasy, and adolescent fiction.

Saint Peter's College. English. Imaginative writing for children and adolescents is treated as literary art, with emphasis on classic works, in CHILDREN'S LITERATURE.

Trenton State College. Education. EXPLORING CHILDREN'S LITERATURE: AN EDUCATOR'S PERSPECTIVE is a multimedia approach to children's literature.

William Paterson College of New Jersey. Education. LITERATURE FOR CHILDREN AND YOUNG ADULTS is a survey of literature past and present, with strategies for bringing students and books together. RECENT TRENDS IN CHILDREN'S LITERATURE focuses on ways to extend literature with children, and on teaching reading and writing through literature. ADVANCED INQUIRY INTO LITERATURE FOR CHILDREN AND YOUTH gives attention to research studies, adaptation of materials for children and youth, and appropriate use in the classroom.

NEW MEXICO

Eastern New Mexico University–Portales Campus. Education. LITERATURE IN EARLY CHILDHOOD includes methods for presenting literary experiences.

New Mexico Highlands University. Education. READING AND CHILDREN'S LITERATURE places emphasis on knowing books and authors for the elementary classroom. READING AND LITERATURE FOR CHILDREN AND YOUNG ADULTS explores and evaluates artistic qualities of literature for all grades, and stresses motivation for developing reading skills through literature.

New Mexico State University–Las Cruces. English. LITERATURE FOR CHILDREN AND YOUNG ADULTS is a comparative historical survey with emphasis on critical evaluation.

University of New Mexico. Education. CHILDREN'S LITERATURE is a survey course with emphasis on literary response and classroom programs. TECHNIQUES OF LITERARY PRESENTATIONS is a storytelling course. Library Science. BOOKS AND RELATED MATERIALS FOR YOUNG ADULTS surveys books and nonbook materials for junior and senior high school age.

Western New Mexico University. Education. CHILDREN'S LITERATURE MATERIALS includes a survey of different types of literature with attention to storytelling and establishment of desirable reading habits. English. CHILDREN'S LITERATURE OF THE SOUTHWEST is a survey of Southwest literature appropriate for use in the elementary or junior high classroom.

NEW YORK

Adelphi University. Education. CHILDREN'S LITERATURE familiarizes students with the literature's history, authors, and the functions it fulfills for children.

Barnard College. English. THROUGH THE LOOKING GLASS. A SURVEY OF CHILDREN'S LITERATURE considers new critical interpretations as well as discussion of purely literary aspects.

Bernard M. Baruch College of the City University of New York. English. CHILDREN'S LITERATURE is a historical survey with consideration of reading for age groups from childhood through adolescence.

Brooklyn College of the City University of New York. Education. TEACHING LITERATURE FOR CHILDREN AND ADOLESCENTS helps students plan balanced programs of reading and use literature in all curriculum areas. English. WRITING FOR CHILDREN AND YOUNG ADULTS includes writing literary and informational materials. LITERATURE FOR YOUNG PEOPLE is a teacher preparation course that addresses basic reading of interest to young people.

Buffalo State College. Education. TEACHING POETRY IN THE ELEMENTARY SCHOOL places emphasis on strategies for bring poetry and children together. English. Three survey courses are offered for teacher preparation: CHILDREN'S LITERATURE, STUDIES IN CHILDREN'S LITERATURE, and LITERATURE FOR THE SECONDARY SCHOOL. The remaining classes are genre-specific and address literary elements in the literature. They are: REALISTIC FICTION FOR CHILDREN, THE HEROIC TRADITION IN CHILDREN'S LITERATURE, CLASSICS OF CHILDREN'S LITERATURE, FANTASY AND THE MODERN LITERATURE FAIRY TALE, POETRY FOR CHILDREN, and FOLKLORE IN CHILDREN'S LITERATURE.

Canisius College. Education. LITERATURE FOR CHILDREN AND YOUNG ADULTS is a survey of genres that focuses on importance of reading to children and uses of children's books across all curriculum areas. English. C. S. LEWIS AND FANTASY LITERATURE includes study of related authors.

College of New Rochelle. Education. CHILDREN'S LITERATURE presents an overview of the field and strategies for classroom use.

College of Saint Rose. Education. LITERATURE FOR CHILDREN is a critical survey of literature that stresses use of literature with children. PRE-SCHOOL LITERATURE AND READING READINESS explores books and practices suited to preparation for reading.

Columbia University. English. ADOLESCENT LITERATURE explores literary works within the context of secondary education curricula.

Concordia College. Education. CHILDREN'S LITERATURE is a general survey with attention to the use of literature to supplement and enrich other curriculum areas. English. LITERATURE AND THE ADOLESCENT EXPERIENCE relates literature to social issues and life.

Dominican College. English. The emphasis is on reading for enjoyment in LITERATURE FOR CHILDREN AND ADOLESCENTS. Treatment of current issues and values is included.

Dowling College. English. WRITING FOR CHILDREN is designed for students interested in writing for the juvenile market.

D'Youville College. Education. CHILDREN'S LITERATURE IN ENGLISH AND IN SPANISH considers folklore and ways to use literature with children.

Elmira College. English. WRITING FOR CHILDREN offers study of works of successful authors and preparation of manuscripts for publication.

Herbert H. Lehman College of the City University of New York. Education. LITERATURE IN THE ELEMENTARY SCHOOL is a critical survey with special emphasis on the use of literature for enriching a basal reading program. English. Selected works in various genres are given critical examination in CRITICAL APPROACHES TO CHILDREN'S LITERATURE.

Hobart and William Smith College. Education. In CHILDREN'S LITERATURE, books are considered from historical, psychological, literary, theoretical, and educational perspectives. The messages in children's literature are explored.

Hofstra University. Education. Effective ways of promoting wider reading are examined in a multimedia study of literary materials in CHILDREN'S LITERATURE. A global perspective and reading in the content area are stressedn LITERATURE IN THE ELEMENTARY SCHOOL. WRITING AND CHILDREN'S LITERATURE provides an in-depth investigation of literature for children as a literary experience which promotes language and writing development. English. Students learn techniques for editing picture books, fiction, and informational books in EDITING CHILDREN'S BOOKS. In WORKSHOP: CHILDREN'S FICTION WRITING discussion includes techniques and themes in contemporary examples of children's fiction.

Iona College. Education. THE USE OF LITERATURE TO IMPROVE LANGUAGE TEACHING AND LEARNING offers techniques to make literature more accessible and interesting to children and young people.

Ithaca College. English. Potential high school teachers study various works of literature with emphasis on presentation in TEACHING LITERATURE IN HIGH SCHOOL.

Keuka College. English. CHILDREN'S LITERATURE is a survey of quality literature past and present.

King's College. Education. In LITERATURE FOR CHILDREN, an historical survey, social and personal values in literature are analyzed.

Long Island University, Brooklyn Campus. Education. A seminar, LITERATURE FOR CHILDREN, seeks to develop a critical awareness and appreciation of children's literature through examination of many genres.

Long Island University, C. W. Post Campus. Education. SEMINAR IN LITERATURE FOR CHILDREN seeks to develop a critical awareness and appreciation of children's literature through examination of many genres.

Manhattanville College. Education. Both novice and master teachers can enhance their knowledge of literature and its use in the curriculum in TEACHING READING THROUGH CHILDREN'S LITERATURE.

Maria College. Education. The importance of dramatic expression, storytelling, creative oral and written expression and the use of media in presenting literature to children are stressed in CHILDREN'S LITERATURE.

Marymount Manhattan College. English. A course for anyone working with children, CHILDREN'S LITERATURE places emphasis on the nature and uses of narrative.

Molloy College. Education. READING AND LANGUAGE ARTS IN THE ELEMENTARY SCHOOL—PART II includes children's literature and storytelling. INDIVIDUALIZED READING THROUGH CHILDREN'S LITERATURE includes the major aspects of pupil-teacher conferences and skill analysis. English. CHILDREN'S LITERATURE is an intensive study of genres and literary devices.

Nazareth College of Rochester. English. Narratives and poetry that has appealed to both children and adults are read in CHILDREN'S LITERATURE.

New York University. Education. LANGUAGE ARTS IN CHILDHOOD EDUCATION relates literature to the elementary curriculum. WRITING FOR CHILDREN includes preparation and submission of manuscripts and consultations with children's book editors. INTERNATIONAL LITERATURE FOR CHILDREN is designed to acquaint students with multicultural characteristics and values from a wide variety of ethnic backgrounds as expressed in children's literature. CHILDREN'S LITERATURE AND CULTURAL VALUES, for teachers, librarians, and publishers, examines children's literature as a reflection and transmitter of cultural values. Ways to stimulate and evaluate response to literature are examined in CRITICAL READING AND RESPONSE TO LITERATURE. Emphasis is placed on helping children acquire the knowledge and strategies to read, comprehend, and interpret texts in LITERATURE-BASED APPROACHES TO TEACHING READING. LITERATURE FOR YOUNGER CHILDREN and LITERATURE FOR OLDER CHILDREN are survey courses with special attention to storytelling and use of literature in the classroom. TEACHING READING IN THE ENGLISH CLASSROOM develops insights into the nature, roles, and creation of narrative. READING AND LITERATURE WITH ADOLESCENTS explores the reasons people read and ways to engage adolescents in meaningful reading.

Niagara University. University Studies. "TWAS BRILLIG": LANGUAGE AND LOGIC IN THE WRITINGS OF LEWIS CARROLL looks at Wonderland from the viewpoint of psychology, political science, religious studies, philosophy, history, physics, and literature and mathematics.

Nyack College. Education. CHILDREN'S LITERATURE is for teachers of elementary school children.

Pace University—New York City Campus. English. LITERATURE FOR YOUNG PEOPLE is a general survey of significant prose and poetry for children and young people.

Saint Bonaventure. Education. Elementary school teachers are offered an overview of the literature available for children and are introduced to the art of storytelling and creative dramatics in READINGS IN CHILDREN'S LITERATURE. The role of adolescent literature in modern society and the literary aspects of young adult books are examined in an honors course, LITERATURE FOR YOUNG ADULTS.

Saint Francis College. Education. Field-centered experience, peer teaching, and the use of audiovisual aids are part of LITERATURE.

Saint John Fisher College. Education. The focus of CHILDREN'S LIT-
ERATURE is the use of children's literature as a curricular tool, including
reading skills.

Saint John's University. Library Science. CONTEMPORARY LITERATURE
FOR CHILDREN AND YOUNG ADULTS is an intensive study of selected
books with emphasis on literary analysis and evaluative critical techniques. PRINT AND NON-PRINT MATERIALS FOR CHILDREN includes
evaluation and selection of materials in elementary school and public
libraries. LIBRARY PROGRAMS AND SERVICES FOR CHILDREN AND YOUNG
ADULTS includes telling stories and book talks.

Skidmore College. Education. INTEGRATING LITERATURE ACROSS THE
CURRICULUM is an extension of children's literature, reading, and
language arts courses. Using literature with science, mathematics, and
social studies is included. CHILDREN'S LITERATURE is an introductory
historical survey.

State University of New York at Binghamton. Education. LITERATURE
FOR CHILDREN AND YOUTH is an overview of all categories of literature
written for students in elementary and middle schools. CULTURAL
IDENTITIES AND THE LITERATURE OF YOUTH examines contemporary
multicultural literature written for and about youth. English. CHIL-
DREN'S LITERATURE is a study of representative works of realistic and
fantasy fiction for children.

State University of New York at Buffalo. Library Science. Two courses,
RESOURCES AND SERVICES FOR CHILDREN and RESOURCES AND SERVICES
FOR YOUNG ADULTS, survey literature and related media, selection, and
presentation.

State University of New York, College at Brockport. Education.
CHILDREN'S LITERATURE explores the conventions of children's literature. INTRODUCTION TO CHILDREN'S LITERATURE familiarizes students
with the wide variety of literature available for use with elementary
school children. READING AND RESPONDING TO LITERATURE, K–12 provides a survey of the major theories of literature interpretation and
methods of applying them. TEACHING CHILDREN'S LITERATURE covers
both traditional and current literature for young children. Books are
considered in terms of their contributions to social growth and to the
curriculum. English. YOUNG ADULT LITERATURE examines the needs of
the young adult reader, genre literature, and literature in the content
areas.

State University of New York, College at Cortland. Education. Literature as a means of enhancing child growth is the object of CHILDREN's LITERATURE IN THE CURRICULUM. In ADOLESCENT LITERATURE IN THE MIDDLE AND SECONDARY SCHOOL CURRICULUM, special consideration is given to the reluctant reader and the disabled reader. English. LITERATURE FOR CHILDREN addresses critical appreciation of books. LITERATURE IN THE SECONDARY SCHOOLS includes works originally intended for adults but widely read by adolescents.

State University of New York, College at Fredonia. Education. INTRODUCTION TO CHILDREN's LITERATURE is designed to assist students to become acquainted with trade books and media. COMPARATIVE CHILDREN's LITERATURE includes recent research and critical analysis of all literary genres. English. Examination of the adolescent experience in books for, by, and about adolescents is the subject of LITERATURE FOR ADOLESCENTS.

State University of New York, College at Oneonta. Education. CHILDREN's LITERATURE AND READING is a survey with emphasis on selection and children's needs. English. LITERATURE FOR THE YOUNG ADULT offers the study of literary materials, the criteria for their selection, and their use in the classroom.

State University of New York, College at Oswego. Education. LITERATURE FOR YOUNG CHILDREN is an in-depth examination of literature relevant for the younger child. USING LITERATURE IN READING INSTRUCTION emphasizes selection and integration of materials for elementary and secondary schools.

State University of New York, College at Potsdam. Education. USING CHILDREN's AND ADOLESCENTS' LITERATURE IN THE TEACHING OF READING provides special attention to the use of literary materials for enriching classroom and individualized reading programs.

State University of New York, College of Arts and Sciences at Genesco. English. CHILDREN's LITERATURE is a study of masterpieces, old to modern, that illustrate literary qualities appealing to children.

State University of New York, College of Arts and Sciences at Plattsburgh. Education. Students in TEACHING READING THROUGH CHILDREN's LITERATURE evaluate books based on psychological and reader response criticism. READING, LITERATURE AND THE YOUNG ADULT provides rationale and methodologies for including young adult reading in content area lessons. Methods of providing appropriate literary experiences for children in the classroom are explored in CREATIVITY IN CHILDREN'S LITERATURE. English. In PINOCCHIO: FIRST 100 YEARS, students learn how editorial and other changes reflect changes in American attitudes toward childhood and children's literature. CHILDREN'S LITERATURE is a study of traditional and modern literature for ages three to sixteen. Emphasis is on the literature as a literary genre.

Syracuse University. Education. Children's Literature covers history, selection, methods of presentation, and use of literature in the reading program.

Utica College of Syracuse University. Education. LITERATURE FOR YOUNG READERS is a survey course with emphasis of criteria for selection and bibliotherapy.

Yeshiva University. Education. LITERATURE FOR CHILDREN AND ADOLESCENTS surveys standard literary works and new materials. English. LITERARY CONSCIOUSNESS III: FRACTURED FAIRY TALES examines the genre from a wide range of approaches, including linguistic, anthropological, psychological, Marxist, and feminist.

York College of the City University of New York. Education. LITERATURE AND STORYTELLING FOR CHILDREN is a critical study that includes field trips.

NORTH CAROLINA

Appalachian State University. Education. Two courses, MEDIA FOR YOUNG PEOPLE and LANGUAGE AND LITERATURE IN THE ELEMENTARY SCHOOL, prepare teachers to select and use literature, films, and television in the curriculum.

Barton College. Education. CHILDREN'S LITERATURE is a survey literature course. English. ADOLESCENT LITERATURE is a teacher preparation course. Reading problems, student response to literature, and design of study guides are topics covered.

Catawba College. Education. One course, LITERATURE FOR CHILDREN AND YOUTH, is offered for teacher preparation.

East Carolina University. English. Four courses are offered for teacher preparation. LITERATURE FOR CHILDREN and LITERATURE FOR HIGH

SCHOOL are survey courses that together cover early childhood through grade 12. LITERATURE FOR THE YOUNGER ADOLESCENT includes purpose and role of literature, criteria for selection, and literature for and about minority groups. ADVANCED STUDIES IN CHILDREN'S LITERATURE emphasizes excellence and suitability of literature for children. Trends, problems, and recent research are studied. Library Science. MATERIALS FOR CHILDREN and MATERIALS FOR YOUNG ADULTS cover the selection, evaluation, and use of both print and nonprint materials. LIBRARY PROGRAMS AND MATERIALS FOR YOUNG CHILDREN and LIBRARY PROGRAMS AND MATERIALS FOR MIDDLE SCHOOL CHILDREN offer advanced study of the selection and evaluation of materials and their use in programs. Also offered is STORYTELLING, which gives special emphasis on folklore.

Elon College. English. CHILDREN'S LITERATURE is a teacher preparation course. Literature is related to modern education requirements.

Fayetteville State University. English. These courses, CHILDREN'S LITERATURE and ADOLESCENT LITERATURE, although intended for teacher preparation, appear to emphasize literature over curriculum and teaching methods.

Gardner-Webb College. Education. The CHILDREN'S LITERATURE course covers classical and current materials for K–9.

Greensboro College. Education. LITERATURE FOR CHILDREN is a teacher preparation course that emphasizes quality in children's books.

Guilford College. English. Literary classics are studied in relation to their use in elementary and middle schools in LITERATURE FOR CHILDREN AND YOUTH.

High Point College. Education. LITERATURE FOR CHILDREN AND ADOLESCENTS examines current literature for literary value and enjoyment value.

Johnson C. Smith University. Education. CHILDREN'S LITERATURE covers history and trends in children's literature, with strategies for integrating literature throughout the curriculum. LITERATURE FOR THE YOUNG CHILD includes storytelling, puppetry, and a variety of media.

Lees-McRae College. Education. LITERATURE FOR CHILDREN/YOUNG ADULTS is a teacher preparation course covering literature and nonprint media.

Lenoir-Rhyne College. Education. In CHILDREN'S LITERATURE and LITERATURE FOR ADOLESCENTS, literature is examined that is appropriate for life styles, needs, and aspirations, and which satisfies modern educational requirements.

Mars Hill College. Education. CHILDREN'S LITERATURE covers principles of selection and evaluation of literature and its use in the curriculum. ADOLESCENT LITERATURE 6–12, offered jointly with English, is a similar course.

Methodist College. English. LITERATURE FOR CHILDREN AND YOUTH is a teacher education course that emphasizes integrating literature in the curriculum.

Montreat-Anderson College. English. LITERATURE ABOUT ADOLESCENTS includes non-print media, appropriate teaching methods, and multi-cultural perspectives. LITERATURE FOR CHILDREN is a general critical and historical survey. Storytelling is included.

North Carolina State University. Education. LITERATURE FOR ADOLESCENTS is a survey course that covers integration of the literature in the curriculum.

North Carolina Wesleyan University. English. CHILDREN'S LITERATURE surveys changing concepts of the nature of childhood as seen in children's literature, and methods of presenting literature to children.

Pembroke State University. English. Two courses, CHILDREN'S LITERATURE (K–6) and LITERATURE FOR ADOLESCENTS (6–12) emphasize methods of teaching literature, pluralistic classrooms, curriculum-correlations, and field experiences.

Queens College. Education. LITERATURE FOR CHILDREN covers selection, integration in the curriculum, and evaluation of types of literature.

Saint Andrews Presbyterian College. Education. Students learn to critique literature and integrate it in the curriculum in LITERATURE FOR CHILDREN AND YOUTH.

Salem College. Education. CHILDREN'S LITERATURE AND DRAMA includes techniques of integrating drama into the basic curriculum.

University of North Carolina-Asheville. Education. Both courses, CHILDREN'S LITERATURE, K-6 and ADOLESCENT LITERATURE, 6-12, discuss teaching literature through appropriate instructional and motivational techniques.

University of North Carolina-Chapel Hill. Library Science. Seven courses are offered. SURVEY AND EVALUATION OF MATERIALS FOR CHILDREN: EARLY CHILDHOOD and SURVEY AND EVALUATION OF MATERIALS FOR CHILDREN: INTERMEDIATE GRADES are designed for prospective teachers. HISTORY OF CHILDREN'S LITERATURE, CHILDREN'S LITERATURE AND RELATED MATERIALS, and YOUNG ADULT LITERATURE AND RELATED MATERIALS are survey courses. Together, they cover the Middle Ages through current material. STORYTELLING: MATERIALS AND METHODS offers experience in selecting, adapting, and presenting materials. SEMINAR IN CHILDREN'S LITERATURE offers advanced study of a selected topic.

University of North Carolina-Charlotte. English. In CHILDREN'S LITERATURE and LITERATURE FOR ADOLESCENTS, emphasis is on the literature rather than on teaching methods, although children's and adolescents' responses to literature are studied. THE WORLDS OF JUVENILE LITERATURE offers analysis of the literary qualities which distinguish the classic from the ephemeral. Library Science. Two courses, READING GUIDANCE AND THE SELECTION OF BOOKS AND MATERIALS FOR CHILDREN and READING GUIDANCE AND THE SELECTION OF BOOKS AND RELATED MATERIAL FOR YOUNG PEOPLE are surveys of library materials, with study of aids and criteria for selection.

University of North Carolina-Greensboro. Education. CHILDREN'S LITERATURE AND INSTRUCTIONAL MEDIA offers a multimedia approach to literature for children. Library Science. MATERIALS FOR ADOLESCENTS and MATERIALS FOR CHILDREN offer study of selection aids and programming based on interests.

University of North Carolina-Wilmington. LITERATURE IN THE ELEMENTARY SCHOOL, (K-9) is a teacher preparation course that includes books and other media, multi-cultural themes, and strategies for curriculum integration. English. LITERATURE FOR CHILDREN and LITERATURE FOR YOUNG ADULTS explore several genres and are intended for future teachers and parents.

Wake Forest University. Education. CHILDREN'S LITERATURE AND READING relates the study of literature to reading problems. ADOLESCENT LITERATURE covers recent fiction.

Warren Wilson College. Education. CHILDREN'S AND ADOLESCENTS' LITERATURE is a course that includes field work to prepare teachers for helping children and adolescents become readers.

Western Carolina University. Education. All three courses, LITERATURE FOR CHILDREN AND YOUTH, ADOLESCENT LITERATURE, and ADVANCED CHILDREN'S LITERATURE, seek to prepare teachers to teach literature and to integrate literature into the curriculum. Library Science. CHILDREN'S AND ADOLESCENTS' LITERATURE is a historical survey course that includes study of illustrators.

Wingate College. Education. In these courses, CHILDREN'S LITERATURE (K–6) and ADOLESCENT LITERATURE (6–9), prospective teachers develop resource files for use in teaching. Dramatic techniques and story reading are included.

Winston-Salem State University. Education. TEACHING OF LANGUAGE ARTS AND CHILDREN'S LITERATURE is a course in teaching language arts with an emphasis on literature. English. CHILDREN'S LITERATURE and ADOLESCENT LITERATURE are survey courses. Classics and contemporary works are studied, with emphasis on standards for judging the worth of works.

NORTH DAKOTA

Dickinson State University. Education. CHILDREN'S LITERATURE is a study of literature for teachers.

Jamestown College. Education. Three courses, CHILDREN'S LITERATURE, ADOLESCENT LITERATURE, and LANGUAGE AND LITERATURE IN EARLY CHILDHOOD, introduce prospective teachers to the world of children's and adolescents' literature and prepares them to present it to pupils.

Maryville State University. Education. A survey course, CHILDREN'S LITERATURE, introduces classics and modern literature. The program of study follows the suggested outline of literary growth in the English language arts curriculum. Library Science. A survey of young adult literature and media for school and public libraries is offered in YOUNG ADULT LITERATURE.

Minot State University. English. Two courses are offered for teacher preparation, LITERATURE FOR CHILDREN and LITERATURE FOR ADOLESCENTS. Library Science. A variety of print and non-print materials is examined in LISTENING, VIEWING, AND READING GUIDANCE.

University of Mary. Education. A survey course for teachers, CHILDREN'S LITERATURE, is offered.

University of North Dakota. English. This CHILDREN'S LITERATURE course covers a variety of genres. Library Science. In INTRODUCTION TO CHILDREN'S LITERATURE and YOUNG ADULT LITERATURE methods of presenting literature are included along with surveys of the material.

Valley City State University. Library Science. Students study the needs and interests of children and adolescents along with library materials in YOUNG ADULT LITERATURE AND MEDIA and CHILDREN'S LITERATURE.

OHIO

Antioch University. Education. Class meetings focus on literary interests of children in CHILDREN'S LITERATURE.

Baldwin-Wallace College. CHILDREN'S LITERATURE is a survey of children's literature adapted to the elementary school.

Bowling Green State University. Education. STORYTELLING offers experience in techniques and selection. English. Problems in children's literature are addressed in STUDIES IN CHILDREN'S LITERATURE. CHILDREN'S LITERATURE and LITERATURE FOR ADOLESCENTS include reading and evaluation of books for use in the classroom.

Capital University. Education. CHILDREN'S LITERATURE is an introductory course and includes theories of learning and child development related to literature.

Cedarville College. Education. Social and personal values of literature are studied in CHILDREN'S LITERATURE, a historical survey.

Central State University. Education. CHILDREN'S LITERATURE is a study of literary merits and educational value of children's literature.

Chatfield College. English. Forms and topics of books are studied from the viewpoint of literature and psychology in CHILDREN'S LITERATURE.

Cleveland State University. Education. LITERATURE FOR ADOLESCENTS is designed for the reading teacher and other school personnel.

CHILDREN'S LITERATURE is a reading course of literature of interest to children.

College of Mount Saint Joseph. Education. CHILDREN'S AND ADOLESCENT LITERATURE AND MEDIA is designed to develop appreciation of the genres through wide exposure and discussion.

Defiance College. Education. CHILDREN'S LITERATURE places emphasis on selection and evaluation of various genres for use with elementary school children.

Franciscan University of Steubenville. Education. Strong emphasis is placed on appreciation of literature for pre-school to adolescence in CHILDREN'S LITERATURE.

Hiram College. Education and Library Science. Uses of literature for promotion of values and to improve reading are included in CHILDREN'S LITERATURE AND READING.

John Carroll University. Education. ELEMENTARY CURRICULUM: LANGUAGE ARTS AND CHILDREN'S LITERATURE gives special emphasis to integrating the curriculum around major themes. CHILDREN'S LITERATURE is a survey course for advanced teacher education and practicing teachers.

Kent State University. English. Two survey courses are offered for teacher education, CHILDREN'S LITERATURE and ADOLESCENT LITERATURE. Library Science. Attention to gifted child and retarded reader is included in LIBRARY MATERIALS AND SERVICES FOR ADOLESCENTS. LIBRARY MATERIALS AND SERVICES FOR CHILDREN addresses selection and use of materials in relation to needs, abilities, and interests of children.

Lake Erie College. Education. Research and field experiences are included in CHILDREN'S LITERATURE.

Malone College. English. CHILDREN'S LITERATURE includes relation of books to the curriculum and children's needs and interests. ADOLESCENT LITERATURE is a critical evaluation of books and their appropriateness to the secondary curriculum.

Marietta College. English. CHILDREN'S LITERATURE is a survey course of various genres.

Miami University. Education. STORYTELLING: TRADITIONAL AND CONTEMPORARY presents principles of storytelling and reading aloud to various age levels in schools and public libraries. Education and English. LITERATURE AND OTHER MEDIA FOR ADOLESCENTS includes evaluation and consideration of adolescent needs. English. CHILDREN'S LITERATURE is a broad study of children's books with emphasis on evaluation.

Mount Union College. English. CHILDREN'S LITERATURE includes methods of presenting and exploring literature with children.

Mount Vernon Nazarene College. Education. CHILDREN'S LITERATURE covers the use of literature with children from preschool to secondary schools.

Muskingum College. Education. CHILDREN'S LITERATURE AND LANGUAGE ARTS is a study of classical and modern children's literature as it relates to the curriculum.

Ohio Dominican College. Education. LITERATURE FOR CHILDREN AND YOUNG ADULTS includes consideration of nonprint media.

Ohio Northern University. Education. CHILDREN'S LITERATURE places emphasis on all genres in children's literature and includes field experience. English. APPROACHES TO CHILDREN'S LITERATURE uses the same critical approaches that are traditionally used to analyze literature for adults.

Ohio State University–Columbus Campus. Education. Nine courses are offered. Use of literature in the preschool and elementary curriculum is covered in INTRODUCTION TO CHILDREN'S LITERATURE, LITERATURE IN EARLY CHILDHOOD EDUCATION, LITERATURE ACROSS THE CURRICULUM, LITERATURE FOR MIDDLE CHILDHOOD and ADVANCED COURSE IN CHILDREN'S LITERATURE. The same topics for junior and senior high school are included in LITERATURE FOR ADOLESCENTS, and ADVANCED LITERATURE FOR ADOLESCENTS. Genre courses are POETRY FOR CHILDREN and ROOTS OF FANTASY FOR CHILDREN. English. Topics vary in STUDIES IN FOLKLORE and sometimes include children's folklore.

Ohio University. Education. Courses cover use of children's literature both in the classroom and in the library. ADOLESCENT MATERIALS AND SERVICES includes consideration of intellectual freedom. LIBRARY SERVICE TO CHILDREN covers storytelling along with other topics.

CHILDREN'S LITERATURE is a genre survey. LITERATURE FOR CHILDREN AND ADOLESCENTS is a seminar in critical analysis of research and theory. English. READINGS IN CHILDREN'S LITERATURE offers consideration of historical development of children's literature and philosophical and ethical issues.

Ohio Wesleyan University. Education. CHILDREN'S LITERATURE AND LANGUAGE ARTS includes research and the classroom application of literature in the areas of language arts.

Otterbein College. Education. CHILDREN'S LITERATURE includes study of folk literature, children's classics, poetry, and modern prose for children. ADOLESCENT LITERATURE includes methods and rationale for presentation as well as topics of concern in the field.

University of Akron. Education. LITERATURE FOR YOUNG CHILDREN concerns use of literature with children ages two through six. CHILDREN'S LITERATURE is a survey of materials for children from early historical periods to modern times.

University of Cincinnati–Clermont College. Education. Two courses are offered to help teachers prepare to present literature in the classroom: CHILDREN'S LITERATURE and LITERATURE IN ECE.

University of Dayton. Education. LITERATURE FOR CHILDREN AND ADOLESCENTS, offered at the graduate and undergraduate levels, is a study of books for preschool through senior high school levels.

University of Toledo. Education. Surveys of materials and their uses in the classroom are included in SURVEY OF LITERATURE FOR CHILDREN, LITERATURE AND STORYTELLING FOR YOUNGER CHILDREN, ANALYSIS AND USE OF LITERATURE FOR OLDER CHILDREN, and USING LITERATURE IN THE CLASSROOM. Specially selected topics are discussed each summer by noted authors, illustrators and editors of children's books in CHILDREN'S LITERATURE INSTITUTE. MULTICULTURAL LITERATURE offers an opportunity for students to gain familiarity with literature for children written by and about American ethnic groups.

Urbana University. English. Attention is given to books and their use in all subject areas in CHILDREN'S LITERATURE.

Ursuline College. Education. CHILDREN'S LITERATURE takes a multimedia approach to the study of the history and types of children's literature. English. THE ADOLESCENT IN LITERATURE is a study of the adolescent character in selected titles.

Westminster College. English. CHILDREN'S LITERATURE, a required course for elementary education majors, is a study of children's literature from traditional origins to modern times.

Wittenberg University. Education. CHILDREN'S LITERATURE offers a survey of genres and a study of current issues and trends. TEACHING LANGUAGE ARTS AND CHILDREN'S LITERATURE IN THE ELEMENTARY AND MIDDLE SCHOOL provides wide acquaintance with children's books and emphasis on their use in all subject and skill areas.

Wright State University. Education. HISTORY OF BOOKS FOR CHILDREN AND YOUNG PEOPLE surveys international children's literature from the eighteenth century to the twentieth century. In SURVEY OF WORLD LITERATURE FOR CHILDREN AND YOUNG PEOPLE, knowledge of international literature is applied to teaching in curriculum areas. Three other courses address study of literature and its application in the classroom: LITERATURE FOR ELEMENTARY CHILDREN, BOOKS AND EDUCATIONAL PROGRAM, and ELEMENTARY SCHOOL CHILDREN'S LITERATURE CURRICULUM AND MATERIALS. CHILDREN'S LITERATURE FOR TEACHERS OF FOREIGN LANGUAGES includes reading information books about the countries where the languages are spoken. Library Science. STORYTELLING includes techniques of adaptation and presentation, with broad foundation in the materials. LITERATURE FOR ADOLESCENTS AND YOUNG ADULTS includes techniques of reading guidance and promotion of books.

Youngstown State University. English. CHILDREN'S LITERATURE and ADOLESCENT LITERATURE survey the works and discuss their uses in the classroom.

OKLAHOMA

Bartlesville Wesleyan College. Education and English. CHILDREN'S LITERATURE is a survey, with evaluation and utilization of books for children.

Cameron University. Library Science. CHILDREN'S LITERATURE is a general survey, with methods of selecting books and introducing them to children. YOUNG ADULT LITERATURE is a survey of adolescent reading patterns.

Central State University. Education. Students in CHILDREN'S LITERATURE look at types of literature used in the grades. Library

Science. LIBRARY MATERIALS FOR ELEMENTARY SCHOOLS places emphasis on building a library collection. LIBRARY MATERIALS FOR SECONDARY SCHOOLS considers reference and curriculum requirements.

East Central University. English. TEACHING OF LITERATURE IN SECONDARY SCHOOL reviews materials for teaching, principles for the selection of literature, and critical study of selected readings.

Northeastern State University. Library Science. Evaluation, selection, and use of multi-media materials in school media centers are the focus of MATERIALS FOR CHILDREN (formerly CHILDREN'S LITERATURE). MATERIALS FOR ADOLESCENTS emphasizes modern literature and reading guidance. ISSUES IN CHILDREN'S LITERATURE is an in-depth approach to specific issues in children's materials, such as sex, divorce, and death.

Northwestern Oklahoma State University. English. CHILDREN'S LITERATURE AND STORYTELLING includes evaluation of materials according to literary value and age placement.

Oklahoma Baptist University. English. Methods of presentation and relation of literature to the development processes of the young adult reader are considered in LITERATURE FOR YOUNG ADULTS.

Oklahoma Christian College. Education. CHILDREN'S LITERATURE is an introduction and relates the use of literature to the language arts.

Oklahoma City University. Education. CHILDREN'S LITERATURE AND THE LIBRARY includes practice in classroom techniques and a survey of old and new prose and verse.

Oklahoma State University. Education. CHILDREN'S LITERATURE stresses extensive reading and a survey of materials for children. ADVANCED STUDIES IN CHILDREN'S LITERATURE includes a historical survey and the tools of research along with a study of book publishing. Library Science. READING GUIDANCE FOR YOUNG PEOPLE gives practice in preparing book talks and other means of motivating young readers.

Oral Roberts University. Education. CHILDREN'S LITERATURE AND THE LIBRARY acquaints students with the best literature for children and its use in the classroom and library.

Phillips University. Education and Library Science. CHILDREN'S LITERATURE looks at enrichment in the classroom provided by literature.

BOOKS FOR ADOLESCENTS surveys literature for use with young adults, 13 to 18.

Rogers State College. English. Emphasis is placed on selection and presentation of literature suitable for young children in CHILDREN'S LITERATURE.

Southeastern Oklahoma State University. English. CHILDREN'S LITERATURE AND STORY TELLING provides a study of the various types of literature appropriate for children. ADVANCED CHILDREN'S LITERATURE continues this course with emphasis on the modern period.

Southern Nazarene University. Education. READING THROUGH LITERATURE is a survey of major classic and modern literature for children. LITERATURE FOR CHILDREN/YOUTH is an investigation of trends, issues, and problems relating to contemporary literature for children and youth.

Southwestern Oklahoma State University. Education. The choice of literature for K–8 grades is the focus of CHILDREN'S LITERATURE. TEACHING LITERATURE IN THE ELEMENTARY SCHOOLS offers practical creative experiences with literature and fine arts. Library Science. BOOKS AND MATERIALS FOR YOUNG PEOPLE provides guidelines for selection and evaluation of books for young people.

University of Central Oklahoma. Education. Types of literature used in the grades are examined in CHILDREN'S LITERATURE. Library Science. LIBRARY MATERIALS FOR ELEMENTARY SCHOLS and LIBRARY MATERIALS FOR SECONDARY SCHOOLS place emphasis on building suitable library collections.

University of Oklahoma. Library Science. BOOKS AND MATERIALS FOR CHILDREN offers in-depth criticism of children's materials and selection of recent literature. BOOKS AND MATERIALS FOR YOUNG ADULTS is a seminar involving thematic-issue approach to reading guidance and twentieth century trends.

University of Science and Arts of Oklahoma. Education. CHILDREN'S LITERATURE offers a wide acquaintance with children's and adolescents' books.

OREGON

Concordia College. Education. CHILDREN'S LITERATURE provides treatment of literature for early childhood through grade 8.

Eastern Oregon State College. Education. CHILDREN'S LITERATURE AND EARLY CHILDHOOD EDUCATION gives the student basic knowledge of literature available for use with young children.

George Fox College. English. A study of criteria for guiding youth into an appreciation of literature is included in LITERATURE FOR CHILDREN AND ADOLESCENTS.

Lewis and Clark College. Education. LANGUAGE ARTS AND LITERATURE, K-8 is an exploration of literature and the development of a theoretical framework for teaching the language arts.

Linfield College. English. CHILDREN'S LITERATURE includes study of literature available in different formats, and its presentation to children.

Oregon State University. Education. BOOKS IN ELEMENTARY SCHOOLS assists students to recognize and evaluate various genres and to incorporate them into the curriculum. English. LITERATURE FOR CHILDREN emphasizes analysis and evaluation of literary works. LITERATURE FOR TEACHERS is a review of approaches to literature for the secondary school.

Pacific University. Education. CHILDREN'S LITERATURE emphasizes motivation and enjoyment of literature in the classroom.

Portland State University. Education. Offered at the graduate and undergraduate levels. CHILDREN'S LITERATURE gives suggestions for the presentation of literature in the elementary school. ENRICHING CHILDREN'S READING is a study of the use of literature in the reading program. READING AND TELLING CHILDREN'S STORIES introduces old folk and modern fanciful tales, with laboratory practice. Library Science. CHILDREN'S LITERATURE surveys the genres and literature that illustrate cultural diversity.

Southern Oregon State College. English. LITERATURE FOR ADOLESCENTS places emphasis on selection and evaluation of books for use in the curriculum.

University of Oregon. Education. STORYTELLING gives fundamental principles and techniques. CHILDREN'S LITERATURE is a study of selection and evaluation of children's books suitable for school libraries.

University of Portland. Education. CHILDREN'S AND ADOLESCENT LITERATURE AND LIBRARY is a survey of literature and its use to enrich the curriculum.

Western Baptist College. English. CHILDREN'S LITERATURE places emphasis on reading and on learning the criteria for evaluating children's literature.

Western Oregon State College. Education. READING, WRITING AND CHILDREN'S LITERATURE I AND II include ways of using children's literature across the curriculum, especially in the language arts and reading. READING AND TELLING CHILDREN'S STORIES includes use of stories for bibliotherapy, crafts, choral reading, and multicultural studies. LITERATURE FOR CHILDREN AND YOUNG ADULTS examines the literature for pre-school through high school.

PENNSYLVANIA

Albright College. Education. CHILDREN'S LITERATURE is an introductory course with focus on history, current issues, and promotion of child development through literature.

Bloomsburg University of Pennsylvania. Education. LITERATURE FOR CHILDREN IN THE ELEMENTARY GRADES is a survey of ways that children may encounter literature.

Cedar Crest College. Education. Consideration of a wide variety of literature for children and its use in the curriculum is the focus of THE TEACHING OF CHILDREN'S LITERATURE AND THE LANGUAGE ARTS.

Chestnut Hill College. Education. CHILDREN'S LITERATURE offers an introduction to the oral traditions of world literature and a study of contemporary literature, with emphasis on its use in the classroom.

Clarion University of Pennsylvania. Education. Students develop teaching strategies to introduce literature to children in CHILDREN'S LITERATURE. English. LITERATURE FOR YOUNG ADULTS introduces future teachers to the field.

College Misericordia. Education. Currriculum topics in elementary literature studies are explored in CHILDREN'S LITERATURE.

Drexel University. Library Science. RESOURCES FOR CHILDREN is a survey of library materials for children. RESOURCES FOR YOUNG PEOPLE surveys materials for school and public libraries.

East Stroudsburg University. Education. CHILDREN'S LITERATURE offers varied ways to get children interested in books. CHILDREN'S LITERATURE FOR ADVANCED STUDENTS gives special attention to social and personal issues and the use of bibliotherapy.

Eastern College. Education. JUVENILE LITERATURE is an introduction to juvenile books and their uses.

Gannon University. Education. Techniques for storytelling and methods of using books are considered in LITERATURE IN EARLY CHILDHOOD EDUCATION. CHILDREN'S LITERATURE is a critical examination of books, writers, and illustrators. ADOLESCENT LITERATURE offers literature program design.

Grove City College. Education. CHILDREN'S LITERATURE is a genre survey for preschool through sixth grade. YOUNG ADULT LITERATURE emphasizes post–1969 publications.

Holy Family College. Education. CHILDREN'S LITERATURE is a study of representative works.

Immaculata College. Education. CHILDREN'S LITERATURE is an introduction to various types of literature, including drama.

Juniata College. Education. Literature as a vehicle for integrating the curriculum is part of CHILDREN'S LITERATURE study.

King's College. Education. CHILDREN'S LITERATURE is designed to inculcate in students an appreciation of the literature created especially for children.

Kutztown University of Pennsylvania. Education. CHILDREN'S LITERATURE is a survey of important children's books, with emphasis on multiculturalism. Library Science. RESOURCES FOR CHILDREN is an introduction to the principles for the development of a library collection. RESOURCES FOR YOUNG ADULTS is a survey and critical evaluation of adolescent literature and related media. FOLK LITERATURE AND STORYTELLING provides a survey of literature and practical experience in storytelling.

La Roche College. Art. ILLUSTRATION OF LITERATURE is a study of the history and techniques of illustrating children's literature. English. CHILDREN'S LITERATURE offers an opportunity to practice creative projects designed to encourage and enrich reading.

La Salle University. English. YOUNG ADULT LITERATURE is aimed at preparing prospective and practicing teachers, librarians, and parents to direct the reading of young adults.

Lebanon Valley College. Education. Extensive examination of books and audiovisual resources is included in CHILDREN'S LITERATURE.

Lehigh University. Education. The use of trade books for instruction in reading is explored in CHILDREN'S LITERATURE IN READING INSTRUCTION.

Lycoming College. Education. Using children's literature as a vehicle for ensuring an appreciation of the creative writing of others is one of the objectives of TEACHING LANGUAGE ARTS AND CHILDREN'S LITERATURE IN THE ELEMENTARY SCHOOL.

Mansfield University of Pennsylvania. Education. Uses of children's literature in the curriculum are the aim of CHILDREN'S LITERATURE.

Marywood College. Education. CHILDREN'S LITERATURE FOR EARLY CHILDHOOD AND ELEMENTARY SCHOOL TEACHERS presents a brief history of children's literature.

Messiah College. Education. CHILDREN'S LITERATURE gives attention to text, illustration, and historical development. English. ADOLESCENT LITERATURE is an introduction for prospective teachers.

Millersville University of Pennsylvania. Education. LITERATURE FOR THE MIDDLE AND SECONDARY SCHOOL introduces teachers to methods of helping young people read with pleasure. Library Science. CHILDREN'S LITERATURE introduces authors, illustrators, and genres.

Moravian College. Education. CHILDREN'S LANGUAGE AND LITERATURE gives special emphasis to the selection and use of quality children's literature.

Neumann College. Education. CHILDREN'S LITERATURE is designed to acquaint students with authors and illustrators. LANGUAGE ARTS AND CHILDREN'S LITERATURE correlates children's literature with language development.

Pennsylvania State University. University Park. Education. CHILDREN'S LITERATURE encourages use of literature-related activities in teaching reading. LITERATURE FOR CHILDREN AND ADOLESCENTS offers approaches for using literature in the school curriculum. ADOLESCENT LITERATURE AND DEVELOPMENTAL READING includes practices suitable for an English class.

Point Park College. Education. CREATIVE STORY TELLING fosters techniques for teaching literature creatively.

Rosemont College. Education. CHILDREN'S LITERATURE considers literature as communication between authors, adult readers, and child readers.

Saint Joseph's University. Education. Students in LITERATURE FOR TODAY'S YOUNG PEOPLE plan experiences with literature for children and adolescents. LITERATURE FOR ADOLESCENTS focuses on themes that reflect development concerns. LITERATURE FOR YOUNG PEOPLE includes study of appropriate social and cultural balance in literature.

Seton Hill College. English. LITERATURE FOR CHILDREN is a study of folklore and contemporary literature, with emphasis on award books.

Shippensburg University of Pennsylvania. Education. STUDIES IN CHILDREN'S LITERATURE is planned to evaluate the role of literature in the elementary classroom.

Susquehanna University. Education. Required for elementary education majors, CHILDREN'S LITERATURE is a survey of the literature and a review of its bibliography.

Swarthmore College. Library Science. LIBRARIES, LITERATURE, AND THE ADOLESCENT includes a study of adolescent literature and the trends affecting its development. LIBRARIES, LITERATURE, AND THE CHILD offers an opportunity to investigate the use of children's literature in school and public libraries. STORYTELLING gives attention to multi-media storytelling. HISTORY OF CHILDREN'S LITERATURE is a survey of the history and development of children's literature through the nineteenth century.

Temple University. English. CHILDREN'S LITERATURE AND FOLKLORE includes readings in classics and addresses literature and its relation to culture.

University of Pennsylvania. Education. CHILDREN'S LITERATURE includes both theoretical and practical aspects of study. English. ADOLESCENT LITERATURE: THE PROBLEM NOVEL examines literature appropriate for grades 5–12. CHILDREN'S LITERATURE includes reading and critical analysis of books for elementary schools. WRITING FOR CHILDREN includes extensive readings in important works as models for writing in juvenile genres.

University of Scranton. Education. Children's literary needs and interests are emphasized in CHILDREN'S LITERATURE.

Villanova University. Education. LITERATURE FOR EARLY CHILDHOOD EDUCATION gives strategies for providing literary experiences for young children. CHILDREN'S LITERATURE addresses the use of children's literature in the elementary school curriculum. FOLK LITERATURE AND STORYTELLING combines a study of traditional literature with practice in presenting it orally. YOUNG ADULT LITERATURE is intended to provide curriculum enrichment in school libraries. English. SEMINAR: METHODS OF TEACHING CHILDREN'S LITERATURE is designed for the practical use of elementary and secondary school teachers.

West Chester University of Pennsylvania. Education. TEACHING READING WITH CHILDREN'S AND ADOLESCENTS' LITERATURE is based on the philosophy that literature should be an integral element of reading programs. LITERATURE FOR THE ELEMENTARY SCHOOL and LITERATURE FOR THE SECONDARY SCHOOL address the content and approach of the literature program. English. LITERATURE FOR YOUNG CHILDREN and CHILDREN'S LITERATURE are teacher preparation courses.

Westminster College. Education. LANGUAGE ARTS AND CHILDREN'S LITERATURE IN THE ELEMENTARY SCHOOL includes the effective use of children's literature as integrated into the curriculum.

Widener University. Education. ADOLESCENT LITERATURE gives specific methods and practices for classrom use. LITERATURE FOR CHILDREN focuses on the application of evaluative criteria in the classroom setting. CHILDREN'S LITERATURE is designed to develop a love for children's literature and a broad knowledge of many literary types.

Wilkes University. Education. CHILDREN'S LITERATURE places emphasis on criteria for selecting literature for the classroom.

RHODE ISLAND

Rhode Island College. Education. CREATIVE DRAMA AND LITERATURE: RESOURCES IN THE CLASSROOM relates these topics to the reading,

English, and social studies curricula. LITERATURE IN THE ELEMENTARY SCHOOL is concerned with the development of literature instruction in the elementary school. CHILDREN AND BOOKS is an introduction to books for children from birth to age 9. English. CHILDREN'S LITERATURE and ADOLESCENT LITERATURE are teacher preparation courses, which relate literature to children's and adolescents' needs and interests.

Roger Williams College. Education. DEVELOPMENT OF LITERACY IN CHILDREN I AND II. Both courses include the use of children's literature in the reading program.

Salve Regina College. Education. DEVELOPMENT OF LITERACY IN CHILDREN I AND II. Both courses include the use of children's literature in the reading program. CHILDREN'S LITERATURE is a critical study of fantasy and realism in children's books.

University of Rhode Island. Education. THE USE OF TRADE BOOKS IN THE READING PROGRAM provides understanding of the use of children's literature as an extension of elementary school textbooks. Library Science. READING INTERESTS OF YOUNG ADULTS gives an overview of young adult literature, with emphasis on building the collection. STORYTELLING gives attention to sources of materials and practice in the art.

SOUTH CAROLINA

Anderson College. Education and English. LITERATURE FOR CHILDREN requires extensive reading and consideration of integrating literature into writing and reading programs.

Benedict College. English. CHILDREN'S LITERATURE surveys literature and addresses methods of teaching it to children of varying backgrounds, abilities, and interests. ADOLESCENT LITERATURE includes study of traditional works as well as literature especially designed for readers grades six through twelve.

Bob Jones University. Education. CHILDREN'S LITERATURE is an interpretive and critical study of literature suitable for children. English. ADOLESCENT LITERATURE is a teacher preparation course.

Central Wesleyan College. Education. CHILDREN'S LITERATURE is a survey course for the preparation of teachers to use literature with children. English. ADOLESCENT LITERATURE is a teacher preparation course.

Charleston Southern. English. ADOLESCENT LITERATURE is a survey of literature appropriate to the needs, interests, and abilities of the adolescent.

The Citadel. Education. CHILDREN'S LITERATURE includes the promotion of reading interests and tastes in the classroom. ADOLESCENT LITERATURE includes methods of introducing the major literary genres. Library Science. CHILDREN'S LITERATURE is a historical survey that requires wide reading. ADOLESCENT LITERATURE is designed for the secondary-school teacher.

Claflin College. Education. LITERATURE FOR CHILDREN includes principles for evaluation and familiarity with resources. English. ADOLESCENT LITERATURE includes creative writing of short stories and poetry.

Clemson University. Education. TEACHING READING THROUGH A LITERATURE EMPHASIS gives strategies for integrating literature into the traditional reading program. English. CHILDREN'S LITERATURE and ADOLESCENT LITERATURE require wide reading in prose and verse. CHILDREN'S LITERATURE FOR TEACHERS and LITERATURE FOR TEACHERS are teacher preparation courses.

Coastal Carolina College. English. CHILDREN'S LITERATURE and ADOLESCENT LITERATURE prepare teachers to share appropriate literature with children and adolescents.

Coker College. English. CHILDREN'S LITERATURE helps prospective teachers develop standards for recommending children's books. ADOLESCENT LITERATURE offers critical reading of books being read by adolescents.

College of Charleston. Education. LITERATURE FOR CHILDREN reviews old and new literary materials and addresses their integration with the curriculum. EARLY CHILDHOOD LITERATURE is a survey of literature with attention to participation books. CHILDREN'S LITERATURE is a historical and genre survey, with attention to reading for pleasure. English. LITERATURE FOR ADOLESCENTS includes study of major literary genres and media.

Columbia Bible College. Education and English. CHILDREN'S LITERATURE gives practice in the use of books in the home and in the classroom.

Columbia College. Education. CHILDREN'S LITERATURE is an intensive study with wide reading required. YOUTH LITERATURE includes selection and evaluation of literary works from standard bibliographies.

Converse College. Education. LITERATURE FOR THE CHILD acquaints the student with traditional and modern literature and its use in the curriculum. TEACHING READING THROUGH LITERATURE is designed to facilitate reading instruction from a literature base. In MYTHOLOGY AND FAIRY TALES FOR ELEMENTARY TEACHERS, the primary focus is on theory and on the mythic tales themselves. English. ADOLESCENT LITERATURE is a teacher preparation course planned to evaluate and read literary works for high school students.

Erskine College. Education. CHILDREN'S LITERATURE includes study of informational books. English. LITERATURE FOR YOUNG ADULTS offers basic critical approaches to literature.

Francis Marion College. English. LITERATURE FOR ADOLESCENTS offers readings in literature appropriate for use in the classroom, especially with poor readers.

Furman University. Education. LANGUAGE AND LITERATURE IN THE ELEMENTARY SCHOOL gives a comprehensive look at the language arts program and its use of literature. ADOLESCENT LITERATURE looks at content of literature and methods of teaching.

Lander College. Education. CHILDREN'S LITERATURE includes selection of book and non-book materials. TEACHING READING THROUGH A LITERATURE EMPHASIS is an introduction to ways literature can be integrated into a reading/language arts program. English. YOUNG ADULT LITERATURE provides the history and background of young adult literature for teachers.

Limestone College. Education. LITERATURE FOR CHILDREN is a study of traditional and modern literature and its use in the classroom.

Morris College. English. LITERATURE FOR CHILDREN AND ADOLESCENTS deals with criteria for selecting works of special interest to children and adolescents.

Newberry College. English. CHILDREN'S LITERATURE is a survey of world literature. ADOLESCENT LITERATURE is a historical survey.

Presbyterian College. Education. LITERATURE FOR CHILDREN includes materials, resources, and techniques for presenting literature to children. ADOLESCENT LITERATURE considers the relation of the teacher to the school library program.

South Carolina State College. English. CHILDREN'S LITERATURE deals with the history of children's literature and criteria for selecting books for children. LITERATURE FOR ADOLESCENTS acquaints prospective teachers of English with literature appropriate for use with high school students.

University of South Carolina. English. CHILDREN'S LITERATURE and ADOLESCENT LITERATURE provide prospective teachers with experience reading and evaluating representative works. Library Science. MATERIALS FOR EARLY CHILDHOOD reviews media resources and techniques for children to age nine. MATERIALS FOR CHILDREN covers reading interests of children and their curricular needs. MATERIALS FOR ADOLESCENTS studies relationships of media to information needs.

University of South Carolina–Beaufort. Education. CHILDREN'S LITERATURE explores reading interests of children and their curricular and developmental needs. English. CHILDREN'S LITERATURE is a course in reading and reporting on works appropriate for the elementary school.

University of South Carolina–Spartanburg. English. CHILDREN'S LITERATURE is a study of works appropriate for the elementary school child. ADOLESCENT LITERATURE examines the characterization of adolescents in literature and the historical development of the literature.

Winthrop College. English. ADOLESCENT LITERATURE is for students preparing to teach in secondary schools. Library Science. BOOKS AND OTHER MEDIA FOR CHILDREN is an introduction to books, magazines, and nonprint adaptations of literature for children. CURRENT TRENDS IN CHILDREN'S LITERATURE is intended to update classroom teachers' knowledge of children's literature. BOOKS AND OTHER MEDIA FOR YOUNG ADULTS is a study of literature and media produced for young people.

Wofford College. English. ADOLESCENT LITERATURE offers principles for selection of works appropriate for study in secondary schools.

SOUTH DAKOTA

Augustana College. Education. CHILDREN'S LITERATURE AND LANGUAGE ARTS includes the evaluation of traditional and modern literature.

Black Hills State University. English. NATIVE AMERICAN CHILDREN'S LITERATURE introduces children's literature written by and about Native Americans. English and Library Media. CHILDREN'S LITERATURE includes study of how to integrate knowledge of children, books, and the learning process. LITERATURE FOR YOUNG ADULTS focuses on the basic genres, with analysis of literary quality and discussion of current issues.

Dakota Wesleyan University. Education. LANGUAGE ARTS AND CHILDREN'S LITERATURE IN THE ELEMENTARY SCHOOL includes study of the types of literature used in the language arts program.

Huron University. Education. TEACHING CHILDREN'S LITERATURE IN ELEMENTARY SCHOOL provides opportunity for the student to become familiar with a wide range of stories and poems.

Mount Marty College. Education. ELEMENTARY SCHOOL LANGUAGE ARTS AND LITERATURE FOR CHILDREN includes study of classic and contemporary literature, experience in book selection, and strategies for presenting literature to children.

Northern State University. Library Media. LITERATURE FOR CHILDREN covers history of children's literature, experience in storytelling, and selection of books for children.

Oglala Lakota College. English. CHILDREN'S LITERATURE presents books and other media and their use in the classroom, with attention to Native American works.

Presentation College. English. CHILDREN'S LITERATURE is a survey course with emphasis on selection of books for children.

Sioux Falls College. Education. LITERATURE FOR CHILDREN AND ADOLESCENTS stresses response to and evaluation of literature by teachers, librarians, and parents. English. LITERATURE FOR CHILDREN AND ADOLESCENTS includes a genre and age-specific survey, as well as discussion of literary elements.

South Dakota State University. English. JUVENILE LITERATURE is a historical and genre survey.

University of South Dakota. Education. ADOLESCENT LITERATURE covers selection of non-curricular reading and reading guidance.

Library Media. CHILDREN'S LITERATURE covers traditional and modern literature and field experience.

TEXAS

Abilene Christian University. English. LITERATURE FOR CHILDREN is a content reading course with special emphasis on historical backgrounds. YOUNG ADULTS LITERATURE includes reading theory and materials for high schools.

Angelo State University. English. CHILDREN'S LITERATURE is a historical survey with book selection for elementary grades.

Baylor University. Library Science. CHILDREN'S LITERATURE traces the development of a distinct literature for children and its selection and use. Both CURRICULUM APPLICATIONS IN CHILDREN'S LITERATURE and LITERATURE FOR CHILDREN AND YOUNG ADULTS address curriculum planning.

Bishop College. Education. LITERATURE FOR CHILDREN provides opportunities for sharing a variety of types of literature.

Corpus Christi University. English. ORAL INTERPRETATION OF CHILDREN'S LITERATURE is strongly oriented toward teaching literature in the elementary school classroom.

East Texas Baptist University. English. CHILDREN'S LITERATURE is a historical survey for elementary education majors.

East Texas State University. English. Two courses are offered. PICTURE BOOKS AND THE ART OF ILLUSTRATION stresses the relationship between art and text. HISTORY AND SURVEY OF CHILDREN'S LITERATURE is an overview emphasizing the development of classic works. Library Science. DEVELOPING GENERAL AND SPECIALIZED COLLECTIONS reviews principles and practices of selection. BOOKS AND RELATED MATERIALS FOR CHILDREN AND YOUNG ADULTS is an in-depth study of materials as they relate to the curriculum. Use of books for development of positive self-identity is part of MULTI-ETHNIC MATERIALS.

East Texas State University at Texarkana. English. STUDIES IN CHILDREN'S LITERATURE, intended for students with background or experience, focuses on specific authors with emphasis on classroom use.

Hardin-Simmons University. Education. LITERATURE FOR THE ELEMENTARY SCHOOL is a study of literature, traditional and modern, for classroom use.

Houston Baptist University. Education. TEACHING READING THROUGH CHILDREN'S LITERATURE focuses on teaching pre-adolescents.

Howard Payne University. English. CHILDREN'S LITERATURE is recommended for teachers and surveys a wide range of readings.

Incarnate Word College. Education. READING AND LITERATURE FOR THE YOUNG ADULT focuses on library materials and development of a recreational reading program. READING AND LITERATURE IN THE ELEMENTARY SCHOOL includes research in reading interests and reading in the content areas.

Lamar University. Education. CHILDREN'S LITERATURE includes materials for motivating children to develop a continuing interest in reading.

Lubbock Christian University. Education. CHILDREN'S LITERATURE is a general survey including standards for selection.

McMurry College. Education and English. CHILDREN'S LITERATURE is a genre survey including the use of literature in the classroom.

Midwestern State University. English. CHILDREN'S LITERATURE focuses on the works of the most important writers and illustrators.

Our Lady of the Lake University. Library Science. CHILDREN'S LITERATURE AND RELATED MEDIA includes multiethnic and multicultural selection and the use of books in the school curriculum.

Pan American University. Education. LANGUAGE ARTS/CHILDREN'S LITERATURE IN THE ELEMENTARY CURRICULUM addresses teaching language arts with special emphasis on literature. CHILD AND ADOLESCENT LITERATURE provides experiences for selecting and presenting literature to children.

Sam Houston State University. Library Science. BOOKS AND RELATED MATERIALS FOR CHILDREN is a historical survey with emphasis on motivational techniques. BOOKS AND RELATED MATERIALS FOR YOUNG PEOPLE includes book talks and the sharing of reading experiences.

LIBRARY MATERIALS FOR YOUNG ADULTS is a study of books based on personal and curriculum-related needs.

Southwest Texas State University. English. CHILDREN'S LITERATURE and ADOLESCENT LITERATURE are surveys that aid teachers in developing a critical philosophy for using literature in the classroom.

St. Philip's College. English. A survey of the history of literature for children is provided for child care workers in CHILDREN'S LITERATURE.

St. Mary's University. Education. Various uses of literature in the classroom are covered in CHILDREN'S LITERATURE.

Sul Ross State University. English. CHILDREN'S AND ADOLESCENT LITERATURE includes the application of literary evaluation to children's and adolescent literature and a survey of resources for teachers.

Texas A & M University. Education. TEACHING READING THROUGH CHILDREN'S LITERATURE includes use of past and contemporary literature. CHILDREN'S LITERATURE AND LITERACY covers integration of reading and response theory into the study of literature. MULTICULTURAL CHILDREN'S LITERATURE AND LITERACY provides concentrated study of Native American, black, and Hispanic children's literature. English. Two courses are provided, LITERATURE FOR CHILDREN and LITERATURE FOR ADOLESCENTS. Both provide comprehensive surveys and pedagogical materials on reading and responding to literature.

Texas Christian University. Education. In both CHILDREN'S LITERATURE and LITERATURE FOR ADOLESCENTS, students read widely and apply principles of selection and use in the curriculum.

Texas Lutheran College. Education and English. CHILDREN'S LITERATURE familiarizes students with the literature and its use with individuals and groups.

Texas Tech University. Education. STUDIES IN CHILDREN'S LITERATURE provides in-depth studies of research and instructional practices, and it may be repeated for credit.

Texas Wesleyan College. English. CHILDREN'S LITERATURE offers history and survey of literature with emphasis on selection and use.

Texas Woman's University. Library Science. LITERATURE FOR CHILDREN and LITERATURE FOR YOUNG ADULTS survey modern and traditional literature, and both courses provide techniques for reading guidance and selection of materials.

University of Dallas. Education. CHILD AND YOUNG ADULT LITERATURE examines the principles necessary for a successful literature program.

University of Houston. Education. LITERATURE FOR CHILDREN covers analysis of fiction and nonfiction and emphasizes criteria for selection.

University of Houston (Clear Lake). Education. CHILDREN'S BOOKS AND READING explores the role of literature in teaching reading and language skills. Library Science. SELECTING LITERATURE AND MATERIALS FOR ADOLESCENTS covers selection of literature for the secondary school. SELECTING LITERATURE AND MATERIALS FOR CHILDREN includes motivational techniques for encouraging interest in reading.

University of North Texas. Library Science. MATERIALS AND READING FOR CHILDREN includes multicultural/multi-ethnic materials and wide reading and use of literature. MATERIALS AND READING FOR YOUNG ADULTS addresses curricular correlations and enrichment.

University of Texas–Arlington. English. CHILDREN'S LITERATURE, designed for prospective teachers, is a survey with analysis of outstanding authors and illustrators.

University of Texas–Austin. Library and Information Science. CHILDREN'S LITERATURE AND RELATED MATERIALS requires extensive reading and is intended to help the student develop a frame of reference for working with children's materials.

University of Texas–El Paso. Education. CHILDREN'S LITERATURE IN THE ELEMENTARY SCHOOL addresses the recreational reading program in relation to the content areas in the elementary school. English. CHILDREN'S LITERATURE is a survey of major genres from the seventeenth century to the present.

University of Texas–San Antonio. Education. Two courses are offered. Field based experiences are included in YOUNG CHILDREN'S LITERATURE AND STORYTELLING. LITERATURE FOR CHILDREN AND ADOLESCENTS emphasizes ways to integrate literature into the curriculum. English. LITERATURE FOR CHILDREN AND ADOLESCENTS is a literary analysis of classics and current materials.

University of Texas-Taylor. English. Two CHILDREN'S LITERATURE courses are offered. Both are designed for teacher preparation and survey the history of the literature.

University of Texas-Tyler. English. CHILDREN'S LITERATURE surveys the history of the literature for teachers.

West Texas State University. Education. TEACHING READING THROUGH CHILDREN'S LITERATURE presents techniques and methods. English. LITERATURE FOR CHILDREN is a general survey with standards for selection and evaluation.

Wiley College. Education and English. CHILDREN'S LITERATURE offers study of a wide range of materials with emphasis on use in the elementary school.

UTAH

Brigham Young University. Education. CHILDREN'S LITERATURE covers trends and practical uses of literature.

College of Eastern Utah. English. CHILDREN'S LITERATURE reviews history, types, and practical uses in the classroom.

Southern Utah State College. English. CHILDREN'S LITERATURE introduces the literature with emphasis on approach. ADOLESCENT LITERATURE places emphasis on literary devices, theme, and social criticism.

University of Utah. Education. CHILDREN'S LITERATURE IN THE SCHOOLS addresses ways of implementing literature in the classroom and integrating it into the total curriculum. ADVANCED CHILDREN'S LITERATURE examines research, reader response, current issues, and literature in the content areas.

Utah State University. English. CHILDREN'S LITERATURE and YOUNG ADULT LITERATURE offer study of prose and poetry for the targeted ages. LITERATURE FOR TEACHERS includes evaluation and selection of materials and methods of presenting literature to students.

Westminster College of Salt Lake City. English. CHILDREN'S LITERATURE emphasizes literary and artistic merit and the place of literature in the curriculum. LITERATURE FOR YOUNG ADULTS is a similar course for this age level.

Weber State College. English. CHILDREN'S LITERATURE is a study of representative literature. YOUNG PEOPLE'S LITERATURE requires extensive reading for prospective teachers.

VERMONT

Castleton State College. English. Six courses are offered, taking a genre or period approach to the literature. In POETRY FOR CHILDREN and FOLK TALES students read widely, considering psychological content, children's language skills, and literary appreciation. NINETEENTH-CENTURY CHILDREN'S LITERATURE and TWENTIETH-CENTURY CHILDREN'S LITERATURE focus on major authors, social contexts, and influences. IMAGES OF THE CHILD IN AMERICAN LITERATURE examines treatment of children in the work of major authors. CHILDREN'S WORDS AND PICTURES compares children's writings with the work of professional authors.

Champlain College. Education. CHILDREN'S LITERATURE emphasizes the selection of good literature and its use in a young child's environment.

Johnson State College. LITERATURE FOR CHILDREN presents trade books and their selection and use in the classroom, home, and library. LITERATURE FOR YOUTH is a genre survey.

Lyndon State College. Education. CHILDREN'S LITERATURE offers principles of selection and evaluation, as well as storytelling.

Norwich University. English. CHILDREN'S LITERATURE gives a background in the field and training in evaluating and presenting literature.

Saint Michael's College. Education. LITERATURE FOR CHILDREN AND YOUTH requires wide reading in all genres, with study of the use of literature in the classroom.

University of Vermont. Education. CHILDREN'S LITERATURE AND LANGUAGE ARTS includes appreciation, evaluation, and selection of literature for use in the language arts program. LITERATURE AND LANGUAGE FOR CHILDREN AND YOUTH offers organization of book units for teaching literature and for content areas. Library Science. SELECTION OF

Books and Materials for Young Adults includes techniques for cross-media approach. SELECTION OF LIBRARY MATERIALS FOR CHILDREN includes use of selection tools and evaluation of materials.

VIRGINIA

Averett College. Education. CHILDREN'S LITERATURE presents techniques for teachers to use for bringing children and books together. English. LITERATURE FOR CHILDREN is the study of a broad spectrum of literature appropriate for children.

Bluefield College. English. LITERATURE FOR CHILDREN AND ADOLESCENTS is a historical/genre survey.

Bridgewater College. English. LITERATURE FOR CHILDREN is a historical survey with attention to problems of reluctant readers.

Christopher Newport College. English. The coming of age theme in contemporary literature is explored in ADOLESCENT LITERATURE.

College of William and Mary. Education. Offered at graduate and undergraduate levels, CHILDREN'S LITERATURE covers all aspects of the field. Education and English. LITERATURE FOR ADOLESCENTS allows participants to read and discuss books and to determine the interests, needs, and abilities of middle and high school age readers.

Eastern Mennonite College. English. LITERATURE FOR CHILDREN AND ADOLESCENTS explores strategies for involving children in every genre.

Emory and Henry College. English. CHILDREN'S LITERATURE is a survey of ancient and modern children's books, with criteria for selection and strategies for presentation.

George Mason University. Education. Historical development and types are studied in CHILDREN'S LITERATURE, with storytelling and techniques of presentation.

Hampton University. English. CHILDREN'S LITERATURE is a survey course that includes experience in storytelling and dramatization.

Hollins College. English. CHILDREN'S LITERATURE introduces traditional and contemporary classics of all genres.

James Madison University. Library Science. Five courses are offered. CHILDREN'S LITERATURE offers use of books with children for teachers and librarians. RESOURCES FOR CHILDREN is a comprehensive survey with attention to curriculum-related materials. RESOURCES FOR YOUNG ADULTS includes study of the research on reading, viewing, and listening interests. CURRENT TRENDS IN CHILDREN'S/YOUNG ADULTS LITERATURE reviews print and nonprint publications of the last ten years. LITERATURE IN THE ORAL TRADITION presents storytelling as a traditional folk art.

Liberty University. Education. CHILDREN'S LITERATURE includes activities to enhance children's interest and enjoyment in their literature.

Mary Baldwin College. Education and English. LITERATURE FOR CHILDREN is a study of classics and contemporary works, with emphasis on evaluation of individual works.

Mary Washington College. Liberal Studies. YOUNG ADULT LITERATURE provides literary analysis of works and the development of teaching rationales.

Marymount University. Education. CHILDREN'S LITERATURE AND INTRODUCTION TO LANGUAGE ARTS offers a brief survey of the literature and its use in the curriculum.

Norfolk State University. Education. CHILDREN'S LITERATURE FOR EARLY CHILDHOOD EDUCATION places emphasis on reading aloud, storytelling, and choral speaking; the course also includes field experience.

Old Dominion University. Education. LITERATURE FOR CHILDREN AND YOUNG ADULTS, offered at graduate and undergraduate levels, provides for the evaluation and use of library materials and resources.

Radford University. Library Science. ADOLESCENT AND YOUNG ADULT LITERATURE emphasizes critical evaluation of books, multi-ethnic materials, and materials for bibliotherapy at the graduate and undergraduate levels.

Randolph-Macon Woman's College. Education. CHILDREN'S LITERATURE includes a laboratory requirement in the public schools.

Roanoke College. Education. CHILDREN'S AND ADOLESCENT LITERATURE is a survey course for prospective teachers.

Saint Paul's College. English. Prospective teachers are prepared to select and evaluate literature in ADOLESCENT LITERATURE.

Southern Seminary College. English. CHILDREN'S LITERATURE reviews the history and development of literature for children and its use with young children.

Sweet Briar College. Education. CHILDREN'S LITERATURE presents the history of children's literature.

University of Richmond. Education. CHILDREN'S LITERATURE, a survey of modern and traditional literature, gives guidance for integrating books into the curriculum. Education and English. ADOLESCENT LITERATURE emphasizes American novels and stories since 1945.

University of Virginia. Education. LITERATURE FOR ADOLESCENTS covers selection of literature for secondary school use.

Virginia Commonwealth University. Education. CHILDREN'S LITERATURE I is designed to give students an appreciation of values and a historical survey. CHILDREN'S LITERATURE II is a genre survey with a focus on the use of literature with children. LITERATURE FOR ADOLESCENTS acquaints the prospective secondary English teacher with the nature, scope, and use of adolescent literature.

Virginia Intermont College. English. CHILDREN'S AND ADOLESCENT LITERATURE is a historical survey that helps teachers select and present the best literature to children.

Virginia Polytechnic Institute and State University. Education. LITERATURE FOR ADOLESCENTS addresses reading interests and needs of adolescents. English. LITERATURE FOR CHILDREN is a general critical and historical survey of traditional and contemporary writing for children.

Virginia State University. Library Science. MEDIA RESOURCES FOR CHILDREN examines trends which affect children's literature and methods of teaching. MEDIA RESOURCES FOR YOUNG ADULTS is a survey of multimedia resources with emphasis on modern literature.

Virginia Wesleyan College. English. CHILDREN'S LITERATURE gives attention to criteria for selecting materials suited to the needs of children. ADOLESCENT LITERATURE is a survey course.

WASHINGTON

Eastern Washington University. English. CHILDREN'S LITERATURE surveys major types of literature for children in the elementary grades. Library Science. CHILDREN'S LITERATURE gives attention to literary value and selection of materials for children. ADOLESCENT LITERATURE is a survey including classics and social problem novels.

Gonzaga University. Education. CHILDREN AND ADOLESCENT LITERATURE surveys classical and contemporary literary works and teaching strategies for their utilization.

Heritage College. English. LITERATURE FOR YOUTH SERIES includes an examination of books viewed in the light of social, psychological, political, and moral implications. LITERATURE FOR CHILDREN emphasizes appropriate content, style, and suitability for various ages. LITERATURE FOR YOUNG ADULTS provides extensive reading and sharing of young adult literature.

Northwest College of the Assemblies of God. English. CHILDHOOD LITERATURE is a survey of major historical classic and contemporary books.

Pacific Lutheran University. English. CHILDREN'S LITERATURE focuses on major authors. SPECIAL TOPICS IN CHILDREN'S LITERATURE may include study of genre, themes, historical periods, or other topics, and the course may be repeated for credit. FAIRY TALES AND FANTASY emphasizes various kinds of fantasy. WRITING FOR CHILDREN is a writing workshop.

Peninsula College. English. CHILDREN'S LITERATURE determines criteria for excellence in books for children.

Pierce College. Education. CHILDREN'S LITERATURE is a historical study, including methods for sharing literature with young children.

Saint Martin's College. Education. LITERATURE FOR CHILDREN AND YOUNG ADULTS reviews the nature, history, and sources of children's books.

Seattle Pacific University. Education. CHILDREN'S/YOUNG ADULT LITERATURE examines trends, issues, and research, with attention to use of trade books in the curriculum.

Seattle University. English. CHILDREN'S LITERATURE includes interpretive and creative writing assignments.

South Pacific University. Education and English. CHILDREN'S BOOKS: READING FOR ALL AGES tests selected books against literary, developmental, and societal criteria.

University of Washington. English. CHILDREN'S LITERATURE RECONSIDERED views books in the light of their social, psychological, political, and moral implications. Library and Information Studies. SURVEY OF CHILDREN'S LITERATURE offers criteria for the selection and utilization of books for family, school, and library enrichment. LITERATURE FOR YOUNG ADULTS offers reading and appraisal of literature appropriate for young adults.

Walla Walla College. Education. LITERATURE IN THE SECONDARY SCHOOL emphasizes choosing literature related to student problems and goals. LIBRARY MATERIALS FOR CHILDREN is an overview study designed to develop the ability to choose library materials. Education and Library Science. LITERATURE IN THE ELEMENTARY SCHOOL is a study of the selection and study of literature on the elementary school level.

Washington State University. Education. TEACHING FOLK LITERATURE TO CHILDREN AND ADOLESCENTS includes curriculum applications. ADVANCED CHILDREN'S LITERATURE reviews trends, issues, and research. TEACHING ADOLESCENT LITERATURE includes evaluating, selecting, and using literature with students.

Western Washington University. Education. READING AND CHILDREN'S LITERATURE uses children's books to teach basic reading skills. Library Science. INTRODUCTION TO CHILDREN'S LITERATURE is an overview. BOOKS AND MATERIALS FOR ELEMENTARY SCHOOLS emphasizes wide reading, literary analysis, and correlation with the curriculum. BOOKS AND MATERIALS FOR YOUNG ADULTS includes review of multicultural self-concept literature and literary analysis. WRITING AND ILLUSTRATING CHILDREN'S BOOKS includes techniques of composition and illustrations.

Whitman College. Education. CRITICAL READING OF LITERATURE FOR CHILDREN AND YOUTH is a genre survey with emphasis on selection and use in the classroom. English and Library Science. LITERATURE IN THE ELEMENTARY SCHOOL is an overview study of library materials.

Whitworth College. Education. EXPLORING CHILDREN'S LITERATURE AND READING GROWTH is a course that prepares teachers to bring children and literature together.

WEST VIRGINIA

Bethany College. Education and English. Students work with children as they learn approaches to using literature in CHILDREN'S LITERATURE. Readings in LITERATURE AND ADOLESCENCE are primarily in novels and short stories, with techniques for presentation.

Bluefield State College. CHILDREN'S LITERATURE covers selection, evaluation and presentation.

Concord College. English. Two courses in CHILDREN'S LITERATURE are offered. Both are for teacher certification. One is a general survey and the other focuses on folktales and myths. ADOLESCENT LITERATURE also is a survey course.

Fairmont State College. English. CHILDREN'S LITERATURE provides wide acquaintance with current books for use with children.

Glenville State College. English. BACKGROUNDS OF CHILDREN'S LITERATURE is an international genre survey with techniques for use in the classroom. Library Science. LIBRARY MATERIALS FOR CHILDREN is a historical survey with emphasis on modern materials. LIBRARY MATERIALS FOR ADOLESCENTS includes means of stimulating interest in reading.

Marshall University. Library Science. MATERIALS SELECTION FOR CHILDREN surveys print and non-print, with standards for selection.

Salem College. Education. CHILDREN'S LITERATURE reviews authors and illustrations.

Shepherd College. English. ADOLESCENT LITERATURE is a genre survey that includes criteria and resources for selection. Library Science. LIBRARY MATERIALS FOR CHILDREN and LIBRARY MATERIALS FOR ADOLESCENTS are surveys with emphasis on modern books and non-print. Practice is provided in storytelling and book talks.

University of Charleston. English. CHILDREN'S LITERATURE introduces teachers to children's reading.

West Liberty State College. Education. CHILDREN'S LITERATURE is a study of representative literary works in all genres. English.

West Virginia State College. English. LITERATURE FOR CHILDREN is a comprehensive survey with emphasis on types and uses.

West Virginia University. English. FICTION FOR ADOLESCENTS, designed for prospective teachers, focuses on recent publications. Library Science. LITERATURE FOR CHILDREN is a survey that includes historical development and recent trends. YOUNG ADULT LITERATURE includes print and non-print materials for high school students.

West Virginia University, Parkersburg. English. CHILDREN'S LITERATURE surveys the development of children's literature with emphasis on modern books and their use in the classroom.

West Virginia Wesleyan College. Library Science. LITERATURE FOR CHILDREN is a survey designed for teachers and librarians in elementary schools.

WISCONSIN

Alverno College. English. LITERATURE FOR THE READING CHILD AND ADOLESCENT, offered at graduate and undergraduate levels, is a critical survey including media presentations.

Beloit College. Education. Reading, evaluating, and using literature in the classroom are the objectives in CHILDREN'S LITERATURE.

Carroll College. Education. LANGUAGE ARTS AND CHILDREN'S LITERATURE includes the use of appropriate literature for pupils of nursery through middle school age.

Carthage College. Education. CHILDREN'S AND EARLY ADOLESCENTS' LITERATURE is a study of story interests of students and the use of literature as an instructional tool for reading.

Concordia College. Education. CHILDREN'S LITERATURE, an extensive reading course, covers use of literature with children. Humanities. ADOLESCENT LITERATURE is a survey of seven modern genres along with a historical overview.

Edgewood College. Education. LITERATURE FOR CHILDREN AND YOUNG ADULTS is a genre survey, an exploration of values and current social issues in literature, and study of criteria for selection. PRE-READING AND LITERATURE FOR THE YOUNG CHILD offers a child development study and techniques for presenting literature.

Lakeland College. Education. CHILDREN'S AND EARLY ADOLESCENT LITERATURE AND ADVANCED READING AND STUDY SKILLS includes selecting, evaluating, and using children's books in classroom settings.

Marian College of Fond du Lac. Education. CHILDREN'S LITERATURE gives techniques for integrating children's literature into reading and writing instruction. ADOLESCENT LITERATURE emphasizes instructional activities designed to stir literary appreciation in young people.

Marquette University. Education. LITERATURE FOR CHILDREN AND ADOLESCENTS identifies and evaluates factors involved in planning and implementing a sequential program of literature.

Northland College. English. CHILDREN'S LITERATURE offers reading and evaluation of a broad range of children's literature.

Ripon College. Education. ELEMENTARY TEACHING: CHILDREN'S LITERATURE is a survey course.

Saint Norbert College. Education. CHILDREN'S LITERATURE requires wide reading in all forms of literature. ADOLESCENT LITERATURE: AN INTERNATIONAL APPROACH places emphasis on literature and contemporary issues of society, with attention to literary elements that appeal to adolescents.

Silver Lake College. Education. LITERATURE FOR CHILDREN K–8 gives consideration to history of literature, social issues, and classroom use. English. LITERATURE FOR ADOLESCENTS includes titles dealing with contemporary issues as well as classics.

University of Wisconsin-Eau Claire. Library Science. CHILDREN'S LITERATURE is a survey of print and non-print formats. LITERATURE FOR ADOLESCENTS AND ADULTS emphasizes contemporary and realistic fiction and fantasy. A special course is LITERATURE FOR PRE-SCHOOL HANDICAPPED CHILDREN, which emphasizes creative ways to extend their book experience. SEMINAR IN CHILDREN'S LITERATURE and SEMINAR IN LITERATURE FOR THE YOUNG ADULT provide opportunities to read, discuss, and evaluate contemporary literature.

University of Wisconsin-Green Bay. Education. CHILDREN'S LITERATURE: CONTEMPORARY PRACTICES IN THE ELEMENTARY SCHOOL examines practices which produce an effective children's literature program. ADOLESCENT LITERATURE IN SECONDARY SCHOOL READING includes current practices in literacy curriculum and criteria for evaluating literature and literature programs.

University of Wisconsin-La Crosse. English. FOLKTALES AND OTHER LORE FOR CHILDREN includes modern adaptations by contemporary authors. English and Library Science. CHILDREN'S LITERATURE is a basic course in literature for teacher preparation. ADOLESCENT LITERATURE is a survey course for teachers. Library Science. CURRENT

TRENDS IN LITERATURE FOR CHILDREN AND YOUNG ADULTS is a course designed to study new and recent trends in literature.

University of Wisconsin-Madison. Education. LITERATURE FOR THE YOUNG covers use of trade books for the very young (age two) through young adults. Library Science. TEACHING CHILDREN'S LITERATURE IN ELEMENTARY AND MIDDLE SCHOOLS gives instructional strategies and curriculum development. YOUNG ADULT LITERATURE FOR SCHOOLS covers use of trade books and other media. CHILDREN'S LITERATURE covers traditional titles and contemporary ones, with techniques of reading guidance. STORY TELLING AND ORAL LITERATURE includes development of story telling programs in library, school and community. YOUNG ADULT LITERATURE places emphasis on reading interests.

University of Wisconsin-Milwaukee. Education. CHILDREN'S LITERATURE aims to acquaint students with a wide range of good books for children. READING INTERESTS OF ADOLESCENTS focuses on recently published materials related to school programs. Books and Pictures for the Young Child examines using picture books to develop verbal fluency and aesthetic awareness. Library Science. LIBRARY MATERIALS FOR CHILDREN and LIBRARY MATERIALS FOR YOUNG ADULTS offer criteria for evaluation and selection of materials.

University of Wisconsin-Oshkosh. English. LITERATURE FOR CHILDREN places emphasis on selecting materials for use with children in the classroom. LITERATURE FOR YOUNG ADULTS offers reading, listening, and viewing guidance techniques appropriate for the classroom. English. LITERATURE FOR YOUNG ADULTS is a study of literature of interest to young people.

University of Wisconsin-Parkside. Education. LANGUAGE ARTS AND CHILDREN'S LITERATURE examines range of children's books for literacy programs. CHILDREN'S LITERATURE emphasizes using trade books for implementing school literature programs.

University of Wisconsin-Platteville. Education. LITERATURE FOR CHILDREN is a study of folk literature and poetry, with ways of presenting literature to children. English. LITERATURE FOR YOUNG PEOPLE is an analysis of selected prose and poetry for junior and senior high school age.

University of Wisconsin-River Falls. English. LITERATURE FOR CHILDREN is a study of picture books and novels for teacher preparation. CHILDREN'S LITERATURE: ISSUES AND TRENDS focuses on current trends and issues in children's books. LITERATURE FOR YOUNG ADULTS covers selection and evaluation of literature for adolescents. Library Science. READING GUIDANCE FOR YOUNG ADULTS covers types of reading materials for young adults in relation to their needs. READING GUIDANCE FOR CHILDREN includes storytelling and dramatization. ADVANCED READING GUIDANCE FOR CHILDREN AND YOUNG ADULTS is an evaluative survey of books and other media with emphasis on developing collections.

University of Wisconsin-Stevens Point. English. LITERATURE FOR EARLY CHILDHOOD covers selection of materials for preschool children. CHILDREN'S LITERATURE is a similar course for elementary school readers.

University of Wisconsin-Stout. English. LITERATURE FOR YOUNG CHILDREN is a critical survey with directed study in presentation methods. LITERATURE FOR THE READING CHILD AND ADOLESCENT includes media presentations of literature.

University of Wisconsin-Superior. Education and English. CHILDREN'S LITERATURE emphasizes the selection and use of children's literature to develop a permanent interest in reading. English and Library Science. ADOLESCENT LITERATURE is a study of various types of literature in the secondary grades.

University of Wisconsin-Whitewater. Education. CHILDREN'S LITERATURE explores evaluation and selection techniques of various genres for the young child. English. LITERATURE FOR ADOLESCENTS explores the history and development of adolescent literature, with emphasis on the period since 1960. Library Science. ADOLESCENT LITERATURE AND RELATED MEDIA places emphasis on adolescent growth and development, with selection of books of interest and appeal. CHILDREN'S LITERATURE AND RELATED MEDIA surveys the historical development of children's literature.

Viterbo College. Education. CHILDREN/EARLY ADOLESCENT LITERATURE introduces various types of literature through reading.

WYOMING

University of Wyoming. Education. TEACHING LITERATURE IN THE SECONDARY SCHOOL considers various genres for use in the English classroom. Library Science. LITERATURE FOR CHILDREN is a survey course to prepare teachers and librarians to provide knowledgeable service in the use of materials with children. LIBRARY-MEDIA MATERIALS FOR THE TEENAGER is for librarians and teachers who wish to strengthen their backgrounds in the utilization of a wide collection of books and other media. STORYTELLING places emphasis on literature for preschool and elementary age children. FIELD STUDIES IN is offered through extension services and includes European study tours. Two courses are for students with a strong background in children's literature. RECENT TRENDS IN CHILDREN'S LITERATURE addresses new developments in the subject matter, settings, and style of children's books. LITERATURE AND READING/WRITING links the use of literature for children with the language arts.

Author/Title Index

References are to entry numbers in Part I.

A to Zoo: Subject Access to Children's Picture Books 13
Adamson, Lynda G. 109, 110
"The Adolescent as 'Mock Reader': Some Thoughts for the Teacher of Literature" 238
"Adventuring with International Literature: One Teacher's Experience" 267
Aitken, David 111
The ALAN Review 30
Alfonso, Sister Regina 112, 113, 114, 115, 116, 117
Allen, Melody Lloyd 118
"American Children's Literature Down Under" 252
"And Who Taught You Children's Literature?" 109
Another Look at Mother Goose: Prior Knowledge or Endangered Species 250
"'Anything Goes' . . . Connecting Children to Literature: A Personal View" 242
Appraisal: Science Books for Children 31
"Approaches to Teaching Children's Literature" 155
Arbuthnot, May Hill 106
Armstrong, Mary K. 192
Ashley, L. F. 83

Atkinson, Dorothy 119
Atkinson, Joan L. 120

Bagnall, Norma 193
Barron, Pamela Petrick 121, 122
Barton, Bob 194
"The Basalization of Trade Books" 255
Bass, Marion 123
Bauer, Caroline Feller 195
"Being Literary in a Literature-Based Classroom" 214
Benne, Mae 124
Best Books for Children: Preschool Through Grade 6 8
Beyond the ABC: Toward a Rhetoric of Children's Literature and Reading 236
The Biggest Bear 261
Bingham, Jane 1
Black Authors and Illustrators of Children's Books: A Biographical Dictionary 25
Blass, Rosanne J. 196
The Book Report 34
Bookbird 32
Booklist 33
Bookpeople: A First Album; Bookpeople: A Second Album 14
Books by African-American Authors

343

and *Illustrators for Children and
Young Adults* 29
"Books for Children Deserve to Be
Part of Literary Studies" 131
"Books in the Classroom: Unweaving
the Rainbow" 266
*Books Kids Will Sit Still For: The
Complete Read-Aloud Guide* 7
*Booktalk: Occasional Writing on
Literature and Children* 199
Booth, David 194
Broderick, Dorothy M. 125
Bromley, Karen D'Angelo 197
*Bulletin of the Center for Children's
Books* 35
Burgan, Mary 198
Burke, Eileen M. 74, 75
Burley, Jennifer Q. 122
Burt, Lesta 233
Bush, Margaret 118
*"'But Don't Go into Mr. McGregor's
Garden': Children's Books in Brit-
ain Today"* 144
Butler, Francelia 76, 126, 127
Butts, Dennis 128

Cain, Melissa 16
Carpenter, Humphrey 2
Carroll, Frances Laverne 3
CBC Features 36
CCL (Canadian Children's Literature)
37
*Celebrate Literature! A Spiraling Cur-
riculum for Grades K–6* 212
Chambers, Aidan 129, 199, 200, 201
Chang, Margaret 130
"Charting Book Discussions: A
Method of Presenting Literature in
the Elementary Grades" 211
*Child and Story: The Literary Con-
nection* 108
"The Child and the Picture Book:
Creating Live Circuits" 224
*The Child as Critic: Teaching Litera-
ture in Elementary and Middle
Schools* 104
Childhood Education 38
Children and Books 106
Children and Literature 105

"Children and Literature Becoming a
Subject of Serious Study in the
Netherlands" 135
*Children's Book Awards International:
A Directory of Awards and
Winners* 27
*Children's Books in England: Five
Centuries of Social Life* 79
"Children's Books in Teacher Educa-
tion—The University of Birming-
ham" 136
"Children's Books in Teacher Educa-
tion at Armidale College of Ad-
vanced Education" 172
"Children's Books in Teacher Educa-
tion at Bulmershe College of
Higher Education" 128
"Children's Books in Teacher Educa-
tion at Craigie College of Educa-
tion, Ayr" 176
"Children's Books in Teacher Educa-
tion at St. Martin's College Lan-
caster" 111
"Children's Books in Teacher Edu-
cation at the University of Cam-
bridge" 187
"Children's Books in Teacher Educa-
tion at the University of Exeter"
138
"Children's Books in Teacher Educa-
tion at the University of Sydney"
190
"Children's Books in Teacher Educa-
tion at Worcester College of Higher
Education" 134
"Children's Books in the Education of
Librarians at the College of Libra-
rianship Wales, Aberystwyth" 157
"Children's Fiction in a College of
Education" 146
Children's Literature 39
*Children's Literature: A Guide to
Reference Sources* 9
*Children's Literature: A Guide to the
Criticism* 10
*Children's Literature: An Annotated
Bibliography of the History and
Criticism* 23
*Children's Literature: An Issues Ap-
proach* 100

"Children's Literature: Books for Teaching It" 188
Children's Literature: Resources for the Classroom 101
Children's Literature: Theory, Research, and Teaching 185
Children's Literature Abstracts 40
"Children's Literature and Teacher Education in Canada" 147
"Children's Literature as an Academic Pursuit: The University of British Columbia Model" 148
"Children's Literature as It Is Taught in University English Departments in the U. S. in 1985" 163
Children's Literature Association Quarterly (ChLA) 41
"Children's Literature Courses" 233
Children's Literature in Education 42
"Children's Literature in New Zealand: New Initiatives in Higher Education" 133
Children's Literature in the Classroom 87
"Children's Literature in the College Classroom" 153
"Children's Literature in the Education of Teachers" 132
Children's Literature in the Elementary School 88
"Children's Literature in the English Department" 164
Children's Literature in the Reading Program 206
Children's Literature Review 4
"The Child's Voice: Literature Conversations" 226
Cianciolo, Patricia J. 202, 203
Cinderella 236
Clark, Beverly Lyon 131
Classroom Uses of Children's Literature: A Research Report 196
Clements, Frank 132
Cochrane, Kirsty 133
Collected Perspectives: Choosing and Using Books for the Classroom 16
College Students as Readers 154
"College Students Reading to Preschoolers" 141
Comics to Classics: A Parent's Guide

to Books for Teens and Preteens 24
Commire, Anne 5
Conlon, Alice 204
Corcoran, Bill 77
"Course Development: From a Gleam in the Eye to a Full-Term Product" 124
Cox, Carole 205
"Creating a School Wide Literature Program: A Case Study" 235
A Critical Handbook of Children's Literature 92
Critical History of Children's Literature: A Survey of Children's Books in English from the Earliest Times to the Present 15
Critical Thinking in the Study of Children's Literature in the Elementary Grades 202
Criticism, Theory, and Children's Literature 89
Crook, Patricia R. 230
"Cross-Cultural Futures: Research and Teaching in Comparative Children's Literature" 151
Croxson, Mary 134
Cullinan, Bernice E. 78, 87, 206
Cullum, Carolyn N. 207
"Curriculum Planning in Literature for Children: Ways to Go" 143

Darton, F. J. Harvey 79
Demers, Patricia 80, 81
"Dialogue with a Text" 245
Dictionary of Literary Biography 6
Donelson, Kenneth L. 82
Duijx, Toin 135

Early Childhood Literature: For Love of Child and Book 74
"Editor's Comments: Teaching Children, or Teaching Subject" 240
Eeds, Maryann 208
"Effective Schools Research and Excellence in Reading: Rationale for Children's Literature in the Curriculum" 230

Egawa, Kathy 209
Egoff, Sheila 83
Emergency Librarian 43
*Engines of Instruction, Mischief, and
    Magic: Children's Literature in
    England from Its Beginnings to
    1839* 90
English Journal 44
"ERIC/RCS Report: Developing
    Children's Appreciation of Litera-
    ture" 232
Evans, Emrys 77
Evans, W. D. Emrys 136
"Everything Considered: Response to
    Literature in an Elementary School
    Setting" 219
"Examining Children's Literature:
    Children's Books at the University
    of Wales" 145
Experiencing Children's Literature 97
*Experts Define the Ideal Elementary
    Literature Program* 203

*The Family of Stories: An Anthology
    of Children's Literature* 93
*Fantasy Literature: Encounters in the
    Globe of Time* 130
Farrell, Edmund J. 84
Fenwick, Geoff 210
*Fifteen Centuries of Children's
    Literature: An Annotated
    Chronology of British and
    American Works in Historical
    Context* 1
Five Kinds of Literary Knowing 246
The Five Owls 45
Flender, Mary G. 211
Foster, John 137
Fox, Carol 212
Fox, Geoff 138
Freeman, Judy 7
*From Instruction to Delight: An An-
    thology of Children's Literature to
    1850* 81

Galda, Lee 213
Gallagher, Mary Elizabeth 85
*A Garland from the Golden Age: An
    Anthology of Children's Literature
    from 1850 to 1900* 80

Gay, Carol 139
Gillespie, John T. 8
"Giving Mrs. Jones a Hand: Making
    Group Storytime More Pleasurable
    and Meaningful for Young Chil-
    dren" 204
Glazer, Joan I. 86
Great Expectations 238
Gross, Elizabeth H. 140
"Guiding Young Students' Response
    to Literature" 223

Hade, Daniel D. 214
Hall, Susan 215
Hancock, Marjorie R. 216
Hannabuss, Stuart 217
"Harnessing the Power of Language:
    First Graders' Literature Engage-
    ment with Owl Moon" 209
Haviland, Virginia 9
Hayes, David 141
Hearne, Betsy 142
Helbig, Alethea 143
*Helping Children to Grow as Critics
    of Literature* 257
Hendrickson, Linnea 10
Hepler, Susan 88, 218
Hickman, Janet 87, 88, 219, 220
The Hobbit 263
The Horn Book 46
*The Horn Book Guide to Children
    and Young Adult Books* 47
The House of Dies Drear 259
"How to Teach a Mass Class in Chil-
    dren's Literature Year After Year"
    126
Huck, Charlotte S. 88
Hunt, Peter 89, 144, 145

I Am Phoenix 226
"Implications of the State-Wide
    Survey of Children's Literature In-
    struction" 191
"Informal Children's Literature Inven-
    tory: Test Yourself" 189
Instructor 48
*International Review of Children's
    Literature and Librarianship* 49
"Interpreting Literature for Young
    Children" 170

"It Was Real Exciting: Adults and Children Studying Literature Together" 193

"'It's Not What You Expect': Teaching Irony to Third Graders" 261

"Jack and Jill No Longer Go Up the Hill: Primary Education in Australia 1986 and Children's Literature" 234

Jackson, Mary V. 90

Jackson, William 146

Jobe, Ronald 147, 148

Johnson, Terry D. 221, 222

Journal of Reading: A Journal of Adolescent and Adult Literacy 50

Journal of Youth Services in Libraries (JOYS) 51

Jump Over the Moon: Selected Professional Readings 122

The Junior Bookshelf 52

Jurenka, Nancy E. Allen 196

Kaminski, Robert 254

Katz, Bill 11

Katz, Linda Sternberg 11

Kaye, Marilyn 149

Kearney, Anthony 111

Kelly, Patricia R. 223

Kiefer, Barbara Z. 224, 225

Kingore, Bertha W. 150

Kinnell, Margaret 151

Kissen, Rita M. 152

Koeller, Shirley A. 226, 227

Kohn, Rita 12

Kutzer, M. Daphne 153

LaBonty, Jan 154

Landes, Sonia 228

Langer, Judith A. 229

Language Arts 53

Laughlin, Mildred Knight 155

"Learning How: Remarks on the Teaching of Children's Literature" 149

Lehman, Barbara A. 230

The Leopard 267

"Letter from England: Summerhouse Blues" 200

"Letter from England: Teaching Children's Literature" 201

"Letter from England: Teaching Children's Literature Part 2" 129

Lewis, Claudia 91

"Library Education and Youth Services: A Survey of Faculty, Course Offerings, and Related Activities in Accredited Library Schools" 118

"Library Education for Young Adult Specialists" 120

Lieberman, Jan 156

Lima, Carolyn W. 13

Lima, John A. 13

Lindauer, Shelley L. Knudsen 231

The Lion and the Unicorn 54

Literacy Through Literature 222

Literary Experience, a Neglected Essential 227

"Literary Gaps Invite Creative Interaction" 269

"The Literary Transaction: Evocation and Response" 173

Literature: Basic in the Language Arts Curriculum 260

Literature and the Child 78

"Literature Anthologies in the US: Impediments to Good Teaching Practice" 271

Literature as Exploration 98

"The Literature Connection: Using Children's Books in the Classroom" 99

Literature for Children: A Short Introduction 102

Literature for the Young Child 75

Literature for Today's Young Adults 82

Literature for Young Children 86

"Literature Response Journals: Insights Beyond the Printed Page" 216

Little Blue and Little Yellow 220

Livingston, Myra Cohn 107

Logan, John W. 232

Lonsdale, Ray 157

"A Look at One Successful Literature Program" 241

Louis, Daphne R. 222
Louis the Fish 269
Lowery-Moore, Hollis 233
Lukens, Rebecca J. 92
Lynch-Brown, Carol 267

McElmeel, Sharron L. 14
Magazines for Young People 11
"Magic Abroad! Children's Literature at the Catholic College of Education Sydney" 184
The Man Without a Country 238
"The Manchester Polytechnic Library's Collection of Children's Books" 178
Many, Joyce E. 205
Masterworks of Children's Literature 17
Mathews, Virginia H. 158
Matte, Gerard 234
May, Jill P. 235
Meacham, Mary 3
"Meaning-Making and the Dragons of Pern" 268
Meek, Margaret 159
Meigs, Cornelia L. 15
Meinbach, Anita Meyer 99
"Metaphors, Morality, and Children's Books" 217
Mikkelsen, Nina 236
Mikkelsen, Vincent 236
Miles, Avi 237
Miles, Betty 237
"Modules for Teaching About Young People's Literature – Module 1: Gender Roles" 112
"Modules for Teaching About Young People's Literature – Module 2: How do the Elderly Fare in Children's Books?" 113
"Modules for Teaching About Young People's Literature – Module 3: Values Children Can Learn from Picture Books" 114
"Modules for Teaching About Young People's Literature – Module 4: Humor" 115
"Modules for Teaching About Young People's Literature – Module 5:

Picture Storybooks vs. Basal Readers" 116
"Modules for Teaching About Young People's Literature – Module 6: Informational Books" 117
Moir, Hughes 16
Monseau, Virginia R. 160, 238
Monson, Dianne L. 97
Moon, Cliff 161
More Creative Uses of Children's Literature 96
More Exciting, Funny, Scary, Short, Different, and Sad Books Kids Like About Animals, Science, Sports, Families, Songs and Other Things 3
Moss, Anita 93
Mother Goose 250
"Moving Toward a Whole Language College Classroom" 174
Moyles, Gordon 81
Moynihan, William T. 17
"Multicultural Education: The Opening of the American Mind" 152
Multi-Cultural Folktales: Stories to Tell Young Children 254
Multicultural Review 55

Naden, Corinne J. 8
National Council of Teachers of English 162
Neumeyer, Peter F. 163, 164
The New Advocate 56
"New Corn from Old Fields: A Study of the Potential Children's Literature to Be Gleaned from English Literature Existing Prior to the Seventeenth Century" 123
The New York Times Book Review 57
The New Yorker 58
"The Newbery Committee That Never Was" 125
Nilsen, Alleen Pace 18, 82
Nineteenth-Century Literature 59
Nix, Kemie 239
Nodelman, Perry 94, 165, 166, 240
Norton, Donna E. 95
Novels of Initiation: A Guidebook

for Teaching Literature to Adolescents 243

O'Brien, Kathy L. 241
Olendorf, Donna 19
"On Producing Brand-New Book Lovers" 239 *Once Upon . . . a Time for Young People and Their Books: An Annotated Resource Guide* 12
"One Children's Literature Course" 179
Only Connect: Readings on Children's Literature 83
"The Onus of Teaching Children's Literature: The Need for Some Reappraisals" 139
Owl Moon 209
Oxford Companion to Children's Literature 2

Paul, Lissa 167
Paulin, Mary Ann 96
Peck, David 243
Pellowski, Anne 20, 21
"The People Behind the Pens" 218
Peterson, Ralph 208
"Petunia and Beyond: Literature for the Kindergarten Crowd" 192
Phaedrus 60
"Picture Books as Contexts for Literary, Aesthetic, and Real World Understandings" 225
"Picture Books as Literature" 228
Pilhjerta, Ritva-Liisa 168
Pilla, Marianne Laino 22
"Planning Programs for Children: A Library School Course" 156
The Pleasures of Children's Literature 94
Pond, Patricia 169
Post, Robert M. 170
Prawat, Richard S. 203
"Presenting Literature to Children" 221
Prest, Julie 244
Prest, Peter 244
Prichard, Mari 2

"Problems and Possibilities: U. S. Research in Children's Literature" 142
Probst, Robert E. 171, 245, 246, 247
"Production of a Telecourse in Library and Information Science: 'Jump Over the Moon: Sharing Literature with Young Children'" 121
Prosak-Beres, Leslie 16
Publications of the Modern Language Association (PMLA) 61
Publishers Weekly 62
Purves, Alan 97

"The Question of Work: Adolescent Literature and the Ericksonian Paradigm" 198

Rahn, Suzanne 23
Raphael, Taffy E. 248
Rasmussen, Bonnie 172
Read for the Fun of It: Active Programming with Books for Children 195
"Readers as Performers: The Literature Game" 249
"Readers, Texts, and Contexts: A Response-Based View of Literature in the Classroom" 213
Readers, Texts, Teachers 77
The Reading Teacher 63
Reed, Arthea J. S. 24
"Research and the Newbery and Caldecott Books" 180
"Research Currents: Researching Children's Response to Literature" 220
"Research Directions: Literature and Discussion in the Reading Program" 248
Resources for Middle-Grade Reluctant Readers: A Guide for Librarians 22
Response and Analysis: Teaching Literature in Junior and Senior High School 247
"Response-Based Teaching of Literature" 171
"Results of the Children's Literature

Assembly's Survey of Teaching in U.S. Colleges and Universities" 110

A Review of Children's Literature Anthologies and Core Texts 91

The Riverside Anthology of Children's Literature 103

"The Role of Children's and Adolescent Literature in the Undergraduate Curriculum" 160

"The Role of Children's Literature in Shaping Professional Aspirations" 127

Rollock, Barbara 25

Rosenblatt, Louise M. 98, 173

Ross, Elinor Parry 174

Rothlein, Liz 99

Rudman, Masha Kabakow 100, 101

Russell, David L. 102

Sadler, Glenn Edward 175

Saltman, Judith 103

Salvner, Gary M. 249

Sandel, Lenore 250

Sarland, Charles 251

Sauer, Margery 212

Sawyer, Wayne 252

Scholt, Grayce 1

The School Librarian 64

School Library Journal 65

School Library Media Quarterly 66

"School Visits: The Author's Viewpoint" 237

Schwartz, Sheila 253

Scott, Anne 176

The Scott, Foresman Anthology of Children's Literature 107

Sensitizing Students to the Selective Tradition in Children's Literature 181

Shachter, Jaqueline 177

Shaner, Mary E. 17

Sharing Literature with Children: A Thematic Anthology 76

Sharp, Patricia 186

Shercliff, W. H. 178

"Should Literary Classics Be Part of Children's Literature?" 186

Sierra, Judy 254

Signal: Approaches to Children's Books 67

Silvey, Anita 255

Slattery, Carole 256

Sloan, Glenna 104, 257

Smith, Edna K. 258

Smith, Laura 27

Snider, Bill 186

Snow, Miriam 179

Something About the Author: Autobiography series 28

Something About the Author: Facts and Pictures About Authors and Illustrators of Books for Young People 19

Spears-Bunton, Linda A. 259

Spink, John 157

"The Spiralled Sequence Story Curriculum: A Structuralist Approach to Teaching Fiction in the Elementary Grades" 262

Spoerl, Dorothy Tilden 180

Squire, James 84

Stanley and Rhoda 228

Stewig, John Warren 105, 260

Stories in the Classroom: Storytelling, Reading Aloud and Roleplaying with Children 194

"Storytelling: A Bridge from the University to the Elementary School to the Home" 150

Storytelling Magazine 68

The Storytime Sourcebook: A Compendium of Ideas and Resources for Storytellers 207

Stott, Jon C. 93, 262, 263, 264, 265, 266

"A Structuralist Approach to Teaching Novels in the Elementary Grades" 263

Stubbs, G. T. 83

Sutherland, Zena 106, 107

Sylvester and the Magic Pebble 221

"Symbolic Outlining: The Academic Study of Children's Literature" 159

Taxel, Joel 181, 182

Taylor, Mary-Agnes 183

"Teacher as Curator: Learning to Talk About Literature" 208

"Teacher Training and Children's Fiction" 161

"Teaching a Unit of Fairy Tales" 165

Teaching Adolescent Literature: A Humanistic Approach 253

"Teaching Children's Literature in Canada" 167

Teaching Children's Literature in Colleges and Universities 162

Teaching Children's Literature in the Primary School 210

"Teaching Children's Literature" 182

"Teaching Children's Literature: An Intellectual Snob Confronts Some Generalizers" 166

Teaching Children's Literature: Issues, Pedagogy, Resources 175

"Teaching Children's Literature—With Paperbacks" 169

Teaching K-8 69

"Teaching Literary Criticism in the Elementary Grades: A Symposium" 264

"The Teaching of Children's Literature" 140

"The Teaching of Children's Literature in Australia" 137

"The Teaching of Children's Literature in Finland" 168

"Teaching Teachers About Children's Books: How, Why, and to What Effect" 119

"Teaching Theme to Elementary Students" 258

"Theory Becomes Practice: Aesthetic Teaching with Literature" 272

"Theory into Practice: Clarifying Our Intentions: Some Thoughts on the Application of Rosenblatt's Transactional Theory of Reading in the Classroom" 244

"Thinking About Folklore: Lessons for Grades K-4" 256

Thomas, Jane Rest 266

Through the Eyes of a Child: An Introduction to Children's Literature 95

Times Literary Supplement 70

Tomlinson, Carl M. 267

"Toward an Understanding of the Aesthetic Response to Literature" 205

Transactions with Literature: A Fifty-Year Perspective 84

Trin, Mary 184

"Understanding Literature" 229

Using Picture Storybooks to Teach Literary Devices: Recommended Books for Children and Young Adults 215

"Using Picture Storybooks to Teach Literary Elements to the Disabled Reader" 270

Vandergrift, Kay E. 108, 185, 268

"Videotaping Children's Authors: Temple University's Unique Teaching Program" 177

Voice of Youth Advocates (VOYA) 71

Watkins, Tony 128

Watson, Jerry J. 186, 269

Watson, Ken 252

Watson, Victor 187

Webbing with Literature: Creating Story Maps with Children's Books 197

Weber, Rosemary 188

Weiss, Adele B. 270

"Welcome to My House: African American and European American Students' Responses to Virginia Hamilton's *House of Dies Drear*" 259

Wendellin, Karla Hawkins 189

Where the Wild Things Are 221

"Which Way to Castle Yonder?" 183

"'Will the Real Dragon Please Stand Up?' Convention and Parody in Children's Stories" 265

Williams, Geoff 190
Williams, Helen E. 29
Wilson Library Bulletin 72
"WNBA Offers a Plan for a Course in Children's Literature" 158
"Wordless Books: An Approach to Visual Literacy" 231
The World of Children's Literature 20
The World of Storytelling 21

Yellow Brick Road 73
Young Adult Literature: Issues and Perspectives 85
Young People Reading: Culture and Response 251
Your Reading: A Booklist for Junior High and Middle School Students 18

Zaharias, Jane Ann 191, 271
Zarillo, James 272

Subject Index

References are to entry numbers in Part I

Activities for Children 7, 14, 73, 78, 96, 119, 192, 195, 196, 207, 221, 232, 242, 249, 257
Activities for Adults 74, 125, 128
Afro-American authors 25, 29
Anthologies 76, 77, 80, 81, 93, 103, 107, 122; reviews 91, 271
Australia, children's literature in 137, 172, 184, 190, 252
Authors: Biography 4, 5, 6, 14, 19, 25, 28, 73; In-depth Study 218; Interviews 69, 177; School Visits 237

Basalization of Books 255
Basic Resources 140
Bibliography, General 12, 16, 40
Book Awards 27, 125, 180
Book Charts 211
Book Clubs 248
Britain, children's literature in 144, 187

Canada, children's literature in 147, 167
Character Development 263
Characteristics of Good Books 260
Children as Literary Critics 257, 264
Children's Interests, Bibliography 3, 7, 8, 26

Children's Literature, Tests 189
Children's Literature Assembly, Survey 109, 110
Classics 123, 131, 186
Comparative Children's Literature 129, 151
Course Design 185, 191
Criticism 4, 61, 83, 149, 183; Bibliography 10, 23

Disabled Reader 270

Early Childhood 74, 75, 78, 86, 87, 88, 95, 104, 182, 192, 204, 207, 231
Elderly, in Children's Literature 113
Encyclopedia 2
English Departments, children's literature in 139, 143, 153, 160, 163, 164, 175, 187
Essays 84, 199, 200

Fairy Tales 165
Fantasy 130
Fiction 161, 221, 243
Finland, children's literature in 168
Folklore 256

Gender Roles, in Children's Literature
112
Genres 102, 105, 106, 122, 212
Grammar of literature 263

History of Children's Literature 1, 5,
6, 15, 17, 23, 79, 90, 101, 106
Humor in Children's Literature 115

Illustrators: Afro-American 29;
Biography 73; Interviews 69
Informational Books 117
International Board on Books for
Young People 233
International Children's Literature
152, 233, 267; Bibliography 20
Irony 261

Language Arts 104, 203, 210, 235, 260
Library Collections 178
Library Education 120, 121, 122, 124,
148, 156, 157; Survey 118
Literary Classroom 213, 214, 219,
220, 226, 227, 232, 239, 241
Literary Connection 265
Literary Elements 92, 104, 108, 166,
181, 193, 208, 212, 215, 241, 270
Literary Studies, children's literature
in 131
Literature Across the Curriculum 87,
99, 190, 203
Literature-based Reading Programs
88, 100, 101, 172, 174, 206, 222, 230
Literature Games 249

Magazines, Bibliography 11
Middle Grades 78, 82, 104, 202, 205,
206, 216, 219, 229, 257, 258, 263,
264, 267, 269, 272; Bibliography 18,
22, 24
Multicultural Children's Literature
152, 254; Reviews 56

National Council of Teachers of
English — Survey 162

The Netherlands, children's literature
in 135
New Zealand, children's literature
in 133

Paperbacks 169
Parody 265
Pern Novels of Anne McCaffrey 268
Picture Books 116, 215, 224, 225, 228,
231, 270; Bibliography 13
Political Factors, in Children's Literature 181, 234
Primary Grades 202, 206, 207, 209,
210, 219, 220, 223, 224, 225, 228,
234, 256, 257, 258, 261, 264, 269
Professional Reading 32, 36, 38, 42,
43, 44, 48, 49, 50, 51, 53, 54, 55,
56, 58, 59, 63, 67, 69, 72
Professions, various, children's literature in 127

Reader Response 77, 84, 89, 94, 97,
98, 171, 173, 182, 193, 199, 201, 205,
208, 209, 212, 213, 216, 219, 223,
224, 227, 229, 236, 240, 244, 245,
246, 247, 251, 253, 259, 266, 268,
269, 272
Reading Aloud 7, 141, 170, 194, 195,
204
Reading for Pleasure 119
Reading Logs 248
Reference, Bibliography 9
Reluctant Readers, Bibliography 22
Research 60, 142, 154, 159, 196, 213,
220, 230, 236, 241, 248
Response Journals 216
Reviews 33, 35, 39, 41, 45, 46, 47,
48, 52, 57, 59, 60, 62, 64, 65, 66,
70, 71

St. Martin's College Lancaster, Course
Description 111
Science books, reviews 31
Scotland, children's literature in 176
Selection 101, 204
Social Factors in Children's Literature
181, 254

Spiralled Sequence Story Curriculum 262, 264
Storytelling 21, 68, 141, 150, 194, 207, 210, 254

Teacher Education 132, 134, 136, 138, 146, 147, 148, 153, 154, 158, 161, 172, 174, 176, 179, 184, 185, 187
Teaching Methods 155
Telecourse Production 121
Textbooks 140; Reviews 91, 188
Theme 253, 258

University of Connecticut, Course Description 126

Values in Children's Literature 100, 114, 198, 217

Wales, children's literature in 145
Webbing 197
Where the Wild Things Are 221

Young Adults 82, 85, 206, 238, 243, 247, 253; Bibliography 24; Reviews 30, 34